BOLTON PUBLIC LIBRARIES

M6593

NOT TO BE TAKEN
FROM THIS ROOM

Any person in whose possession this book may be
found after it has been taken from this room is liable
to prosecution.

BOLTON PUBLIC

REFERENCE
LIBRARY

BIOGRAPHY

NATIONAL MARITIME MUSEUM
CATALOGUE OF THE LIBRARY
VOLUME TWO   PART TWO

Biography

LONDON: HER MAJESTY'S STATIONERY OFFICE 1969

© *Crown copyright 1969*

SBN 11 290004 6

016·359092
LON
59974 ·①
RS

BOLTON PUBLIC
REFERENCE
LIBRARY
LIBRARIES

Printed in England for Her Majesty's Stationery Office
by Eyre and Spottiswoode Limited at Grosvenor Press Portsmouth

Contents

PART TWO

Reference
Index

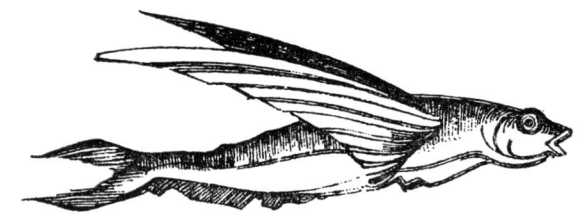

Sources

A Asimov, Isaac: *Asimov's biographical encyclopaedia of science and technology.* (London; Allen & Unwin; 1966)

AE Jose, Arthur W., & Carter, Herbert J.: *The Illustrated Australian Encyclopaedia,* 2 vols. (Sydney; Angus & Robertson; 1925)

B Boase, Frederick: *Modern English Biography.* 6 vols. (London; Frank Cass; 1965)

CE *Chambers's Encyclopaedia.* New [*i.e.* third] edition. 15 vols. (London; Newnes; [1959])

ch Charnock, John: *Biographia Navalis . . .* 6 vols. (London; R. Faulder; 1794–8)

chb Chubb, Thomas: *The Printed maps in the atlases of Great Britain and Ireland: a bibliography, 1579–1870 . . . and biographical notes on the map makers, engravers and publishers by T. Chubb, assisted J. W. Skells and H. Beharell.* (London; Homeland Association; 1927)

DAB Hopkins, Joseph G. E. [general editor]: *Concise Dictionary of American Biography.* (New York; Charles Scribner/London; Oxford University Press; 1964)

DAuB [Pike, Douglas [general editor]]: *Australian Dictionary of Biography.* 2 vols. (Melbourne; Melbourne University Press; 1966–7)

DCB Brown, George W. [general editor]: *Dictionary of Canadian Biography. volume I* (Toronto; University of Toronto Press; 1966)

DNB *Dictionary of National Biography.* Second edition. 27 vols. (London; Smith, Elder & Oxford Press; 1908 *et seq.*)

H *A Naval encyclopaedia: comprising a dictionary of nautical words and phrases, biographical notices, and records of naval officers . . .* (Philadelphia; L. R. Hamersly; 1881)

M Marshall, *Lieut* John: *Royal Naval Biography . . .* 8 vols. in 12 (London; Longman, Hurst, Rees . . . ; 1823–35)

Md Michaud, Louis G.: *Biographie Universelle (Michaud) ancienne et moderne . . .* Second edition. 45 vols. (Paris; Madame C. Desplaces/Leipzig; F. A. Brockhaus; 1843–65)

MDC Wallace, W. Stewart [editor]: *The Macmillan dictionary of Canadian biography.* Third edition (London & Toronto; Macmillan/New York; St. Martin's; 1963)

NA [Harris, Joseph]: *The Naval Atalantis . . . By Nauticus Junior.* 2 vols. (London; J. Ridgway; 1788–89)

NC *The Naval Chronicle.* volumes I–XL (London; 1799–1840)

R Ralfe, James: *The Naval Biography of Great Britain . . .* 4 vols. (London; Whitmore & Sons; 1828)

S Six, *Professor* Georges: *Dictionnaire biographique des généraux & amiraux français de la Revolution et de l'Empire, (1792–1841).* 2 vols. (Paris; Librarie Historique et Nobilière; 1934)

T i Taylor, *Professor* Eva G. R.: *The Mathematical practitioners of Tudor & Stuart England.* (Cambridge University Press for the Institute of Navigation; 1954)

T ii Taylor, *Professor* Eva G. R.: *The Mathematical practitioners of Hanoverian England, 1714–1840.* (Cambridge University Press for the Institute of Navigation; 1966)

Tr Mackenzie, *Col* Robert H.: *The Trafalgar Roll . . .* (London; George Allen; 1913)

ACLAND, Hugh Dyke (1791–1834)
Served as a volunteer, 1st Class aboard the 'Ajax' at Trafalgar   T 235

ACLAND, James (1799–1876)
Ran a packet on the Humber between Hull and Barton, charging less than half fare   B i 10

ACONTIUS, Jacobus [ACONZIO, ACONCOI, *or* CONCIO, Jacopo]
(1500?–1566?)
Philosopher, theologian and engineer; recovered land from the Thames at Erith,
Plumstead and Lesnes   DNB i 63

ACOSTA, Joseph d' (*d* 1600)
Spanish Jesuit and traveller. Author of: 'Historia natural y moral de las Indias' (1590),
which was reproduced by de Bry in his collection of voyages   Md i 128

A'COURT, *Capt* Edward Henry, RN (*b* 1783)   M x 345

ACTON, *Capt* Edward, RN (*d* 1707)   ch iii 60; DNB i 66

ACTON, Ferdinand (1832–91)
Neapolitan naval commander   B iv 25

ACTON, *Sir* John Francis Edward (1736–1811)
Served in the Tuscan naval service, later re-organised the Neapolitan fleet   CE i 53; DNB i 67

ACTON, *Capt* Thomas, RN (*d* 1689 *or* 1698)   ch ii 379

ACUNA, *Don* Pedro d' (*d* 1606)   Md i 135

ADAIR, *Capt* Charles William, RM (1776–1805)   Tr 22

ADAIR, *Gen Sir* Charles William, KCB, RM (1822–1897)   B iv 26

ADAIR, John (*d* 1722)   CE i 53; CHb 419;
Cartographer   DNB i 70; T i 278

ADAIR, William, *Master's Mate*, RN (1790–1806)   Tr 305

ADAM, *Adm Sir* Charles, KCB (1751–1839)   B i 13

ADAM, *Adm Sir* Charles, KCB (1780–1853)   DNB i 85; M iii 222

ADAM, Mathew (*fl* 1822–1823)
Inventor of artificial horizon tested by Royal Navy   T ii 412

ADAMS, Arthur, *Surgeon*, RN (1820–1878)   B i 15

ADAMS, *Lieut* Charles A., USN (*fl* 1863–1873)   H 956

ADAMS, Clement (*ca* 1519–1587)
Mathematician, travel writer, map-block cutter   T i 169

ADAMS, Dudley (*ca* 1760–1827)
Globe and telescope-maker   T ii 303

ADAMS, George (*d* 1773)
Writer on navigation, instrument-maker. Instruments at National Maritime Museum   DNB i 97; T ii 152

ADAMS, George (*junior*) (1750–1795)
Instrument-maker; compass-maker for Admiralty   T ii 277

ADDICKS, *Lieut* Joseph T., USN (*fl* 1869–1880)   H 996

ADDINGTON, *Cdr* William Silvester, RN (*fl* 1807–1830)   M viii 358

ADDISON, John (*fl* 1820–1838)
Globe-maker   T ii 412

ADEAN, William, *Master* RN (*d* 1822)   Tr 313

ADELAER [*or* ADELER], Curt Sivertsen (1622–1675)
Venetian naval commander; later admiral in the Danish fleet   CE i 63; Md 169

ADEY [*or* ADY], *Lieut* Henry, RN (*fl* 1661–1664)   ch i 142

ADIE, Alexander James (1775–1858)
Optical instrument maker; instruments at National Maritime Museum B i 21; T ii 354

ADLEY, Charles Coles (1830/1–1896)
Civil engineer; author of: 'The port of Calcutta' (1864)   B iv 44

ADLINGTON, *Capt* James, RN (*d* 1709/10)   ch iii 329

AERNOUTSON [*or* AERNOUTSZ], Jurriaen (*fl* 1674)
Dutch naval captain; conqueror of Acadia   DCB i 39

AFFLECK, *Adm Sir* Edmund (1723?–1788)   ch vi 209; DNB i 171;
                                                                    NA i 117; NC xxxi
                                                                    445; R i 222

AFFLECK, *Adm* Philip (1726–1799)   ch vi 346; DNB i 171;
                                                                    NA i 155; NC xxi 455

AGAR, *Cdr* William Gapper, RN (*d* 1833)   Tr 296

AGASSIZ, Alexander (1835–1910)
Oceanographer   CE i 149; DAB 9

AGASSIZ, *Capt* James John Charles, RN (*fl* 1806–1826)   M vi 297

AGRAMONTE, Juan de (*fl* 1511)
Catalan seaman; explorer of Newfoundland   DCB i 41

AINSLIE, John (*fl* 1772–1813)
Scottish land-surveyor, engraver and cartographer   CE i 170; chb 419

AIRE, *Capt* James, RN (*fl* 1678–1682)   ch ii 34

AIRY, *Sir* George Biddle, KCB (1801–1892)
Astronomer Royal   A 247; B iv 53;
                                                                    CE i 207; DNB xxii 22;
                                                                    T ii 412

AITCHISON, George (1792–1861)
Clerk of works to St Katherine's Dock Company, 1827   B i 35

AITCHISON, George (1825–1910)
Joint architect to the London and St Katherine's Dock Company   DNB xxiii a 28

AITCHISON, *Rear-Adm* Robert (1798–1861)   B iv 56; M v 299

ALEXANDER, *Capt* John, RN (*fl* 1807–1840)   M vii 4

ALEXANDER, *Cdr* Nicholas, RN (*fl* 1799–1816)   M vii 360

ALEXANDER, Stephen (1806–1883)
Astronomer   DAB 15

ALEXANDER, *Rear-Adm* Thomas (*fl* 1790–1819)   M ii 771

ALEXANDER, *Capt* Thomas, CB, RN (*d* 1825)   M xi 410

ALEXANDER, *Sir* William, *Earl of Stirling* (1567 or 1577–1640)
Promoter of colonisation, poet, proprietor of Nova Scotia   DCB i 50; MDC 718

ALEXANDER, *Sir* William (1602–1638)
Privateering captain; founder of Port-Royal colony   DCB i 54

ALEXANDER, William (1767–1816)
Artist; illustrated; Barrow's: 'Voyage to Cochin China' (1806). Completed drawings from
Daniell's sketches which illustrated Vancouver's: 'Voyage to the North Pacific' (1813)   DNB i 281

ALEXANDER, William (*d* 1884)
Surveyor of shipping to the Liverpool underwriters   B i 45

ALEXANDER-SINCLAIR, *Adm Sir* Edwyn Sinclair, GCB (1865–1945)   DNB xxvii 9

ALFRED, *King* (849–901)   CE i 251; DNB i 152;
                                                               Md i 459

ALFRED ERNEST ALBERT, *Duke of Edinburgh & Duke of Saxe-Coburg &*
Gotha, Adm of the Fleet, KT, GCB, GCSI, GCMG (1844–1900)   B iv 80; DNB xxii 34

ALINGHAM, William (*fl* 1694–1710)
Writer on and teacher of mathematics and navigation   T i 289

ALLAN & CAITHNESS (*fl* 1802–1820)
Makers of chromometers tested by Captain Buchan in 1818   T ii 380

ALLAN, Andrew (1822–1901)
Canadian capitalist, president of the Montreal Ocean Steamship Co; chairman of the
Montreal Harbour Commissioners   MDC 7

ALLAN, *Sir* Hugh (1810–1882)
Scottish capitalist, shipbuilder and shipowner; founder of the Allan Line   B i 48, MDC 7

ALLAN, *Sir* Hugh Montague (1860–1951)
Canadian capitalist and shipowner   MDC 8

ALLAN, James (*d* 1874)
First secretary of the Peninsular Steam Navigation Co.; 1837, and of the Peninsular &
Oriental Co., 1840   B i 48

ALLAN, James (1826–1882)
Shipowner   B iv 84

ALLAN, Peter (1798–1849)
Excavated caves at Marsden's Rock near Sunderland, whence he moved in 1828.
Allan spent the rest of his life there, during which time he rescued several vessels
in distress   DNB i 296

ALLEN, William (1790?–1856)
Master mariner and philanthropist   DAUB i 7

ALLEN, *Rear Adm* William (1793–1864)   B i 53; DNB i 322

ALLEN, William (*fl* 1805–1848)
Served as volunteer aboard the 'Naiad' at Trafalgar   Tr 297

ALLEN, *Capt* William Edward Hughes, RN (1787–1855/6)   M viii 307; Tr 53

ALLEN, *Cdr* William Henry, USN (1784–1813)   DAB 17

ALLIBONE, *Lieut* Charles O., USN (*fl* 1863–1880)   H 952

ALLIN, *Adm Sir* Thomas (1612–1685)   ch i 4; DNB i 332

ALLINGTON, *Capt* Argentine [*or* Argenton], RN (*fl* 1668–1669) ch i 313

ALLISON, *Lieut* John, RN (*fl* 1794)   M viii 172

ALLISON, Thomas (*fl* 1697)
Arctic voyager   DNB i 333

ALLISON, *Rear-Adm* Thomas (*d* 1776)   ch v 422

ALLPORT, *Sir* James Joseph (1811–1892)
Managing director of Palmer's Shipbuilding Company, 1857–1860 B iv 102

ALLTOFF, Thomas, *Master's Mate*, RN (*fl* 1805–1816)   Tr 31

ALMEIDA, Francisco de (*d* 1509)   CE i 284

ALMONDE, Philippe van (1646–1711)
Dutch Vice-Admiral   Md i 572

ALMS, *Capt* James, RN (1728–1791)   ch vi 546; DNB i 342

ALMY, *Rear-Adm* John Jay, USN (1815–1895)   DAB 19; H 29

ALSTON, *Cdr* Alfred Henry, RN (1830–1874)   B iv 105

ALZATE Y RAMIREZ, *Don* Joseph-Antoine (*d* 1796)
Mexican astronomer and geographer   Md i 550

AMADAS [*or* AMIDAS], *Adm* Philip (1550–1585)   DAB 20; H 31

AMBLER, James Markham Marshall (1848–1881)
Surgeon on the 1879–1881 'Jeanette' Arctic expedition   DAB 20

AMBLIMONT, Fuschemberg, *Comte* d' (*d* 1797)
French naval officer and writer. Author of: 'Tactique navale' (1788) Md i 566

AMBROSE, *Rear-Adm* John, RN (*d* 1771)   ch iv 252; DNB i 351

AMBROSE, *Lieut* Prosper, RN (*d* 1848)   Tr 287

AMES, *Capt* Joseph (1619–1695)
Naval commander during the Commonwealth   DNB i 352

AMES, *Cdr* Sulivan D., USN (*b* 1840)   H 909

AMFREVILLE
Three brothers at La Hogue action (1692)   Md i 584

AMHERST, *Adm* John (1718?–1778)   ch v 275; DNB i 359

ANDERSON, *Capt* Robert, RN (*fl* 1665)   ch i 142

ANDERSON, Robert, *Asst-Surgeon* RN (*d* 1856)   B i 65

ANDERSON, *Sir* Samuel Lee (1837–1886)
Marshall of the High Court of Admiralty in Ireland, 1866–1868   B iv 123

ANDERSON, William (1757–1837)
Marine painter   DNB i 393

ANDERSON, William (*d* 1778)
Surgeon and naturalist; accompanied Cook's second and third voyages   DNB i 393

ANDOE, *Cdr* Robert, RN (*fl* 1801–1821)   M viii 58

ANDREADE, Ferdinand d' (*fl* 1518)
Portuguese admiral   Md i 661

ANDRÉE, Salomon August (1854–1897)
Swedish engineer; attempted to reach North Pole by balloon   CE i 411

ANDREW, *Rear-Adm* John William, CB (*d* 1854)   B i 67; M xi 115

ANDREW, Charles (1829–1864)
Admiralty resident engineer at Malta, 1864–1873   B iv 131

ANDREWS, *Capt* George, RN (*b* 1778)   M x 49

ANDREWS, Henry (1743–1820)
Astronomical calculator; worked for the 'Nautical Almanac' for over forty years   DNB i 406; T ii 252

ANDREWS, Henry, *Master* RN (*d* 1859)   Tr 296

ANDREWS, *Capt* Isaac, RN (*d* 1702)   ch iii 62

ANDREWS, James (1774–1833)
Writer on, and teacher of navigation   T ii 328

ANDREWS, *Capt* John, RN (*fl* 1664–1666)   ch i 88

ANDREWS, John (*fl* 1766–1809)
Geographer, map-seller and engraver   chb 419

ANDREWS, *Capt* Thomas, RN (*fl* 1670–1672)   ch i 329

ANDREWS, *Capt* Thomas, RN (*d* 1756)   ch v 360

ANDREWS, *Capt* William, RN (*fl* 1666–1673)   ch i 214

ANGAS, George Fife (1789–1879)
Merchant banker and philanthropist; founded the shipping business G. F. Angus & Co.,
London, 1825; helped his brother William found the Bethel Mission for Seamen;
became a director of the British & Foreign Sailors' Society, 1833   AE i 57; B i 69; DAuB
                                                                           i 15; DNB i 413

ANGAS, William Henry (1781–1832)
Sailor and missionary; worked for the British & Foreign Seamen's Friend Society &
Bethel Union, 1822–1832   DNB i 413

ANGELL, *Capt* Henry, RN (*d* 1777)   ch vi 152

APRENDESTIGUY [*or* ARPENTIGNY *or* DAPRANDESTEGUY],
Martin d', *Sieur de Martignon* (1616–1689)
French sea-captain and fur-trader   DCB i 66

APRÈS de MANNEVILLETTE, Jean Baptiste Nicolas Denis d' (1707–1780)
French hydrographer   M*d* ii 127

ARABIN, *Rear-Adm* Septimus (*d* 1856)   B iv 148; M v 69

ARBUCKLE, John (1839–1912)
American merchant and shipowner   DAB 27

ARBUTHNOT, *Adm* Marriott (*d* 1794)   *ch* vi 1; DNB i 537;
                                                                       MDC 17; NA i 48;
                                                                       NC xxiii 265; R i 129

ARBUTHNOT, *Adm Sir* Robert Keith, KCB (1864–1916)   DNB xxv 11

ARBUTHNOTT, *Adm Sir* Alexander Dundas Young (*d* 1871)   B i 78; Tr 125;
                                                                       M v 195

ARDECKNE, Andrew (1822–1871)
Commodore of the Royal London Yacht Club for eighteen years   B i 80

ARCHER, *Capt* Anthony, RN (*fl* 1664)   *ch* i 88

ARCHER, Colin (1832–1921)
Shipbuilder; constructed Nansen's 'Fram'   DA*u*B i 22

ARCHER, *Capt* John, RN (*fl* 1670–1673)   *ch* i 239

ARDEN, *Capt* Samuel, RN (*fl* 1781–1796)   M iii 73

ARENTSON, Jurriaen: *see* AERNOUTSON

ARGALL [*or* ARGOLL], *Sir* Samuel (*d* 1626)   DAB 27; DCB i 67;
                                                                       DNB i 551; MDC 18

ARGELANDER, Friedrich Wilhelm August (1799–1875)
German astronomer   CE i 574

ARGLES, *Capt* George, RN (*fl* 1794–1813)   M iv 719

ARISTARCHUS OF SAMOS (*ca* 310–250 B.C.)
Astronomer   CE i 587

ARMS, Frank A., *Paymaster*, USN (*fl* 1862–1880)   H 993

ARMSTRONG, *Sir* Alexander, RN (1818–1899)
Director-general of the medical department of the navy, 1869–1880   B iv 163; DNB xxii 61

ARMSTRONG, *Cdre* James, USN (1794–1868)   H 43

ARMSTRONG, John (1674–1742)
Part author of: 'Report with proposals for draining the Fens and amending the port of
King's Lynn . . .'   DNB i 566

ARMSTRONG, Lancelot, *Surgeon*, RN (*d* 1848)   Tr 236

ARMSTRONG, Mostyn John (*fl ca* 1771–1791)
Geographer and publisher   *chb* 419

ARTHUR, *Cdr* William Stephens, RN (*fl* 1811–1824)   M viii 146

ARUNDEL, *Capt* Charles, RN (*d* 1723)   ch iv 38

ARUNDELL, *Sir* John (*d* 1379)
Naval commander   DNB i 618

ARUNDELL, *Sir* John (1495–1561)
Naval commander   DNB i 618

ASHBY, *Capt* Arthur, RN (*d* 1666)   ch i 214

ASHBY, *Capt* Arthur, RN (*d* 1691)   ch ii 306

ASHBY, *Adm Sir* John (*d* 1693)   ch i 302; DNB i 638;
                                                                       M*d* ii 325

ASHFORD, *Capt* Andrew, RN (*fl* 1660–1664)   ch i 7

ASHLEY, *Sir* Anthony (1551–1628)
Translator of Waghenaer's: 'Spieghel der Zeevaardt'   DNB i 642

ASHLEY, Wilfred William, *Baron Mount Temple* (1867–1938)
Politician; president of the Navy League for several years   DNB xxvi 26

ASHMORE, *Maj-Gen* John, RM (*d* 1865)   B iv 183

ASHTON, Henry (*b* 1794)
Served as a clerk aboard the 'Colossus' at Trafalgar   Tr 171

ASHTON, *Sir* Robert de (*d* 1385)
Naval officer; Admiral of the Narrow Seas, 1369   DNB i 651

ASHTON, *Capt* Thomas, RN (*fl* 1678–1688)   ch ii 134

ASHWORTH, *Lieut* Henry, RN (1785–1811)   DNB i 659; NC xxxiii
                                                                       265

ASKEW, *Cdr* Charles Crackenthorpe, RN (*fl* 1798–1828)   M xii 396

ASKEW, *Capt* Robert, RN (*d* 1756)   ch vi 8

ASKEY, *Cdr* James, RN (*b* 1775)   M vii 249

ASLETT, *Col* Thompson, RM (*d* 1851)   B i 99

ASLETT, *Maj-Gen* William Stratton, RM (*d* 1876)   B i 99

ASPINWALL, William Henry (1807–1875)
Shipowner   DAB 32

ASPLEY, John (*fl* 1624)
Writer on navigation and mathematician   T i 209

ASSHETON, Richard (*fl* 1659)
Instrument-maker; carpenter's joint-rule at National Maritime Museum T i 246

ASTLE, *Capt* George, RN (*fl* 1794–1798)   M iii 152

ASTLEY, *Capt Sir* Edward William Corry, RN (*b* 1788)   M vi 81

ASTON, Albert, *Chief Engineer*, USN (*d* 1881)   H 1009

ASTON, *Capt* John, RN (*fl* 1697–1698)   ch iii 155

ATCHERLEY, *Capt* James, RN (*d* 1834)   Tr 155

ATCHISON, *Capt* Arthur, RN (*d* 1818)   Tr 40

ATHERTON, Charles (1805–1875)
Resident engineer of the River Clyde, 1832–1834; chief engineer, Woolwich Dockyard, 1847–1848 and 1851–1862, and at Devonport, 1849–1851   B i 101

ATHERTON, *Sir* William (1806–1864)
Judge advocate of the fleet and counsel to the Admiralty, 1854–1859   B i 101

ATHILL, *Cdr* James, RN (*d* 1825)   M vii 213

ATHY, *Capt* Richard, RN (*fl* 1693–1695)   *ch* iii 4

ATKINS, *Capt* Charles, RN (*fl* 1672–1675)   *ch* ii 10

ATKINS, George (*fl* 1817–1822)
Inventor of instruments for finding longitude at sea   T ii 381

ATKINS, *Capt* James, RN (*fl* 1692–1696)   *ch* iii 5

ATKINS, John, *Surgeon*, RN (1685–1757)   DNB i 692

ATKINS, *Rear-Adm* Samuel (*d* 1755 *or* 1765)   *ch* iv 68

ATKINS, Samuel (*fl* 1787–1808)
Marine painter   DNB i 693

ATKINS, Samuel Elliott (1807–1898)
Chronometer-maker   B iv 192

ATKINSON, *Capt Sir* Henry Esch, RN (1792–1857)   B i 103; M viii 218

ATKINSON, James (*fl* 1667–1711)
Writer on, and teacher of navigation; book and chart-seller; instrument-maker   T i 254

ATKINSON, *Cdr* James Charles, RN (1783–1882)   B i 103

ATKINSON, Thomas, *Master*, RN (*d* 1836)   Tr 14

ATTWOOD, Matthias (*d* 1851)
Chairman of the General Steam Navigation Company   B i 105

ATWELL, Robert (*fl* 1795–1848)
Midshipman on the 'Prince' at Trafalgar   Tr 81

AUBERT, Alexander (1730–1805)
Astronomer and naval architect; chairman of Ramsgate Harbour Commission   DNB i 715; T ii 279

AUBERT, Thomas (*fl* 1504–1508)
French sea-captain and explorer   DCB i 72

AUCHMUTY, Robert (*d* 1750)
Judge of the Admiralty Court, Massachusetts, 1733–1741   DAB 33

AUDLEY, *Capt* Robert, RN (*d* 1696/7)   *ch* iii 5

AUDUS, James (1781–1867)
Began a coasting trade between Selby and London, 1826, and by 1830 had eighteen schooners employed in the trade   B i 107

AULICK, Hampton, *Surgeon*, USN (*fl* 1870–1880)   H 980

AULT, Joseph, *Purser*, RN (*d* 1817)   Tr 171

AURIN, *Capt* David, RN (*d* 1735/6)   *ch* iv 211

AUSTEN, *Rear-Adm* Charles John, CB (1779–1852)   B i 107; M x 74

AUSTEN, *Adm of the Fleet Sir* Francis William, GCB (1774–1865)   B i 107; DNB i 730;
                                                                         M iii 274

AUSTEN, *Lieut* Sylvester, RN (*fl* 1801–1816)   Tr 42

AUSTIN, *Vice-Adm Sir* Horatio Thomas, KCB (1801–1865)   B i 109; CE i 785;
                                                                         M viii 369

AUSTIN, James (1776–1831)
Established a ferry across the River Derwent, Australia   DAuB i 42

AUTRIDGE, *Capt* William, RN (*d* 1825)   M xi 106

AUVERGNE, *Capt* Corbet James d', RN (*d* 1825)   M x 414

AUVERGNE, *Vice-Adm* Philip, *Prince of Bouillon* (*b* 1754)   NC xiii 169

AUWERS, George Friedrich Julius Arthur (1838–1915)
German astronomer   CE ii 1

AVERY, John (*fl* 1695)
Pirate   DNB i 747

AYALA, Juan Manuel de (*fl* 1775)
Spanish navigator   DAB 36

AYLEN, *Capt* Jonathan, RN (1798–1874)   B i 112

AYLES, *Maj-Gen* John George Augustus, RM (1808–1883)   B i 112

AYLETT, *Capt* John, RN (*fl* 1664–1668)   *ch* i 89

AYLLON, Lucas Vasquez de (*ca* 1475–1526)
Spanish navigator   DAB 36

AYLMER, *Adm* Frederick Whitworth, KCB, *sixth Baron Aylmer* (1777–1858) B i 112; M iv 947

AYLMER, *Capt.* George, RN (*fl* 1677–1688)   *ch* ii 61

AYLMER, *Capt* Henry, RN, *third Baron Aylmer* (1718–1766)   *ch* v 64

AYLMER, *Adm* John (*fl* 1782–1809)   M i 234

AYLMER, *Adm of the Fleet* Matthew, *first Baron Aylmer* (*d* 1720)   *ch* ii 35; DNB i 755

AYLWIN, John Cushing, USN (*ca* 1780–1813)   DAB 36

AYRES, Joseph G., *Surgeon*, USN (*fl* 1866–1880)   H 978

AYRES, Samuel L. P., *Chief Engineer*, USN (*fl* 1858–1880)   H 1007

AYSCOUGH, *Adm* John (1775–1863)   B i 115; M ix 123

AYSCUE, *Adm Sir* George (*fl* 1646–1671)   *ch* i 38; DNB i 770;
                                                                         Md ii 320

AZARA, *Don* Felix d' (1746–1811)
Spanish engineer and South American explorer   Md ii 535

BAFFIN, William (*ca* 1584–1622)   A 82; CE ii 49;
                                                                        DCB i 74; DNB i 861;
                                                                        H 58; MDC 28;
                                                                        M*d* ii 607

BAGGE, Jacques (*b* 1499)
Swedish admiral   M*d* ii 610

BAGOT, *Adm* Henry (1810–1877)   B i 125

BAGUE, *Cdr* George, RN (*d* 1856)   Tr 168

BAGWELL, *Cdr* Paul Piercy, RN (*fl* 1813–1830)   M viii 351

BAGWELL, William (*fl* 1665)
Writer on astronomy   DNB i 878

BAHARIE, A. (*fl ca* 1840)
Instrument-maker; sextant at National Maritime Museum   T ii 466

BAIKIE, William Balfour (1825–1864)
Naval surgeon and African explorer   B i 126; CE ii 54;
                                                                        DNB i 878

BAILEY, Frank Harvey, USN (1851–1921)   DAB 40

BAILEY, Solomon Irving (1854–1931)
Astronomer   DAB 40

BAILEY, *Rear-Adm* Theodorus, USN (1805–1877)   DAB 40; H 59

BAILLIE, Charles William (1844–1899)
Marine superintendent of the Meteorological Office, 1888–1899   B iv 227

BAILLIE, *Capt* Thomas, RN (*d* 1802)   *ch* vi 214; DNB i 878

BAILLIE, *Adm* Thomas (1811–1889)   B iv 230

BAILLIE-HAMILTON, *Adm* Cospatrick (1817–1892)   B iv 230

BAILLY, Jean Aylvain (1736–1793)
French astronomer   CE ii 55

BAILY, *Capt* Edward Seymour, RN (*fl* 1780–1809)   M x 52

BAILY, Francis (1774–1844)
Astronomer and writer on longitude   A 210; CE ii 56;
                                                                        DNB i 899; T ii 919

BAIN, Alexander (1810–1877)
Patented an apparatus for registering the progress of a ship, 1844   B i 130; DNB i 904

BAIN, *Adm* Henderson (*d* 1862)   B i 131; M ii 123

BAIN, *Sir* William (1771–1853)
Master RN, 1811; later commanded G.S.N.C. vessels; harbour master of Granton on
the Firth of Forth for ten years   B i 131; T ii 382

BAKER, *Capt* James, RN (*d* 1765) ch vi 290

BAKER, *Adm* James Vashon (1798–1875) B i 137

BAKER, *Adm* John (1661–1716) ch ii 379; DNB i 932

BAKER, *Capt* John, RN (*d* 1845) M x 267

BAKER, *Capt* John Popham, RN (*fl* 1802–1829) M viii 51

BAKER, Robert (*fl* 1563)
Voyager to Guinea DNB i 936; M*d* ii 655

BAKER, Robert (*fl* 1685–1712)
Teacher of practical mathematics and navigation T i 28

BAKER, *Lieut-Cdr* Samuel H., USN (*fl* 1861–1880) H 926

BAKER, *Vice-Adm Sir* Thomas, KCB (1771?–1845) DNB xxii 105;
M ii 829; R iv 237

BAKER, *Cdr* Thomas, RN (*fl* 1815–1833) M viii 389

BAKER, Thomas (*fl* 1830–1835)
Chronometer-maker T ii 443

BAKER, Thomas Palmer, CB (*d* 1876)
*Chief engineer at Chatham dockyard, 1856–1868; appointed chief inspector of machinery
afloat, 1866* B i 138

BAKEWELL, Thomas (1730–1764)
Bookseller, map and print-seller ch*b* 420

BALBI, Gaspar (*fl* 1579–1588)
Venetian voyager M*d* ii 663

BALBOA, Vasco Nunez de (1475–1517) CE ii 85; M*d* ii 66

BALCH, *Rear-Adm* George Beall, USN (1821–1908) DAB 43; H 60

BALCHEN, *Capt* George, RN (*d* 1745) ch v 4

BALCHEN, *Adm Sir* John (1670–1744) ch iii 155; DNB i 946;
NC xxviii 89

BALD, William (1803–1857)
*Civil engineer; at one time a draughtsman at the Admiralty; resident engineer to the
trustees of the River Clyde, 1839–1845* B i 139

BALDCOCK, *Rear-Adm* Thomas (*d* 1871) B i 140

BALDWIN, *Lieut* Abraham, RN (*d* 1815) T*r* 80

BALDWIN, *Adm* Augustus Warren (1776–1866) B i 140; M xii 138;
MDC 30

BALDWIN, *Cdr* Charles H., USN (*b* 1822) H 61

BALDWIN, Edward (*fl* 1704)
Teacher of navigation T i 300

BALDWIN, Evelyn Brigge (1862–1933)
Arctic explorer DAB 43

BALMAIN, William (1762–1803)
*Joined the Royal Navy as a surgeon's mate in 1786; appointed assistant surgeon to
New South Wales in 1786*   DAuB i 51

BAMBER, *Cdr* William Richard RN (*d* 1843)   M vi 406

BAMBER, James (*fl* 1820)
Inventor of ship's log   T ii 413

BAMFF, *Lord* Alexander Ogilvie (*d* 1748)   ch 5 66

BANCROFT, *Capt* Gherardi, USN (*b* 1832)   H 885

BANKERT, Adrien (*d* 1684)
Dutch vice-admiral   M*d* iii 12

BANKERT, Joseph van Trappen (*fl* 1622–1646)
Dutch vice-admiral   M*d* iii 12

BANKHEAD, *Capt* John Pine, USN (*b* 1821)   H 63

BANKS, *Cdr* Francis, RN (*d* 1777)   ch vi 386

BANKS, *Cdr* Francis, RN (*fl* 1798–1813)   M vii 120

BANKS, *Cdr Sir* Jacob, RN (*d* 1724)   ch ii 306

BANKS, *Sir* Joseph (1743–1820)   A 155; AE i 128; CE ii
                                                                                        106; DAuB i 56; DNB i
                                                                                        1049; M*d* iii 13;
                                                                                        T ii 155

BANKS, *Cdr* John, RN (*d* 1859)   M vii 72

BANNERMAN, *Sir* Alexander (1788–1864)
Aberdeen merchant and shipowner; a commissioner of Greenwich Hospital, 1841   B i 153

BANT, Thomas, *Midshipman*, RN (*b* 1786)   Tr 205

BARBARO, Josaphat (*d* 1494)
Venetian traveller   M*d* iii 37

BARBAROSSA, I. [Horush *or* Arauj *or* Koruk] (1473?–1518)
Turkish corsair   CE ii 117; M*d* iii 55

BARBAROSSA, II. [Khair ed-Din *or* Khairreddin] (1466?–1546)
Turkish corsair   CE ii 117; M*d* iii 56

BARBER, *Capt* Daniel, RN (*fl* 1810–1825)   M v 223

BARBER, *Cdr* Edward, RN (*d* 1762?)   ch vi 153

BARBER, *Lieut-Cdr* Francis M., USN (*fl* 1861–1880)   H 932

BARBER, J. (*fl* 1770–1800)
Engraver   ch*b* 420

BARBER, *Capt* James, RN (*d* 1691)   ch i 385

BARBER, *Capt* Robert, RN (*d* 1784)   ch vi 348

BARBIE DU BOCAGE, Jean-Denis (1760–1825)
Cartographer and geographer   M*d* iii 60

BARKER, *Lieut* George Alexander, RN (*fl* 1804–1817)   Tr 226

BARKER, *Capt* James, RN (1772–1838)   DNB i 1121; M xi 96

BARKER, *Capt* Jedediah, RN (*d* 1702)   *ch* ii 407

BARKER, *Capt* John, RN (*d* 1653)   DNB i 1122

BARKER, *Capt* John, RN (*d* 1776)   *ch* v 361

BARKER, Josiah (1763–1847)
Shipbuilder   DAB 48

BARKER, Matthew Henry (1790–1846)
Served in both the Royal Navy and the East India Company's service before turning
to writing in 1825. Published sea tales under the pseudonym: 'The Old Sailor'   DNB i 1127

BARKER, *Lieut* Thomas Dobbins, RN (*fl* 1801–1806)   Tr 233

BARKLEY, Charles William (1759–1832)
Sea-captain and explorer   MDC 34

BARLOW, *Capt* Charles Anstruther, CB, RN (1800–1855)   B i 167

BARLOW, Peter (1776–1862)
Mathematician; invented a method of compensating compass errors in ships   B i 168; DNB i 1143;
                                                                         T ii 330

BARLOW, *Adm Sir* Robert, GCB (1757–1843)   DNB xxii 127; M iii 44

BARLOW, Roger (*d* 1554)
Cartographer and navigator with Sebastian Cabot   T i 166

BARLOW, William (1544–1625)
Navigation expert   T i 176

BARLOW, William Henry (1812–1902)
Civil engineer; reported on lighthouses at the mouth of the Bosphorus and wrote a
thesis on the illumination of lighthouses, 1837   DNB xxiiia 98

BARNABY, *Sir* Nathaniel, KCB (1829–1915)
Naval architect   DNB xxiv 28

BARNARD, *Adm* Edward (*d* 1863)   B i 170; M xii 142;
                                                                         Tr 161

BARNARD, Edward Emerson (1857–1923)
American astronomer   CE ii 129; DAB 49

BARNARD, Edward George (*d* 1851)
Shipbuilder   B i 170

BARNARD, *Vice-Adm* Frederick Lamport (1813–1880)   B i 170

BARNARD [*or* BERNARD], *Capt* George, RN (*fl* 1661)   *ch* i 53

BARNARD, *Lieut* John James, RN (*d* 1851)   B iv 272

BARNARD, William (1774–1849)
Mezzotint engraver; produced four portraits of Nelson, after Abbott   DNB i 1162

BARNES, *Cdr* Butler, RN (*fl* 1666–1668)   *ch* i 215

BARROS, Jean de (*ca* 1491–1570)
Portuguese historian, author of: 'L'Azia Portugueza', 14 vols. (1552)   Md iii 167

BARROW, Henry (*fl* 1838)
Instrument-maker; compass and gunner's rule at National Maritime Museum   T ii 466

BARROW, John (*fl* 1735–1774)
Teacher of mathematics and navigation and writer on same   T ii 169

BARROW, John (*fl* 1756)
Geographical compiler   DNB i 1225

BARROW, *Sir* John (1764–1848)
Secretary to the Board of Admiralty; writer on exploration   DNB i 1225; T ii 304

BARROW, John (1808–1898)   B iv 286

BARROW, *Cdr* William, RN (*fl* 1829–1834)   M viii 383

BARRY, *Lieut* Edward B., USN (*fl* 1865–1880)   H 959

BARRY, *Cdre* John, USN (1745–1803)   DAB 51; DNB i 1245;
                                                                                     H 66

BARRY, Richard, (*fl* 1799–1820)
Chart-seller and instrument-maker   T i 331

BARRY, William W., *Assist-Paymaster*, USN (*fl* 1870–1880)   H 996

BART, Jean (1651–1702)   CE ii 141; H 67
French naval officer and privateer   Md iii 174

BARTELOT [*or* BARTLET], John (*fl* 1540–1546)
Hydrographer   T i 168

BARTER, *Capt* John, RN (*d* 1708)   ch iii 307

BARTHOLOMEW, *Cdr* Charles, RN (*fl* 1777–1809)   M x 52

BARTHOLOMEW, *Capt* David Ewen, CB, RN (*d* 1821)   DNB i 1253; M xii 444

BARTHOLOMEW, John (1831–1893)
Cartographer   B iv 292; CE ii 142

BARTHOLOMEW, John George (1860–1920)
Cartographer   DNB xxiv 33

BARTHOLOMEW, Thomas, *Midshipman*, RN (1792–1805)   Tr 227

BARTLEMAN, Richard Milner, *Engineer*, USN   H 1004

BARTLETT, Charles H., *Assist-Paymaster*, USN (*fl* 1869–1880)   H 996

BARTLETT, *Capt* Henry Anthony, USMC (*fl* 1861–1880)   H 1015

BARTLETT, *Cdr* John R., USN (*fl* 1859–1880)   H 914

BARTLETT, John Sharren, *Surgeon*, RN (1790–1863)   B i 186

BARTLETT, Robert Abram (1875–1946)
Canadian Arctic explorer   MDC 36

BATE, *Capt* William Thornton, RN (1820–1857)   B i 190

BATEMAN, *Adm* Charles Philip Butler (1776–1857)   B i 190; M ix 178

BATEMAN, John (1789–1833)
Merchant; established the Fremantle Whaling Company   DAuB i 66

BATEMAN, John (1824–1909)
Promoter of Fremantle's claims as a harbour   DAuB i 66

BATEMAN, John Frederick La Trobe [*formerly* John Frederick Bateman]
(1810–1889)
*Civil engineer; associated with several dock and harbour trusts throughout the
British Isles*   DNB xxii 138

BATEMAN, *Capt* Nathaniel, RN (*fl* 1760–1780)   ch vi 386

BATEMAN, *Capt the Hon* William RN (*d* 1783)   ch v 362

BATES [*or* BATTS], *Cdr* George, RN (*fl* 1660–1666)   ch v 362

BATES, *Sir* Henry Elly (1879–1946)
Liverpool merchant and shipowner; chairman of the Cunard Company, 1930–1946   DNB xxvii 65

BATES, Newton L., *Surgeon*, USN (*fl* 1861–1880)   H 973

BATES, Thomas (*fl* 1704–1719)
*Served five years as a naval surgeon; author of: 'Enchiridion of fevers common to
seamen in the Mediterranean' (1709)*   DNB i 1319

BATHURST, Ralph (1620–1704)
*Employed as physician to the sick and wounded in the navy during the English
Civil War*   DNB i 1330

BATHURST, *Capt* Walter, RN (1764?–1827)   DNB i 1332; M iii 239

BATTELL, Andrew (*fl* 1589–1614)
English voyager   DNB i 1335; Md iii 264

BATTEN [*or* BATTIN], *Capt* William RN (*fl* 1653–1660)   ch i 8

BATTEN, *Adm Sir* William (*d* 1667)   DNB i 1338

BATTENBERG FAMILY   CE ii 161

BATTENBERG, *Adm of the Fleet Prince* Louis Alexander, *later* Louis
Alexander Mountbatten, *first Marquess of Milford Haven* (1854–1921)   DNB xxiv 394

BATTERS, *Cdr* Christopher, RN (*fl* 1660)   ch i 215

BATTS [*or* BATES], *Cdr* George, RN (*fl* 1660–1666)   ch i 8

BAUDIN, François André, *Baron* (1774–1842)   s i 60

BAUDIN, Thomas Nicholas (1754–1803)
Cartographer   DAuB i 71; Md iii 278

BAUER, Ferdinand Lukes (1760–1826)
Botanist; accompanied Flinders in the 'Investigator', 1800–1803   DAuB i 73

BAUGH, *Capt* Henry, RN (*fl* 1793–1841)   M vi 367

BAUGH, *Rear-Adm* Thomas Folliott (*fl* 1784–1846)   M x 266

BAUGHMAN, George E., *Assist-Paymaster*, USN (*fl* 1870–1880) — H 997

BAUMGARDT, *Cdre* William Augustus, RN (*fl* 1806–1820) — M vii 342

BAUZA, *Don* Filippo (*d* 1833)
Spanish hydrographer and cartographer — M*d* iii 319

BAVIN, Thomas (*fl* 1582–1583)
Surveyor with Sir Humphrey Gilbert — T i 184

BAXENDELL, Joseph (1851–1887)
Meteorologist and astronomer; served at sea between the ages of fourteen and twenty — B iv 309; DNB xxii 145

BAYER, Johann (1572–1625)
German astronomer — CE ii 169; M*d* iii 337

BAYFIELD, *Adm* Henry Wolsey (1795–1885) — B iv 311; M viii 530; MDC 37

BAYFORD, James Heseltine (*ca* 1805–1871) — B iv 312

BAYLEE, John Tyrell (*fl* 1823)
Teacher of mathematics and writer on longitude — T ii 413

BAYLER, William (1727–1810)
Astronomer; sailed with Cook, 1772; assistant to Maskelyne — T ii 223

BAYLEY, *Cdr* James, RN (*b* 1785) — M viii 302

BAYLEY, *Capt* John, RN (*fl* 1793–1813) — M xi 166

BAYLY [*or* BAILY *or* BALEY], Charles (*fl ca* 1630–1680)
First overseas governor of Hudson's Bay Company — DCB i 81

BAYLY, George (1807–1888)
An elder brother of Trinity House, 1857-1888 — B iv 315

BAYLY, *Capt* James, RN (*d* 1857) — T*r* 278

BAYLY, *Adm Sir* Lewis, KCB, KCMG (1857–1938) — DNB xxvi 54

BAYLY, *Lieut* Robert Sutton, RN (1787–1832?) — T*r* 53

BAYLY, William (1757–1810)
Astronomer — DNB i 1372

BAYNE, *Capt* William, RN (*d* 1782) — *ch* vi 387; DNB i 1374

BAYNES, *Adm Sir* Robert Lambert, KCB (1796–1869) — B i 202; M vi 42

BAYNES, *Col* Simcoe (*d* 1875)
Served as midshipman, Royal Navy, 1810 — B i 202

BAYNTUN, *Adm Sir* Henry William, GCB (1766–1840) — DNB i 1377; M ii 543, 859, 871; T*r* 191

BAYS, Peter Payne (*d* 1864)
Mercantile marine sailing master; author of: 'A narrative of the wreck of the Minerva whaler of Port Jackson' (1831) — B i 202

BAZALGETTE, *Cdr* Joseph William, RN (*ca* 1783–1849) — M vii 197

BAZELY, *Capt* Henry, RN (*b* 1786) — M iii 250

BAZELY, *Vice-Adm* John (1740/1–1790)   NC xiv 177

BAZELY, *Capt* John, RN (*fl* 1783–1814)   M iii 27

BEACH, *Capt Sir* Richard, RN (*d* 1692)   *ch* i 51

BEAL, Samuel, *Chaplain*, RN (1825–1889)   B iv 320

BEALE, *Cdre* Joseph, USN (*fl* 1837–1876)
Chief of USN Bureau of medicine and surgery, 1873–1876   H 980

BEAMAN, Charles Cotesworth (1840–1900)
Lawyer; acted for the U.S.A. in the 'Alabama' claims case, 1871–1873   DAB 59

BEAMAN, George, *Paymaster*, USN (*fl* 1862–1880)   H 990

BEARDMORE, Nathaniel (1816–1872)
Engineer to the Thames Conservancy Board   B i 209; DNB ii 16

BEARDMORE, William, *Baron Invernairn* (1856–1936)
Shipbuilder   DNB xxvi 55

BEARDSLEE, *Cdr* Lester A., USN (*fl* 1850–1879)   H 899

BEARE, *Capt* Amos, RN (*fl* 1664–1668)   *ch* i 94

BEARE, James (*fl* 1577–1585)
Ship's master, with Frobisher 1577–1578; cartographer   DCB i 85

BEATSON, Robert (1742–1818)
Author of: 'Naval and military memoirs of Great Britain' (1790)   DNB ii 21

BEATTY, *Adm of the Fleet* David, *first Earl Beatty* (1871–1936)   CE ii 177; DNB xxvi 56

BEATTY, Francis, *Purser*, RN (*d* 1822)   Tr 155

BEATTY, *Gen* George, RM (*d* 1857)   B i 211

BEATTY, *Sir* William, *Surgeon*, RN (*d* 1842)   DNB ii 27; Tr 21

BEAUCHAMP, Joseph (1752–1801)
Astronomer   Md iii 362

BEAUCHESNE, Robert, *Chevalier de*, (1686–1731)
French-Canadian buccaneer   MDC 38

BEAUCLERK, *Adm Lord* Amelius, GCB, GCH (1771–1846)   DNB ii 33; M ii 484

BEAUCLERK, *Capt Lord* Aubrey, RN (1710?–1741)   *ch* iv 221; DNB ii 34

BEAUCLERK, *Cdr Lord* Frederick Charles Peter, RN (*b* 1808)   M viii 392

BEAUCLERK, *Capt* Vere, *Baron Vere*, RN (1699–1781)   *ch* iv 89

BEAUFORT, *Rear-Adm Sir* Francis, KCB (1774–1857)   B i 212; CE ii 178;
                                                                  DNB ii 39; M viii 52,
                                                                  x 82; T ii 331

BEAUFORT, John, KG, *first Earl of Somerset & Marquis of Dorset* (1373?–1410)
Naval commander   DNB xxii 158

BEAUFORT, *Sir* Thomas, KG, *Duke of Exeter* (*d* 1427)
Naval commander   DNB ii 49

BEDFORD, *Adm Sir* William (1764?–1827)   DNB ii 113; M ii 574, 871

BEDINGFIELD, *Vice-Adm* Norman Bernard (1824–1884)   B iv 338

BEDOUT, *Contre-Amiral* Jacques (1751–1818)   M*d* iii 439; S i 72

BEEBE, Charles William (1877–1962)
U.S. naturalist; pioneer of submarine zoology; inventor of bathysphere   A 472

BEECHEY, *Rear Adm* Frederick William (1796–1856)   B i 220; DNB ii 121; M v 302; T i 383

BEECHEY, *Vice-Adm* Richard Brydges (1808–1895)   B iv 339

BEECHING, James (1788–1858)
Inventor of 'self-righting' lifeboats   B i 220; DNB ii 123

BEEHLER, *Lieut* William H., USN (*fl* 1864–1880)   H 958

BEER, *Cdr* John, RN (*fl* 1660)   *ch* i 8

BEER, *Cdr* John, RN (*d* 1701)   *ch* ii 383

BEER, *Cdr* Thomas, RN (*b* 1787)   M viii 171

BEERBOHM, Julius Ewald (1809–1892)
Founded 'Beerbohm's Morning Shipping List' (1869)   B iv 340

BEECROFT, *Cdr* Charles, RN (*d* 1825)   M vi 393

BEESTON, *Sir* William (*fl* 1702)
Lieutenant-governor of Jamaica   DNB ii 125

BÉGON, Michel, *Sieur de la Picardière* (ca 1674–1740)
Inspector-general of the French navy; intendant of New France   MDC 44

BÉHAGUE, Jean-Pierre-Antoine, *Comte de* (*fl* 1744–1802)
French general and colonial governor   M*d* iii 511

BEHAIM, Martin (1459–1507)
German geographer   CE ii 202; M*d* iii 511

BEHM, Ernest (1830–1884)
German geographer   CE ii 208

BEHRING, Vitus: *see* BERING

BEKE, Charles Tilstone (1800–1874)
Explorer of Abyssinia; edited de Veer's: 'True description of three voyages by the north east towards Cathay and China' (1852)   DNB ii 138

BELBIN, *Cdr* Peter, RN (*fl* 1672–1677)   *ch* i 385

BELCHER, *Adm Sir* Edward, KCB (1799–1877)   B i 223; CE ii 210; DNB ii 142; H 73; M viii 322; MDC 45; T ii 414

BELCHER, *Cdr* Nathaniel, RN (*fl* 1794–1830)   M vi 401

BELDEN, *Lieut* Samuel, USN (*fl* 1862–1880)   H 941

BENEDICT, Erastus Cornelius (1800–1880)
Lawyer; specialist in Admiralty cases   DAB 66

BENETT, *Cdr* Charles Cowper, RN (*fl* 1801–1814)   M vii 271

BENHAM, Henry Washington, USA (1813–1884)
In charge of New York and Boston harbour defences, 1865–1882   DAB 66

BENJAMIN OF TUDELA (*d* 1173)   CE ii 253

BENHAM, *Capt* Andrew E. K., USN (*b* 1832)   H 887

BENNET, *Capt* Edward, RN (*d* 1732)   ch iv 223

BENNET, *Capt* John, RN (*d* 1716)   ch iii 92

BENNET, Roelof Gabriel (1775–1829)
Dutch naval officer and marine writer   Md iii 639

BENNETT, *Capt* Charles, RN (*d* 1842)   M vi 411; Tr 88

BENNETT, Floyd, USN (1890–1928)   DAB 67

BENNETT, George, RN (1804–1893)   AE i 155

BENNETT, George John (1800–1879)
Actor; served in the Royal Navy, 1813–1817   B i 241

BENNETT, *Cdr* James Cooper, RN (1801–1852)   M viii 211

BENNETT, *Adm* Thomas (1785–1870)   B i 235; M iv 58

BENSON, Edward Frederic (1867–1940)   DNB xxvi 70

BENSON, *Lieut* John, RM (*fl* 1804–1815)   Tr 172

BENSON, *Sir* John (1812–1874)
Architect and engineer; appointed engineer to the Cork harbour Commissioners in 1850   DNB ii 257

BENSON, *Rear-Adm* William Shepherd, USN (1855–1932)   DAB 68

BENT, *Lieut* Silas, USN (1820–1887)   DAB 69

BENTHAM, *Vice-Adm* George (1787–1862)   B i 246; M xii 112

BENTHAM, *Brig-Gen Sir* Samuel (1757–1831)
Naval architect and engineer; appointed superintendent of the shipbuilding yard at Kritchev by Potemkin, 1783; returned to England in 1795 and was inspector-general of navy works, 1795–1807 and a commissioner of the navy, 1807–1812   DNB ii 281

BENTINCK, *Capt* John, Albert, RN (1737–1775)   ch vi 294; DNB ii 289

BENTINCK, *Capt* William, RN (*fl* 1788)   NA ii 124

BENTLEY, *Vice-Adm Sir* John (*d* 1772)   ch v 280; DNB ii 305

BENZONI, Jérome (*fl ca* 1519)
Italian traveller, whose history of the New World was reproduced in de Bry   Md iii 680

BERESFORD, *Adm* Charles William de la Poer (1846–1919)   CE ii 260; DNB xxiv 41

BERESFORD, *Adm Sir* John Poo, KCB (1766–1844)   DNB ii 329; M ii 666; R iv 97

BERRY, *Adm Sir* Edward, KCB (1768–1831)   DNB ii 396; M ii 774;
                                                                           NC xv 177; Tr 266

BERRY, *Adm Sir* John (1635–1690)   *ch* i 143; DCB i 92;
                                                                           DNB ii 398; M*d* iv 114

BERRY, *Lieut* John, RN (*d* 1809)   Tr 197

BERRY, *Lieut* Robert M., USN (*fl* 1862–1880)   H 944

BERRY, *Capt* Thomas, RN (*d* 1689)   *ch* i 385

BERRY, *Capt* William, RN (*fl* 1664–1666)   *ch* i 94

BERRY, William (*fl* 1669–1708)
Globe-maker   *ch*b 420; T i 259

BERTHON, Edward Lyon (1813–1899)
Inventor; experimented with a two-bladed screw propeller, 1835; devised 'Burton's
log' – a means of measuring a ship's speed, and later a collapsible boat   B iv 383; DNB xxii
                                                                           184

BERTIE, *Adm Sir* Albemarle, KCB (1755–1824)   DNB ii 402; M i 195

BERTIE, *Capt Lord* Montagu, RN (*d* 1753)   *ch* v 4

BERTIE, *Capt* Peregrine, RN (1677–1709)   *ch* iii 213

BERTIE, *Capt the Hon* Peregrine, RN (1741–1790)   *ch* vi 515

BERTIE, Robert, *first Earl of Lindsey* (1582–1642)
Admiral of the ship-money fleet and general of the King's forces   DNB ii 408

BERTIE, *Capt Lord* Thomas, RN (*d* 1749)   *ch* v 283

BERTIE [*formerly* HOAR], *Adm Sir* Thomas (1758–1825)   DNB ii 409; M i 300;
                                                                           M*d* iv 155; NC xxvi 1

BERTIUS Petrus [BERTS, Pierre] (1565–1629)
Flemish cartographer and geographer   M*d* iv 170

BERTRAM, *Capt* Charles, RN (*b* 1777)   M xi 300

BERTRAM, John (1796–1882)
Sea-captain and merchant   DAB 71

BESSEL, Friedrich Wilhelm (1784–1846)
German astronomer   CE ii 284

BESSEMER, *Sir* Henry (1813–1898)   CE ii 284; DNB xxi
                                                                           185

BEST [*or* BESTE], George (*d* 1583)
Navigator; accompanied Frobisher's voyages in search of a North-West Passage,
1576–1578   DCB i 93; DNB ii 415

BEST, *Capt* John, RN (*fl* 1665)   *ch* i 156

BEST, *Capt* Robert, RN (*d* 1677)   *ch* i 279

BEST, *Capt* Thomas, RN (1570?–1638?) — DNB ii 418

BEST, *Vice-Adm* Thomas (1799–1864) — B i 262; M vi 158

BEST, *Capt* William, RN (*fl* 1674–1678) — *ch* ii 1

BESTON, *Capt* William, RN (*fl* 1671) — *ch* i 325

BETHELL, *Capt* Christopher, RN (*d* 1795) — *ch* vi 295

BETHUNE, *Vice-Adm* Charles Ramsay Drinkwater, CB (1802–1884) — B i 264

BETHUNE, *Col* John Drinkwater [*formerly* John Drinkwater] (1762–1844)
Took part in the defence of Gibraltar and published: 'A History of the siege of Gibraltar, 1779–1783' (1785); witnessed the battle of St Vincent and published anonymously: Narrative of the battle of St Vincent' (1797) — DNB ii 433

'BETHUNE, *Surgeon Lieut* Norman, RCN (1899–1939) — MDC 54

BETTESWORTH, *Capt* George Edmund Byron, RN (1780–1808) — DNB ii 441; NC xxxix 425

BETTESWORTH, John (*fl* 1770–1788)
Teacher of navigation and seamanship — T ii 280

BETTY, *Cdr* Christopher William, RN (*d* 1850) — Tr 71

BEULING, Frederick (*fl* 1838)
Chart seller — T ii 467

BEVAN, *Capt* Rowland, RN (*fl* 1794–1810) — M ix 361

BEVERLEY, Charles James (1788–1868)
Assistant-surgeon in the Navy, 1810 — B i 267; DNB ii 448

BEVERLEY, *Cdr* John, RN (*d* 1699) — *ch* i 386

BEVERLEY, *Capt* Thomas, RN (*d* 1721) — *ch* iv 3

BEVERLEY, Thomas (*fl* 1826)
Writer on latitude — T ii 414

BEVIANS, *Cdr* William, RN (*fl* 1797–1823) — M vi 261

BEVIS [*or* BEVANS], John (1693–1771)
Astronomer — DNB ii 451; T ii 111

BEVIS, *Cdr* Thomas, RN (*fl* 1797–1863) — M viii 333

BIANCHINI, Francesco (1662–1729)
Italian astronomer — CE iii 293

BIANCHO [*or* BIANCO], Andrea (*fl* fifteenth century)
Venetian geographer — Md iv 274

BIBB, *Capt* Edward, RN (*fl* 1691–1701) — *ch* ii 384

BICKEL, Luke Washington (1866–1917)
Sea-captain — DAB 72

BICKERTON, *Vice-Adm Sir* Richard (1727–1792) — *ch* vi 349; DNB ii 468; NA i 158; NC xiii 33; R ii 277

BICKERTON, *Adm Sir* Richard Hussey (1759–1832)   DNB ii 469; M i 125, ii 864; M*d* iv 288

BICKHAM, George, *senior* (1684–1758)
Author and engraver   C*hb* 421; DNB ii 470

BICKHAM, George, *junior* (*d* 1771)
Engraver and publisher, son of the above   C*hb* 421; DNB ii 470

BICKHAM, John (*fl* 1733–1743)
Engraver and publisher   C*hb* 421

BICKNALL, *Lieut* George A., USN (*fl* 1861–1880)   H 945

BIDDER, George Parker (1806–1878)
Civil engineer; constructed the Royal Victoria Docks, London   B i 271; DNB ii 474

BIDDER, Samuel Parker (1843–1878)
Assistant manager of the Victoria Docks Graving Company   B i 272

BIDDLE, *Capt* James, USN (1783–1848)   DAB 72; H 75

BIDDLE, *Capt* Nicholas, USN (1750–1778)   DAB 72; H 76

BIDDLE, Richard Junius (1832–1882)
Marine artist   B i 272

BIDDLECOMBE, *Capt Sir* George, CB, RN (1807–1878)   B i 272; DNB ii 478

BIELLE, Gabriel, *Surgeon*, RN (*d* 1819)   Tr 155

BIENCOURT DE SAINT-JUST, Charles de (*ca* 1591–*ca* 1624)
Vice-admiral of Acadia, commander of Port-Royal settlement, fish and fur trader,
explorer   DCB i 99; MDC 55

BIENVILLE, Jean Baptiste Le Moyne, *Sieur de* (1680–1768)
French naval officer, governor of Louisiana   MDC 56

BIESTER, John Peter (*fl* 1726–1736)
Astronomer, writer on longitude   T ii 153

BIGGAR, Henry Percival (1872–1938)
Canadian historian; writer on Cartier, Champlain, and trading companies of New
France   MDC 56

BIGLAND, *Vice-Adm* Wilson Braddyll (1788–1858)   B i 275; M xii 287

BIGNALL, *Capt* George, RN (1786–1863)   Tr 114

BIGNELL, *Cdr* George, RN (*b* 1786)   M vii 400

BILES, *Sir* John Haward, KCIE (1854–1933)   DNB xxvi 78

BILL, John (*d* 1630)
Printer and bookseller   C*hb* 422

BILL, Robert (1754–1827)
Inventor; recommended use of iron tanks for preserving water aboard ship (1795);
promoted Massey's logs and published: 'A Short Account of Massey's Patent Log and
Sounding Machine' (1806)   DNB ii 490

BIRD, *Adm* Edward Joseph (*d* 1881)   B i 284

BIRD, Frederick Vincent Godfrey, RM (1842–1899)   B iv 405

BIRD, *Sir* James, OBE (1883–1946)
Naval and aircraft constructor; owner of Supermarine Aviation Works, Southampton,
1923–1928   DNB xxvii 81

BIRD, John (1709–1776)
Mathematical instrument maker; constructed instruments for the Royal Greenwich
Observatory   DNB ii 539; T ii 169

BIRD, *Cdr* Matthew, RN (*fl* 1672)   ch i 329

BIRKHEAD, *Cdr* Henry Hutchings, RN (*fl* 1783–1806)   M vi 253

BIRMINGHAM, John (1816–1884)
Astronomer   DNB ii 547

BIRNIE, James (1762?–1844)
Australian merchant and shipowner   DAuB i 104

BISCOE, John (1794–1843)   DAuB i 105

BISHOP, Alexander McC., *Paymaster*, USN (*fl* 1862–1870)   H 998

BISHOP, Charles (1765?–1810)
Trader; spent his 'teens in the Royal Navy, later commander of the trader
'Ruby Major'   DAuB i 107

BISHOP, George (1562–1611)
Bookseller and printer   chb 422

BISHOP, George (1785–1861)
Astronomer   B i 289; DNB ii 552

BISHOP, *Capt* Henry J., USMC (*fl* 1861–1890)   H 1016

BISHOP, *Cdr* Henry William, RN (*fl* 1806–1830)   M viii 357

BISHOP, *Lieut-Cmdr* Joshua, USN (*fl* 1854–1880)   H 930

BISHOP, *Maj* Peter, KH (*fl* 1803–1829)
Soldier and explorer; accompanied Major Edmund Lockyer on the 'Mermaid's' voyage
of exploration up the Brisbane river, 1825   DAuB i 108

BISSELL, *Cdr* William, RN (*d* 1826)   M vi 379

BISSETT   *Cdr* George, RN (*fl* 1810–1832)   M viii 360

BISSETT, *Rear-Adm* James (*fl* 1791–1813)   M ii 608

BISSON, Hippolyte (*d* 1827)
French naval lieutenant   Md iv 375

BIXLER, *Lieut* Lewis E., USN (*fl* 1865–1880)   H 959

BJARNI, Herjolfsson (*fl ca* 986)
Norse explorer and coloniser, first European to sight east coast of North America   DCB i 103

BJÖRNSTAAL, Jacob Jonas (1731–1779)
Swedish voyager   Md iv 353

BLAGDEN, *Sir* Charles (1748–1820)
Scientist, writer on thermal navigation   DNB ii 617; T ii 256

BLAGG [*or* BLAGUE] *Cdr* William, RN (*fl* 1673–1680)   ch ii 41

BLAIR, *Cdr* Charles, RN (*fl* 1822–1830)   M viii 366

BLAIR, Robert (*fl* 1783–1823)
Professor of astronomy, contributor to the 'Nautical Almanac'; inventor of the
'aplanatic' telescope   DNB ii 628; T ii 305

BLAIR, *Capt* William, RN (1741–1782)   DNB ii 629

BLAKE, Charles Paget, *Surgeon*, RN (1819–1896)   B iv 421

BLAKE, *Adm* George Charles (*d* 1872)   B i 303; M viii 66

BLAKE, *Cdre* George S., USN (*d* 1871)   H 79

BLAKE, *Cdre* Homer Crane, USN (1822–1880)   DAB 81; H 79

BLAKE, *Cdr* James, RN (*fl* 1665)   ch i 156

BLAKE, *Cdr* John RN (*fl* 1665–1668)   ch i 215

BLAKE, *Adm* Patrick John (1797–1884)   B i 303; M viii 349

BLAKE, *Adm* Robert (1599–1657)   CE ii 353; DNB ii 632;
                                                                             H 80; NC xxxi 1;
                                                                             Md iv 401

BLAKE, *Capt* Thomas, RN (*d* 1703)   ch iii 5

BLAKE, *Cdr* William, RN (*fl* 1661–1663)   ch i 53

BLAKELY, *Capt* Johnston, USN (1781–1814)   DAB 81; H 80; DNB ii
                                                                             646

BLAKISTON, *Cdr* Thomas, RN (1790–1855)   M viii 60

BLAMEY, *Capt* George William, RN (*b* 1768)   M x 272

BLANCARD, Pierre (1741–1826)
French navigator   Md iv 408

BLANCKLEY, *Capt* Edward (*d* 1845)   M viii 178

BLANCKLEY, *Maj-Gen* Horatio Charles Nelson, RM (1831–1899)   B iv 425

BLANCKLEY, Thomas Riley (*fl* 1750)
Perhaps a mariner; marine lexicographer   T ii 224

BLAND, William, *Surgeon*, RN (1789–1868)   AE i 170

BLANDFORD, *Cdr* James, RN (*d* 1867)   Tr 108

BLANE, *Sir* Gilbert (1749–1834)
Private physician to Rodney 1779, and to the fleet 1779–1783; did much to improve
the sanitary conditions of the navy; wrote: 'On the most effectual means for preserving
the health of seamen' (1780); commissioner for sick and wounded seamen, 1795–1802   DNB ii 664

BLANKETT, *Adm* John (*d* 1801)   DNB ii 667

BOLTON PUBLIC REFERENCE LIBRARY LIBRARIES

BLOW, *Capt* John Aitken, RN (*d* 1849)   M viii 180

BLOWERS, *Cdr* William, RN (*d* 1720)   *ch* iii 162

BLOXHAM, *Rev* Andrew (1801–1878)
Naturalist aboard HMS 'Blonde', 1824–1826   B i 317; DNB ii 726

BLOYE, *Rear-Adm* Robert (*d* 1847)   M xi 154

BLOYS, *Capt* William, RN (*d* 1720)   *ch* iii 162

BLUETT, *Capt* Auckland Stirling, RN (*d* 1845)   M xi 102

BLUETT, *Cdr* Richard, RN (*fl* 1793–1816)   M vii 417

BLUNDEL, William (1647–1723)
Writer on longitude   T ii 111

BLUNDERVILLE, Thomas (*fl* 1560–1602)
Teacher of navigation; author of: 'M. Blunderville his exercises containing six
treatises . . . in cosmographie, astronomie and geographie, as also in the arte of
Navigation, &c.' (1594)   DNB ii 734; T i 173

BLUNT, Charles (*fl* 1811–1818)
Instrument-maker; instruments at National Maritime Museum   T ii 384

BLUNT, Edmund March (1770–1862)
Hydrographer   DAB 85

BLUNT, George William (1802–1878)
Hydrographer   DAB 85

BLUNT, John (*fl* 1767)
Compass-maker and ship-chandler   T ii 256

BLYTH, *Cdr* Samuel, RN (1783–1813)   NC xxxii 441

BOAD, Henry (*fl* 1733)
Teacher of navigation, gunnery, and use of globes   T ii 170

BOAZIO, Baptista (*fl* 1585–1603)
Cartographer   CE ii 387

BOCCANERA [*or* BOCCANEGRA], Simone *and* Gilles
Genoese admirals   M*d* iv 488

BODE, Johann Elert (1747–1826)
German astronomer   CE ii 389

BOGER, *Capt* Edmund, RN (*fl* 1789–1815)   M ix 153

BOGER, *Cdr* Richard, RN (*d* 1824)   M vi 249

BOGERT, Edward S., *Surgeon*, USN (*fl* 1861–1880)   H 973

BOGGS, *Rear-Adm* Charles Stuart, USN (1811–1888)   DAB 86

BOGGS, Laurence G., *Asst-Paymaster*, USN (*fl* 1869–1880)   H 996

BOHAM, *Lieut* Jeremiah William, RN (*d* 1840)   Tr 193

BOILEAU, John Theophilus (1805–1886)
Astronomer   B iv 445

BONNE, Rigobert (1727–1794)
Cartographer   M*d* v 23

BONNER, John (*ca* 1643–1725/6)
Mariner, shipowner and shipbuilder   DAB 88

BONNER, *Cdr* William, RN (*fl* 1667)   *ch* i 279

BONNIVET-GOUFFIER, Guillaume, *Seigneur de* (*fl* 1507–1525)
French admiral   M*d* v 42

BONTEKOE, Willem Ijsbrandt (*fl* 1618)
Dutch navigator   M*d* v 53

BOOK, *Lieut* George M., USN (*fl* 1861–1880)   H 937

BOONE, *Cdr* John, RN (*fl* 1666–1673)   *ch* i 215

BOOTH, Charles (1840–1916)
Shipowner   CE ii 434; DNB xxiv 48

BOOTH, *Sir* Felix (1775–1850)
Promoter of Arctic exploration   DNB ii 839

BOOTH, George, *Purser*, RN (*d* 1839)   Tr 91

BOOTH, *Capt* James Richard, RN (*fl* 1805–1846)   M viii 347

BOOTH, *Cdr* Thomas, RN (*fl* 1672–1677)   *ch* i 387

BOOTH, *Capt Sir* William, RN (*d* 1703)   *ch* i 387; DNB ii 853

BORCHGREVINK, Carsten Egeberg (1864–1934)
Antarctic explorer   CE ii 439

BORDA, Jean Charles (1733–1799)
French navigator   H 87

BORDONI, Benedetto (1460–1539)
Italian geographer and miniaturist   M*d* v 75

BORLASE, *Vice-Adm* John, CB (1811–1895)   B iv 455

BOROUGH, Christopher (*fl* 1579–1587)   DNB ii 861

BOROUGH, *Capt* John À. (*fl* 1533–1542)
Navigation and gunnery expert   T i 167

BOROUGH, Stephen (1525–1584)
Master of Chancellor's ship, 1553; chief pilot to Muscovy Company   CE ii 439; DNB ii 864; M*d* vi 211; T i 171

BOROUGH, William (1536–1599)
Served with Drake and Chancellor, Treasurer of the Queen's Ships, Comptroller of the Navy, hydrographer and teacher of navigation   CE ii 451; DNB ii 866; T i 173

BORROWDELL [*or* BARRADALL], *Capt* Blumfield, RN (*d* 1749)   *ch* v 279

BORTHWICK, *Cdr* Alexander, RN (*fl* 1795–1818)   M viii 24

BOUGHEY, *Vice-Adm* Charles Fenton Fletcher (1823–1894)   B iv 461

BOUGUER, Pierre (1698–1758)
Professor of hydrography at Le Havre; sailed on La Condamine's expedition   A 125; Md v 207

BOUGUEREAU, Maurice (*fl* 1594)
French map publisher   CE ii 469

BOUILLÉ, Francois-Claude-Amour, *Marquis de* (1739–1800)
French soldier and colonial governor   Md v 213

BOULTBEE, *Capt* Frederick Moore, RN (*fl* 1811–1841)   M viii 320

BOURCHENU, Jean-Pierre Moret de, *Marquis de Valbonnais* (1651–1730)
French traveller and historian   Md v 291

BOURCHIER, *Rear-Adm* Henry (*d* 1852)   B i 349

BOURCHIER, *Capt* Thomas, RN (1791–1849)   M vi 15

BOURCHIER, *Cdr* William, RN (*d* 1844)   M vii 400

BOURDAGES, Louis (1764–1835)
French-Canadian merchant seaman, member of legislative assembly of Lower Canada   MDC 74

BOURDE de VILLEHUET, Jacques (*ca* 1730–1789)
French writer and strategist   Md v 295

BOURDIN, Martial (1867–1894)
Anarchist; intended to destroy the Royal Observatory with bomb; fatally wounded when
the bomb exploded in his pocket as he neared the observatory   B iv 463

BOURDON, Jean, *Sieur de Saint-François* (*ca* 1601–1668)
French engineer, surveyor, cartographer and explorer   DCB i 111; MDC 74

BOURDON D' AUTRAY, Jacques (1652–1688)
French-Canadian officer and explorer   DCB i 113

BOURDON DE DOMBOURG, Jean-François (1647–1694)
French-Canadian merchant sea-captain   DCB i 114

BOURDON de VATRY, Marc-Antoine (1761–1828)
Ministère de la Marine et des Colonies 1799–1801   Md v 305

BOURDONNAIS, Bertrand F. de (*fl* 1746)
French naval officer   H 89

BOURMASTER, *Capt* John, RN (*fl* 1788)   NA ii 61

BOURN, *Cdr* George William, RN (*d* 1844)   Tr 256

BOURNE, Gilbert Charles (1861–1933)
Zoologist and oarsman   DNB xxvi 93

BOURNE, *Cdr* Henry, RN (*fl* 1801–1830)   M vii 132

BOURNE, *Adm* Nehemiah, RN (*ca* 1611–1691)   DAB 93; DNB ii 939

BOWER, *Capt* George Henry Kerr, CB, RN (1817–1883)   B i 356

BOWERS, *Capt* Edward Carrington, USN (*fl* 1828–1867)   H 898

BOWKER, *Capt* John, RN (*b* 1770)   M X 429

BOWLER, *Capt* Robert, RN (*d* 1734)   *ch* iii 378

BOWLER, Thomas William (*d* 1869)   DNB ii 975

BOWLES, Carrington (1724–1793)
Map and print seller   *chb* 424

BOWLES, *Capt* Edward, RN (*d* 1695)   *ch* iii 63

BOWLES, John (*b* 1701)
Map and print seller   *chb* 424

BOWLES, *Capt* Phineas, RN (*d* 1698)   *ch* ii 408

BOWLES, Thomas (*d* 1767)
Map and print seller   *chb* 424

BOWLES, *Cdr* Valentine, RN (*fl* 1693–1698)   *ch* iii 92

BOWLES, *Adm of the Fleet Sir* William, KCB (1780–1869)   B i 360; M ix 258

BOWMAN, *Lieut* Charles G., USN (*fl* 1865–1880)   H 958

BOWMAN, James (1784–1846)
Entered Royal Navy as an assistant-surgeon in 1808; served as surgeon on convict
transports, 1816–1818   DAuB i 137

BOWRING, Benjamin (1778–1846)
British and Newfoundland shipowner, founder of Bowring Bros.   MDC 77

BOWRING, *Sir* Edgar Rennie (1858–1943)
Newfoundland shipowner, chairman of Bowring Bros.   MDC 77

BOWRY, *Cdr* John, RN (*fl* 1660)   *ch* i 9

BOWRY, *Cdr* Matthew, RN (*fl* 1667)   *ch* i 279

BOWYER, *Rear-Adm Sir* George (1740–1800)   *ch* vi 511; R i 374

BOWYER, *Capt* Richard Runwa, RN (*d* 1823)   M iii 136

BOWYER, *Rear-Adm* William Bohun (1789–1859)   B i 354; M vi 124

BOXER, *Adm Sir* Edward, KCB (1784–1855)   B i 364; DNB ii 995;
                                                                     M v 92

BOXER, *Capt* James, RN (*d* 1847)   M xi 399

BOXER, *Cdr* William, RN (*d* 1842)   M viii 125

BOYCE, *Cdr* Frederick, RN (*fl* 1810–1824)   M viii 138

BOYCE [*or* BOYS], *Capt* Philip, RN (*d* 1826)   *ch* iii 220

BOYCE [*or* BOYS], *Capt* William, RN (*d* 1774)   *ch* v 233

BOYCE, *Cdr* William Henry T., RN (*d* 1866)   Tr 124

BOYD, *Lieut* Arthur, USN (*fl* 1862–1880)   H 950

BRADLEY, *Cdr* Thomas, RN (*d* 1741)   *ch* iv 261

BRADFORD, *Cdr* Robert F., USN (*fl* 1852–1880)   H 901

BRADFORD, William (1598/90–1657)   DAB 100

BRADLEY, George P., *Asst-Surgeon*, USN (*fl* 1870–1880)   H 979

BRADLEY, James (1693–1762)
Astronomer Royal, 1742–1762   A 119; CE ii 487;
                                                                                        DNB ii 1074; M*d* v
                                                                                        404; T ii 112

BRADLEY, John (*fl* 1710–1716)
Teacher of navigation   T ii 112

BRADLEY, John, *Purser*, RN (*fl* 1742–1772)
Teacher of mathematics; assistant to James Bradley   T ii 198

BRADLEY, *Capt* John, RN (*d* 1829)   M xii 120

BRADLEY, Michael, *Medical Inspector*, USN (*fl* 1861–1880)   H 972

BRADLEY, Thomas (*fl* 1484–1505)
Sailed with John Cabot (1498), as representative of Henry VII   DCB i 121

BRADLEY, *Cdr* Thomas, RN (*d* 1741)   *ch* iv 261

BRADLEY, *Rear-Adm* William (1757–1833)   DA*u*B i 145

BRADSHAW, *Capt* James, RN (*d ca* 1833)   M ix 308

BRADSHAW, *Vice-Adm* Richard, CB (1829–1899)   B iv 480

BRADY, *Sir* Antonio (1811–1881)
Admiralty official; first superintendent of the contract department, 1869–1870   B i 376; DNB ii 1098

BRAGG, *Sir* William Henry, OM, KBE (1862–1942)
English physicist, worked on invention of hydrophone for submarine detection   A 423; DNB xxvii 99

BRAHE, Tycho (1546–1601)
Danish astronomer   CE ii 388; M*d* v 412

BRAIMER, *Capt* David, RN (*d* 1838)   M xii 126

BRAITHWAITE, *Capt* James, RN (*d* 1693)   *ch* ii 409

BRAITHWAITE, John (1700?–1768?)
Historian; served with the fleet during the reign of Queen Anne   DNB ii 1109

BRAITHWAITE, John (*d* 1818)
Engineer; constructor of one of the earliest successful forms of diving bell   DNB ii 1109

BRAITHWAITE, *Rear-Adm* Richard (*d ca* 1805)   *ch* v 430

BRAITHWAITE, *Capt* Samuel (*d* 1751)   *ch* iv 96

BRAKEL, Jan*de* (1618–1690)
Dutch naval officer   M*d* v 416

BRAMLEY-MOORE, John (1800–1886)
Appointed chairman of Liverpool Docks Board, 1842   DNB xxii 255

BREMER, *Rear-Adm Sir* James Gordon, KCH, KCB (1786–1850)   AE i 201; DAuB i 148;
                                                                 DNB ii 1164; M vi 436

BREMNER, James (1784–1856)
*Engineer and ship-raiser; established a shipbuilding yard at Pultney Town;
reconstructed the harbour there and constructed Keiss harbour 1818, Lossiemouth and
Pitullie harbours. Raised 236 vessels sunk in Scottish waters*   B i 389; DNB ii 1165

BRENAN, *Cdr* Alexander, RN (1790–1862)   Tr 54

BRENDAN, *Saint: see* BRÉANAINN

BRENNAN, Louis, CB (1852–1932)
Mechanical engineer; designed a dirigible torpedo for coastal defence   AE i 201; DNB xxv
                                                                 101

BRENTON, *Capt* Edward Pelham, RN (1774–1839)   DNB ii 1172; M ix 411

BRENTON, *Vice-Adm Sir* Jahleel, KCB (1770–1844)   DNB ii 1173; M iii
                                                                 261; R iv 292

BRENTON, *Capt* John, RN (*b* 1782)   M xii 419

BRERETON, John (*fl* 1603)
*Voyager; accompanied first party of English settlers to New England who returned
home the same year, 1603*   DNB ii 1175

BRERETON, *Capt* William, RN (*fl* 1758–1778)   ch vi 298

BRETNOR, Thomas (*fl* 1605–1619)
Professor of mathematics, teacher of navigation and almanack-maker   T i 197

BRETT, *Capt* John, RN (*d* 1785)   ch v 67; DNB ii 1190

BRETT, John Watkins (1805–1863)
Originated scheme of submarine telegraphy   B i 391; DNB ii 1191

BRETT, *Adm Sir* Piercey (1709–1781)   ch v 239; DNB ii 1191

BRETT, *Cdr* Piercy, RN (*b* 1785)   M vii 34

BRETT, *Capt* Timothy, RN (*d* 1739)   ch iv 145

BRETT, *Capt* William, RN (*d* 1769)   ch vi 27

BREWER, George (1774–1871)
Served in the Royal Navy 1793–1791; later became a waterman at Gosport   B i 393

BREWER, George (*b* 1766)
*Miscellaneous writer; served as a midshipman in the Royal Navy and later became a
lieutenant in the Swedish Navy in 1791*   DNB ii 1200

BREWER, Henry (1739–1796)
*Joined the Royal Navy as a volunteer when aged nearly 40; was midshipman of the
'Sirius' in the 'First Fleet'; on arrival at Sydney he was appointed provost-marshal*   DAuB i 149

BREWSTER, *Sir* David (1781–1868)
Inventor of sea-thermometer   DNB ii 1207; T ii 357

BRIGGS, Henry Perronet (1791?–1844)
Subject and portrait painter; his works include: 'George III presenting the Sword to Lord Howe on board the "Queen Charlotte"' (1794)   DNB ii 1235

BRIGGS, *Lieut* John B., USN (*fl* 1865–1880)   H 958

BRIGGS, *Sir* John Henry (1808–1897)
Chief clerk of the Admiralty, 1865–1870   B iv 495

BRIGGS, *Sir* John Thomas (1781–1865)
Accountant-general of the Navy, 1832–1854   B i 398; DNB ii 1237

BRIGGS, *Adm Sir* Thomas, GCMG (1780–1852)   M i 398; M iii 417

BRIGHAM, Albert Perry (1855–1932)
Geographer   DAB 107

BRIGHT, *Sir* Charles Tilston (1832–1888)   B iv 495; CE ii 554;
                                                                                DNB xxii 271

BRIGHT, George A., *Surgeon*, USN (*fl* 1864–1880)   H 977

BRIGHT, Henry Arthur (1830–1884)
Shipowner   B i 399

BRIGHT, *Rev* Mynors (1818–1883)
Decipherer of Pepys' Diary   B i 399; DNB ii 1241

BRIGHT, Robert (1795–1869)
Shipowner   B i 400

BRIGSTOCKE, *Cdr* Thomas Robert, RN (*d ca* 1869)   M viii 53

BRINDLEY, James (1716–1772)
Canal engineer   CE ii 557; DNB ii 1253

BRINE, *Rear-Adm* Augustus, RN (*d* 1840)   M iv 666

BRINE, *Adm* George (*d* 1864)   B i 402; M xii 201

BRINKLEY, John (1763–1835)
Royal Astronomer of Ireland; writer on longitude   DNB ii 1255; T ii 305

BRION de la TOUR, Louis (*fl* 1795)
Engineer and geographer   M*d* v 549

BRION, Louis (1782–1821)
Dutch adventurer and admiral of the Colombian navy   M*d* v 550

BRISBANE, *Rear-Adm Sir* Charles, KCB (1769?–1829)   DNB ii 1260; M ii 730,
                                                                                881; NC xx 81; R iv
                                                                                84

BRISBANE, *Cdre Sir* James, CB, RN (1774–1826)   AE i 205; DNB ii 1261;
                                                                                M iii 400

BRISBANE, *Adm* John (*d* 1807)   Ch vi 447

BRISBANE, *Gen Sir* Thomas Makdougall, KCB (1773–1860)
Soldier and astronomer   CE ii 558; DNB ii 1261

BROMLEY, *Sir* Richard Madox, KCB (1813–1865)
Civil servant; accountant-general of the navy, 1854–1863; a commissioner o
Greenwich Hospital   B i 412; DNB ii 1308

BROMLEY, *Adm Sir* Robert Howe (1778–1808)   B i 413; M iv 550

BROODBANK, *Sir* Joseph Guiness (1857–1944)   DNB xxvii 110

BROOKE, *Capt* Edward, RN (*d* 1783)   ch iv 193

BROOKE, Henry, KG, *eighth Lord Cobham* (*d* 1619)
Appointed lord warden of the Cinque Ports, 1597   DNB ii 1331

BROOKE, *Sir* James, KCB (1803–1868)
Rájáh of Sarawak   B i 417; DNB ii 1336

BROOKE, John Mercer (1826–1906)
Served in the United States Navy, 1841–1861 and Confederate States Navy, 1861–1865 DAB 109

BROOKE, R., *Master*, RN (*fl* 1801)
Inventor of log   T ii 357

BROOKE-PECHELL, *Rear-Adm* Sir Samuel John, CB (1785–1849)   M ix 361

BROOKES, Christopher (*fl* 1649–1651)
Seaman and instrument-maker   T i 234

BROOKES, *Capt* John, RN (*fl* 1666)   ch i 215

BROOKES, *Cdr* John, RN (*d ca* 1672)   ch i 216

BROOKING, Charles (1723–1759)
Marine artist   DNB ii 1344

BROOKING, *Capt* Samuel, RN (*b* 1755)   M iii 38; NC X 177

BROOKS, *Capt* Caesar, RN (*d* 1708/9)   ch iii 395

BROOKS, Francis (*fl* 1681–1692)
Bristol mariner   Md v 608

BROOKS, *Capt* John, RN (*d* 1792)   ch vi 510

BROOKS, *Capt* Packington, RN (*fl* 1661–1664)   ch i 81

BROOKS, Richard (1765?–1833)
Mariner, merchant and Australian settler   DAUB i 156

BROOKS, Robert (1799–1882)
London merchant and shipowner   B i 420

BROOKS, William Alexander (1802–1877)
Resident engineer to the Tees Navigation Co., 1828; investigated the feasibility of a
ship canal across the isthmus of Darien, 1876   B i 421

BROOKS, William B., *Chief Engineer*, USN (*fl* 1852–1880)   H 1002

BROOKS, William Robert (1844–1921)
Astronomer   DAB 110

BROOME, *Lieut-Col* John L., USMC (*fl* 1848–1879)   H 1012

BROOME, *Cdr* Samuel, RN (*fl* 1678–1679)   ch ii 41

BROWN, *Lieut* Robert M. G., USN (*fl* 1864–1878) H 953

BROWN, S. Augustine, *Asst-Surgeon*, USN (*fl* 1871–1880) H 979

BROWN, *Capt* Samuel, RN (1776–1852) DNB iii 27; M vii 20

BROWN [*or* BROWNE], Thomas (*fl* 1627–1653)
Instrument-maker T i 210

BROWN, *Rear-Adm* Thomas (*d ca* 1848) M ix 105

BROWN, *Adm* Thomas (*d* 1857) B i 439

BROWN, *Adm* William (1777–1857) B i 440; DNB iii 36

BROWN, *Rear-Adm* William (*d* 1814) DNB iii 35

BROWN, *Cdr* William Cheselden, RN (*d ca* 1847) M viii 384

BROWN, *Capt* William R., USMC (*fl* 1861–1880) H 1016

BROWN, Zachary, *Asst-Paymaster*, USN (*fl* 1870–1880) H 997

BROWN-GRIEVE, *Gen* John Tatton, CB, RM (1795–1880) B i 441; iv 515

BROWN-RAMSAY, James Andrew, KT, *first Marquis of Dalhousie* (1812–1860)
*Became an elder Brother of Trinity House 1846, and lord warden of the Cinque Ports,
1853* B i 803

BROWNE, Christopher (*fl ca* 1684–1712)
Cartographer and publisher chb 425

BROWNE, *Rear-Adm* Edward Walpole (1767–1847) M iv 685

BROWNE, *Cdr* Henry, RN (*fl* 1666) ch i 216

BROWNE, *Cdr* John, RN (*fl* 1660) ch i 9

BROWNE, John (*fl* 1750)
Compass-maker and ship's-chandler T ii 224

BROWNE, John M., *Medical-Director*, USN (*b* 1831) H 968

BROWNE, *Vice-Adm* Philip (1772–1860) B i 445; M x 95

BROWNE, Robert (*fl* 1705–1731)
Writer on longitude T i 301; ii 113

BROWNE, Samuel T., *Paymaster*, USN (*d* 1881) H 991

BROWNE, *Vice-Adm* Thomas (*d* 1851) B i 445; M iv 706

BROWNE, *Cdr* William, RN (*d* 1774) ch vi 118

BROWNE, *Adm* William Cheselden (1805–1881) B i 446

BROWNE, William George (1768–*ca* 1813) Md v 656

BROWNE, *Cdr* William Henry James, RN (*d* 1871) B i 447

BROWNE, *Cdr* Zachary (*fl* 1666–1667) ch i 94

BROWNING, Colin Arnott (1791–1856)
*Naval surgeon; was surgeon-superintendent of convict ships, 1831–1849; author of:
'The Convict Ships' (1844)* B i 447; DAuB i 169

BRYAN, *Sir* Francis (*d* 1550)
Courtier and diplomatist; captained a ship-of-war, 1513   DNB iii 150

BRYANT [*née* BROAD], Mary (*b* 1765)   DAUB i 173

BRYANT, *Capt* Thomas (*d* 1694)   ch iii 63

BRYANT, William (*d* 1791)
Fisherman   AE i 211

BRYCE, George (1844–1931)
Canadian historian; writer on Hudson's Bay Co., colonisation and exploration   MDC 89

BRYDGES, *Maj-Gen* George, RMA (1831–1896)   B iv 528

BRYDONE, James Marr, *Surgeon*, RN (1799–1866)   Tr 243

BUACHE, Jean-Nicolas (1741–1825)
Cartographer   Md vi 82

BUACHE, Philippe (1700–1773)
French geographer; author of: 'Considerations sur les nouvelles découvertes de la
grande mer' (1753)   CE ii 633; Md vi 81

BUC, Jean-Baptiste du (1717–1795)
Caribbean colonial administrator   Md vi 87

BUCHAN, *Capt* David, RN (*d ca* 1839)   M v 83

BUCHANAN, *Cdr* Archibald, RN (*d* 1822)   M vii 273

BUCHANAN, *Capt* Franklin, USN (1800–1874)   DAB 118; H 95

BUCHANAN, George (1790?–1852)
Civil engineer; harbour constructor   DNB iii 193

BUCHANAN, *Sir* George Cunningham, KCIE (1865–1940)
Civil engineer; chief engineer to the Dundee Harbour Trust (1896–1901) and the
Rangoon Port Trust (1901–1915)   DNB xxvi 114

BUCHANAN, *Capt* William, RN (*d ca* 1838)   M x 50

BUCHANAN, *Capt* William, RN (1777–1859)   M vii 72; Tr 182

BUCK, *Capt* James, RN (*d* 1691)   ch ii 307

BUCK, *Capt* Richard, RN (*d ca* 1830)   M x 350

BUCKHILL, *Cdr* Thomas, RN (*fl* 1661)   ch i 53

BUCKINGHAM, *Lieut* Benjamin H., USN (*fl* 1865–1880)   H 958

BUCKLE, *Adm Sir* Claude Henry Mason, KCB (1803–1894)   B iv 532; DNB xxii
                                                                       330

BUCKLE, *Adm* Henry Thomas (1770–1855)   B i 463

BUCKLE, *Adm* Matthew (*d* 1784)   ch v 365

BUCKLE, *Vice-Adm* Matthew (1770–1855)   M iv 565

BUCKLEY, *Capt* Cecil William, VC, RN (*d* 1872)   B i 464; DNB iii 213

BUCKMASTER, Thomas (*fl* 1566)
Divine and astronomer DNB iii 216

BUCKNER, *Adm* Charles (*d* 1811) *ch* vi 577

BUCKNEY, Thomas (1838–1900)
Designed electric contacts for marine chronometers; constructed the sidereal standard
clock at Greenwich, 1871 B iv 534

BUCKOLL, *Capt* Richard, RN (1771–1798) NC ii 85

BUDD, George (1808–1882)
Surgeon to the 'Dreadnought' hospital ship, 1837–1840 B i 466

BUDGE, William (*d* 1811)
Commissioner of the Navy NC XXXV 1; 89

BUEHLER, William G., *Chief Engineer*, USN (*fl* 1857–1880) H 1005

BUFORD, *Lieut* Marcus B., USN (*fl* 1861–1880) H 937

BUGDEN [*or* BRIDGEN], *Capt* Edmond, RN (*fl* 1797) *ch* iii 163

BUGG, Thomas (1740–1815)
Danish astronomer M*d* vi 122

BUGNON, Didier (*fl* 1707–1725)
Geographer, cartographer and engineer M*d* vi 123

BULKELEY, *Lieut* Richard, RN (*fl* 1803–1810) Tr 17

BULLARD, *Rear-Adm* William Hannum Grubb, USN (1866–1927) DAB 123

BULLEN, *Adm Sir* Charles, GCB, KCH (1769–1853) B i 469; DNB iii 291;
M iv 590; viii 444;
Tr 39

BULLEN, *Adm* Joseph (1761–1857) B 469; M iii 34

BULLER, *Vice-Adm Sir* Edward (1764–1824) M i 350; NC xix 177

BULLER, *Cdr* Thomas Wentworth, RN (*d* 1852?) M vii 417

BULLEY, *Cdr* George, RN (*d* 1817) Tr 168

BULLOCH, James Dunwody (1823–1901)
Served in the United States Navy 1839–1859; Confederate States Navy agent in
the United Kingdom, 1861–1865 DAB 123

BULLOCK, *Adm* Frederick (*d* 1874) B i 471; M viii 335

BULLY, *Cdr* William, RN (*d* 1746) *ch* v 367

BUMPSTEAD, *Cdr* John, RN (*d* 1691) *ch* i 10

BUNCE, *Cdr* Francis M., USN (*fl* 1852–1880) H 904

BUNDOCK, William, *Purser*, RN (*d* 1841) Tr 236

BUNGAREE [BONGAREE *or* BOUNGAREE]
Aborigine; accompanied Flinders in 1801–1802 becoming the first aborigine to
circumnavigate the Australian continent DA*u*B 1 177

BUNKER, Eber (1762–1836)
Sea-captain; master of the 'William and Ann', a transport in the 'Third Fleet' which arrived at Sydney in 1791; discoverer of the Bunker Islands off the Queensland coast; has been called 'the father of Australian whaling' DAuB i 178

BUNN, *Capt* Thomas, RN (*fl* 1660) ch i 10

BURBANK, Charles H., *Medical Inspector*, USN (*fl* 1861–1880) H 972

BURCHETT, Josiah (1666?–1745)
Secretary of the Admiralty, 1698–1742 DNB iii 291

BURCKHARDT, Jean-Louis (1784–1819)
Traveller Md vi 166

BURDETT, *Capt* George, RN (*d* 1832) M iv 576

BURDICK, *Cdr* John, RN (*fl* 1672) ch i 329

BURE, Anders [*or* BURAEUS, Andreas] (1571–1646)
Swedish cartographer CE ii 728; Md vi 172

BURGESS, Edward (1848–1891)
Yacht designer DAB 124

BURGESS, *Capt* Samuel, RN (1781–1851) M vi 162; Tr 79

BURGESS, *Cdr* William, RN (*d* 1840) M vi 250

BURGH, *Sir* John (1562–1594)
Military and naval commander DNB iii 322

BURGHERS, Michael (*fl* 1672–1720)
Dutch draughtsman and engraver chb 425

BURGOYNE, *Capt* Frederick William, RN (1778–1848) M xii 103

BURGOYNE, *Capt* Hugh Talbot, VC, RN (1833–1870) B i 479; DNB iii 338; H 98

BURKE, Walter, *Purser*, RN (*d* 1815) Tr 22

BURKE, *Capt* William, RN (*fl* 1665–1674) ch i 310; ii 1

BURLEY, Richard (*fl* 1631–1661)
Mathematical lecturer and ship-keeper, Chatham Dockyard T i 213

BURN, George, RN (1810–1881)
Inspector-general of hospitals and fleets B i 482

BURNABY, *Cdr Sir* William, RN (*d* 1776) ch v 131

BURNABY, *Cdr Sir* William Crisp Hood, RN (*d* 1853) B i 484; M vii 199

BURNAP, George J., *Chief Engineer*, USN (*fl* 1861–1880) H 1011

BURNE, Charles, *Chaplain*, RN (*d* 1852) Tr 65

BURNET, *Cdr* Charles, RN (*d ca* 1870) M viii 387

BURNET, *Capt* Thomas, RN (*d* 1784) ch vi 216

BURNETT, John C., *Assist Paymaster*, USN (*fl* 1869–1880) H 996

BURSTAL, Richard, *Master*, RN (*d* 1838)   Tr 71

BURSTON, John (*fl* 1658–1666)
Marine hydrographer and chart-maker; charts at National Maritime Museum   T i 245

BURT, *Cdr* Edward, RN (*d ca* 1858)   M vi 366

BURT, *Lieut* George, RN (*d* 1815)   T 226

BURT, John (1814–1886)
Designer and builder of canals; patented a new type of canal lock   DAB 129

BURT, N. (*fl* 1658–1666)
Teacher of navigation   T ii 332

BURT, Peter (*fl* 1813–1827)
Inventor of sounding apparatus, compass and steam-engine   T ii 385

BURTIS, Arthur, *Paymaster*, USN (*fl* 1862–1880)   H 990

BURTON, *Capt* Alfred, RM (*d* 1840)   Tr 186

BURTON, *Capt* Casibe Cain, RN (*fl* 1666–1674)   ch i 329

BURTON, Charles Edward (1846–1882)
Astronomer; photographer to the transit of Venus expedition, 1874   B i 494; DNB iii 454

BURTON, George (*fl* 1772–1815)
Instrument-maker; supplied Cook, etc.   T ii 282

BURTON, *Rear-Adm* George Guy (*d ca* 1849)   M vii 334

BURTON, *Capt* James Ryder, RN (1795–*ca* 1870)   B i 494; M v 178

BURTON, Mark (*fl* 1758–1775)
Instrument-maker; supplied Cook   T ii 225

BURTON, *Cdr* Richard, RN (*d* 1836)   M vii 75; Tr 305

BURTON, *Capt* Thomas, RN (*d* 1843)   M x 294

BURTON, *Capt* William, RM (*fl* 1803–1834)   Tr 66

BURTON, *Sir* William Westbrook (1784–1888)
*Entered the navy in 1807, wounded at Toulon; left the navy to study Law, called
to the bar 1824*   AE i 217

BURWELL, *Lieut* William T., USN (*fl* 1862–1880)   H 944

BURY, Edward (1794–1858)
Introduced improved engines for steamboats employed on the Rhône   B i 498; DNB iii 476

BURY, *Vice-Adm* Richard Incledon (*d* 1825)   M i 409; NC xxix 177

BURY, *Capt* Thomas, RN (*d* 1748)   ch v 134

BURY, *Cdr* Thomas, RN (*d* 1831)   M vii 268

BUSBY, John (1765–1857)
*Civil engineer and surveyor; successfully refloated the New Zealand government brig
'Elizabeth Henrietta' which was aground on Goulburn Island, 1825*   DAuB i 188

BYLOT, Robert (*fl* 1610–1616)
Navigator; explorer of the North-West Passage; sailed with Hudson 1610–1611,
Button 1612–1613 and Gibbons 1614   DCB i 145; DNB iii 566

BYNARD, *Cdr* Walter, RN (*fl* 1672–1677)   ch ii 13

BYNG, *Adm of the Fleet* George, *Viscount Torrington* (1663–1733)   CE xiii 684; ch ii 194;
                                                                                         DNB iii 567; Md vi
                                                                                         273; R iii 319

BYNG, *Vice-Adm* Henry Dilkes (1784–1860)   B i 505; M xi 242

BYNG, *Adm* John (1704–1757)   CE ii 728; ch iv 145;
                                                                                         DNB iii 970; Md v
                                                                                         274

BYNNING, *Cdr* Thomas, RN (*fl* 1672–1678)   ch i 389

BYRD, *Rear-Adm* Richard Evelyn USN (1888–1957)   A 517; CE ii 728

BYRON, *Adm* George Anson, *seventh Baron Byron* (1789–1868)   B i 507; M xii 373;
                                                                                         NA ii 81; DNB iii 613

BYRON, *Vice-Adm the Hon* John (1723–1786)   ch v 423; Md vi 278
                                                                                         R i 60

BYRON, *Rear-Adm* Richard (1769–1837)   M iv 619

BYWATER, John (*fl* 1816–1835)
Compass-maker, nautical instrument repairer and writer on longitude   T ii 385

CABEZA DE VACA, Alvar Nunez (*fl* 1540–1544)
Spanish navigator and colonial governor   Md vi 308

CABOT, George (1752–1823)
Merchant and shipowner   DAB 134

CABOT [*or* CABOTO], John (*fl* 1461–*ca* 1498)   CE ii 753; DCB i 146;
                                                                                         H 101; Md vi 309;
                                                                                         MDC 100

CABOT, Sebastian (*ca* 1484–1557)   CE ii 753; DCB i 152;
                                                                                         DNB iii 618; H 101;
                                                                                         Md vi 309

CABRAL [*or* CABRERA], Pedro Alvares (*ca* 1467–*ca* 1520)   CE ii 753; H 101;
                                                                                         Md vi 312

CABRILLO, Juan Rodriguez (*d* 1543)   DAB 134

CACHIN, Joseph-Marie-François (1757–1825)
French engineer, especially of coastal fortifications and canals   Md vi 317

CADAMOSTO, Alvise [*or* Luigi] (1432?–1511?)
Venetian navigator and explorer   Md vi 318

CALLENDER, *Sir* Geoffrey Arthur Romaine (1875–1946)
Naval historian and first director of the National Maritime Museum   DNB xxvii 128

CALLENDER, John (*fl* 1802)
Inventor of a sea telescope   T ii 415

CALLIS, *Rear-Adm* Smith (*d* 1761)   *ch* v 136

CALMADY, *Capt* Warwick, RN (*d* 1757 or 1759)   *ch* v 244

CALVER, *Capt* Edward Killwick, RN (1813–1892)   B iv 583

CALVERT, George, *first Baron Baltimore* (*ca* 1580–1632)
Coloniser of Newfoundland   DCB i 162; DNB iii
                                                                                     721; MDC 32

CAMARGO, Alfonso de (*fl* 1539)
Spanish navigator   Md vi 443

CAMBIS, *Contre-Adm* Joseph, *Vicomte de* (1748–1825)   s i 181

CAMDEN, William (1551–1623)
Antiquarian and cartographer   *chb* 426; DNB iii 729;
                                                                                     Md vi 468

CAMERON, *Lieut* Allan, RN (*fl* 1805–1812)   Tr 80

CAMERON, *Cdr* Verney Lovett, CB, RN (1844–1894)   CE ii 813

CAMMILLERI, *Cdr* Joseph, RN (*b* 1794)   M viii 319

CAMOCK, *Capt* George, RN (*fl* 1692–1719)   *ch* iii 221; DNB iii 757

CAMPBELL, *Capt* Alexander, RN (*fl* 1751–1754)   T ii 225

CAMPBELL, *Cdr* Alexander, RN (*d* 1798)   *ch* vi 220

CAMPBELL, Alexander (1805–1890)
Farmer and mariner; engaged in the Australian whaling industry 1836–1849; and
later became the first harbour master at Melbourne   DAuB i 197

CAMPBELL, *Capt* Alexander, RN (*fl* 1806–1828)   M vi 29

CAMPBELL, *Capt* Alexander, RN (*d* 1825)   M iv 902

CAMPBELL, *Capt* Charles, RN (*fl* 1795–1799)   M iii 233

CAMPBELL, *Rear-Adm* Colin (1787–1850)   M xi 62; Tr 135

CAMPBELL, *Capt* Colin, RN (*fl* 1796–1814)   M xi 315

CAMPBELL, *Adm* Colin York (1812/13–1893)   B iv 590

CAMPBELL, *Rear-Adm* Donald (1778–1856)   B i 528; M x 399

CAMPBELL, *Lieut* Donald, RN (*fl* 1804–1848)   Tr 271

CAMPBELL, Frederick Archibald Vaughan, *third Earl Cawdor* (1847–1911)   DNB xxiiia 299

CAMPBELL, *Capt* George, RN (*fl* 1789)   NA ii 120

CAMPBELL, George Douglas Glassell, *eighth Duke of Argyll*, KG, KT (1823–1900)
Elder brother of Trinity House 1862–1900   B iv 157

CAMPBELL, *Rear-Adm the Hon* George Pryse (1793–1858)   M xii 230

CAMPBELL, William Douglas (1770–1827)
Mariner, shipowner and island trader; first Australian shipmaster engaged in
Tahitian salt pork trade, 1805 and the Tuamotu pearl fisheries, 1809   DA*u*B i 208

CAMPBELL, William Wallace (1862–1938)
American astronomer   CE iii 5; DAB 141

CAMPBELL-BANNERMAN, *Sir* Henry, GCB (1836–1908)
British statesman; secretary to the Admiralty, 1882–1884   CE iii 5; DNB xxiiia
                                                                                302

CAMPION, *Capt* Thomas, RN (*fl* 1692–1704)   *ch* iii 244

CANAGA, Alfred Bruce (1850–1906)
Naval engineer   DAB 141

CANDLER, *Capt* Bartholomew, RN (*d* 1722)   *ch* iii 329

CANE, Diogo (*fl* late 15th century)
Portuguese navigator   CE iii 76

CANN, James E., *Assist-Paymaster*, USN (*fl* 1870–1880)   H 997

CANNING, *Capt* George, RN (*d* 1677)   *ch* i 330

CANNING, George (1770–1827)
Statesman; treasurer of the navy, 1804–1806   DNB iii 872

CANNING, *Cdr* George, RN (*d* 1842)   M vii 227; Tr 160

CANNING, *Capt* Richard, RN (*d* 1726)   *ch* iii 228

CANNING, *Sir* Samuel (1823–1908)
A pioneer of submarine telegraphy   DNB xxiiia 312

CANNON, Annie Jump (1863–1941)
American astronomer   CE iii 61

CANNON, *Adm* Edward St Leger (1803–1881)   B i 537

CANO, Juan Sebastián del (*d* 1526)
Spanish navigator   A 57; CE iii 61; M*d* vi
                                                                                559

CANTELLI, Giacomo (*d* 1695)
Cartographer and globe-maker   M*d* vi 580

CAPEL, *Cdr* Algernon Henry Champagné, RN (1807–1886)   M viii 369

CAPEL, *Adm Sir* Thomas Bladen, GCB (1776–1853)   B i 539; DNB iii 927;
                                                                                M iii 195; Tr 285

CAPELL, *Capt* Bartholomew, RN (*fl* 1661)   *ch* i 156

CAPELLE, Eduard von (1855–1931)
German naval officer   CE iii 76

CAPPELLE, Jan van der (1624/5–1679)
Dutch marine painter   CE iii 88

CARLETTI, Francisco (*fl* 1592–1602)
Florentine voyager and circumnavigator   Md vi 681

CARLI(S)LE, *Capt* Charles, RN (*fl* 1682)   ch ii 91

CARLILL, John (*fl* 1837)
Nautical instrument maker   Tii 468

CARLIN, *Lieut* James W., USN (*b* 1848)   H 957

CARLSTAKE, *Capt* Martin (*fl* 1665–1669)   ch i 157

CARLTON, *Capt* John [*or* James], RN (*d* 1712?)   ch iii 230

CARLTON [*or* CHARLTON], *Capt* St John (*d* 1742)   ch iv 6

CARLYON, *Rear-Adm* William (*fl* 1773–1800)   M iii 70

CARMAN, *Capt* John, RN (*fl* 1679)   ch ii 60

CARMICHAEL, James Wilson (1800–1868)
Marine artist   B i 551; DNB iii 1048

CARMICHAEL, *Cdr* Sir Thomas Gibson, RN (1817–1855)   B i 552

CARMODY, John R., *Paymaster*, USN (*fl* 1864–1880)   H 995

CARMODY, *Lieut* Robert E., USN (*fl* 1860–1880)   H 949

CARNAC, *Vice-Adm* John Rivett (1796–1869)   B i 552; M viii 226

CARNEGIE, *Adm* George, *sixth Earl of Northesk* (1716–1792)   ch v 109

CARNEGIE, *Adm* Swynfen Thomas, CB (1813–1879)   B i 552

CARNEGIE, *Adm* William, GCB, *seventh Earl of Northesk* (1758–1831)   DNB iii 1048; NC xv
                                                                         441; R ii 400

CARNEY, Thomas (*fl* 1805–1848)
Served as midshipman aboard the 'Prince' at Trafalgar   Tr 81

CARPENTER, *Capt* Charles C., USN (*fl* 1850–1880)   H 895

CARPENTER, *Capt* Edward John, RN (*fl* 1813–1846)   M viii 231

CARPENTER, *Adm* James (*d* 1845)   DNB iii 1063; M ii 528

CARPENTER, James (1840–1899)
Employed at the Royal Greenwich Observatory 1854–1872, and by John Penn &
Sons, marine engineers, 1872–1890   B iv 606

CARPENTER, James N., *Pay Inspector*, USN (*fl* 1860–1879)   H 998

CARPENTER, John B., *Chief Engineer*, USN (*fl* 1861–1880)   H 1009

CARPENTER, *Capt* John Cook, KH, RN (*fl* 1781–1846)   M xii 289

CARPENTER, *Capt* Robert, RN (*d* 1773)   ch vi 390

CARPIN [*or* CARPINI], *Friar* Jean du Plan (*ca* 1220)
Mediaeval traveller   Md vii 35

CARR, Debney Smith (1802–1854)
Diplomat; naval officer of Baltimore, Md., 1829–1843   DAB 145

CARR, *Capt* Overton, USN (*fl* 1827–1867)   H 897

CARTWRIGHT, *Cdr* John, RN (1740–1824)   DNB iii 1133; M vi
                                                               409

CARTWRIGHT, Joseph (1789?–1829)
Marine painter   DNB iii 1134

CARVER, Isaac (*fl* 1667–1708)
Instrument-maker; designer of a log-line   T i 254

CARVER, John (1575?–1621)
Leader of the 'Pilgrim Fathers'; sailed from Leyden aboard the 'Mayflower', 1620   DAB 149; DNB iii 1145

CARVERTH [*or* KERWORTH], *Capt* Richard, RN (*d* 1728)   ch ii 394

CARVETH, *Capt* Henry, RN (*fl* 1672–1681)   ch i 393

CARY, George (*fl* 1821–1859)
Globe-maker   T ii 385

CARY, *Cdr* Henry, RN (*d* 1847)   Tr 18

CARY, John (*ca* 1754–1835)
Cartographer   CE iii 151; T ii 282,
                                                               385

CARY, *Adm Sir* Plantaganet Pierrepont, *eleventh Viscount Falkland* (1806–1886)   B v 266

CARY, William (1759–1825)
Optical and mathematical instrument-maker; instruments at National Maritime Museum   T ii 306

CARYSFORT, *Adm* Granville Leveson Proby, *third Earl of* (1781–1868)   B i 567

CASABIANCA, Louis (*ca* 1755–1798)
French naval officer   CE iii 152; Md vii 93

CASAMAJOR, Arsène Augustus Joseph (*d* 1861)
Oarsman   B i 567

CASE, *Rear-Adm* Augustus Ludlow, USN (*b* 1813)   H 116

CASE, *Capt* William, RN (*fl* 1790–1846)   M vii 73

CASEY, *Cdr* Silas, Jr., USN (*b* 1841)   H 910

CASS, George Washington (1810–1888)
Engineer; organised the first steamboat service on the Monongahela river   DAB 150

CASSIN, *Cdre* Stephen, USN (1783–1857)   H 117

CASSINI, Jacques (1667–1756)
Astronomer and geographer   Md vii 136

CASSINI, Jean-Dominique (1625–1712)
Astronomer   Md viii 133

CASSINI de THURY, César Francois (1714–1784)
Geographer and cartographer; produced first map of France, surveyed by triangulation   Md vii 136

CASTLE, *Lieut* George, RN (*fl* 1805–1827)   Tr 32

CASTLE, *Capt* John, RN (*d* 1706)   ch iii 307

CEELEY [*or* SEALE *or* SEELEY], *Capt* William, RN (*d* 1666/7)   ch i 157

CELSIUS, André (1701–1744)
Swedish astronomer   Md vii 315

CESSART, Louis Alexandre de (1719–1806)
Engineer   Md vii 370

CHABERT, Joseph-Bernard, *Marquis de* (1724–1805)
French naval officer and hydrographer   Md vii 381

CHADS, *Adm Sir* Henry, KCB (1819–1906)   DNB xxiiia 343

CHADS, *Adm Sir* Henry Ducie, GCB (1788?–1868)   B i 580; DNB iii 1343;
                                                                          M v 237

CHADS, *Capt* James, RN (*d* 1781)   ch vi 582

CHADS, *Maj* John Cornell, RM (*d* 1854)   B i 580

CHADWICK, *Rear-Adm* French Ensor, USN (1844–1919)   DAB 152; H 926

CHADWICK, *Capt* Richard, RN (*d* 1746)   ch v 284

CHADWICK [*or* CHUNDWICK], *Capt* Robert, RN (*d* 1719)   ch iv 22

CHADWICK, *Capt* Samuel, RN (*d* 1728)   ch iv 68

CHAFFAULT DE BESNÉ, *Le Comte du* (ca 1707–1794)
French admiral   Md vii 397

CHALLIS, James (1803–1882)
Astronomer   B i 582; CE iii 258;
                                                                          DNB iii 1347

CHALMERS, *Cdr* Charles William, RN (*fl* 1799–1815)   M vii 239

CHALMERS, William, *Master*, RN (*d* 1805)   Tr 31

CHAMBER, John (1546–1604)
Writer on astronomy   DNB iv 1

CHAMBERLAIN, *Rear-Adm* Charles (*d* 1737)   ch iv 139

CHAMBERLAIN, *Capt* Clifford, RN (*d* 1691)   ch ii 307

CHAMBERLAIN, *Capt* Peter, RN (*d* 1720)   ch iii 244

CHAMBERLAIN, *Capt* Thomas, RN (*fl* 1672–1673)   ch i 330

CHAMBERLAIN, *Rear-Adm* William Charles (1818–1878)   B i 585

CHAMBERLAINE, Joseph (*fl* 1627–1628)
Teacher of navigation; almanac-maker   T i 211

CHAMBERLAYNE, *Cdr* John, RN (*fl* 1814–1828)   M viii 306

CHAMBERS, George (1803–1840)
Marine artist   DNB iv 17

CHAMBERS, John Graham (1843–1883)
Oarsman   B i 586

CHAPPE, Claude (1763–1805)
Pioneer in signal telegraphy   Md vii 493

CHAPPE, Ignace Urbain Jean (1760–1828)
Pioneer in signal telegraphy   Md vii 494

CHAPPE d'AUTEROCHE, Jean (1722–1769)
Voyager and astronomer   Md vii 492

CHAPELL, *Cdr* Charles, RN (1782–1865)   Tr 15

CHAPPELL, *Capt* Edward, RN (*fl* 1804–1840)   M viii 182

CHAPPELL, *Capt* George, RN (*fl* 1664)   ch i 95

CHAPPELLE, *Capt* John, RN (*d* 1666)   ch i 158

CHARCOT, Jean Baptiste (1867–1936)
French polar explorer   CE iii 280

CHARLES, *Lieut* Claudius, RN (*fl* 1804–1825)   Tr 33

CHARLEWOOD, *Adm* Edward Philips (1814–1894)   B iv 645

CHARLTON [or CARLTON], *Capt* St. John (*d* 1742)   ch iv 6

CHARNOCK, John (1756–1807)
Author of: 'Biographia Navalis' (1794–1798) and: 'History of Marine Architecture'
(1801–1802)   Md vii 671; DNB iv
                                                                                             132

CHARRINGTON, *Lieut* Harold, RN (*d* 1883)   B i 596

CHARY, Chintamanny Ragoonatha (*d* 1880)
Astronomer   B i 597; DNB iv 139

CHASMAN, *Cdr* William, RN (*d* 1828)   M viii 52; Tr 14

CHASTILLON, Claude de (1547–1616)
Engineer and topographer   Md viii 12

CHÂTEAU-REGNAUD, *Vice-Adm* François-Louis de Rousselet, *Comte de*
(1637–1716)   Md viii 17

CHATFIELD, *Adm of the Fleet* Alfred Ernle Montacute, *first Baron Chatfield*
(1873–1967)   CE iii 304

CHATTERTON, *Lady* Henrietta Georgiana Maria Lascelles (1806–1876)
Miscellaneous author; wrote: 'Memorials of Admiral Lord Gambier' (1861)   DNB iv 143

CHAUMONT, *Capitaine le Chevalier de* (*fl* 1635)   Md viii 44

CHAUNCEY, Isaac, USN (1772–1840)   DAB 160

CHAUNCEY, *Cdre* John S., USN (*d* 1874)   H 125

CHAUVENET, William (1820–1870)
Astronomer   DAB 160

CHAUVIN DE LA PIERRE, Pierre (*fl* 1603–1613)
French naval captain; temporary commandant at Quebec   DCB i 208

BOLTON PUBLIC REFERENCE LIBRARY LIBRARIES

CHILCOTT, *Cdr* John, RN (*d* 1829)   M vi 296

CHILD, *Cdr* John, RN (*fl* 1790–1800)   M vi 292

CHILD, *Sir* Josiah (1630–1699)
Writer on trade; naval store dealer at Portsmouth, 1655   DNB iv 244

CHILDS, *Maj-Gen* Joseph, RM (1787–1870)   B i 610; DA*u*B i 220

CHILDERS, Hugh Culling Eardley (1827–1896)
First lord of the Admiralty, 1868–1871   B iv 655; DNB xxii
                                                                                  423

CHILDERS, Robert Erskine, DSC (1870–1922)
Author and politician; during the First World War was employed as an intelligence
officer and in training officers in reconnaissance work in the RNAS. He was the
author of: 'The Riddle of the Sands' (1903)   DNB xxv 180

CHILLEY [*or* CHILLY], *Capt* John, RN (*d* 1734)   *ch* iii 379

CHILLINGWORTH, John (*d* 1445)
Astronomer   DNB iv 252

CHILLY [*or* CHILLEY], *Capt* John, RN (*d* 1734)   *ch* iii 379

CHIMLEY, *Cdr* John, RN (*fl* 1797–1829)   M viii 332

CHIMMO, *Capt* William, RN (1828–1891)   B iv 656

CHIPP, *Lieut* Charles W., USN (*fl* 1863–1880)   H 955

CHISWELL, Richard (1639–1711)
Bookseller and publisher   *chb* 427; DNB iv 265

CHOQUET DE LINDU (1713–1790)
Marine engineer   M*d* viii 200

CHORIS [*or* KHORIS], Louis (*b* 1795)
Russian painter and voyager   M*d* viii 201

CHOUART DES GROSEILLIERS, Médard (1618–*ca* 1696)
French explorer; one of the founders of the Hudson's Bay Company   DCB i 223; MDC 137

CHRISTIAN, *Capt* Edward, RN (*d* 1758)   *ch* vi 99

CHRISTIAN, Fletcher (*fl* 1789)
'Bounty' mutineer   DNB iv 277

CHRISTIAN, *Rear-Adm* Hood Hanway (*b* 1784)   M ix 119

CHRISTIAN, *Rear-Adm Sir* Hugh Cloberry (1747–1798)   DNB iv 278; NC xxi
                                                                                  177; R ii 265

CHRISTIAN, *Cdr* Jonathan, RN (*fl* 1793–1820)   M vii 32

CHRISTIE, Alexander (*ca* 1841–1895)
Merchant marine captain   B iv 661

CHRISTIE, George (1794–1837)
Inventor of a sea telescope   T ii 333

CHRISTIE, James, *Schoolmaster*, RN (*fl* 1805–1848)   Tr 185

CLARK, Alexander Russell (1809–1894)
*Surveyor; emigrated to Australia in 1832; joint owner of the steamer 'Governor
Arthur', 1837–1841; constructed in partnership with John Watson, the engine for the
paddle-steamer 'Native Youth' – probably the first marine steam engine to be
built in Tasmania, 1842*   DAuB i 224

CLARK, Alvan (1804–1887)
Astronomer   DAB 165

CLARK, Alvan Graham (1832–1897)
Astronomer   DAB 165

CLARK, Ambrose I., *Paymaster*, USN (*fl* 1861–1880)   H 988

CLARK, Arthur Hamilton (1841–1922)
Master mariner   DAB 165

CLARK, *Lieut-Cdr* Charles E., USN (*fl* 1862–1880)   H 922

CLARK, *Capt* Edward, RN (*d* 1764)   ch vi 305

CLARK, Ezra W. (*b* 1839)
Chief of the US Revenue Marine   H 131

CLARK, *Sir* James, KCB (1788–1870)
Physician; served as a surgeon, Royal Navy, 1809–1815   DNB iv 402

CLARK, James Edgar, USN (1843–1922)   DAB 165

CLARK, *Capt* John, RN (1711–1789)   ch vi 303

CLARK, *Cdr* John, RN (1777–1849/50)   Tr 241

CLARK, John, *Surgeon's Mate*, RN (*d* 1864)   Tr 73

CLARK, Josiah Latimer (1822–1898)
*Engineer; worked with C. T. Bright on cable-laying; assisted G. B. Airy in devising
a method of indicating Greenwich Mean Time throughout the country, 1857*   B iv 671; DNB xxxii
                                                                                451

CLARK, Ralph (*d* 1794)
Royal Marine officer; was aboard the 'Friendship' in the 'First Fleet'   DAuB i 226

CLARK, Robert H., *Paymaster*, USN (*fl* 1857–1880)   H 986

CLARK, *Cdr* Samuel, RN (*d* 1834)   Tr 167

CLARK, William Tierney (1783–1852)
Civil engineer; engineer of the Thames and Medway Canal   DNB iv 411

CLARKE, *Lieut-Gen Sir* Andrew, GCMG, CB, CSI, RE
*Director of engineering works at the Admiralty, 1864–1873; recommended the
purchase of the Suez Canal by an English company, 1870; as governor of the Straits
Settlements, suppressed piracy there, 1873–1875; advocated the widening of the
Suez Canal, 1880–1882*   DNB xxiiia 362

CLARKE, *Lieut* Charles Ansyl, USN (*fl* 1861–1880)   H 962

CLARKE, *Rear-Adm* Edward (*d* 1778/9)   ch vi 37

CLEBURNE, Richard (1799–1864)
Merchant; opened the first direct trade between Melbourne and Hobart; active
promoter of the Tasmanian Steam Navigation Company   DAUB i 229

CLELAND, *Rear-Adm* John (*fl* 1744–1781)   *ch* vi 353

CLELAND, *Capt* William, RN (*d* 1744)   *ch* iv 424

CLEMENT, *Capt* Benjamin, RN (*d* 1836)   M viii 453; x 391;
                                                                                       Tr 80

CLEMENTS, *Capt* Bartholomew, RN (*fl* 1700)   *ch* iii 199

CLEMENTS, *Cdr* George, RN (*d* 1707)   *ch* iii 65

CLEMENTS, *Cdr* John, RN (*d* 1694)   *ch* iii 9

CLEMENTS, *Capt* John, RN (*d* 1704)   *ch* i 279; ii 9

CLEMENTS, *Rear-Adm* John, RN (*fl* 1794–1814)   M ii 609

CLEMENTS, *Rear-Adm* Michael (*d* 1796)   *ch* vi 220; DNB iv
                                                                                       490

CLEMENTS, *Capt* Richard, RN (*d* 1775)   *ch* vi 60

CLEPHAN, *Capt* James, RN (*d* 1851)   M vii 6; Tr 114

CLEPHANE, *Capt* Robert, RN (*d* 1827)   M x 314

CLERK, *Sir* George (1787–1867)
Statesman; a lord of the Admiralty, 1819–1827   B i 645; DNB iv 494

CLERK, John (1728–1812)
Author of: 'Essay on naval tactics' (1790)   CE iii 638; DNB iv 497

CLERKE, Agnes Mary (1842–1907)
Astronomer   CE iii 639; DNB xxiiia
                                                                                       371

CLERKE, *Capt* Charles, RN (1741–1779)   DNB iv 502; M*d* viii
                                                                                       436

CLERKE, *Capt Sir* John, RN (*d* 1775)   *ch* vi 438

CLEVELAND, *Capt* Archibald, RN (*d* 1766)   *ch* vi 158

CLEVELAND, Richard Jeffry (1773–1860)   DAB 173

CLEVELAND, *Capt* William, RN (*d* 1735)   *ch* iii 66

CLEVELEY, John (1747–1786)
Marine artist   DNB iv 509

CLEVELEY, Robert (1747–1809)
Marine artist   DNB iv 509

CLIFF, William (1811/2–1891)
Chairman of the West India & Pacific Steam Ship Co, 1884–1891   B iv 688

CLIFFORD, *Adm Sir* Augustus William James, CB (1788–1877)   B i 648; DNB iv 514;
                                                                                       M viii 453; xi 77

COAKLEY, *Cdr* Thomas, RN (1780–1851)   Tr 52

COAL, *Capt* Thomas, RN (*d* 1710)   ch ii 97

COBB, *Lieut* Charles, RN (*d* 1811)   Tr 288

COBB, Elijah (1768–1848)
Sea-captain   DAB 176

COBB, *Cdr* Smith, RN (*b* 1786)   M vii 80

COBBE, *Cdr* William, RN (*fl* 1797–1825)   M vii 214

COBBIE, Walsall (*fl* 1676–1682)
Sea-captain and carpenter with Hudson's Bay Co   DCB i 232

COCHET, *Adm* John (1760–1851)   B i 660; M ii 756

COCHRAN, George, *Paymaster*, USN (*fl* 1861–1880)   H 988

COCHRANE, *Adm the Hon Sir* Alexander Forrester Inglis, KB (1758–1832)   DNB iv 615; M i 257; R ii 435

COCHRANE, Archibald, *ninth Earl of Dundonald* (1749–1831)
*Chemical manufacturer; as a youth served both in the army and navy; urged the
Admiralty to use coal-tar to protect ships' hulls*   DNB iv 616

COCHRANE, Henry Clay, USMC (1842–1913)   DAB 177; H 1017

COCHRANE, *Adm Sir* Thomas, GCB, *tenth Earl of Dundonald* (1775–1860)   CE iv 664; DNB iv 621; NC xxii 1; M*d* viii 510

COCHRANE, *Adm of the Fleet Sir* Thomas John, GCB (1789–1860)   B i 661; DNB iv 631; M ix 135; MDC 145

COCK [*or* COCKS *or* COX], Christopher (*fl* 1660–1696)
Optical instrument-maker; instruments at National Maritime Museum   T i 248

COCK, George (*d* 1679)
Steward for sick and wounded seamen, 1664   DNB iv 632

COCK, Robert, *Master*, RN (*fl* 1794–1809)   Tr 242

COCK, *Cdr* Robert, RN (*d* 1855)   Tr 242

COCK, *Capt* William, RN (*fl* 1699–1715)   ch iii 196

COCKAYNE, *Capt Sir* Samuel, RN (*d* 1735)   ch iv 209

COCKAYNE, William (1717–1798)
Astronomer   DNB iv 632

COCKBURN, *Adm of the Fleet Sir* George, GCB (1772–1853)   B i 663; DNB iv 640; H 146; M ii 518; R iii 257

COCKBURN, *Capt* John, RN (*d* 1731)   ch iii 379

COCKBURN, William (1669–1739)
Physician; appointed physician to the fleet and to Greenwich Hospital, 1731   DNB iv 648

COCKBURNE, *Capt* Andrew, RN (*d* 1768)   ch vi 100

COKE, *Sir* John (1563–1644)
Commissioner of the Navy, 1621–1636   DNB iv 700

COLBERT, Jean Baptiste (1619–1683)
French statesman; secretary of state for the navy   CE iii 717

COLBERT DE MAULEVRIER, Edouard Charles Victurnin *Comte de*
(1758–1820)   M*d* viii 562

COLBY, *Cdr* David, RN (*b* 1782)   M ix 666

COLBY, *Lieut* Harrison G. O., USN (*fl* 1862–1880)   H 951

COLBY, Henry G., *Paymaster*, USN (*fl* 1863–1880)   H 994

COLBY, *Capt* Stephen, RN (*d* 1779)   *ch* vi 159

COLBY, *Cdr* Thomas, RN (1782–1864)   M vii 196; Tr 242

COLBY, *Maj-Gen* Thomas Frederick, RE (1784–1852)   B i 669; DNB iv 711

COLCHESTER, *Adm Lord*: *see* ABBOT, Charles

COLE, *Capt* Ambrose, RN (*d* 1711)   *ch* iv 22

COLE, Benjamin (senior) (1695–1755)
Instrument-maker, writer on quadrants; instruments at National Maritime Museum   T ii 114

COLE, Benjamin (junior) (1727–1813)
Instrument-maker; quadrant at National Maritime Museum   T i 291; ii 199

COLE, *Capt Sir* Christopher, KCB, RN (1770–1887)   DNB xxii 465; M iv
                                                                    501; R iv 352

COLE, *Capt* Edward, RN (*fl* 1697)   *ch* iii 163

COLE, George Ward (1793–1879)
Merchant; served in the Royal Navy (1807–1817) before joining the merchant
service; constructed Cole's Wharf, Melbourne, 1840; operated paddle-steamers on the
Yarra River and in Port Phillip Bay; built the 'City of Melbourne', first screw
steamer south of the equator, 1851   AE i 281; B i 670;
                                                                    DA*u*B i 233

COLE, Humfray (*ca* 1530–1591)
Instrument-maker who supplied Drake and Frobisher; designer of a mechanical log   DNB iv 726; T i 171

COLE, John, *Purser*, RN (*fl* 1812–1829)   T ii 386

COLE, *Lieut-Col* Nathaniel, RM (*d* 1837)   Tr 195

COLE, *Cdr* Thomas Edmund, RN (*fl* 1797–1834)   M viii 83

COLE, William (*fl* 1818)
Teacher of mathematics and writer on navigation   T ii 386

COLE, *Capt* William John, RN (*fl* 1802–1838)   B i 672; M viii 299

COLEBY, *Capt* Charles, RN (*d* 1772)   *ch b* 84

COLEMAN, George (*fl* 1802–1820)
Teacher of navigation   T ii 360

COLEMAN, *Capt* James, RN (*fl* 1665)   *ch* i 158

COLLINS, *Lieut-Col* David, RM (1756–1810)   AE i 281; DAuB i 236;
                                                              DNB iv 822

COLLINS, *Cdr* Edward, RN (*b* 1792)   M vii 223

COLLINS, Edward Knight (1802–1878)   DAB 181

COLLINS, Enos (1774–1871)
Canadian privateer, banker and merchant   MDC 149

COLLINS, Grenville (*fl* 1679–1693)
Hydrographer   CE iii 729; *ch* ii 60;
                                                              DNB iv 823; T i 259

COLLINS, *Capt* James, RN (*fl* 1781–1812)   M x 206

COLLINS, John (1625–1683)
*Mathematician; served in a merchantman 1642–1649; author of: 'The Description
and uses of a general quadrant' (1658)*   DNB iv 824; T i 228

COLLINS, *Lieut* John B., USN (*fl* 1866–1880)   H 965

COLLINS, Michael, *Midshipman*, RN (*fl* 1801–1805)   Tr 117

COLLINS, *Rear-Adm* Napoleon, USN (1814–1875)   DAB 181; H 148

COLLINS, *Capt* Richard, RN (*fl* 1672)   *ch* i 331

COLLINS, *Rear-Adm* Richard (*d* 1779)   *ch* v 285

COLLINS, *Capt* Richard, RN (*d* 1780)   *ch* vi 353

COLLINS, *Lieut* Samuel, RN (*fl* 1805–1806)   Tr 219

COLLINS, *Capt* William, R N (*fl* 1678)   *ch* ii 49

COLLINS, William (1760?–1819)
Naval officer, shipowner and explorer   DAuB i 236

COLLINSON, *Adm Sir* Richard, KCB (1811–1883)   B i 683; CE iii 730;
                                                              DNB iv 839

COLLUM, *Capt* Richard S., USMC (*fl* 1861–1880)   H 1016

COLOHAN, *Lieut* Charles E., USN (*fl* 1865–1880)   H 961

COLOMB, *Sir* John Charles Ready, KCMG (1838–1909)
Writer on imperial defence; served in the Royal Marines, 1854–1869   DNB xxiiia 392

COLOMB, *Vice-Adm* Philip Howard (1831–1899)   B iv 721; DNB xxii
                                                              474

COLPOYS [*formerly* GRIFFITH], *Adm* Edward Griffith (*fl* 1778–1821)   M ii 548; R iii 164

COLPOYS, *Adm Sir* John, GCB (1742?–1821)   DNB iv 855; Md viii
                                                              662; NA ii 31; NC xi
                                                              265; R ii 3

COLQUITT, *Cdr* Goodwin, RN (*d* 1826)   M vi 248

COLQUITT, *Rear-Adm* Samuel Martin (*fl* 1788–1846)   M x 268

CONDAMINE, Charles Maria de la (1701–1774)
French geographer; went on voyages to Africa, Asia and South America   A 123; M*d* ix 6

CONDON, *Capt* David, RN (*d* 1692)   ch ii 308

CONEY, *Capt* William, RN (*d* 1707)   ch iii 289

CONGREVE, *Sir* William (1772–1828)
Inventor of the Congreve Rocket   DNB iv 934; M*d* ix 35

CONN, *Capt* John, RN (1764–1810)   T*r* 69

CONNER, *Capt* David, USN (1792–1856)   DAB 184

CONNER, *Cdr* Richard, RN (*fl* 1808–1828)   M viii 294

CONNINGSBY, *Capt* Humphrey, RN (*fl* 1660–1662)   ch i 81

CONNOLLY [*or* CONOLLY], *Capt* Matthew, RN (*b* 1776)   M vii 135

CONNOLLY, *Lieut* Peter, RM (*d* 1835)   T*r* 208

CONNOLLY, *Gen* William Hallett, RM (*d* 1861)   B i 693

CONRAD, Joseph [*née* Teodor Josef Konrad KORZENIOWSKI]
(1857–1923)   CE iv 24; DNB XXV
                                                                               205

CONSETT, *Capt* Matthew, RN (*d* 1749)   ch iv 93

CONSTABLE, *Capt* Charles, RN (*d* 1716)   ch iii 395

CONSTABLE, *Capt* John, RN (*fl* 1692–1701)   ch ii 409

CONSTABLE, *Capt* William, RN, *fourth Viscount Dunbar* (*d* 1718)   ch ii 142

CONTARINI, Giovanni Matteo (*fl* 1506)
Italian cartographer   CE iv 81

CONTRECOEUR, Claude Pierre Pécaudy, *Sieur de* (1701–1774)
French-Canadian captain in the Marine   MDC 152

CONVERSE, *Lieut-Cdr* George A., USN (*fl* 1861–1880)   H 932

CONWAY, Hugh Seymour [*afterwards Lord* Hugh Seymour] (1759–1801)   NA ii 78; NC ii 357;
                                                                               R ii 126

CONY, *Capt* William, RN (*d* 1707)   DNB iv 985

CONYNGHAM, Gustavus (*ca* 1744–1819)
American naval officer and privateer   DAB 186; H 171

COODE, *Sir* John, KCMG (1816–1892)
Civil engineer; associated with important harbour works in various parts of the world   B iv 733; DNB xxii
                                                                               477

COODE, *Vice-Adm Sir* John Henry, KCB (1779–1858)   B i 698; M x 276

COOK, *Lieut-Cdr* Francis A., USN (*fl* 1860–1880)   H 922

COOK, Frederick Albert (1865–1940)
Polar explorer   DAB 186

COOK, *Capt* Hugh, RN (*d* 1834)   M ix 160; T*r* 251

COOPER, *Rear-Adm* Bransby Blake (1792–1853)   B i 708

COOPER, Daniel (1785–1853)
Merchant; founder of Cooper and Levey, who sent ships from Australia to New
Zealand, Samoa Islands and India; also a pioneer in shipping wool to England   DAUB i 245

COOPER, Edward Joshua (1798–1863)
Astronomer   DNB iv 1067

COOPER, *Capt* Francis, RN (*d* 1733 *or* 1736)   ch iv 28

COOPER, *Cdre* George H., USN (*fl* 1837–1880)   H 172

COOPER, James Fenimore (1789–1851)   CE iv 101; DAB 188;
                                                                     H 172

COOPER, *Capt* John, RN (*d* 1728)   ch iii 125

COOPER, *Cdr* Philip H., USN (*fl* 1860–1879)   H 917

COOPER, Robert (1835–1899)
Oarsman   B iv 748

COOPER, *Capt* Thomas, RN (*d* 1770)   ch iv 375

COOPER, William (*d* 1872)
Wrote on yachting under the pseudonym 'Vanderdecken'   B iv 750

COOTE, Richard, *first Earl of Bellamont* (1636–1701)
Appointed governor of New England, with a special mission to suppress piracy, 1695;
with others fitted out the 'Adventure' and gave Kidd powers to arrest pirates; arrested
Kidd for piracy 1699 and sent him for trial in England, 1700   DAB 191; DNB iv 1088

COOTE, *Adm* Robert, CB (1820–1898)   B iv 752

COOTE, *Cdr* William, RN (*d* 1857)   M vi 364; Tr 267

COPE, Charles John (*fl* 1814–1830)
Chronometer-maker; instruments at National Maritime Museum   T ii 387

COPE, Thomas Pym (1768–1854)
Shipowner   DAB 191

COPELAND, Charles W. (1815–1895)
Naval engineer   DAB 191

COPELAND, Ralph (1837–1907)
Astronomer   DNB xxiiia 411

COPELAND, *Capt* Richard, RN (*b* 1792)   M vii 370

COPEMAN, Edward Stephens (*d* 1891)
Partner with R. E. Pinhet as patentees of marine life-saving appliances   B iv 754

COPOW, *Capt* William, RN (*fl* 1665–1677)   ch i 394

COPPERTHWAITE, *Lieut* Arthur, RN (*fl* 1803–1809)   Tr 110

COPPIN, *Capt* John, RN (*d* 1666)   ch i 11

COPPINGER, Richard William, *Staff Surgeon*, RN (1847–1910)   DNB xxiiia 416

CORNISH-BOWDEN, *Adm* William (1857–1896)   B iv 761

CORNWALL, *Capt* Frederick, RN (*d* 1786)   *ch* v 288

CORNWALL, *Cdr* John, RN (*b* 1795)   M viii 212

CORNWALL, *Capt* Thomas, RN (*d* 1796)   *ch* vi 222

CORNWALL, *Capt* Woolfran, RN (*d* 1719)   *ch* ii 141

CORNWALLIS, *Adm Sir* William, GCB (1744–1819)   *ch* vi 533; DNB iv
                                                                   1169; M*d* ix 249; NC
                                                                   vii 1; R i 387

CORNWELL, *Lieut* Charles C., USN (*fl* 1864–1880)   H 953

CORONELLI, Vincenzo Maria (1650–1718)
Italian cartographer   CE iv 138; M*d* ix 252

CORREÁ DE SAA, Salvador (*fl* 1516)
Portuguese admiral and governor of Brazil   M*d* ix 257

CORRIE, *Capt* F. H., USMC (*fl* 1861–1880)   H 1015

CORRY, *Rear-Adm* Armar Lowry, KCB (*d* 1855)   B i 724; M xii 314

CORRY, Henry Thomas Lowry (1803–1873)
*Junior lord of the Admiralty, 1841–1845; secretary 1845–1846, 1858–1859, and
first lord 1867–1868*   DNB iv 1179

CORSALI, Andrea (*fl* 1516)
Florentine navigator and explorer   M*d* ix 264

CORT, Henry (1740–1800)
*Ironmaster; in partnership with Adam Jellicoe undertook contracts to supply the navy
with rolled iron; on Jellicoe's death it was found that he had embezzled naval funds
to finance Cort's factory*   CE iv 145; DNB iv
                                                                   1182

CORTE-REAL, Gaspar (*fl* 1502)
Portuguese explorer   DCB i 234; M*d* ix 270;
                                                                   MDC 155

CORWIN, William A., *Assistant-Surgeon*, USN (*fl* 1869–1880)   H 978

CORY, John (1828–1910)
Philanthropist; coal merchant and shipowner   DNB xxiiia 423

CORYTON, *Gen* John Rawlins, RM (1790–1867)   B i 724; Tr 118

COSA, Juan de la (*d* 1509)
Spanish navigator   CE iv 147

COSBY, Frank, *Pay-Inspector*, USN (*fl* 1861–1880)   H 988

COSBY, *Capt* Henry, RN (*d* 1753)   *ch* v 368

COSBY, *Adm* Phillips (1727?–1808)   *ch* vi 435; DNB iv
                                                                   1188; NC xiv 354

COSMAO-KERJULIEN, *Contre Amiral* Julien Marie, *Baron* (1761–1825) s i 265

COUNTRY, *Capt* Richard, RN (*fl* 1661–1673)   *ch* i 54

COURAND, *Contre Amiral* Jean François (1751–1816)   s i 268

COURCY, *Cdr* Michael de, RN (*d* 1813)   Tr 115

COURCY, *Adm* Michael de (*d* 1824)   M i 332; NA ii 122

COURCY, *Adm* Michael de (1811–1881)   B i 846

COURCY, *Cdr* Nevinson de (1780–1845)   M xii 317

COURCY, *Lieut-Col* Nevinson Willoughby de, CB, RM (1823–1885)   B i 846

COURTEN [*or* COURTEENE], *Sir* William (1572–1636)
Merchant; owned a fleet of twenty ships trading with Guinea, Spain and West Indies;
one of his ships discovered Barbados in 1624   DNB iv 1258

COURTENAY, *Vice-Adm* George William Conway (1795–1863)   B i 733; M vi 27

COURTHOPP, Nathaniel (*d* 1620)
Captain in the East India Company's service   DNB iv 1273

COURTIS, *Lieut* Francis, USN (*fl* 1862–1880)   H 943

COURTNAY, *Capt* Francis, RN (*d* 1673)   *ch* i 222

COUSINS, *Lieut* Stephen, RN (*fl* 1805–1819)   Tr 297

COVELL, *Capt* Allen, RN (*fl* 1661)   *ch* i 54

COVENTRY, John (1735–1812)
Telescope manufacturer   DNB iv 1284

COVERDALE, William Hugh (1871–1949)
Canadian engineer; consulting engineer to Canada Steamships' Company   MDC 158

COWAN, *Cdr* Malcom, RN (*fl* 1790–1809)   M vi 298

COWAN, *Capt* Thomas, RN (*fl* 1798–1802)   M iv 656

COWAN, *Cdr* Thomas, RN (*fl* 1812–1827)   M viii 232

COWDRY, *Capt* John, RN (*fl* 1665–1667)   *ch* i 158

COWE, *Capt* John, RN (*d* 1704)   *ch* iii 245

COWELL, *Capt* Henry, RN (*d* 1765)   *ch* vi 422

COWELL, John Leathley [*formerly* Hawkins Witchett] (1792–1863)
Actor; served as a midshipman, RN, 1805–1808   B i 735; DNB iv 1301

COWES, *Capt* Richard, RN (*fl* 1660)   *ch* i 11

COWLES, *Lieut* William S., USN (*fl* 1863–1880)   H 952

COWLEY, *Capt* Ambrose (*fl* 1683–1686)
English circumnavigator   Md ix 413

COWLEY, *Capt* William, RN (*d* 1740)   *ch* iv 35

COX, Christopher: *see* COCK

COX, *Capt* Douglas, RN (*fl* 1800–1841)   M viii 4

COX, *Gen* Edmund Henry, RMA (1828–1893)   B iv 782

CRANSTON, *Capt* James, RN (*d* 1790)   ch vi 469

CRANSTOUN, *Capt* James, RN, *eighth Lord Cranstoun* (1755–1796)   DNB v 32

CRAVEN, *Cdr* Charles H., USN (*fl* 1860–1880)   H 917

CRAVEN, *Rear-Adm* Thomas (*d* 1772)   ch v 439

CRAVEN, *Rear-Adm* Thomas Tingey, USN (1808–1887)   DAB 199; H 181

CRAVEN, *Cdr* Tunis Augustus Macdonough, USN (1813–1864)   DAB 199; H 182

CRAWFORD, *Adm* Abraham (1788–1869)   B i 754; M vi 77

CRAWFORD, *Capt the Hon* Charles, RN (*d* 1745)   ch iv 223

CRAWFORD, Edmund Thornton (1806–1885)
Marine artist   DNB v 51

CRAWFORD, *Capt* James Coutts, RN (*b* 1760)   M iv 667

CRAWFORD, *Capt* John, RN (*fl* 1667)   ch i 280

CRAWFORD [*or* CRAFORD], *Capt* John, RN (*d* 1740)   ch iv 426

CRAWFORD, William (1788–1847)
Philanthropist; employed at the Naval Transport Office, 1804–1815   DNB v 57

CRAWLEY, *Vice-Adm* Edmund (*fl* 1790–1814)   M i 386; ii 865

CRAWLEY, *Capt* Jeremiah [*or* Jeremy], RN (*fl* 1667)   ch i 280

CRAWLEY, *Capt* Thomas, RN (*d* 1700–1701)   ch ii 307

CREAGH, *Cdr* James, RN (*b* 1798)   M viii 216

CREASE, *Cdr* Henry, RN (*fl* 1798–1821)   M viii 56

CREESY, Josiah Perkins (1815–1871)
Sea-captain   DAB 200

CREIGHTON, *Cdre* Johnston B., USN (*fl* 1838–1879)   H 182

CREMER [*or* CREMOR], *Cdr* Henry, RN (*d* 1707)   ch iii 329

CRESPI, Juan (1721–1782)
Franciscan missionary and American explorer   DAB 201

CRESPIGNY, *Cdr* Augustus James de, RN (*b* 1825)   Tr 117

CRESSWELL, *Maj* Heneage William, RM (*d* 1826)   Tr 218

CRESSWELL, *Capt* Samuel Gurney, RN (*d* 1867)   B i 758

CREUZE, Augustin Francis Bullock (1800–1852)
Naval architect   B iv 801

CREYKE, *Capt* Richard, RN (1746–1826)   M iii 72

CREYKE, *Capt* Richard, RN (*fl* 1800–1846)   M xi 414

CRICHTON, *Capt* James Augustus Seymour, RN (*fl* 1799–1813)   M vii 75

CRICHTON, Robert, *Surgeon*, RN (*d* 1827)   Tr 136

CRIRIE, *Cdr* John, RN (*fl* 1809–1825)   M viii 157

CRISP, *Lieut* George, RN (1770–1831)   Tr 194

CROSBY, Thomas (*fl* 1740–1780)
Teacher of and writer on navigation   T ii 202

CROSLEY, John (*fl* 1790–1804)
Astronomer; assistant to Maskelyne at Greenwich   T ii 333

CROSMAN, *Capt* Robert, RN (*fl* 1664)   *ch* i 95

CROSS, *Capt* George, RN (*d* 1689)   *ch* ii 385

CROSS, *Capt* William, RN (*d* 1746)   *ch* ii 385

CROSSLEY, John Sydney (1812–1879)
Engineer to the Leicester Canal Co, 1832   B i 774

CROSSMAN, *Maj-Gen Sir* William, KCMG, RE (1830–1901)
First inspector of submarine mining defences, 1876–1881   DNB xxiiia 452

CROSWELL, William (*fl* 1791)
Teacher of navigation, compiler of longitude tables   T ii 334

CROUCH, *Cdr* Edward Thomas, RN (*b* 1816)   M viii 77

CROUCHER, Joseph (*fl* 1800)
Marine chronometer maker   T ii 361

CROUT, Henry (*fl* 1612–1617)
Newfoundland settler and explorer   DCB i 240

CROW, *Capt* Anthony, RN (*fl* 1677–1688)   *ch* ii 13

CROW, Francis (*fl* 1813–1832)
Compass and octant-maker; instruments at National Maritime Museum   T ii 387

CROW, *Capt* George, RN (*fl* 1665–1667)   *ch* i 280

CROW, Hugh (1765–1829)
Captain of a merchant vessel employed in the African trade   DNB v 236

CROW, *Capt* Josiah, RN (*d* 1714)   *ch* ii 387

CROW, *Capt* Leonard, RN (*d* 1705)   *ch* iii 10

CROW, *Capt* Thomas, RN (*fl* 1666–1671)   *ch* i 222

CROWDER, *Sir* Richard Budden
Judge-advocate of the Fleet, 1849–1854   DNB v 237

CROWDY, *Adm* Charles (1786–1870)   B i 774; M viii 528

CROWE, *Sir* Eyre Alexander Barby Wichart, KCMG, CB (1864–1925)
Diplomat; British delegate at the international maritime conference held at London, 1908   DNB xxv 219

CROWINSHIELD, *Cdr* Arrant S., USN (*fl* 1860–1880)   H 917

CROWINSHIELD, Benjamin Williams (1772–1851)
Secretary of the US Navy, 1814–1818   DAB 204

CROWINSHIELD, George (1766–1817)
Sea-captain and pioneer yachtsman   DAB 204

CROWINSHIELD, Jacob (1770–1808)
Sea-captain   DAB 205

CUNDETT, *Capt* John, RN (*d* 1724)   *ch* iv 93

CUNHA, Nuno da (1487–1539)
Portuguese navigator   Md ix 566

CUNHA, Tristan da (*fl* 1460–1540)
Portuguese navigator   Md ix 565

CUNIGHAM [*or* CUNINGHAM], Jacob (*fl* 1661)
Instrument-maker; telescope at National Maritime Museum   T i 249

CUNN, Samuel (*fl* 1714–1722)
Teacher of navigational mathematics   T i 304

CUNNINGHAM, *Capt* Alexander, RN (*fl* 1805–1812)   M xi 114

CUNNINGHAM, *Adm of the Fleet* Andrew Browne, KT, DSO, *Viscount
Cunningham of Hyndehope* (1883–1963)   CE iv 298

CUNNINGHAM, *Rear-Adm Sir* Charles (1755–1834)   DNB v 316; M iii 75

CUNNINGHAM, George (*b* 1788)
Midshipman aboard the 'Neptune' at Trafalgar   Tr 62

CUNNINGHAM, Henry Duncan Preston, *Paymaster*, RN (1815–1875)   B iv 824

CUNNINGHAM, John (1575–1651)
Scotsman, Danish naval captain, explorer   DCB i 243

CUNNINGHAM, John S., *Pay Director*, USN (*fl* 1857–1880)   H 986

CUNNINGHAM, Peter Miller, *Surgeon*, RN (1789–1864)   B i 788; DAuB i 267
                                                                                        DNB v 316

CUNNINGHAM, *Cdr* Thomas, RN (*fl* 1765–1823)   M vi 394

CUNNINGHAM, William (*fl* 1805–1848)
Midshipman aboard the 'Prince' at Trafalgar   Tr 81

CUPPAGE, *Cdr* Adam, RN (*b* 1792)   M viii 361

CUPPAGE, *Capt* William, RN (*fl* 1807–1830)   M vi 158

CURLE, *Capt* Edmund, RN (*fl* 1661)   *ch* i 54

CURRAN, *Cdr* John Bartholomew Hoar, RN (*fl* 1806–1817)   M vii 27

CURRIE, *Sir* Donald, GCMG (1825–1909)
Founder of the Castle Steamship Company   DNB xxiiia 452

CURRIE, *Vice-Adm* Mark John (1795–1874)   B i 792; M viii 125

CURRY, *Adm* Richard, CB (1772–1855)   B i 792; M iii 459

CURRY, *Capt* Roger Carley, RN (*fl* 1810–1834)   M viii 385

CURSETJEE, Ardaseer (1808–1877)
In charge of the shipbuilding yard at Mazagon, 1828; assistant shipbuilder there, 1833 B i 792

CURTIS, Anthony (1796–1853)
*Merchant and whaler; in early life served in Royal Navy; became first person to
trade between Western Australia and Ceylon, in his schooner 'Vixen'*   DAuB i 272

DABOLL, Nathan (1750–1818)
Teacher of navigation   DAB 211

DACOSTA, Benjamin (*b* 1782)
Midshipman aboard the 'Téméraire' at Trafalgar   Tr 54

DACRE, Ranulph (1797–1884)
Master mariner and Australian merchant   DAuB i 275

DACRES, *Vice-Adm* James Richard (1749–1810)   NC xxvi 265

DACRES, *Vice-Adm* James Richard (1788–1853)   B i 796; M iv 972

DACRES, *Capt* Richard, RN (*b* 1761)   M iii 29; NC xxvi 353,
                                                                     441

DACRES, *Adm Sir* Sidney Colpoys, GCB, KLH, KTS (1805–1884)   B i 799; DNB V 375

DADE, Francis C., *Chief Engineer*, USN (*fl* 1849–1880)   H 1001

D'AETH, *Adm* George William Hughes (1786–1873)   B i 79; M xii 22

DAHLGREN, *Rear-Adm* John Adolphus Bernard, USN (1809–1870)   DAB 211; H 192

DAIMLER, Gottlieb (1834–1900)
*German inventor of four-cycle internal combustion engine, which he first applied
practically to a boat, 1883*   A 332

DALBARADE, *Contre-Amiral* Jean (1743–1819)
Privateer captain and minister of marine   s i 280

DALBY, *Cdr* Thomas, RN (*fl* 1778–1798)   M vi 251

DALE, *Sir* David (1829–1906)
Ironmaster and shipbuilder   DNB xxxiiia 461

DALE, *Capt* Richard, USN (1756–1826)   DAB 212; H 193

DALE, *Sir* Thomas (*d* 1619)
Naval commander   DNB V 385

DALE, *Capt* William, RN (*fl* 1660–1673)   ch i 12

DALGLEISH, *Cdr* James, RN (*d* 1846)   M vii 135

DALLAS, *Cdr* Francis G., USN (*fl* 1841–1869)   H 919

DALLING, *Capt* John Windham, RN (*d* 1853)   M vi 22; Tr 184

DALRYMPLE, Alexander (1737–1808)   AE i 355; CE iv 353;
                                                                     DAuB i 275; DNB V
                                                                     402; Md x 49; T ii 227

DALRYMPLE, *Capt* Hugh, RN (*d* 1779/80)   ch vi 527

DALRYMPLE, *Adm* John (*d* 1798)   ch vi 306; NA i 145

DALRYMPLE-HORN-ELPHINSTONE, *Sir* James (1805–1886)
Retired from the H.E.I.C. naval service in 1834 with the rank of commander   B v 9

DALTON, *Capt* James Robert, RN (*d* 1860)   M vi 396

DALY, *Rear-Adm* Cuthbert Featherstone, CB (*fl* 1794–1846)   M ix 383

DANSON, John Towne (1817–1898)
An authority on marine insurance · B v 18

DANVERS, Frederic Charles (1833–1906)
Author of: 'List of marine records of the late East India Company' (1897) · DNB xxiiia 466

DAPPER, Oliver (*d* 1690)
Dutch geographer · M*d* x 151

D'APRANDESTEGUY, Martin : *see* APPRENDESTIGUY

DARBY, *Vice-Adm* George (*d* 1790) · *ch* vi 39; DNB v 493; NA i 53; NC xxiii 89; R i 156

DARBY, *Adm Sir* Henry D'Esterre, KCB (1781–1819) · M i 268

DARCY, *Capt* Thomas, RN (*fl* 1661–1672) · *ch* i 95

DARE, *Capt* Jeffery, RN (*d* 1666) · *ch* i 222

DARLEY, *Capt* Arthur, RN (*fl* 1806–1846) · M viii 255

DARLEY, *Capt* Edward, RN (*d* 1702) · *ch* iii 99

DARLING, Grace Horsley (1815–1842) · CE iv 379; DNB v 507

DARLING, William (1786–1865) · B i 816

DARTON, William (*fl* 1806–1822)
Geographer and publisher · *chb* 429

DARWIN, Charles Robert (1809–1882) · A 256; CE iv 381; DNB v 522

DARWIN, *Sir* George Howard, KCB (1845–1912)
Mathematician and astronomer · DNB xxiv 144

DASSIÉ, F. (*fl* 1677–1683)
French naval architect · M*d* x 151

DASHWOOD, *Vice-Adm Sir* Charles, KCB (*b* 1765) · M iii 450

DASHWOOD, George Frederick, RN (1806–1881) · DA*u*B i 287

DASHWOOD, *Adm* William Bateman (1790–1869) · B i 820; M xii 186

DAUMONT DE SAINT LUSSON, Simon François (*d* 1677)
French army officer and explorer · DCB i 248; MDC 664

DAUPHIN DE MONTORGUEIL (*d ca* 1694)
Lieutenant, French Navy · DCB i 250

DAVDET, N. (*fl* 1722–1733)
French engineer and geographer · M*d* x 161

DAVENPORT, *Lieut-Cdr* Francis O., USN (*fl* 1842–1870) · H 935

DAVENPORT, *Lieut* Richard G., USN (*fl* 1864–1880) · H 959

DAVIES, William Henry (1824/5–1898)
First officer on the 'Great Eastern' on her maiden voyage to New York, 1862; later
P. & O. agent at Aden   B v 36

DAVIS [or DAVYS], *Capt* Arthur, RN (*d* 1743)   *ch* iv 206

DAVIS, *Rear-Adm* Charles Henry, USN (1807–1877)   H 194

DAVIS, *Rear-Adm* Charles Henry, USN (1845–1921)   DAB 218; H 928

DAVIS, *Lieut* Daniel W., USN (*fl* 1861–1880)   H 945

DAVIS, Edward (*fl* 1683–1702)
Pirate and buccaneer   DNB v 614; M*d* x 216

DAVIS, George Leonard, *Pay Inspector*, USN (*fl* 1861–1880)   H 987

DAVIS, *Lieut-Cdr* George T., USN (*fl* 1860–1880)   H 924

DAVIS, *Capt* Henry, RN (*fl* 1796–1822)   M vi 406

DAVIS [or DAVYS], John (*ca* 1552–1605)
Navigator and Arctic explorer; writer on exploration; inventor of standard backstaff   CE iv 392; DCB i 251;
                                                                           DNB v 656; H 194;
                                                                           M*d* x 215; MDC 175;
                                                                           T i 178

DAVIS, John (*d* 1622)
Navigator   CE iv 392; DNB v 617

DAVIS, *Capt* John Edward, RN (1815–1877)   B i 831

DAVIS, *Rear-Adm* John Lee, USN (1825–1889)   DAB 220; H 877

DAVIS, Raymond Cazallis (1836–1919)
Mariner   DAB 221

DAVIS, *Capt* Richard, RN (*d* 1718)   *ch* iv 41

DAVIS, Robert (*ca* 1800–1838)
Commander of schooner 'Anne' in Upper Canada rebellion of 1837–1838   MDC 176

DAVIS, *Capt* William, RN (*fl* 1665)   *ch* i 161

DAVISON, Alexander (1750–1829)
Government contractor; prize-agent and friend of Nelson   DNB v 624

DAVISON, Gregory Caldwell, USN (1871–1935)   DAB 221

DAVY, *Cdr* John, RN (*fl* 1809–1814)   M vii 301

DAVYS [or DAVIS], *Capt* Arthur, RN (*d* 1743)   *ch* iv 206

DAWES, *Capt* Henry, RN (*d* 1667)   *ch* i 161

DAWES, *Capt* Philip, RN (*fl* 1692–1710)   *ch* iii 11

DAWES, *Lieut* William, RM (1762–1836)   AE i 364; DAuB i 297

DAWES, William Rutter (1799–1865)
Astronomer   B i 837; DNB v 667

DAWKINS, *Cdr* William Robert, RN (*fl* 1810–1821)   M vii 398

DEAS, *Sir* David, KCB, RN (1804–1876)
Inspector-general of hospitals and fleets, 1855–1872   B i 843; DNB v 711

DEASE, Peter Warren (1788–1863)
Canadian fur-trader and explorer; with Franklin in 1825; led Arctic expedition of
1836–1839 with Simpson   MDC 179

DEBENHAM, *Cdr* John, RN (*b* 1772)   M vii 312, 432

DECATUR, Stephen (1779–1820)   CE iv 408; DAB 225;
H 197

DECOEURDOUX, *Cdr* George Lacy, RN (*d* 1850)   Tr 124

DECRÈS, Denis (1762–1820)   H 198; M*d* x 263; s i
305

DEE, John (1527–1608)
Expert on mathematics and navigation   DNB v 721; M*d* x 267;
T i 170

DEECKER, *Capt* Samuel Bartlett, RN (*fl* 1805–1818)   M xii 346

DEERING [*or* DERING], *Capt* Daniel, RN (*d* 1706)   c*h* vi 310

DEERING, George A., *Assist-Paymaster*, USN (*fl* 1870–1880)   H 997

DEERING, *Capt* Griffin, RN (*d* 1740/41)   c*h* iv 378

DEFOE, Daniel (1661?–1731)   CE iv 413; DNB v 730

DEGAULLE, Jean Baptiste (1782–1810)
Marine engineer   M*d* x 276

DEGRAVES, Peter (1778–1852)
Engineer and shipbuilder; established ship-building yard in Tasmania, 1841   DA*u*B i 302

DELACOMB, *Gen* Henry Isatt, CB, RM (*d* 1878)   B i 849

DELAFONS, *Cdr* Thomas, RN (*b* 1772)   M vii 153

DELAFOSSE, *Capt* Edward Hollingworth, RN (*b* 1788)   M viii 2

DELAHAYE, Guillaume Nicolas (1725–1802)
Cartographer   M*d* x 293

DELAMATER, Cornelius Henry (1821–1889)
Mechanical engineer; shipbuilder   DAB 227

DELAMBRE, Jean Baptiste Joseph (1749–1823)
Astronomer and scientist   M*d* x 297

DELANO, Amassa (1763–1823)
Ship captain   DAB 227

DELANO, Francis H., USN (*fl* 1863–1880)   H 955

DELAVAL, *Capt* Francis Blake, RN (*d* 1752)   c*h* iv 81

DELAVAL [*or* DELAVALL], *Capt* George, RN (*d* 1723)   c*h* iii 96

DELAVAL [*or* DELAVALL], *Adm Sir* Ralph (*d* 1707)   c*h* ii 1; DNB v 767

DENNET [or DENNIS], *Capt* Thomas, RN (*fl* 1713)   ch iv 41

DENNETT, John (1790–1852)
Inventor and man of science; invented a life-saving pocket apparatus for conveying a
rope from the shore to a shipwrecked crew, 1832; this system was used by several
coastguard stations in 1834   B i 859; DNB v 817

DENNIS, *Rear-Adm* Henry (*d* 1767)   ch v 86

DENNIS [or DENNET], *Capt* Thomas, RN (*fl* 1713)   ch iv 41

DENNISON, *Capt* Charles, RN (*d* 1742)   ch iv 338

DENNISTON, Henry M., *Paymaster*, USN (*fl* 1861–1880)   H 987

DENNY, *Sir* Archibald (1860–1936)
Shipbuilder   DNB xxvi 221

DENNY, Peter (1821–1895)
Shipbuilder   B v 76

DENNY, William (1847–1887)
Shipbuilder   B i 860

DENNYS, *Cdr* Lardner, RN (1791–1864)   Tr 163

DENT, *Adm* Charles Bayley Calmady (1832 1894)   B v 77

DENT, *Rear-Adm* Charles Calmady (1793–1872)   B i 861; M viii 256

DENT, *Capt* Cotton, RN (*d* 1761)   ch v 440

DENT, *Capt* Digby, RN (*d* 1737)   ch iv 57

DENT, *Capt* Digby, RN (*d* 1761/2)   ch iv 378

DENT, *Rear-Adm Sir* Digby (*fl* 1758–1816)   ch vi 310

DENT, *Capt* Digby, RN (*d* 1861)   M viii 51; Tr 162

DENT, Edward John (1770–1853)
Chronometer-maker; instruments at National Maritime Museum   B i 861; DNB v 827;
                                                                 T ii 388

DENT, Frederick (*d* 1860)
Chronometer maker   B v 77

DENYS, Jean (*fl* 1506)
French sea-captain and explorer   DCB i 256

DENYS, Nicolas (1598–1688)
French navigator, merchant, fisherman, shipbuilder, coloniser DCB i 256; MDC 184

DENYS DE FRONSAC, Richard (*ca* 1654–1691)
French coloniser, trader, fisherman and administrator   DCB i 259

DENYS DE LA TRINITÉ, Simon (1599–*ca* 1680)
French naval captain; fisherman and tax official   DCB i 261

DERBY, Elias Hasket (1739–1799)
Shipowner and merchant   DAB 229

DEVILLE, Edouard Gaston (1849–1924)
French naval hydrographer, surveyor-general of Dominion lands, Canada   MDC 187

DEVIS, Arthur (1711?–1787)
Portrait painter; restored Sir James Thornhill's paintings in the Painted Hall at Greenwich   DNB v 897

DEVIS, Arthur William (1763–1822)
Portrait painter; draughtsman on the 'Antelope's' voyage, 1783; painted: 'The death of Vice-Admiral Lord Nelson'   DNB v 898

DEVLIN, Charles Ramsay (1858–1914)
Minister of colonisation, mines and fisheries, Quebec   MDC 188

DEVON, *Capt* Thomas Barker, RN (*b* 1784)   M v 227

DEVONSHIRE, *Rear-Adm Sir* John Ferris, KGH (*d* 1839)   M iii 411; vi 180

DEVONSHIRE, *Rear-Adm* Richard (*b* 1781)   M vii 329

DEW, *Capt* Anthony, RN (*fl* 1664–1665)   ch i 163

DEWEY, *Adm of the Navy* George, USN (1837–1917)   DAB 231; H 905

DIAMOND, *Capt* Thomas, RN (*fl* 1660)   ch i 12

DIAZ, Bartholomew (*fl* late 15th century)
Portuguese navigator   CE iv 495; Md xi 9

DIAZ, Michael (*fl* 1485–1512)
Voyager, accompanied Columbus on his second voyage   Md xi 10

DIBDIN, Charles (1745 1814)   DNB v 907

DICEARCHUS (*ca* 325–285 B.C.)
Greek geographer and cartographer   A 20

DICK, *Adm* John (*d* 1854)   B i 871; M iv 558

DICK, *Vice-Adm* Thomas (*fl* 1793–1856)   M xi 357

DICKENS, John (*d* 1851)
Clerk in the navy pay office at Portsmouth and Chatham dockyards to 1822   B i 873

DICKENS, *Capt* Samuel Trevor, RN (*b* 1788)   M vii 153

DICKENSON, Dwight, *Surgeon*, USN (*fl* 1869–1879)   H 978

DICKENSON, *Capt* Richard, RN (*fl* 1665–1699)   ch i 290

DICKENSON [*or* DICKINGSON *or* DICKINSON], *Capt* Samuel, RN (*fl* 1665)   ch i 163

DICKIE, George William (1844–1918)
Engineer and shipbuilder   DAB 233

DICKINS, *Lieut-Cdr* Francis W., USN (*b* 1844)   H 928

DICKINSON, *Capt* Richard, RN (*fl* 1806–1830)   M vi 31

DICKINSON [*or* DICKINGSON *or* DICKENSON], *Capt* Samuel, RN (*fl* 1665)   ch i 163

DIGGES, Thomas (*d* 1595)
Mathematician; overseer of the works and fortifications at Dover harbour for several
years; commissioned, with others to equip an expedition to explore 'Cathay and
Antarctic seas', 1590   DNB v 976; T i 175

DILKE, Charles Wentworth (1789–1864)   B i 878

DILKE, *Capt* William, RN (*d* 1756)   *ch* v 87

DILKES, *Capt* Charles, CB, RN (1779–1846)   M ix 451

DILKES, *Vice-Adm* John (*fl* 1790–1808)   M i 360

DILKES, *Rear-Adm Sir* Thomas (1667?–1707)   DNB v 983; *ch* ii 242

DILLON, Jacques Vincent Marie de la Croix (1760–1807)
French hydraulic engineer   M*d* xi 65

DILLON, *Capt* Peter (1788–1847)
Adventurer; spent his youth in the Royal Navy; later served on vessels trading
between Sydney, New Zealand, Fiji and the Society Islands, 1809–1813. In 1827
he discovered remnants at Vanikoro, New Hebrides, which established the fate of
La Pérouse and his expedition, wrecked there in 1788   AE i 371; DA*u*B i 306;
                                                                       DNB xxii 558

DILLON, *Lieut* Stephen, RN (*fl* 1805–1821)   T*r* 115

DILLON, *Adm Sir* William Henry (1779–1857)   B i 880; DNB v 994;
                                                                       M ix 295

DIONNE, Narcisse Eutrope (1848–1917)
French-Canadian historian of exploration of Canada; biographer of Cartier and
Champlain   MDC 190

DISTON, John (*fl ca* 1760–1780)
Trinity House pilot, cartographer and writer on navigation   T ii 259

DITTON, Humfrey (1675–1715)
Teacher of mathematics and writer on longitude   T i 293; ii 116

DITTY, *Capt* John, RN (*fl* 1665)   *ch* i 163

DIX, *Capt* Edward, RN (*fl* 1790–1815)   M x 55

DIX, Thomas (*d* 1822)
Surveyor, geographer and schoolmaster   *ch*b 429

DIXEY, George *and* Charles (*fl* 1825–1838)
Optical instrument makers; instruments at National Maritime Museum T ii 418

DIXIE, *Capt Sir* Alexander, RN (1780–1857)   B v 113; M vii 207;
                                                                       T*r* 287

DIXON, George (*fl ca* 1770–1800)
Sailed with Cook; writer on navigation and voyages; explorer   DNB v 1028; MDC
                                                                       191; T ii 284

DIXON, *Cdr* George Farhill, RN (*fl* 1823–1833)   M viii 333

DODINGTON, George Bubb, *Baron Melcombe* (1691–1762)
Treasurer of the navy, 1744, 1755 and 1757   DNB V 1071

DODSON, James (*d* 1757)
Mathematician; author of: 'An Account of the methods used to describe lines on
Dr Halley's chart of the terraqueous globe' (1758)   DNB V 1079

DODSON, *Sir* John (1780–1858)
Advocate of the Admiralty, 1829–1834   B i 889; DNB V 1080

DOGGETT, Thomas (*d* 1721)
Actor; founded the Doggetts Coat and Badge race for Thames watermen   DNB V 1089

DOILEY [*or* DORLEY], *Capt* George, RN (*d* 1707)   ch iii 330

DOLEMAN [*or* DOLMAN], *Capt* George, RN (*d* 1705)   ch iii 292

DOLLAR, Robert (1844–1932)
Scot; shipowner in Canada, founder of Dollar Steamship Line   DAB 240; MDC 192

DOLLING, *Capt* William Brooking, RN (*d* 1843)   M x 384

DOLLOND, George (1774–1852)
Born George Huggins; instrument maker, inventor of ship's binnacle light; instruments
at National Maritime Museum   DNB V 1100; T ii 335

DOLLOND, John (1706–1761)
Optician; inventor of the achromatic telescope   DNB V 1101

DOLLOND, Peter (1730–1820)
Optical instrument-maker, supplied Cook and Board of Longitude; instruments at
National Maritime Museum   DNB V 1103; T ii 229

DOLMAN [*or* DOLEMAN], *Capt* George, RN (*d* 1705)   ch iii 292

DOMBRAIN, *Sir* James (1793–1871)
Deputy comptroller-general of the English coast guard, 1816; and of the Irish
coast guard, 1819–1849   B i 891

DOMETT, *Cdr* George, RN (*fl* 1812–1814)   M vii 406

DOMETT, *Adm Sir* William, GCB (1754–1828)   DNB V 1105; M i 243;
                                                           NC XV I; R ii 419

DOMVILLE, Henry Jones, CB, RN (*d* 1888)
Inspector-general of hospitals and fleets, 1875–1878   B i 892

DOMVILLE, James (1842–1921)
Canadian shipbuilder, navigator and businessman   MDC 192

DOMVILLE, William Thomas, CB, RN (*d* 1879)
Inspector-general of hospitals and fleets   B i 892

DONALDSON, David, *Master*, RN (*d* 1807)   Tr 236

DONKIN, William Fishburn (1814–1869)
Astronomer   B i 895; DNB V 1125

DONKLEY, *Capt* John (*d* 1758)   ch vi 162

DOUGHARTY, John (1677–1755)
Mathematician, land surveyor and writer on navigation   DNB V 1162; T ii 117

DOUGLAS [DOUGLASS *or* DUGLAS *or* DOWGLASSE], *Capt*
Andrew, RN (*d* 1725)   *ch* ii 387; iv 28;
                                                                           DNB V 1164

DOUGLAS, Andrew (1736–1806)
Physician; served as a surgeon, Royal Navy, 1756–1775   DNB V 1165

DOUGLAS, *Capt Sir* Andrew Snape, RN (1761–1797)   NC XXV 353

DOUGLAS, *Capt* Archibald, RN (*d* 1667)   DNB V 1190

DOUGLAS, *Capt the Hon* Arthur James, RN (*b* 1802)   M viii 345

DOUGLAS, Charles, KG, *third Duke of Queensberry & Second Duke of Dover*
(1698–1778)
Vice-admiral of Scotland   DNB V 1191

DOUGLAS, *Rear-Adm Sir* Charles (*d* 1789)   *ch* vi 427; DNB V
                                                                           1194

DOUGLAS, *Capt* Francis, RN (*b* 1772)   M X 217

DOUGLAS, *Capt the Hon* George, RN (1788–1838)   M xi 57

DOUGLAS, *Cdr* Henry, RN (*d* 1885)   Tr 55

DOUGLAS, *Vice-Adm Sir* Henry Percy, KCB (1876–1939)   DNB XXV 236

DOUGLAS, *Gen Sir* Howard, GCB, GCMG (1775–1861)   B i 902; DNB V 1203

DOUGLAS, *Cdr* Hugh Donald Cameron, RN (*fl* 1807–1827)   M viii 242

DOUGLAS, *Adm Sir* James (1703–1787)   *ch* v 290; DNB V 1237

DOUGLAS, *Adm* James (*b* 1755)   M i 123

DOUGLAS [*or* DOWGLAS], *Capt* John, RN (*d* 1697)   *ch* iii 70

DOUGLAS, *Capt* John, RN (*d* 1787)   *ch* v 441

DOUGLAS, *Cdr* John, RN (*fl* 1794–1802)   M vi 297

DOUGLAS, *Lieut* John Alexander, RN (*fl* 1802–1809)   Tr 203

DOUGLAS, *Adm* John Erskine (*fl* 1778–1841)   M ii 651

DOUGLAS, *Vice-Adm* Peter John (1787–1858)   B V 141; M X 447

DOUGLAS, *Capt* Pringle Home, RN (1784–1859)   M vii 199

DOUGLAS, *Capt* Richard, RN (*d* 1866/7)   M viii 128; Tr 162

DOUGLAS, *Capt* Stair, RN (*d* 1789)   *ch* vi 488

DOUGLAS, *Rear-Adm* Stair (*fl* 1795–1802)   M ii 846

DOUGLAS, *Capt* William, RN (*d* 1741)   *ch* iv 207

DOUGLAS, William, KT, *third Earl of March and fourth Duke of Queensberry*
(1724–1810)
Vice-admiral of Scotland, 1767–1776   DNB V 1278

DRAKE, *Vice-Adm* Francis William (*d* 1788/9)   ch vi 61; NA i 63

DRAKE, *Lieut* Franklin J., USN (*fl* 1863–1880)   H 945

DRAKE, *Capt* John, RN (*d* 1697)   ch iii 128

DRAKE, *Vice-Adm* John (1788–1864)   M viii 251; Tr 136

DRAKE, John Poad (1794–1883)
Inventor and artist; devised improvements in shipbuilding   B i 914; DNB V 1352

DRAPER, *Capt* John, RN (*d* 1697)   ch iii 99

DRAPER, *Capt* John, RN (*d* 1743)   ch v 88

DRAPER, Thomas (*fl* 1670–1681)
Hudson's Bay Company sea-captain   DCB i 280

DRAPER, *Capt* Thomas, RN (*fl* 1672–1678)   ch ii 49

DRAYTON, *Capt* Percival, USN (1812–1865)   H 224

DREBBEL, Cornelius (1572–1633)
Maker of instruments to King James I; inventor of a submarine; served on
La Rochelle expedition, 1627   CE iv 634; DNB vi 13;
                                                                  T i 191

DRENNAN, M. C., *Surgeon*, USN (*fl* 1863–1879)   H 978

DREW, *Adm* Andrew (1792–1878)   B i 916; M viii 145;
                                                                  MDC 198

DREW, John (1809–1857)
Astronomer   B i 917; DNB vi 16

DREYER, John Luis Emil (1852–1926)
Danish astronomer   CE iv 637; DNB xxv
                                                                  273

DRIGGS, *Lieut* William Hale, USN (*fl* 1865–1879)   H 961

DRINKWATER, *Capt* Charles Ramsay, RN (*fl* 1823–1830)   M vi 159

DRING & FAG (*fl* 1798–1870)
Instrument-makers; instruments at National Maritime Museum   T ii 336

DRUCOURT, Augustin de (*ca* 1700–1762)
Captain French navy; governor of Louisbourg   MDC 198

DRUMMOND, *Vice-Adm Sir* Adam, KCH (*fl* 1780–1837)   M iii 240

DRUMMOND, *Rear-Adm* Charles (*d* 1771)   ch iv 305

DRUMMOND, *Adm Sir* James Robert, GCB (1812–1895)   B V 156

DRUMMOND, John (*fl* 1808–1823)
Australian public servant; appointed naval officer at Hobart Town in 1814   DAuB i 327

DRUMMOND, *Cdr Sir* John Forbes, RN (*d* 1829)   M vi 267

DRUMMOND, *Capt* Patrick, RN (*d* 1792)   ch vi 511

DRUMMOND, Thomas (1797–1840)   DNB vi 41

DUFF, *Adm Sir* Alexander Ludovic, KCB (1862–1933)   Tr 124

DUFF, *Adm* Archibald (*d* 1858)   B i 924; M viii 450; ix 47

DUFF, *Capt* George, RN (1764–1862)   M xii 238; NC xv 265; Tr 122

DUFF, *Vice-Adm* Norwich (*d* 1862)   B i 925; M xii 382; Tr 127

DUFF, *Vice-Adm* Robert (*d* 1786)   *ch* v 444; DNB vi 131

DUFF, *Sir* Robert William, GCMG (1835–1895)
A Lord of the Admiralty, 1886   AE i 387; B v 161; DNB xxii 585

DUFOUR, Guillame Henri (1787–1875)   CE iv 655

DUGDALE, ... (*fl* 1732–1733)
Writer on geography and navigation   T ii 174

DU GUA [*or* GUAST] DE MONTS, Pierre (*ca* 1668–1628)
French explorer, trader, coloniser, governor of Acadia   DCB i 291

DUGUAY-TROUIN, René (1673–1736)
French mariner and privateer   CE iv 655; H 228; M*d* xi 452

DUIGAN, Daniel John, CB, RN (*d* 1884)
Inspector-general of hospitals and fleets, 1876   B i 926

DULAGUE, Vincent François Jean Noel (1729–1805)
Hydrographer   M*d* xi 482

DUILLIER, Nicholas Facio de: *see* FACIO DE DUILLIER

DUMANOIR LE-PEPPEY, *le Comte* Pierre Étienne René Marie (1770–1829)
French vice-admiral   M*d* xi 502; S i 391

DUMARESQ, *Rear-Adm* John Saumarez, RN (1873–1922)   AE i 390

DUMAS, Jean Daniel (*fl* 1750–1780)
French inspector-general of troupes de la marine in Canada   MDC 204

DUMBRECK, *Lieut* William, RN (1789–1862)   Tr 184

DUMONT D'URVILLE, Jules Sébastian César (1790–1842)
Admiral and navigator   CE iv 661; M*d* xi 531

DUNBAR, Duncan (1804–1862)
Shipowner; deputy chairman of Lloyd's Register, 1857–1861   B v 166

DUNBAR, *Capt* James (*fl* 1672–1679)   *ch* ii 60

DUNBAR, *Capt Sir* James, RN (*fl* 1790–1814)   M iv 613

DUNBAR, *Capt Sir* James Alexander, RN (1821–1883)   B v 167

DUNBAR, *Capt* Robert, RN (*fl* 1697)   *ch* iii 164

DUNKIN, Richard (1823–1895)
*Astronomer; employed at the Royal Greenwich Observatory from 1838; assistant
in the Nautical Almanac Office, 1847*   B v 171

DUNLAP, *Lieut* Andrew, USN (*fl* 1862–1880)   H 951

DUNLOP, *Adm* Hugh, CB (*d* 1887)   B i 938

DUNLOP, James (1793–1848)
Astronomer   DAuB i 338; DNB vi
                                                                               206

DUNLOP, *Cdr* Robert Graham, RN (*fl* 1816–1822)   M viii 102

DUNN, Edward T., *Paymaster-General*, USN (*fl* 1831–1874)   H 230

DUNN, *Capt* Nicholas James Cuthbert, RN (1785–1858)   M vii 152

DUNN, *Cdr* Pascoe, RN (*fl* 1809–1826)   M vii 271

DUNN, Samuel (1723–1794)
Writer on navigation, seamanship and cartography   DNB vi 210; T ii 204

DUNNAGE, William Marriott (1836–1899)
Oarsman and yachtsman   B v 175

DUNNETT, John, *Gunner*, RN (*d* 1807)   Tr 237

DUNSFORD, *Lieut* George, RN (*d* 1838/9)   Tr 193

DUNSTERVILLE, *Cdr* Edward, RN (1796–1873)   B i 940; DNB vi 233

DUNTHORNE, Richard (1711–1775)
Astronomer   DNB vi 235

DUNTZE, *Adm* John Alexander (1805–1882)   B i 941; M vi 110

DUPERRÉ, Guy Victor, *baron* (1775–1846)
Admiral and minister of marine   Md xi 583; S i 402

DUPETIT-THOUARS, *Capt* Aristide (1760–1798)
Naval officer and navigator   Md xi 598

DUPLEIX, Joseph, *Marquis* (*d* 1763)
Administrator and governor; soldier in India   Md xii 12

DU PLESSIS-BOCHART, Charles (*fl* 1633–1636)
French naval officer   DCB i 296

DU PONT, *Rear-Adm* Samuel Francis, USN (1803–1865)   DAB 253; H 230

DUPONT-GRAVÉ: *see* GRAVÉ DU PONT

DU PORT, William Javrin (1834–1891)
*Civil engineer; resident engineer of the Birkenhead docks, government engineer to
the harbour works at Alexandria, 1870–1879*   B v 177

DUPUY, Jean Cochon (1674–1757)
Naval surgeon   Md xii 57

DUQUESNE, Abraham, *Marquis* (1610–1688)
Celebrated French naval officer
CE iv 672; H 231;
M*d* xii 63

DURAND, *Lieut-Cdr* George R., USN (*fl* 1861–1880)
H 930

DURAND, Jean Baptiste Léonard (1742–1812)
Colonial governor and voyager
M*d* xii 73

D'URBAN, *Capt* William, RN (*fl* 1795–1805)
M iv 845

DURELL, *Capt* George, RN (*d* 1754)
ch v 375

DURELL, *Capt* John, RN (*d* 1748)
ch iv 262

DURELL, *Vice-Adm* Philip (*d* 1766)
ch v 167; MDC 210

DURELL, *Capt* Thomas Philip, RN (*fl* 1778–1802)
M iv 581

DURHAM, *Adm Sir* Philip Charles Henderson Calderwood, GCB (1763–1845)
DNB vi 256; M ii 450,
867; R iii 38

DURRELL, *Capt* Thomas, RN (*d* 1741)
ch iv 82

DURY, Andrew (*fl* 1761–1810)
Cartographer
CE iv 678

DURYEA, Harmanus Barkulo (1863–1916)
Yachtsman
DAB 255

DU TIEL, *Capt Sir* John, RN (*fl* 1665–1671)
ch i 163

DUTTON, *Cdr* Thomas, RN (*fl* 1800–1813)
M vii 33

DUTTON, William (*ca* 1729–1791)
Chronometer-maker
T ii 230

DUTTON, William (1811–1878)
Sea-captain
AE i 391; DA*u*B i 340

DUVAL, *Capt* Francis, RN (*fl* 1799–1851)
M vii 270

DUVAL, Marius, *Medical Director*, USN (*fl* 1842–1880)
H 983

DUVAL, Pierre (1618–1683)
Geographer and cartographer
M*d* xii 153

DUVAL, Pierre-Jean (1731–1800)
Economist and writer
M*d* xii 157

DWYER, *Maj-Gen* Thomas Peard, RMLI (*d* 1863)
B i 945

DYER, *Lieut* George L., USN (*fl* 1866–1879)
H 964

DYER, *Cdr* George Shepherd, RN (*fl* 1823–1832)
M viii 217

DYER, Joseph Chessborough (1780–1871)
Inventor; constructed an unsinkable lifeboat at an early age
DNB vi 287

DYER, *Rear-Adm* Nehemiah Mayo, USN (1839–1910)
DAB 257; H 924

DYER, *Capt* Nicholas, RN (*d* 1697)
ch iii 128

DYER, *Capt Sir* Thomas Swinnerton, RN (*b* 1770)
M vi 396

DYKAR, William, *Surgeon*, RN (*d* 1829) Tr 107

DYSON, *Sir* Frank Watson, KBE (1868–1939)
Astronomer Royal, 1910–1933 DNB xxiv 247

DYVE [*or* DRYCE], *Rear-Adm* Henry (*d* 1779) *ch* v 375

EADS, James Buchanan (1820–1887)
Engineer; inventor of a diving bell; built armour-plated gunboats for the Union
during the Civil War; opposed the Panama Canal and advocated a ship-railway as a
more suitable alternative DAB 258

EAGER, *Cdr* John, RN (*d ca* 1864) M viii 153

EAGLE, *Cdre* Henry, USN (*fl* 1818–1866) H 233

EAGLE, *Lieut* James William, RN (*d* 1822) Tr 144

EARDLEY-WILMOT, *Vice-Adm* Arthur Parry, CB (1815–1886) B iii 1399

EARLE, Augustus (1793–1838)
Artist and traveller; accompanied the voyage of H.M.S. 'Beagle', October 1831–
August 1832 DAUB i 348

EARLE, *Cdr* John, RN (*fl* 1664–1668) *ch* i 163

EARLE, *Rear-Adm* Ralph, USN (1874–1939) DAB 259

EARNSHAW, Thomas (1749–1829)
Watchmaker; chronometer manufacturer; improved and simplified Graham's transit
clock at the Royal Greenwich Observatory DNB vi 325; T ii 284

EAST, *Cdr* William, RN (*fl* 1673) *ch* ii 49

EASTLAKE, William (1820–1881)
Judge-advocate of the Fleet, 1851–1881 B i 954

EASTMAN, John, *Midshipman*, RN (*b* 1777) Tr 54

EASTMAN, John Robie (1836–1918)
Astronomer DAB 260

EASTMAN, *Cdr* Thomas H., USN (*fl* 1853–1880) H 904

EASTON, Peter (*fl* 1610–1620)
English seaman and pirate DCB i 300

EASTWICK, Robert William (1772–1865) B v 191

EASTWOOD, *Cdr* Henry Neville, RN (*d ca* 1834) M viii 241

EASTWOOD, *Cdr* Joseph, RN (*fl* 1809–1832) M vii 371

EASTY, John (*fl* 1786–1793)
Royal Marine; accompanied the 'First Fleet' to Australia DAUB i 349

EATON, *Cdr* James, RN (1783–1856/7) Tr 53

EATON, *Lieut* Joseph G., USN (*fl* 1863–1880) H 947

EATON, *Capt* Nicholas, RN (*d* 1729) *ch* iv 8

EDWARDS & KILBINGTON (*fl* 1789)
Compass-makers for Revenue cutters   T ii 310

EDWARDS, Edwin (1823–1879)
Painter and etcher; at one time an examining proctor in the Admiralty; author of: 'A
Treatise on the jurisdiction of the High Court of Admiralty'   DNB vi 535

EDWARDS, *Capt* Henry, RN (1780–1826)   B i 965; M v 284

EDWARDS, *Capt* John, RN (*d* 1726)   *ch* iii 100

EDWARDS, *Capt* John, RN (*d* 1731)   *ch* iv 179

EDWARDS, John (*fl* 1781–1803)
Optical instrument-maker; inventor of mariner's compass and instruments for obtaining
position at sea   T ii 310

EDWARDS, *Cdr* John, RN (*fl* 1787–1832)   M vi 249

EDWARDS, *Cdr* John, RN (*d* 1823)   M vi 252

EDWARDS, *Cdr* John, RN (1776?–1838)   M vii 143; Tr 79

EDWARDS, *Cdr* Peter, RN (*fl* 1662–1672)   *ch* i 81

EDWARDS, *Cdr* Richard, RN (*d* 1723)   *ch* ii 310

EDWARDS, *Capt* Richard, RN (*d* 1773)   *ch* v 16

EDWARDS, *Adm* Richard (*d* 1794)   *ch* vi 105; NA i 80

EDWARDS, *Cdr* Richard, RN (*fl* 1801–1854)   M viii 304

EDWARDS, *Cdr* Richard Flanigan, RN (*fl* 1847)   M vii 328

EDWARDS, *Lieut* Robert, RN (*fl* 1805–1809)   Tr 32

EDWARDS, *Adm* Sampson (*d* 1840)   M i 173; R ii 367

EDWARDS, Thomas (1775?–1845)
Legal writer; compiler of: 'Reports of cases argued in the High Court of
Admiralty . . .' (1812)   DNB vi 548

EDWARDS, *Cdr* Thomas A., RN (*d* 1826)   M vii 304

EDWARDS, *Rev* Thomas Wynne (1796–1877)
Oarsman   B i 967

EDWARDS, *Capt* Timothy, RN (*d* 1780)   *ch* vi 355

EDWARDS-MOSS, Tom Cottenham (1855–1893)
Oarsman   B ii 999

EDYE, Joseph, *Paymaster-in-Chief*, RN (1791–1866)   B v 206

EFFRITH, *Cdr* Robert, RN (*fl* 1673)   *ch* i 394

EGAN, Thomas Selby (1814/5–1893)
Oarsman   B v 207

EGERTON, Francis, *third Duke of Bridgewater* (1736–1803)   DNB vi 569; CE ii 551

EGERTON, John, KB, *third Earl of Bridgewater* (1646–1701)
First lord of the Admiralty, 1699–1701   DNB vi 575

ELKIN, William Lewis (1855–1933)
Astronomer   DAB 268

ELKINS [*or* EKINS], *Cdr* Thomas, RN (*fl* 1695–1712)   ch iii 100

ELLERMAN, *Sir* John Reeves (1862–1933)
Shipowner   DNB xxvi 255

ELLERY, *Cdre* Frank, USN (1794–1871)   DAB 268

ELLERY, Robert Lewis John, CMG (1827–1908)
Astronomer   AE i 404; DNB xxiiia
                                                                         617

ELLET, Charles (1810–1862)
Engineer; author of: 'Coast & harbour defences' (1855)   DAB 268

ELLICE, *Capt* Alexander, RN (*d ca* 1853)   M viii 477

ELLICOTT, *Rear-Adm* Edward (1768–1847)   M xi 94

ELLIOT BROTHERS (*fl ca* 1840)
*Instrument-makers; quintant and mathematical instruments at National Maritime
Museum*   T ii 470

ELLIOT, *Adm* Charles (1801–1875)   B i 977; DNB vi 669;
                                                                         M vi 57

ELLIOT, *Adm of the Fleet Sir* Charles Gilbert, KCB (1818–1895)   B v 215

ELLIOT, *Cdr* Christopher, RN (*d* 1704)   ch iii 246

ELLIOT, *Cdr* Edmund, RN (*d* 1725)   ch ii 143

ELLIOT, *Capt* Elliot, RN (*d* 1745)   ch v 298

ELLIOT, *Capt* George, RN (*d* 1795)   ch v 298

ELLIOT, *Adm Sir* George, KCB (1784–1863)   B i 978; DNB vi 669;
                                                                         M iv 844

ELLIOT, *Adm Sir* George Augustus, KCB (1813–1901)   DNB xxiiia 619

ELLIOT, *Maj* Gilbert, RM (*d* 1820)   Tr 244

ELLIOT, Gilbert, GCB, *second Earl of Minto* (1782–1859)
First lord of the Admiralty, 1835–1841   DNB vi 675

ELLIOT, *Cdr* James Burnett, RN (1791–1872)   Tr 82

ELLIOT, *Adm* John (*d* 1808)   ch vi 224; DNB vi
                                                                         679; NC ix 425

ELLIOT, Richard, *Midshipman*, RN (*b* 1793)   Tr 54

ELLIOT, *Rear-Adm* Robert (*b* 1769)   M ix 382

ELLIOT, *Capt* Robert, RN (*fl* 1822–1833)   DNB vi 689

ELLIOT, *Cdr* Robert James, RN (*d* 1849)   M viii 339

ELLIOT, *Cdr* Stephen, RN (*d* 1701)   ch iii 101

ELLIOT, *Lieut* William, RN (*d* 1792)   DNB vi 689

ELPHINSTONE, John (*fl* 1745)
Cartographer   CE V 149

ELPHINSTONE, *Capt* William Buller Fullerton, RN, *fifteenth Baron Elphinstone* (1828–1893)   B V 226

ELSDALE, Robinson (1744–1783)
Joined the Royal Navy as a midshipman, but left because of slowness of promotion; served aboard a privateer, 1762–1779   DNB vi 752

ELTON, *Capt* Henry, RN (*d* 1858)   M vii 212

ELTON, *Capt* Jacob, RN (*d* 1745)   ch v 88

ELTON, John (*fl* 1730–1732)
Instrument-maker, quadrant designer; quadrant at National Maritime Museum   T ii 175

ELTON, John (*d* 1751)
Adventurer in Russia; sea-captain in the Russian service; later became admiral in the Caspian   DNB xxii 610

ELWES, *Capt* Gerrard, RN (*fl* 1688–1707)   ch ii 388

EMANUEL, M. & E. (*fl* 1820–1825)
Instrument-makers; instruments at National Maritime Museum   T ii 420

ELYOT, Hugh: *see* ELIOT

EMERIAUD, *Vice-Adm* Maurice Julien, *Comte* (1762–1845)   Md xii 430; S i 423

EMERSON, William (1701–1782)
Mathematician and writer on navigation   T ii 157

EMERY, Caleb J., *Pay Director*, USN (*fl* 1855–1880)   H 985

EMERY, Charles Edward (1838–1898)
Engineer; consultant to the United States Navy on steam engines   DAB 274

EMERY, *Lieut* James, RN (*fl* 1805–1810)   Tr 269

EMMETT, J. B. (*fl* 1817)
Mathematician, designer of navigational instruments   T ii 390

EMMONS, *Rear-Adm* George Foster (1811–1884)   DAB 274; H 245

EMMS, *Capt* Fleetwood, RN (*d* 1693)   ch ii 412

EMO, Angelo (1731–1792)
Venetian admiral and statesman   Md xii 446

EMORY, *Lieut* William H., USN (*fl* 1862–1880)   H 946

ENCISO, Martin Fernandez de (1470?–1528)
Spanish navigator   Md xii 453

ENCKE, Johann Franz (1791–1865)
German astronomer   CE V 177

ENDERBY, *Capt* Samuel, RN (1789–1873)   Tr 185

ENDICOTT, Mordecai Thomas (1844–1926)
Naval engineer; chief of the bureau of yards and docks, 1898–1907   DAB 274

ERSKINE, *Capt* Robert, RN (*d* 1766)   *ch* v 170

ERSKINE, Thomas, KT, *first Baron Erskine* (1750–1823)
Served as a midshipman Royal Navy in the West Indies, 1764–1768   DNB vi 853

ERWIN, *Cdr* George, RN (*fl* 1664)   *ch* i 97

ESCHELS-KROON, Adolf (1739–1793)
Danish voyager   M*d* xiii 5

ESCHSCHOLTZ, Johan Frederik (1793–1831)
Russian voyager and naturalist   M*d* xiii 20

ESCOTT, Albert (1850–1891)
Revised Riddle's: 'Treatise on navigation & nautical astronomy' (*1871*)   B v 240

ESPEJO, Antonio (*fl* 1582)
Spanish navigator   M*d* xiii 51

ESPINOSA Y TELLO, *Don* José de (1763–1815)
Spanish admiral and hydrographer   M*d* xiii 64

ESTAING, *Adm* Charles Henri Théodat, *Comte d'* (1729–1794)   CE v 399; M*d* xiii 90; s i 430

ESTRÉES, Victor Marie *Duc d'* (1660–1737)
French admiral   M*d* xiii 125

ETHERIDGE, *Adm* Thomas (1810–1890)   B v 242

ETHERSEY, *Capt* Richard, RIN (*d* 1857)   B v 243

ETTRICK, . . . (*fl* 1836)
Instrument-maker, improver of mariner's compass   T ii 470

EVAN-THOMAS, *Adm Sir* Hugh, GCB (1862–1928)   DNB xxv 291

EVANCE, *Cdr* William Devereux, RN (*d* 1860)   M viii 14

EVANS, *Capt* Andrew Fitzherbert, RN (*d* 1824)   M iii 125

EVANS, *Capt Sir* Frederick John Owen, KCB, RN (1815–1885)   B i 1003; DNB vi 925

EVANS, *Adm* George (*d* 1870)   M viii 295

EVANS, *Rear-Adm* Henry (*d ca* 1841)   M iii 41

EVANS, *Capt* John, RN (*fl* 1641–1715)   *ch* ii 389

EVANS, *Vice-Adm* John, RN (*d* 1794)   *ch* vi 62; NA i 68

EVANS, John, *Assist-Surgeon*, RN (*fl* 1799–1818)   T*r* 44

EVANS, Lewis (*ca* 1700–1756)
American cartographer   CE v 488; DAB 278

EVANS, *Capt* Robert, RN (*d* 1827)   M x 237

EVANS, Robert, *Surgeon*, RN (*d* 1846)   T 91

EVANS, *Rear-Adm* Robley Dunglison, USN (1846–1912)   DAB 278; H 916

EYRIÈS, Jean Baptiste Benoit (1767–1846)
French geographer and writer   Md xiii 240

EYTON [or EATON], *Capt* William, RN (d 1698)   ch iii 70

EYTON, *Cdr* William Wynne, RN (d 1857)   Tr 64

FABIAN, *Capt* Charles Montague, RN (d 1826)   M x 268

FABRICUS, David (1564–1617)
German astronomer   CE v 561

FACIO DE DUILLIER, Nicholas (1664–1753)
Swiss mathematician; writer on navigation   T ii 117

FADEN, William (1750–1836)
Geographer to the King, cartographer, chart-seller   T ii 286

FAGAN, *Capt* Louis E., USMC (fl 1862–1880)   H 1016

FAGUNDES, Joâo Alvares (fl 1521)
Portuguese explorer; voyager to Newfoundland   DCB i 303

FAHIE, *Adm Sir* William Charles, KCB (1763–1833)   DNB vi 985; M ii 715,
                                                                           880; R iv 34

FAIR, *Cdr* Robert, RN (d ca 1837)   M viii 130

FAIRBAIRN, Stephen (1862–1938)
Oarsman   DNB xxvi 267

FAIRBORNE, *Adm of the Fleet Sir* Stafford (d 1742)   ch ii 143; DNB vi 990

FAIRBORNE, *Cdr* William, RN (d 1708)   ch iii 246

FAIRBURN, *Sir* William (1789–1874)
Founded a shipbuilding yard at Millwall   B i 1014; CE v 568

FAIRER, *Capt* Robert, RN (fl 1664)   ch i 97

FAIREY, Richard (fl ca 1790–1827) and Joseph (fl ca 1790–1846)
Instrument-makers; quadrant at National Maritime Museum   T ii 337

FAIRFAX, *Rear-Adm* Donald McNeill, USN (1821–1894)   DAB 281; H 270

FAIRFAX, Edward (fl 1818)
Mariner; inventor of deep-sea lead   T ii 391

FAIRFAX, *Adm Sir* Henry, KCB (1837–1900)   B v 262

FAIRFAX, *Rear-Adm* Robert (1666–1725)   ch ii 312; DNB vi
                                                                           1002

FAIRFAX, *Vice-Adm Sir* William George (1739–1813)   DNB vi 1014; M iv
                                                                           485; NC v 465

FAIRLEY, *Capt* George, RN (fl 1714–1724)   ch iv 41

FAIRLOUGH, *Lieut* Henry Blacker, RM (fl 1804–1848)   Tr 110

FARMER, *Capt* William, RN (*fl* 1677–1680)   *ch* ii 14

FARMER, William (*ca* 1750)
Instrument-maker; mariner's compass at National Maritime Museum   T ii 231

FARNCOMB, Thomas (*d* 1865)
London shipowner and merchant   B i 1022

FARQUHAR, *Adm Sir* Arthur, CB (1772–1843)   DNB vi 1084; M iv
                                                                             929

FARQUHAR, *Cdr* Norman H., USN (*b* 1840)   H 907

FARQUHARSON, *Lieut* Edward Riou Owen, RN (*d* 1846)   Tr 153

FARR, *Capt* Charles, RN (*fl* 1667)   *ch* i 292

FARRAGUT, *Adm* David Glasgow, USN (1801–1870)   CE v 595; DAB 284;
                                                                             H 272

FARRAGUT, George, *Master*, USN (1755–1817)   DAB 284

FARRANT, *Cdr* John, RN (1789–1849)   Tr 33

FARRE, *Capt* . . . , RN (*fl* 1669)   *ch* i 314

FARRINES, *Capt* Henry, RN (*fl* 1665)   *ch* i 164

FARWELL, *Cdr* Charles, RN (*d* 1837)   M vii 65

FASEBY, *Capt* William, RN (*d* 1711)   *ch* i 55

FAULKNER, *Adm* Jonathan (*d* 1795)   *ch* bi 361; NA i 153

FAULKNER, *Capt* Robert, RN (*d* 1769)   *ch* vi 228

FAULKNER, *Capt* Samuel, RN (*d* 1744)   *ch* iv 306

FAULKNER, *Capt* William, RN (*d* 1724/5)   *ch* iii 382

FAULKNOR, *Capt* Robert, RN (1763–1795)   DNB vi 1109; NC xvi
                                                                             1; R iii 308

FAULKNOR, *Capt* Samuel, RN (*d* 1758)   *ch* v 448

FAURE, Félix (1841–1899)
French statesman; minister for the navy, 1888; 1894–1895   CE v 603

FAVELL, *Cdr* Thomas, RN (*d* 1835)   M viii 245

FAWLER, *Capt* John, RN (*d* 1766)   *ch* v 375

FEAD, *Capt* Francis, RN (*d* 1847)   M v 288

FEAKES, *Cdr* Tobias, RN (*fl* 1666–1667)   *ch* i 292

FEARN, John (1768–1837)
Philosopher who served in the navy   DNB vi 1137

FEARON, Samuel (*fl* 1738–1755)
Marine surveyor; published first chart with Greenwich meridian   T ii 176

FEATHERSTONE, *Cdr* Samuel, RN (*fl* 1800–1815)   M vi 249

FEBIGER, *Cdre* John C., USN (*fl* 1838–1880)   H 274

FERNANDES, Joâo (*fl* 1486–1505)
Portuguese explorer, voyager to America, namer of Labrador   DCB i 304

FERNANDEZ, Alvaro (*fl* 1446)
Portuguese voyager   M*d* xiii 590

FERNANDEZ, Juan (16th century)
Spanish pilot and navigator   M*d* xiii 591

FERRARIS, Joseph Johann, *Compte de* (1726–1814)
Cartographer   CE v 628

FERRELO, Bartolomeo (*fl* 1542)
Spanish pilot and navigator   M*d* xiv 6

FERRER MALDONADO, Lorenzo (*fl* 1588–1625)
*Spanish sea captain, navigator and adventurer; voyager to America and Polar regions;
writer on travel and navigation; claimed to have accomplished North-West passage
in 1588*   DCB i 676

FERRIE, *Cdr* William, RN (*d* 1816)   Tr 96

FERRIER, *Vice-Adm* John (*d ca* 1830)   M i 401

FERRIS, *Rear-Adm* Abel (*b* 1776–1859)   M x 360; Tr 79

FERRIS, *Cdr* Thomas, RN (*d ca* 1850)   M vii 401

FESTING, *Capt* Benjamin Morton, RN (1794–1865)   B i 1039; M viii 214;
                                                                                Tr 82

FESTING, *Maj-Gen Sir* Francis Worgan, KCMG, CB, RMA (1833–1886)   B i 1039; DNB vi 1256

FESTING, *Adm* Robert Worgan George, CB (*d* 1862)   B i 1039; M x 446

FEYNES, H. de (*fl* 1606–1630)
French voyager and traveller   M*d* xiv 81

FFARINGTON, *Adm* William (1777–1862)   B i 1040

FFOULKES, Charles John, CB, OBE (1868–1947)
*Served in R.N.V.R. and later as major, Royal Marines in World War One; first
director of the Imperial War Museum (1917–1933)*   DNB xxvii 247

FICHBOHM, *Lieut* Herman F., USN (*fl* 1866–1880)   H 959

FIELD, *Capt* Arthur, RN (*d* 1726)   *ch* iv 29

FIELD, *Adm Sir* Arthur Mostyn, KCB (1855–1950)   DNB xxvii 249

FIELD, Cyrus West (1819–1892)
Financier; promoted the first Atlantic cable   A 306; DAB 290

FIELD, *Lieut* Edward A., USN (*fl* 1865–1880)   H 949

FIELD, *Adm of the Fleet Sir* Frederick Laurence, GCB, KCMG (1871–1945)   DNB xxvii 249

FIELD, Joshua (1786–1863)
Civil engineer; partner of the marine engineering firm, Maudslay, Sons & Field B i 1042; DNB vi 1272

FIELD, *Col* Thomas Y., USMC (*fl* 1847–1880)   H 1012

FISH, *Cdr* Gregory, RN (*fl* 1683)   *ch* ii 98

FISH, Hamilton (1808–1893)
American statesman; secured arbitration of the 'Alabama' claims   CE v 690; DAB 293

FISH, *Adm* John (*d ca* 1830)   M i 154

FISH, Preserved (1766–1846)
Shipowner   DAB 294

FISHBOURNE, *Adm* Edmund Gardiner, CB (1811–1887)   B i 1052

FISHER, Clark, *Chief Engineer*, USN (1837–1903)   DAB 294

FISHER, *Capt* George, RN (*d* 1705)   *ch* iii 309

FISHER, George (1794–1873)
Astronomer; served as chaplain and astronomer on Parry's Arctic expedition, 1821–1823;
headmaster of the Greenwich Hospital School, 1834–1860 and principal, 1860–1863   B i 1053; DNB vii 56;
                                                                                                         T ii 392

FISHER, *Cdr* John, RN (*d ca* 1843)   M vii 209

FISHER, *Adm of the Fleet* John Arbuthnot, OM, GCB, *first Baron Fisher of*
Kilverstone (1841–1920)   CE v 695; DNB xxiv
                                                                                                         182

FISHER, *Capt* Peter, RN (*d* 1844)   M xi 237

FISHER, *Capt* Thomas, RN (*fl* 1666)   *ch* i 13

FISHER, *Capt* Thomas, RN (*d* 1697)   *ch* iii 128

FISHER, *Adm* Thomas (1810–1891)   B v 299

FISHER, Thomas, *Surgeon*, RN (*d* 1861)   Tr 109

FISHER, *Rear-Adm* William (1780–1852)   B i 1054; DNB vii 75;
                                                                                                         M x 359

FISHER, *Adm Sir* William Wordsworth, GCB, GCVO (1875–1937)   DNB xxvi 279

FISKE, John (1744–1797)
Commander in the Massachusetts Navy during the American Revolution   DAB 295

FITCH, H. W., *Chief Engineer*, USN (*fl* 1859–1880)   H 1007

FITCH, John (1743–1798)
American writer on navigation; builder of one of the first steamships in 1787   A 180; DAB 296; T ii
                                                                                                         337

FITCH, Ralph (1550?–1611)
Voyager   DNB vii 77; Md xiv
                                                                                                         161

FITHIAN, Edwin, *Chief Engineer*, USN (*fl* 1848–1880)   H 1001

FITTON, *Capt* Henry, RN (*fl* 1672)   *ch* i 394

FITTON, *Lieut* Michael, RN (1766–1852)   B i 1055; DNB vii 83

FLAMSTEED, John (1646–1719)
Astronomer Royal (1675–1719)   A ii 3; CE v 720; DNB
vii 241; M*d* xiv 194;
T i 255; ii 118

FLANDERS, Henry (1824–1911)
Author of works on maritime law   DAB 298

FLANIGAN, John (*fl* 1830)
Teacher of navigation   T ii 449

FLETCHER, *Capt* John, RN (*fl* 1660–1672)   *ch* i 13

FLAWES, *Capt* William, RN (*fl* 1665–1677)   *ch* i 165

FLEEMING, *Vice-Adm the Hon* Charles Elphinstone (*d* 1840)   M ii 577

FLEMING, *Capt* Humphrey, RN (*fl* 1669)   *ch* i 314

FLEMING, *Cdr* John, RN (*d* 1849)   M vii 337

FLEMING, *Cdr* Richard Howell, RN (*b* 1789)   M vii 412

FLEMING, *Sir* Sandford, KCMG (1827–1915)
Canadian engineer; concerned with the laying of the Pacific cable, 1902   DNB xxiv 190

FLEMING, Williamina Paton Stevens (1857–1911)
Astronomer   DAB 299

FLEMMING, *Capt* William Henry, RN (*d* 1771)   *ch* iv 194

FLETCHER, *Lieut* Arthur H., USN (*fl* 1861–1880)   H 937

FLETCHER, *Capt* John, RN (*d* 1697)   *ch* iii 103; DCB i 308

FLETCHER, *Capt* John, RN (*d* 1704)   *ch* ii 413

FLETCHER, *Capt* John, RN (*d* 1758)   *ch* iv 30

FLETCHER, John (*fl* 1830)
Chronometer-maker; instruments at National Maritime Museum   T ii 449

FLETCHER, *Adm* John Venour (1801–1877)   B i 1069

FLETCHER, Montgomery, *Chief Engineer*, USN (*fl* 1850–1880)   H 1001

FLETCHER, *Capt* William, RN (*d* 1846)   M vi 80

FLEURIEU, Charles Pierre Claret, *Comte de* (1738–1810)
Voyager and scientist; instructor and authority on navigation   M*d* xiv 228

FLINDERS, *Capt* Matthew, RN (1774–1814)   AE i 472; CE v 731;
DA*u*B i 389; DNB vii
325; M*d* xiv 242; NC
xxxii 177; T ii 338

FLINT, Albert Stowell (1853–1923)
Astronomer   DAB 300

FLINT, James M., *Surgeon*, USN (*b* 1838)   H 977

FORBES, *Rear-Adm* Henry (*d* 1855)   M xii 222; Tr 289

FORBES, *Cdr* Hugh, RN (*d* 1750)   *ch* v 277

FORBES, *Adm of the Fleet the Hon* John (1714–1796)   *ch* 338; DNB iv
                                                                           404; NC xxv 265

FORBES, *Sir* John, *Assist-Surgeon*, RN (1787–1861)   B i 1078; M vii 65

FORBES, Robert Bennet (1804–1889)   DAB 303

FORBIN, Claude (1656–1733)
French admiral and privateer   H 290; M*d* xiv 375

FORD, *Sir* Francis Clare, GCB, GCMG (1828–1899)   DNB xxii 649

FORDE, Henry Charles (1827–1897)
Civil engineer; partner in the firm Clark, Forde & Taylor, which laid five Atlantic
cables   B v 324

FORDER, *Cdr* Robert, RN (*d* 1844)   M viii 76

FORDHAM, *Sir* Herbert George (1854–1929)
Writer on cartography; authority on John Cary   DNB xxv 311

FORDYCE, *Capt* Alexander Dingwall (1800–1864)   B i 1081

FORFAIT, Pierre Alexandre Laurent (1752–1807)
Engineer and naval architect   M*d* xiv 395

FORMAN, Simon (1552–1611)
Claimed to have discovered method of finding longitude at sea   DNB vii 438; T i 182

FORMAN, *Capt* Walter, RN (*d ca* 1830)   M vi 417; T ii 420

FORNEY, *Lieut* James, RM (1861–1880)   H 1014

FORREST, *Capt* Arthur, RN (*d* 1770)   *ch* v 380; DNB vii
                                                                           441; NC xxv 441

FORREST, *Sir* Digory, *Purser*, RN (*d* 1846)   Tr 118

FORREST, *Capt* French, USN (1796–1866)   DAB 305; H 292

FORREST, Thomas (1729?–1802?)
Navigator; surveyed the coasts of New Guinea and Sulu Archipelago, 1774–1776;
discovered the Forrest Strait, 1790   DNB vii 443; M*d* xiv
                                                                           409; T ii 206

FORREST, *Capt* Thomas, RN (*d* 1844)   M x 29

FORRESTER, *Capt* Lord George, RN (*d* 1748)   *ch* v 16

FORRESTER, *Capt* John, RN (*d* 1737)   *ch* iv 194

FORSE, *Lieut* Charles T., USN (*fl* 1864–1880)   H 955

FORSTER, George (*d* 1792)
Voyager   DNB vii 454; M*d*
                                                                           xiv 417

11BII

FREEMAN-THOMAS, Freeman, GCIE, GBE, GCSI, GCMG, *first Marquess of Willingdon* (1866–1941)
Lord Warden of the Cinque Ports, 1931–1941   DNB xxvii 279

FREMANTLE, *Adm Sir* Charles Howe, GCB (1800–1869)   B i 1105; M v 285

FREMANTLE, *Adm Sir* Edward Robert, CB, CMG (1836–1929)   DNB xxvii 317

FREMANTLE, *Vice-Adm Sir* Thomas Francis, GCB (1764–1819)   DNB vii 688; Tr 59

FREMINVILLE, Christopher Paulin de la Poix, *Chevalier de* (1787–1848)
Naval officer and writer   Md xv 140

FRENCH, *Capt* George, RN (*b* 1785)   M xii 399

FRENCH, James Moore (*fl* 1810–1838)
Chronometer-maker for Admiralty   T ii 393

FRENCH, John (*d* 1687)
Clergyman at sea with Hudson's Bay Co   DCB i 315

FRENCH, John (*fl* 1690–1715)
Mathematician and writer on longitude; possibly schoolmaster RN   T ii 118

FRERE, *Capt* John James Bartholomew Edward, RN (1812–1864)   B v 36

FRESNEL, Augustin Jean (1788–1827)
French physicist; designed lenses for lighthouses   A 220

FREYCINET, Louis Claude de Saulces de (1779–1842)
Navigator   CE vi 83; DAuB i 71;
                                                                 Md xv 175

FREYCINET, Louis Henri Desaulses *Baron* de (1777–1840)
Rear-admiral and circumnavigator   Md xv 168

FRÉZIER, Amédée François (*b* 1682)
Engineer and voyager   Md xv 185

FRIEND, *Cdr* Matthew Curling, RN (1792–1871)   DAuB i 417

FRIEND, *Capt* Richard, RN (*fl* 1671)   ch i 325

FRITZ, Samuel (1653–1728)
Explorer   Md xv 211

FROBISHER, *Sir* Martin (1539–1594)   CE vi 90; DCB vii 721;
                                                                 H 297; Md xv 216;
                                                                 MDC 251

FRODSHAM, Charles (*fl* 1830–1831)
Chronometer-maker for Admiralty   T ii 449

FRODSHAM, Henry (*fl* 1828–1837)
Chronometer-maker   T ii 421

FROES, Luis (1528–1597)
Portuguese Jesuit and missionary   Md xv 223

FYNMORE, *Lieut-Col* James, RM (*d* 1887)   B i 1114; Tr 258

FYOT, F. M. (*fl* 1785)
French professor of mathematics; inventor of marine chair, cyclometer and graphometer   T ii 311

FYTCHE, *Cdr* Robert, RN (*d* 1740)   ch iv 224

GABOURG, F. (*fl* 1784–1797)
Optical instrument-maker; octant at National Maritime Museum   T ii 311

GABRIEL, *Capt* James Wallace, KH, RN (*b* 1783)   M vi 166, 453

GADBURY, Timothy (*fl* 1656–1661)
Teacher of navigation, author of: 'Young Seamans Guide'   T i 243

GAGE, Thomas (*d* 1656)
Voyager   DNB vii 793; M*d* xv
                                                                                      350

GAGE, *Adm of the Fleet Sir* William Hall, GCB (1777–1864)   B i 1115; DNB vii 797;
                                                                                      M ii 836

GAGELIN, François Isidore (1799–1833)
French missionary to Indo-China   M*d* xv 353

GAGEN, Robert Ford (1847–1926)
English marine and landscape painter, settled in Canada   MDC 253

GAILLARD, David du Bose (1859–1913)
Given charge of dredging and excavation of the Panama Canal, 1907   DAB 323

GAILLARD, Mathieu (*fl* 1683–1694)
Commissary in ordinary to the Navy at Montreal   DCB i 320

GALANTI, Luigi Mario (1765–1836)
Geographer   M*d* xv 383

GALBRAITH, *Rear-Adm* James (*d* 1784)   ch vi 167

GALBRAITH, William (*fl* 1827–1843)
Mathematician; compiler of tables for navigation   T ii 421

GALEN, Jan van (*fl ca* 1600–1653)
Dutch mariner   M*d* xv 393

GALI, Francisco (*fl* 1584)
Spanish navigator   M*d* xv 399

GALILEI, Galileo (1564–1642)   CE VI 150; M*d* xv 411

GALLAWAY, *Cdr* Alexander, RN (1792–1873)   Tr 243

GALLISSONIÈRE, Roland Michel Barrin, *Marquis de la* (1693–1756)
French admiral   M*d* xv 456

GALLOP [*or* GALLOPP], *Capt* George, RN (*fl* 1664–1672)   ch i 333

GARDNER, *Rear-Adm* Alan Hyde, KCB, *second Baron Gardner* (1772–1815)   NC xxi 357

GARDNER, David, *Surgeon*, RN (d 1810)   Tr 258

GARDNER, James (*fl* 1830)
Instrument-maker; instruments at National Maritime Museum   T ii 450

GARDNER, *Cdr* James Baynton, RN (d 1823)   M vii 359

GARDNER, M. (*fl* 1800–1837)
Instrument-maker; octant at National Maritime Museum   T ii 450, 455

GARDNER [*or* GARDINER], *Capt* Martin, RN (*fl* 1692–1697)   ch iii 164

GARDNER, *Capt* Thomas, RN (d 1699)   ch ii 63

GARDNER, *Lieut-Cdr* Thomas M., USN (*fl* 1861–1880)   H 931

GARGOT DE LA ROCHETTE, Nicolas (1619–1664)
French naval captain   DCB i 323

GARGRAVE, George (1710–1758)
Mathematician; contributed papers on the transit of Venus to the 'Gentleman's
Magazine', 1761 and 1769, and a memoir of Abraham Sharp, 1781   DNB vii 875

GARLAND, *Cdr* James, RN (d 1830)   M viii 472

GARLAND, *Capt* Joseph Culston, RN (b 1781)   M xii 38

GARLAND, Thomas (*fl ca* 1678–1687)
Seaman with Hudson's Bay Co   DCB i 324

GARLING, Frederick (1806–1873)
Australian customs official and marine artist   DAuB i 427

GARLINGTON, *Capt* Richard, RN (d 1743)   ch iv 43

GARNEAU, Pierre (1823–1905)
Canadian merchant and politician; president of Quebec Steamship Company   MDC 258

GARNER, William (*fl* 1732–1737)
Instrument-maker; backstaffs at National Maritime Museum   T ii 178

GARNETT, Joseph (1771–1861)
Employed at the Royal Greenwich Observatory, where he designed and completed a
semaphore for signalling astronomical messages   B i 387

GARNIER, Francis (1839–1873)
French sailor   CE vi 173

GARRARD, William (*fl* 1781–1808)
Quartermaster of instruction, Royal Naval Asylum, Greenwich; writer on navigation   T ii 311

GARRETT, *Cdr* Edward William, RN (1781–1860)   M vi 371; Tr 123

GARRETT, *Vice-Adm* Henry (1774–1846)   M iii 238

GARRETT, *Cdr* Henry, RN (1786–1865)   Tr 97

GARRETT, *Cdr* John, RN (*fl* 1810–1833)   M viii 392

GARRETY, *Cdr* James Henry, RN (d 1827)   M vii 7

GELLIBRAND, Henry (1597–1636)
Professor of astronomy; researcher into compass variations and longitude   DNB vii 996; T i 205

GEMELLI-CARERI, Jean François (*b* 1651)
Italian voyager   M*d* xvi 131

GEMINI, Thomas, *pseud: see* LAMBRIT, Thomas

GEMMA FRISIUS (1508–1555)
Dutch mathematician and traveller   M*d* xvi 137

GENEVOIS, Jean Alexandre (*fl* 1760–1761)
Swiss scientist; writer on mechanical propulsion of ships   T ii 261

GENS, *Capt* John de, RN (*fl* 1660–1661)   *ch* i 12

GENTLEMAN, Tobias (*fl* 1614)
Writer on the herring fishery   DNB xxii 698

GEORGE V, *King* (1865–1936)   DNB xxvi 313

GEORGE, Prince of Denmark (1653–1708)
Lord high admiral   DNB vii 1083

GEORGE, William Frederick Charles, KG, KP, GCB, GCMG, GCH, *second
Duke of Cambridge, Earl of Tipperary and Baron Culloden* (1819–1904)
Field-marshal and commander-in-chief of the army; an elder brother of Trinity House DNB xxiiib 94

GEORGE, *Capt* John, RN (*fl* 1672–1684)   *ch* ii 98

GEORGE, *Capt Sir* Rupert, RN (1749–1832)   M iii 70

GERARD, Charles, *first Baron Gerard of Brandon and Earl of Macclesfield* (*d* 1694)
Vice-admiral of the fleet at Helvoetsluys, 1648   DNB vii 1096

GERRITSZ, Dirk (*fl* 1599)
Dutch navigator   M*d* xvi 340

GETHING [*or* GETHINGS], *Capt* John, RN (*fl* 1664–1665)   *ch* i 97

GHEEN, *Lieut* Edward H., USN (*fl* 1862–1880)   H 951

GHERARDI, *Rear-Adm* Bancroft, USN (1832–1903)   DAB 337

GIBB, John (1776–1850)
*Civil engineer; assisted Rennie in the construction of Greenock harbour; repaired
the Crinan canal, 1817*   DNB vii 1126

GIBBES, *Lieut* Francis Blower, RN (*d* 1842)   Tr 30

GIBBONS, *Capt* Anderson, RN (*fl* 1667)   *ch* i 292

GIBBONS, *Sir* George Christie (1848–1918)
Chairman of the Canadian section of the International Waterways Commission   MDC 263

GIBBONS, *Capt* William, RN (*fl* 1612–1614)
Seaman, Arctic explorer   DCB i 329

GIBBONS, *Lieut* William, RM (*fl* 1804–1807)   Tr 228

GIBBS, Benjamin F., *Surgeon*, USN (*fl* 1858–1880)   H 971

GILBERT, William *and* Thomas (*fl* 1810–1842)
Navigational instrument makers and sellers; instruments at National Maritime Museum   T ii 393

GILBY, *Capt* Robert, RN (*fl* 1664–1668)   ch i 225

GILCHRIST, *Capt* James, RN (*d* 1777)   ch vi 122; DNB vii
                                                                                           1220

GILCHRIST, John (1803–1866)
Merchant, associated with the Australian whaling trade   DAuB i 442

GILES, Alfred (1816–1895)
Civil engineer; chief engineer at Southampton Docks Co., for many years   B v 409

GILES, Francis (1787–1847)
Civil engineer; surveyed the Thames, Mersey and other rivers under the direction
of Rennie   DNB vii 1226

GILES, *Cdr* Robert, RN (*d* 1824)   M vii 64

GILL, *Capt* Charles, CB, RN (*fl* 1801–1822)   M ix 433

GILL, *Lieut* Clifford B., USN (*fl* 1862–1880)   H 947

GILL, *Sir* David (1843–1914)
Astronomer   CE vi 351; DNB xxiv
                                                                                           212

GILL, *Capt* John, RN (*fl* 1666)   ch i 225

GILL, *Cdr* Joseph Collings, RN (*d* 1858)   Tr 163

GILL, *Capt* Thomas, RN (1782–1874)   B i 1149; M vii 239

GILLAM, *Capt* Thomas (*d* 1693)   ch ii 253

GILLAM, Zachariah (1636–1682)
Captain, Hudson's Bay Company   DCB i 336

GILLERY, *Capt* James (*d* 1679)   ch ii 61

GILLIES, James, *Surgeon*, RN (*d* 1827)   Tr 185

GILLINGS [*or* GURLING], *Capt* Thomas, RN (*fl* 1666–1667)   ch i 225

GILLIS, *Capt* James H., USN (*b* 1831)   H 889

GILLISS, *Capt* James Melville, USN (1811–1865)   DAB 343

GILMAN, *Capt* Augustus J., USN (*fl* 1861–1879)   H 986

GILMER, Thomas Walker (1802–1844)
Secretary of the United States Navy, 1844   DAB 344

GILMORE, *Lieut* Fernando P., USN (*fl* 1863–1880)   H 948

GILMORE, Joseph (*fl* 1718–1726)
Inventor of a perpetual log   T ii 119

GILMOUR, *Cdr* David, RN (1775–1829)   M vi 274

GILPATRICK, *Lieut* W. W., USN (*fl* 1862–1880)   H 947

GILPIN, *Capt* Bernard, RN (*fl* 1660–1665)   ch i 13

BOLTON PUBLIC REFERENCE LIBRARY LIBRARIES

GILPIN, George (*fl* 1766–1810)
Clerk; assistant to Maskelyne at Greenwich and to William Wales on Cook's second voyage; secretary to the Board of Longitude   T ii 262

GIOIA [*or* GIOJA], Flavia (*b* seventeenth century)
Pilot, ship's captain and alleged inventor of the compass   Md xvi 490

GIRARD, Pierre Simon (1765–1835)
Hydraulic engineer   Md xvi 527

GIRARDIN, Alexandre Louis Robert *comte* de (1776–1855)
Admiral and soldier   Md xvi 567

GISBORNE, Lionel (1823–1861)
Civil engineer; projected several of the long-distance submarine cables, between 1851–1861   B i 1154

GLAISHER, James (1809–1903)
Head of the meteorological department at the Royal Greenwich Observatory, 1838–1874   DNB xxiiib 117

GLAISHERM, James Whitbread Lee (1848–1928)
Astronomer   DNB xxv 339

GLAS, George (1725–1765)
Mariner   DNB vii 1294

GLASCOCK, *Capt* William Nugent, RN (1787?–1847)   DNB vii 1297; M viii 490

GLASS, *Cdr* Henry, USN (*fl* 1860–1879)   H 917

GLASS, *Sir* Richard Atwood (1820–1873)
Superintended the manufacture of the Atlantic cables, 1865–1866   B i 1156; DNB vii 1298

GLASSE, *Adm* Frederick Henry Hastings (*d* 1884)   B i 1156

GLASSFORD, John (1715–1783)
Glasgow merchant and shipowner   DNB vii 1301

GLASSON, *Cdre* John J., USN (*fl* 1823–1864)   H 312

GLEAVES, *Adm* Albert, USN (1858–1937)   DAB 346

GLEMHAM, Edward (*fl* 1590–1594)
Voyager; in his ship, the 'Edward and Constance', destroyed two Spanish vessels, repulsed four galleys and captured a rich Venetian merchantman, 1590   DNB vii 1304

GLEN, *Cdr* Nisbet, RN (*d* 1824)   M vii 145

GLIDDON, *Lieut-Cdr* George D. B., USN (*fl* 1860–1880)   H 924

GLIEMANN, Jean George Theodor (1793–1828)
Danish geographer   Md xvi 636

GLISSON, *Rear-Adm* O. S., USN (*fl* 1826–1871)   H 313

GLOVER, *Capt* Bonovier, RN (*d* 1780)   ch vi 564

GLOVER, *Capt Sir* John Hawley, GCMG, RN (1829–1885)   B i 1159; DNB viii 4

GLYN, *Vice-Adm* Henry Carr (1829–1884)   B i 1161

GLYNN, *Adm* Henry Richard (1768–1856)   B i 1161; M ii 812

GLYNN, *Cdre* James, USN (1801–1871)   DAB 347

GOATE, *Capt* William, RN (*fl* 1790–1809)   M x 35

GOATER, Henry (*fl* 1777–1792)
Optical and mathematical instrument-maker; octants at National Maritime Museum   T ii 287

GOATER, J. (*fl ca* 1760)
Ship's instrument-maker   T ii 262

GOATER, Robert (*fl* 1769–1797)
Ship's instrument-maker; octant at National Maritime Museum   T ii 262

GOBLE, Thomas (1788–1869)
Master's mate aboard the 'Victory' at Trafalgar   Tr 16

GODBY, *Capt* John Hardy, RN (*fl* 1794–1846)   M xi 396

GODDARD, *Capt* Richard, RN (*fl* 1802)   M iv 552

GODDARD, Robert Hutchings (1882–1945)
United States physicist and rocket pioneer; devised system of rocket assisted take-off
for U.S. naval aircraft   A 493

GODDARD, *Capt* Samuel, RN (*d* 1762)   ch v 247

GODEFROY, Jean-Paul (*ca* 1602–*ca* 1668)
French naval commander; businessman and shipowner   DCB i 339

GODENCH, *Cdr* James, RN (*d* 1825)   M vi 253

GODFRAY, *Capt* William, CB, RN (*d* 1835)   Tr 78

GODFREY, Thomas (1704–1749)
'True inventor of Hadley's quadrant'   DAB 347

GODFREY, Thomas (*fl* 1725–1734)
Instrument-maker; inventor of mariner's bow   T ii 178

GODFREY, *Capt* William, RN (*fl* 1665–1673)   ch i 165

GODFREY, *Capt* William, CB, RN (*d* 1835)   M ix 465

GODFREY, *Capt* William M'Kenzie, RN (*fl* 1809–1822)   M xii 397

GODOLPHIN, John (1617–1678)
Appointed a judge of the Admiralty, 1653   DNB viii 41

GODON, *Rear-Adm* Sylvanus W., USN (*d* 1879)   H 313

GODSLAVE, *Rear-Adm* Henry (*d* 1765)   ch v 90

GODWIN, *Adm* Matthew (*b* 1766)   M iv 889

GODWYN [or GOODWYN], John (*fl* 1597–1600)
Teacher of mathematics and instrument-maker: sector at National Maritime Museum   T i 194

GOETHALS, *Maj-Gen* George Washington, USA (1858–1928)
Chief engineer of the Panama Canal, 1907–1914   DAB 348

GOOCH, William (*fl* 1791)
Astronomer with Captain Vancouver   T ii 339

GOOD, *Capt* Edward, RN (*d* 1710)   *ch* ii 254

GOOD, John (*fl* 1706–1733)
Teacher of navigation and surveyor   T i 301

GOODALL, *Adm* Samuel Granston (*d* 1801)   *ch* vi 458; DNB viii
                                                                  116; R i 335

GOODALL, Thomas (1767–1832?)
Privateer; the 'Admiral of Hayti'   DNB viii 117

GOODDAY, B. (*fl* 1723–1725)
Writer on navigation   T ii 159

GOODE, *Sir* William Athelstane Meredith, KBE (1875–1944)
*Journalist; representative of the Associated Press of America on Sampson's flagship
throughout the Spanish-American War; author of: 'With Sampson through the
War'* (*1899*)   DNB xxvii 303

GOODENOUGH, *Cdre* James Graham (1830–1875)   AE i 563; B i 1173;
                                                                  DNB viii 137

GOODENOUGH, *Adm Sir* William Edmund, GCB, MVO (1867–1945)   DNB xxvii 304

GOODERE, *Capt* Samuel, RN (1678–1741)   *ch* iv 241; DNB viii
                                                                  125

GOODFELLOW, James (*fl* 1778–1794)
Teacher of mathematics; compiler of tables for calculating cargo stowage   T ii 287

GOODHEART, *Capt* Abraham, RN (*fl* 1666–1672)   *ch* i 225

GOODLAD, *Lieut* Edward, RN (*d* 1849)   Tr 64

GOODLAD, *Capt* Richard, RN (*fl* 1665)   *ch* i 165

GOODLOE, *Lieut* Green Clay, USN (*fl* 1869–1880)   H 1012

GOODRICH, *Lieut-Cdr* Casper F., USN (*fl* 1861–1880)   H 926

GOODRICKE, John (1764–1786)
Astronomer   DNB viii 140

GOODRICKE, Thomas (*fl* 1805–1811)
Carpenter's mate aboard the 'Colossus' at Trafalgar   ..   Tr 171

GOODSONN, *Vice-Adm* William (*fl* 1634–1662)   DNB viii 140

GOODWIN, *Lieut* Richard Merrish, RN (*fl* 1805–1813)   Tr 125

GOODWIN, *Lieut* Walton, USN (*fl* 1863–1880)   H 949

GOODWIN, William Lushington (1798?–1862)
Journalist; arrived at Sydney in 1831 as master of the convict ship 'Kains'   DAUB i 457

GOOLD, *Cdr* Hugh, RN (*b* 1786)   M viii 358

GOOS, Abraham (*fl* 1614–1630)
Dutch Cartographer   CE vi 551

GORDON, Thomas (*fl* 1705–1726)
RN officer 1705–1715, later flag-officer in the Russian service   ch iii 309

GORDON, *Capt* Thomas, RN (*d* 1761)   ch vi 446

GORDON, *Lieut-Col* Thomas, RM (1790–1855)   Tr 127

GORDON, *Rear-Adm Sir* William (*d* 1768)   ch v 299

GORDON, *Vice-Adm* William (1785–1858)   B i 1183

GORDON, *Adm the Hon* William (1792–1869)   M x 70

GORDON, *Cdr* William, RN (*fl* 1812–1815)   M vii 371

GORDON, *Vice-Adm* William Elrington (1831–1897)   B v 450

GORE, *Capt the Hon* Edward, RN (1797–1879)   M viii 299

GORE, *Capt* Henry, RN (*d* 1725/6)   ch iii 247

GORE, *Vice-Adm Sir* John, KCB (1772–1836)   DNB viii 238; M ii
                                                                                   609; x 466; R iv 460

GORE, *Capt* John, RN (*fl* 1789–1746)   M vii 289

GORE, *Adm* John (*d* 1869)   B i 1184; M v 271

GORE, John Ellard (1845–1910)
Astronomical writer   DNB xxiiib 132

GORE, *Cdr* Robert, RN (*fl* 1805–1821)   M viii 92

GORE, *Capt* Robert, RN (1810–1854)   B i 1184

GORGAS, Albert C., *Surgeon*, USN (*fl* 1856–1880)   H 970

GORGES, *Sir Arthur* (*d* 1625)
Poet; commanded the 'Warspite', Ralegh's flagship on the 1597 Islands voyage   DNB viii 241

GORGES, *Sir Ferdinand* (1566?–1647)
Naval and military commander   DNB viii 241

GORMAN, Arthur Pue (1839–1906)
Chairman of the Chesapeake and Ohio Canal Company   DAB 356

GORRINGE, *Lieut-Cdr* Henry Honeychurch, USN (1841–1885)   B i 1185; DAB 356;
                                                                                   H 925

GORST, Thomas (*fl ca* 1668–1687)
Employee of Hudson's Bay Co., purser and travel writer   DCB i 343

GOSCHEN, George Joachim, *first Viscount Goschen* (1831–1907)   CE vi 445; DNB xxiii
                                                                                   b. 134

GOSLING, *Capt* George, RN (*b* 1790)   M v 273; vi 444

GOSLING, Harry (1861–1930)
*Trade-union leader; elected general secretary of the Amalgamated Society of Watermen
& Lightermen of the River Thames, 1893; a member of the Port of London
Authority, 1908–1930*   DNB xxv 352

GRAHAM, *Capt the Rt Hon Lord* George, RN (*d* 1747)   ch v 22

GRAHAM, George (1673–1751)
Partner and successor to Thomas Tompion; mural quadrant and zenith sectors at
Greenwich   T i 289; ii 120

GRAHAM, *Cdr* James, USN (*fl* 1857–1880)   H 912

GRAHAM, *Sir* James Robert George (1792–1861)   DNB viii 380

GRAHAM, John (*b* 1800?)   DAuB i 468

GRAHAM, *Capt* John George, RN (*fl* 1815–1825)   M v 278

GRAHAM, *Capt* Mitchell, RN (*d* 1795)   ch vi 398

GRAHAM, *Cdr* Philip, RN (*fl* 1803–1820)   M viii 170

GRAHAM, Richard (*fl* 1720–1745)
Scientist; writer on latitude   T ii 160

GRAHAM [*or* GROEME], *Capt* William, RN (*d* 1717)   ch iv 44

GRAHAM, William Alexander (1804–1875)
Secretary of the USN, 1850–1852   DAB 360

GRANDMONT (*d* 1686)
Pirate   M*d* xvii 338

GRANGER, Thomas (*fl* 1710)
Instrument-maker; nocturnal at National Maritime Museum   T i 303

GRANGER, *Vice-Adm* William (*fl* 1785–1837)   M iii 230

GRANT, *Rear-Adm* Albert Weston, USN (1856–1930)   DAB 361

GRANT, Alexander (1734–1813)
RN, merchant navy, and army officer; commodore of the Western Lakes at Detroit;
administrator of Upper Canada   MDC 276

GRANT, Charles, *Viscount de Vaux* (*fl* 1774–1808)
French major-general of English descent; writer on longitude at sea; inventor of log
and other instruments   T ii 287

GRANT, Charles, *Baron Glenelg* (1778–1866)
Treasurer of the navy, 1827–1828   DNB viii 380

GRANT, *Capt* Charles, CB, RN (*fl* 1790–1821)   M iii 300

GRANT, *Capt* Charles Cathcart, RN (*d* 1769)   . .   ch vi 420

GRANT, *Capt* Francis, RN [*later* Francis Grant GORDON] (*fl* 1753–1770) ch vi 576

GRANT, *Cdr* Gregory, RN (*fl* 1795–1812)   M vi 403

GRANT, *Adm* Henry Duncan, CB (1834–1896)   B v 471

GRANT, James (*fl before* 1779)
Marine surveyor; contributor to: 'The Atlantic Neptune'   T ii 288

GRANT, *Cdr* James, RN (1772–1833)   AE i 574; DAuB i 468;

                                                                           M vi 322

GRAVES, Samuel Robert (1818–1873)
Merchant and shipowner at Liverpool; chairman of Liverpool Shipowners' Association
and the local marine board, 1856   B i 1213

GRAVES, *Rear-Adm* Thomas (*d* 1755)   *ch* iv 43

GRAVES, *Adm* Thomas, *first Baron Graves* (1725–1802)   *ch* vi 126; DNB viii
                                                                                      437; NA i 83; NC v
                                                                                      377; R i 175

GRAVES, *Adm Sir* Thomas, KCB (1747?–1841)   DNB viii 440; NC viii
                                                                                      353; 463

GRAVES, *Capt* Thomas, RN (*d* 1856)   B i 1213; M X III

GRAVINA, Charles, *Duc de* (1747–1806)
Spanish admiral   Md xvii 402

GRAY [*or* GAY], *Capt* Charles, RN (*d* 1712)   *ch* iv 48

GRAY, *Capt* Charles, RM (1782–1851)   B i 1214; DNB viii 447

GRAY, *Lieut* Francis, RN (*d* 1851)   Tr 216

GRAY, *Capt* John, RN (*fl* 1711)   *ch* iv 30

GRAY, John, *Surgeon*, RN (1768–1825)   Md xvii 407

GRAY, John (*fl* 1805–1854)
Instrument-maker   T ii 364

GRAY, John (*fl* 1830–1838)
Instrument-maker   T ii 422

GRAY, Thomas (*d* 1890)
Permanent assistant secretary, marine department, Board of Trade, 1867–1890   B i 1219

GRAY, *Capt* William, RN (*fl* 1705)   *ch* iii 310

GRAY, William (1750–1825)   DAB 365

GRAYDON, *Capt* George, RE (*fl* 1820–1839)   T ii 422

GRAYDON, *Lieut* James W., USN (*fl* 1865–1880)   H 963

GRAYDON, *Vice-Adm* John (*d* 1727)   *ch* ii 158; DNB viii
                                                                                      471

GREATHEAD, Henry (1757–1816)
Lifeboat inventor   DNB viii 473

GREATWOOD, *Lieut* William, RN (*fl* 1810–1828)   Tr 82

GREAVES, John (1602–1652)
Professor of geometry; expert on longitude and navigation   DNB viii 481; T i 208

GREELY, *Maj-Gen* Adolphus Washington, USN (1844–1935)   CE vi 577; DAB 367

GREEN, *Vice-Adm Sir* Andrew Pellat, KCH (*d* 1858)   B i 1222; M xi 250;
                                                                                      Tr 62

GREEN, *Capt* Charles, RN (*fl* 1667)   *ch* i 292

GREER, *Rear-Adm* James Augustin, USN (1833–1904)   DAB 372; H 887

GREGORY, David (1661–1708)
Astronomer   DNB viii 536

GREGORY, *Capt* Edward, RN (*d* 1743)   ch iv 81

GREGORY, *Rear-Adm* Francis H., USN (1789–1866)   H 324

GREGORY, Henry (*fl* 1750–1792)
Mathematical and optical instrument-maker, compass designer; supplied compasses
to Cook; compass card at National Maritime Museum   T ii 232

GREGORY, Henry, *and* WRIGHT (*fl* 1783–1792)
Instrument-makers and sellers; octant at National Maritime Museum   T ii 312

GREGORY, John Uriah (1830–1913)
Canadian civil servant; representative of department of marine and fisheries at Quebec   MDC 283

GREGORY, *Capt* Robert, RN (*d* 1774)   ch vi 518

GREGORY, *Capt* Thomas, RN (*d* 1747)   ch v 91

GREGORY, *Cdr* Thomas, RN (*fl* 1810–1833)   M viii 387

GREGORY, *Capt* William, RN (*fl* 1664)   ch i 97

GREGORY, *Cdr* William, RN (*fl* 1803–1833)   M vii 5

GREIG, John (1759–1819)
Teacher of geography; writer on use of globes   DNB viii 549; T ii 313

GREIG, *Sir* Samuel (1735–1788)
Served in the Royal Navy up to 1763, when he became an admiral in the Russian
service   DNB viii 549

GRENFELL, Hubert Henry (1845–1906)
Expert on naval gunnery   DNB xxiiib 165

GRENFELL, John Pascoe (1800–1869)
Admiral in the Brazilian navy   B i 1236; DNB viii 553

GRENFELL, *Adm* Sidney, CB (1807–1884)   B i 1236

GRENFELL, *Sir* Wilfred Thomason, KCMG (1865–1940)
Medical missionary, maritime writer, superintendent of Mission to Deep-Sea
Fishermen   CE vi 588; DNB xxvi
                                                                             364; MDC 283

GRENIER, Jacques Raimond, *Vicomte de* (1736–1803)
French admiral   Md xvii 487

GRENVILLE, George (1712–1770)
First lord of the Admiralty, 1762–1763   CE vi 589; DNB viii
                                                                             556

GRENVILLE , *Sir* Richard (1541?–1591)   CE vi 589; DNB viii
                                                                             565; H 324; Md xvii
                                                                             418

GRIFFITH, Piers (*d* 1628)
Naval adventurer   DNB viii 678

GRIFFITH, *Capt* Richard (*fl* 1668–1678)   ch i 334

GRIFFITH, *Capt* Richard, RN (*d* 1719)   ch ii 415; DNB viii
                                                                            679

GRIFFITH, *Cdr* Richard, RN (*fl* 1828)   M viii 311

GRIFFITH, *Capt* Walter, RN (*d* 1779)   ch vi 365; DNB viii
                                                                            682

GRIFFITHS, *Capt* Anselm John, RN (*fl* 1780-1810)   M iv 573

GRIFFITHS, John Willis (1809?–1882)
Naval architect   DAB 374

GRIFFITHS, Jonathan (1766?–1840?)
Shipowner and shipbuilder   DAuB i 485

GRIFFITHS, *Cdr* Joseph, RN (*b* 1776)   M viii 32

GRIFFITHS, Robert (1805–1883)
Inventor; patented screw propeller, 1849   DNB viii 689

GRIGG, *Lieut* Nathaniel Batt, RM (*d* 1823)   Tr 146

GRIJALVA, Juan de (*fl* 1548)
Spanish voyager and adventurer   Md xvii 541

GRIMALDI, Antonio (*fl* 1332–1353)
Genoese admiral   Md xvii 548

GRIMALDI, Giovanni (*fl* 1431)
Genoese admiral   Md xvii 548

GRIMDITCH, *Capt* John, RN (*fl* 1685–1688)   ch ii 163

GRIMES, *Lieut* James M., USN (*fl* 1863–1880)   H 953

GRIMOUARD, *Vice-Adm* Nicolas René Henri, *Comte de* (1743–1794)   s i 529

GRINDALL, *Lieut* Festing Horatio, RN (1787–1812)   Tr 17

GRINDALL, *Vice-Adm Sir* Richard (1750–1820)   Tr 78

GRINNELL, Henry Walton, USN (1843–1920)   DAB 375

GRINNELL, Moses Hicks (1803–1877)
Merchant and shipowner   DAB 376

GRINT, *Capt* William, RN (*d* 1851)   M viii 27; Tr 42

GRISCOM, Clement Acton (1841–1912)
Shipowner; organised the International Mercantile Marine Company   DAB 376

GRIST, *Capt* William, RN (*fl* 1672–1673)   ch i 334

GROEME [*or* GRAHAM], *Capt* William, RN (*d* 1717)   ch iv 44

GROIGNARD, Antoine (1727–1797)
Naval architect and engineer   Md xvii 580

GUNMAN DE VALLE, *Capt* Christopher, RN (*d* 1682)   *ch* i 225; T i 253

GUNMAN, *Capt* James, RN (*d* 1756)   *ch* iii 397

GUNNELL, Francis M., *Surgeon*, USN (*fl* 1849–1880)   H 967

GUNNING, *Cdr* Orlando George Sutton, RN (*b* 1799)   M viii 352

GUNTHER, Edmund (1581–1626)
Professor of astronomy; mathematician; writer on, and inventor of navigational and
surveying instruments   DNB viii 793; T i 196

GUPPY, Thomas Richard (1797–1882)
Aided I. K. Brunel in the construction of the 'Great Western' and 'Great Britain';
invented the cellular type of shipbuilding   B i 1259

GURLING [*or* GILLINGS], *Capt* Thomas, RN (*fl* 1666–1667)   *ch* i 225

GURNEY, *Capt* Edward, RN (*d* 1694/5)   *ch* ii 392

GURNEY, *Sir* Goldsworthy (1793–1873)
Inventor; author of: 'Observations pointing to means by which a seaman may
identify lighthouses' (1864)   DNB viii 801

GUTHRIE, *Lieut* Robert, RM (*fl* 1804–1809)   Tr 128

GUTIERREZ, Diego (*fl* 1562)
Cartographer   CE vi 667

GUTZLAFF, Karl (1803–1851)
German missionary and voyager   Md xviii 274

GUY, John (*d ca* 1629)
Bristol merchant venturer; explorer and coloniser; governor of Newfoundland   DCB i 349; DNB viii
                                                                                                        832; MDC 287

GUY, *Capt* John, RN (*d* 1697)   *ch* ii 392

GUY, *Capt* Leonard, RN (*fl* 1667)   *ch* i 293

GUY, *Capt* Thomas, RN (*fl* 1665–1674)   *ch* i 166

GWARD, Alexander (*fl ca* 1832–1852)
Writer on navigation   T ii 472

GWILT, George (1746–1807)
Architect to the West India Dock Co   DNB viii 840

GWYN, *Gen* Hamond Weston, RM (1824–1898)   B v 532

GWYN, Stephen (1684–1720)

Professor of navigation, St Petersburg Naval Academy   T ii 123

GWYNE, *Lieut* Laurence, RN (*fl* 1798–1806)
Teacher of mathematics; writer on navigation   T ii 340

GWYNN, *Capt* Richard, RN (*d* 1766)   *ch* vi 44

GYLENHIELM, Carl, *Baron de* (1574–1650)
Swedish admiral   Md xviii 302

HAILS [or HAILES], William Anthony (1766–1845)
Miscellaneous writer; formerly a shipwright   DNB viii 885

HAILSTONE, Edward (1818–1890)
Law clerk to the Leeds and Liverpool canal for forty years   B i 1275

HAINSSELIN, D. F. (d 1852)
British seaman; the last survivor of Keppel's action, 1778   B i 1275

HAKLUYT, Richard (1552–1616)   CE vi 694 DNB viii
                                                                              895; Md xviii 356

HALBERT [or HERBERT], *Capt.* Samuel, RN (*fl* 1695)   ch iii 105

HALDANE, James Alexander (1768–1831)
Religious author; served in the H.E.I.C. marine service, 1785–1794   DNB viii 897

HALDANE, *Capt* Robert, RN (d 1761)   ch vi 64

HALE, George Ellery (1868–1938)
Astronomer   CE vi 695; DAB 383

HALE, *Capt* Jeffrey, RN (1803–1864)   MDC 292

HALE, *Rear-Adm* John (d 1791)   ch vi 144

HALES [or HAILES], *Capt* John, RN (d 1693)   ch ii 314

HALGAN, Emmanuel (1771–1852)
French vice-admiral   Md xviii 360

HALKETT, *Adm Sir* Peter (d 1839)   M ii 572; R iii 329

HALL, Asaph (1829–1907)
Professor of astronomy, U.S. Naval Observatory, Washington, D.C.   A 315; DAB 385

HALL, *Capt* Basil, RN (1788–1841)   CE vi 699; DNB viii
                                                                              942; M xii 142; T ii
                                                                              365

HALL, *Capt* Charles, RN (d 1863)   Tr 218

HALL, *Sir* Charles, KCMG (1843–1900)
British representative to the international maritime conference at Washington, 1889   DNB xxii 802

HALL, Charles Francis (1821–1871)
Arctic explorer   DAB 385

HALL, *Capt* Edward, RN (*fl* 1786–1846)   M vii 75

HALL, James (d 1612)
*Navigator; made two voyages to Greenland, 1605–1606, as a pilot to Danish
expeditions*   DCB i 360; DNB viii
                                                                              951

HALL, James, *Surgeon*, RN (b 1784)   DAuB i 503

HALL, *Cdr* James, RN (d 1810)   Tr 80

HALL, *Sir* John, KCH (1779–1861)
Secretary to the St Katherine's Dock Company, 1824–1853   B i 1286

HALSE, *Sir* Nicholas (*d* 1636)
Inventor; addressed two discourses on the Dutch fisheries to James I, 1608 and 1609   DNB viii 1008

HALSEY, *Adm Sir* Lionel, KCMG (1872–1949)   DNB xxvii 345

HALSEY, *Adm* William Frederick, USN (1882–1959)   CE vi 704

HALSTED, *Cdr* George, RN (*fl* 1796–1809)   M vi 379

HALSTED, *Cdr* George Anthony, RN (*fl* 1816–1834)   M viii 241

HALSTED, *Capt* John, RN (*b* 1768)   M ix 406

HALSTED, *Adm* Sir Lawrence William, GCB (1764–1841)   M i 429; ii 866

HALTON, Immanuel (1628–1699)
Astronomer   DNB viii 1009

HALTON, *Cdr* Thomas, RN (*fl* 1797–1798)   M vi 268

HAMAR, *Rear-Adm* Joseph (*d* 1773)   ch v 92

HAMBLY, *Capt* Peter Simpson, RN (1788–1848)   M viii 33; Tr 80

HAMBLY, *Lieut* Richard, RN (*d* 1832)   Tr 306

HAMEL, Hendrik (*fl* 1653–1668)
Dutch voyager   Md xviii 399

HAMELIN, *Contre-Amiral* Jacques Félix Emmanuel, *Baron* (1768–1854)   Md xviii 400; s i 554

HAMILTON, Alexander (*d* 1732?)
Merchant and sea-captain   DNB viii 1017

HAMILTON, *Capt* Archibald, RN (*fl* 1707)   ch iii 392

HAMILTON, *Capt Lord* Archibald (*d* 1754)   ch iii 15

HAMILTON, Archibald, *Master's Mate*, RN (*fl* 1750–1766)   T ii 232

HAMILTON, *Adm* Arthur Philip (*d* 1877)   B i 1299; M xii 110

HAMILTON, *Adm Sir* Charles, KCB (1767–1849)   DNB viii 1024; M 411; ii 865

HAMILTON, *Adm* Charles Powell (*d* 1825)   M i 100

HAMILTON, *Adm Sir* Edward, KCB (1772–1851)   B i 1300; DNB viii 1029; M ii 821; viii 439; NC v 1; R iv 132

HAMILTON, *Lady* Emma (*ca* 1765–1815)   CE vi 708; DNB viii 1032

HAMILTON, *Capt* Gawen William, CB, RN (*fl* 1801–1828)   M x 447

HAMILTON, *Capt* George, RN (*d* 1760)   ch vi 367

HAMILTON, *Lord* George Francis (1845–1927)
First lord of the Admiralty, 1885–1886   DNB xxv 388

HAMILTON, *Capt* James [*or* John], RN (*d* 1708)   ch iii 392

HAMILTON, *Capt* James, RN (*d* 1747)   ch vi 45

HANFORD, *Lieut* Franklin, USN (*fl* 1862–1880)   H 944

HANHAM, *Cdr Sir* William, RN (1798–1877)   B V 561

HANHAM [*or* HANNAM], *Capt* Willoughby, RN (*d* 1672)   *ch* i 13

HANKERSON, *Rear-Adm* Thomas (*d* 1779)   *ch* vi 144

HANLAN [*properly* HANLON], Edward (1855–1908)
Champion oarsman   DNB xxiiib 196; MDC
                                                                          297

HANMER, *Capt* Job, RN (*fl* 1808–1823)   M xii 399

HANN, James (1799–1856)
Mathematician; at one time a calculator in the Nautical Almanac Office   DNB viii 1184

HANNAM, *Lieut* Thomas, RN (1786–1830)   Tr 72

HANNAM [*or* HANHAM], *Capt* Willoughby, RN (*d* 1672)   *ch* i 13

HANNAY, James (1827–1873)
Man of letters; entered the Royal Navy in 1840 and was dismissed in 1845   DNB viii 1188

HANNAY, *Lieut* Peter, RN (1788–1819)   Tr 136

HANNEN, *Sir* James, *Baron Hannen* (1821–1894)
Arbitrator upon the issue between Great Britain and the United States over seal
fishing rights in the Behring Sea, 1892   DNB xxii 811

HANNO (*fl* 500 B.C.)
Carthaginian navigator, possible circumnavigator of Africa   A 8; Md xviii 418

HANSEN, Peter Andrews (1795–1874)
Astronomer   CE vi 731

HANWAY, *Capt* Jonas, RN (*d* 1737)   *ch* iii 248

HANWAY, Jonas (1712–1786)
Founder-member of the Marine Society   CE vi 732; DNB viii
                                                                          1196; T ii 179

HANWAY, *Capt* Thomas, RN (*d* 1772)   *ch* v 305

HANWELL, *Vice-Adm* Joseph (*b* 1759)   M ii 540

HANWELL, *Capt* William, RN (*fl* 1793–1810)   M iii 198

HARADEN, Jonathan (1744–1803)
American naval officer and privateer   DAB 396

HARBERT, *Lieut* Giles R., USN (*fl* 1865–1880)   H 958

HARBORD, John Bradley, *Chaplain of the Fleet* (1828–1896)   B V 566

HARCOURT, *Adm* Frederick Edward Vernon (1790–1883)   B i 1323

HARCOURT, *Vice-Adm* Octavius Henry Cyril Vernon (1793–1863)   B i 1324

HARDCASTLE, William John (1831–1890)
Engineer-in-chief of ports and lighthouses in Egypt, 1875–1879; deputy controller-
general of ports and lighthouses in the Mediterranean and Red Sea, 1879–1890   B V 568

HARLAND, *Sir* Edward James (1831–1895)
Shipbuilder; a founder partner of Harland & Wolff B V 577

HARLAND, *Capt* Robert, RN (*d* 1751) *ch* iii 293

HARLAND, *Adm Sir* Robert (1715?–1784) *ch* v 454; DNB viii 1275

HARLEY [*or* HARLY], *Capt* John, RN (*fl* 1667) *ch* i 293

HARLOW, *Capt* Thomas, RN (*d* 1673) DNB viii 1294

HARLOW, *Capt* Thomas, RN (*d* 1741) *ch* ii 314

HARMAN, *Capt* James, RN (*d* 1677) *ch* i 395

HARMAN, *Rear-Adm Sir* John (*fl* 1665–1672) *ch* i 97

HARMAN, *Adm Sir* John (*d* 1741) DNB viii 1294

HARMAN, *Capt* Thomas, RN (*d* 1677) *ch* i 335

HARMAN, *Capt* William, RN (*d* 1694) *ch* ii 255

HARMAN, *Capt* William, RN (*d* 1766) *ch* v 457

HARMANSEN, Wolphart (*d ca* 1607)
Dutch navigator Md xviii 480

HARMONY, *Capt* David S., USN (*fl* 1847–1880) H 887

HARMSWORTH, Harold Sidney, *first Viscount Rothermere* (1868–1940)
Newspaper proprietor; appointed Air Minister in 1917 with the special task of amalgamating the RNAS and the RFC CE xii 6; DNB xxvi 400

HARNAGE [*formerly* BLACKMAN], *Cdr Sir* George, RN (1792–1866) B V 579; M viii 49

HARNESS, John (*b* 1754)
Medical Commissioner of the Navy NC xxxv 265

HARNESS, *Cdr* Richard Stephens, RN (*b* 1792) M vii 330

HARPER, *Capt* John, RN, CB (*b* 1772) M xi 326

HARRINGTON, *Lieut* Daniel, RN (1776–1837) Tr 20

HARRINGTON, Mark Walrod (1848–1926)
Astronomer DAB 402

HARRINGTON, *Lieut-Cdr* Purnell F., USN (*fl* 1861–1880) H 921

HARRIOT, Thomas (1560–1621)
Mathematician and navigation expert; cartographer; teacher of navigation; adviser to Raleigh CE vi 755; DNB viii 1321; H 339; Tr 183

HARRIOTT, John (1745–1817)
Projector of the Thames Police and resident magistrate at the Thames Police Court, 1798–1816; served in the Royal Navy, ca 1762–1766, and later in the mercantile marine; patented improvement in ship's pumps which was subsequently adapted by the Royal Navy, 1797; suggested improvement in the organisation of sea and river fencibles DNB viii 1323

HARRIS, *Sir* William Snow (1791–1867)
Electrician; contributed a series of papers on the defence of ships from lightning to the
'Nautical Magazine' in 1834, and papers on this subject, 1830–1847   B i 1351; DNB ix 31

HARRISON, *Lieut* Edward, RN (*fl* 1686–1700)   T i 281

HARRISON, *Vice-Adm* Henry (*d* 1759)   ch v 24

HARRISON, John (1693–1776)
Inventor of the chronometer   A 120; CE vi 756;
                                                                            DNB ix 35; T i 305;
                                                                            ii 125

HARRISON, John, *Purser*, RN (*fl* 1766)
Astronomer; sailed with Captain Wallis   T ii 263

HARRISON, *Rear-Adm* John, RN (*d* 1791)   ch vi 145

HARRISON, John (*fl* 1837)
Chronometer-maker; chronometers at National Maritime Museum   T ii 475

HARRISON, Joseph (*fl* 1734)
Sea captain   T ii 179

HARRISON, *Capt* Joseph, RN (*fl* 1799–1833)   M viii 485

HARRISON, *Capt* Mark, RN (*fl* 1660–1672)   ch i 14

HARRISON, *Capt* Napoleon B., USN (1823–1870)   H 339

HARRISON, Richard (*fl* 1759)
Teacher of mathematics; publisher of solar tables for seamen   T ii 233

HARRISON, *Capt* Robert, RN (*d* 1739)   ch iv 250

HARRISON, *Capt* Thomas, RN (*d* 1752)   ch v 308

HARRISON, *Capt* Thomas, RN (*d* 1768)   ch vi 234

HARRISON, Thomas Elliott (1808–1888)
Civil engineer; designed and constructed the Jarrow docks at South Shields,
1855–1859 and the Hartlepool docks   B i 1356; DNB ix 46

HARRISON, William (*fl ca* 1750)
Sea captain   T ii 233

HARRISON, William (1812–1860)
Commander of the 'Great Eastern', 1856–1860   DNB ix 48

HARROD, Benjamin Morgan (1837–1912)
Member of the Panama Canal Commission   DAB 408

HART, *Cdr* Francis, RN (*d* 1845)   M viii 367

HART, *Rear-Adm Sir* Henry, KCH (1781–1856)   B i 1359; M x 413

HART, James W. (*d* 1899)
Astronomer   B v 595

HART, *Capt* John, RN (*fl* 1664–1671)   ch i 102

HART, John, *Master*, RN (1809–1873)   AE i 602

HARVEY, *Adm Sir* John, KCB (1772–1837) — DNB ix 90; M ii 613, 804; viii 414

HARVEY, *Capt* John, RN (1793–1882) — B v 599; M viii 29

HARVEY, *Lieut* Robert, RN (*d* 1808) — Tr 234

HARVEY, *Vice-Adm Sir* Thomas, KCB (*d* 1841) — DNB ix 92; M ii 797

HARWARD, *Capt* Richard, RN (*d* 1845) — M x 32

HARWOOD, *Rear-Adm* Andrew Allen, USN (*fl* 1818–1872) — H 339

HARWOOD, *Adm Sir* Henry Harwood, KCB, OBE (1888–1950) — DNB xxvii 365

HARWOOD, *Capt* Robert, RN (*d* 1747) — ch iv 45

HARWOOD, *Capt* Thomas, RN (*fl* 1664–1672) — ch i 166

HASELDEN, Thomas (*d* 1740)
Mathematician; at one time designated himself as 'teacher of mathematics to His Majesty's volunteers in the navy' — DNB ix 106; T ii 127

HASELGRAVE, *Capt* John, RN (*fl* 1666) — ch i 235

HASSEL, Johann Georg Heinrich (1770–1829)
German geographer — Md xviii 376

HASTIE, James (1849–1897)
Oarsman — B v 602

HASTINGS, *Capt* Anthony, RN (*d* 1692) — ch ii 10

HASTINGS, *Lieut* Frank, RN (*d* 1819) — Tr 64

HASTINGS, Frank Abney (1794–1828)
Served in Royal Navy from about 1805, later became a Greek naval commander — DNB ix 122

HASTINGS, *Vice-Adm* George Fowler, CB (1814–1876) — B i 1373; DNB ix 124

HASTINGS, *Capt* Hans Francis, RN, *eleventh Earl of Huntingdon* (1779–1828) — DNB ix 124

HASTINGS, John, *second Earl of Pembroke* (1347–1375)
Naval commander — DNB ix 131

HASTINGS, *Adm Sir* Thomas, KCB (1790–1870) — B i 1374; DNB ix 136; M vi 157

HASWELL, Charles Haynes (1809–1907)
Chief engineer, USN, 1844–1852 — DAB 411

HASWELL, *Lieut-Cdr* Gouverneur K., USN (*fl* 1859–1876) — H 935

HASWELL, *Lieut* John Davies, RN (*d* 1868) — Tr 72

HASWELL, *Cdr* William Henry, RN (*d* 1848) — DNB ix 124; Tr 288

HASWELL, *Vice-Adm* William Henry (1818–1900) — B v 603; M viii 359

HATFULL, Edward, *Purser*, RN (*d* 1829) — Tr 128

HATHORN, *Capt* Robert, RN (*d* 1789) — ch vi 368

HATLEY, *Capt* John, RN (*fl* 1782–1806) — M iv 585

HATLUB, *Capt* Robert, RN (*fl* 1664) — ch i 103

HAWKINS, *Capt* James, RN (*fl* 1789)   NA ii 98

HAWKINS, *Sir* John (1532–1595)   CE vi 774; DNB ix
                                                                              212; M*d* xviii 592;
                                                                              NC xxxvii 1

HAWKINS, John (*fl* 1686–1707)
Teacher of navigation   T i 282

HAWKINS, John Croft (1798–1851)
Entered the marine service of the H.E.I.C., 1812. Commodore of the Persian Gulf
squadron, 1845–1847; acting superintendent and commander-in-chief of the Indian
Navy, 1848–1849   B i 1389

HAWKINS, *Sir* Richard (1562?–1622)   CE vi 774; DNB ix
                                                                              223; M*d* xvii 593

HAWKINS, *Capt* Richard, RN (*b* 1768)   M iv 655

HAWKINS, *Lieut* Samuel Holditch, RN (*fl* 1797–1808)   Tr 118

HAWKINS, Thomas Fitzherbert (1781–1837)
Naval officer and pioneer   DA*u*B i 524

HAWKINS, William (*d* 1554?)
Sea-captain and merchant   DNB ix 227

HAWKINS [*or* HAWKYNS], William (*d* 1589)
Sea-captain and merchant   DNB ix 228

HAWKINS [*or* HAWKYNS], William (*d* 1613)
Sea-captain and merchant   DNB ix 229; M*d* xviii
                                                                              593

HAWKSHAW, *Sir* John (1811–1891)
Civil engineer; consulting engineer to the original Channel Tunnel Company;
surveyed the site of the Suez Canal, 1863; member of the international conference
at Paris which considered the proposed inter-oceanic canal across Central America,
1879; engineer to the Amsterdam Ship Canal, 1862–1876   B v 610; DNB xxii 827

HAWKSMOOR [*or* HAWKSMORE], Nicholas (1661–1736)
Architect; clerk of works at Greenwich Hospital from 1698 until shortly
before his death   CE v 775; DNB ix 229

HAWLEY, *Lieut-Cdr* Charles E., USN (*fl* 1849–1869)   H 935

HAWLEY, *Lieut* John M., USN (*fl* 1863–1880)   H 956

HAWTAYNE, *Rear-Adm* Charles Sibthorp John (*fl* 1793–1841)   M ix 263

HAXTON, *Capt* Milton, USN (*fl* 1841–1880)   H 891

HAY, *Capt* George James, CB, RN (*fl* 1806–1846)   M viii 318

HAY, *Rear-Adm* James (*d* 1857)   M xii 205; Tr 136

HAY, *Adm* James Beckford Lewis (1797–1892)   B v 612; M viii 386

HAY, *Rear-Adm* John (1793–1831)   B i 1394; DNB ix 272;
                                                                              M xii 202

HAZLEWOOD, John (*ca* 1726–1800)
American naval officer   DAB 420

HEAD, *Capt* Michael, RN (*fl* 1804–1814)   M xi 319

HEAD, Richard (1637?–1686?)
Author of: 'The Red Sea, a description of the sea-fight between the English and the
Dutch, with an elegy on Sir C. Minnes' (1666)   DNB ix 328

HEAD, *Capt* Richard John, RN (*fl* 1804–1814)   M viii 32

HEALD, *Lieut* Eugene D. F., USN (*fl* 1863–1880)   H 949

HEAP, Samuel Davies, *Surgeon*, USN (1781–1853)   DAB 420

HEARD, Augustine (1785–1868)
Sea-captain and merchant   DAB 420

HEARDER, Jonathan Nash (1809–1876)
Patented improvements in submarine telegraph cables, 1858   B i 1409

HEARLE, John (*b* 1792)
Served as a volunteer, first class, aboard the 'Téméraire' at Trafalgar   Tr 55

HEARNE, Samuel (1745–1792)
Arctic explorer   CE vi 787; DNB ix
                                                                                                      335; M*d* xix 2; MDC
                                                                                                      309

HEASLOP, *Cdr* John Colpoys, RN (*fl* 1805–1817)   M vii 419

HEATH, *Adm Sir* Leopold George, KCB (1817–1907)   DNB xxiiib 234

HEATH, Thomas (*fl* 1714–1765)
Military engineer; astronomer; writer on longitude at sea   DNB ix 349; T ii 180

HEATH, *Capt* Thomas, RN (*d* 1693)   *ch* ii 256

HEATH, Thomas (*fl* 1714–1765)
Instrument-maker; book and instrument seller; writer on navigation   T 129, 208

HEATH, W. (*fl ca* 1830)
Instrument-maker; instruments at National Maritime Museum   T ii 451

HEATHCOTE, *Adm* Edmund (1814–1881)   B i 1412

HEATHCOTE, *Capt* Gilbert, RN (*b* 1739)   M ix 165

HEATHCOTE, *Adm Sir* Henry (1777–1851)   B i 1412; M iii 123

HEATHCOTE, *Capt* John, RN (*fl* 1672)   *ch* i 337

HEATHE, *Capt* John, RN (*fl* 1661–1678)   *ch* i 103

HEATHER, William (*fl* 1763–1815)
Nautical book and chart-seller   T ii 263

HEBB, *Lieut-Col* Clement D., USMC (*fl* 1856–1880)   H 1013

HEBER, Reginald (1783–1826)
Anglican bishop and voyager   DNB ix 355; M*d* xix
                                                                                                      10

HENDERSON, *Capt* Robert, RN (*fl* 1799–1808)   M ix 114; NC xxxviii 177

HENDERSON, *Capt* Thomas, RN (*b* 1795)   M viii 393

HENDERSON, Thomas (1798–1844)
Astronomer   DNB ix 404

HENDERSON, Thomas (*d* 1895)
A founder of the Anchor Line   B v 631

HENDERSON, *Rear-Adm* William Wilmott, CB (1782–1854)   B i 1426; M xii 104; Tr 98

HENDERSON-CALDERWOOD-DURHAM, *Adm Sir* Philip Charles
(1763–1845)   Tr 134

HENDRA, *Capt* Thomas, RN (*fl* 1665)   ch i 168

HENDRY, *Capt* William, RN (*b* 1777)   M xii 398

HENLEY, *Capt* Robert, USN (1783–1828)   DAB 425

HENLEY, William Thomas (1813?–1882)
Telegraphic engineer; began constructing submarine cables at Greenwich in 1857   DNB ix 421

HENN, *Lieut* William, RN (1847–1894)   B v 632

HENNIKER, *Rear-Adm* Major Jacob (1780–1843)   M ix 64

HENRY, *Adm* John (*b* 1731)   M i 64

HENRY, William (1729–1786)
Gunsmith; built an unsuccessful stern-wheel steamboat   DAB 428

HENRY THE NAVIGATOR, *Prince* (1394–1460)
Portuguese prince; promoter of navigation and exploration   A 49; CE vii 23

HENSHAW, John (*fl* 1696–1707)
Mathematical instrument-maker; compass-maker for the Navy   T i 293

HENVY, *Cdr* William, RN (*fl* 1813–1826)   M viii 212

HEPENSTALL, *Cdr* William, RN (*d* 1809)   Tr 304

HEPMAN, Benjamin Franklin (1814–1874)
Served with the Royal Navy until 1840 when he was given command of the Western
Australia colonial schooner 'Champion'; later appointed harbour master of Warrnambool   DAuB i 529

HERBERT, Alfred (*d* 1861)
Marine artist   B i 529

HERBERT, *Adm of the Fleet* Arthur, *third Earl of Torrington* (1647–1716)   ch i 258; DNB ix 620

HERBERT, *Capt* Charles, RN (*fl* 1662–1678)   ch i 103

HERBERT, *Rear-Adm* George Flower (*d* 1868)   M viii 296; Tr 63

HERBERT, George Robert Charles, *thirteenth Earl of Pembroke* (1850–1895)
Vice-commodore of the Royal Cinque Ports Yacht Club   B ii 1446

HERSCHEL, *Sir* John Frederick William, KHG (1792–1871)   A 232; B i 1447; CE vii 73; DNB ix 714

HERVEY, *Vice-Adm* Augustus John, *third Earl of Bristol* (1724–1779)   *ch* vi 27; DNB ix 728

HERVEY, *Capt Lord* John Augustus, RN (*d* 1796)   NA ii 95

HERVEY, *Capt the Hon* William, RN (1699–1776)   *ch* iv 180

HESKETH, *Sir* Peter, *first Baronet Fleetwood* (1801–1866)
Projected and began construction of the port and town of Fleetwood, 1836   B i 1067, 1452

HEVELIUS [HEVEL *or* HÖVELKE], Johann (1611–1687)   CE vii 80

HEWELL, *Capt* John, RN (*fl* 1666)   *ch* i 236

HEWES, Joseph (1730–1779)
First executive head of the navy of the United States   DAB 432

HEWES, *Capt* Thomas Oldacres, RN (*fl* 1794–1842)   M vii 13

HEWET, *Capt Sir* William, RN (*d* 1749)   *ch* v 32

HEWETT, *Capt Sir* William, RN (*d* 1761)   *ch* vi 368

HEWETT, *Cdr* William, RN (*fl* 1805–1826)   M viii 211

HEWETT, *Adm Sir* William Nathan Wrighte, VC, KCB, KCSI (1834–1888)   B i 1454; DNB ix 756

HEWIT, *Capt* Charles, RN (*fl* 1781–1814)   M xi 371

HEWITT, *Capt* W., RN (*fl* 1820–1833)   T ii 423

HEWSON, *Vice-Adm* George (1776–1860)   M xii 121; Tr 70

HEXT, *Capt* William, RN (*fl* 1780)   M vi 382

HEYERMAN, *Lieut-Cdr* Oscar Frederick, USN (*fl* 1861–1878)   H 928

HEYES, Thomas (*fl ca* 1830)
Chronometer-maker   T ii 451

HEYL, Theodore C., *Surgeon*, USN (*fl* 1870–1880)   H 979

HEYN, Piet (1578–1629)
Dutch naval officer   CE vi 823

HEYWOOD, *Lieut* Charles, USN (*fl* 1858–1880)   H 1013

HEYWOOD, *Capt* Peter, RN (*fl* 1673–1680)   *ch* ii 49

HEYWOOD, *Capt* Peter, RN (1773–1831)   DNB ix 787; M iv 746; Md xix 412

HIATT, *Lieut* Henry, RN (*fl* 1805–1815)   Tr 65

HIBBERT, George (1757–1837)
West India merchant; instrumental in originating and maturing plans for the establishment of the West India docks   DNB ix 794

HIBBERT, *Cdr* Stephen D., USN (*fl* 1851–1880)   H 1002

HICHBORN, *Rear-Adm* Philip, USN (1839–1910)   DAB 433

HILL, *Sir* Edward Maurice (1862–1934)
Judge of the Probate, Divorce and Admiralty division, 1917–1930, tried many
Admiralty cases arising out of the First World War   DNB xxvi 428

HILL, George William (1838–1914)
Astronomer   DAB 436

HILL, *Capt* Henry, RN (*fl* 1787–1810)   M iii 319

HILL, James (1734–1811)
Shipbuilder   DAB 436

HILL, *Rear-Adm* John (*d* 1773)   *ch* v 392

HILL, *Rear-Adm Sir* John (1774–1855)   B i 1471; *ch* v 392

HILL, *Capt* Marcus Samuel, RN (*fl* 1793–1802)   M iii 488

HILL, Nathaniel (*fl* 1746–1766)
Instrument and globe-maker   T ii 208

HILL, *Capt* Nicholas, RN (*fl* 1665–1667)   *ch* i 168

HILL, *Reverend* Pascoe Grenfell (1804–1882)
Served as a chaplain RN, 1836–1845   B i 1473

HILL, *Cdr* Thomas, RN (*fl* 1794–1802)   M vi 294

HILL, William (*fl* 1634–1638)
Sea-captain and coloniser; governor of Lord Baltimore's colony in Maryland   DCB i 369

HILL, *Capt* William, RN (*fl* 1661–1667)   *ch* i 57

HILL, *Capt* William, RN (1783–1840)   M xii 118; Tr 161

HILLARY, *Sir* Edmund Percival, KBE (*b* 1919)
New Zealand Antarctic explorer   A 617

HILLARY, *Sir* William (1771–1847)
Founder of the Royal National Lifeboat Institution   DNB xxii 847

HILLIER, *Cdr* Curry William, RN (*b* 1778)   M vii 205

HILLIER, *Cdr* George, RN (*fl* 1787–1824)   M viii 131

HILLS, *Lieut* Alexander, RN (*b* 1780)   Tr 14

HILLS, Arnold Frank (1857–1927)
Shipbuilder; a director of the Thames Ironworks & Shipbuilding Company   DNB xxv 418

HILLS, *Capt* George, RN (*b* 1777)   M xi 301

HILLSOME, *Capt* George, RN (*fl* 1666)   *ch* i 236

HILLYAR, *Adm Sir* Charles Farrel, KCB (1818–1888)   B i 1478; v 662

HILLYAR, *Adm* Henry Schanck, CB (1820–1893)   B v 662

HILLYAR, *Rear-Adm Sir* James, KCB, KCH (*d* 1843)   DNB ix 883; M iv 849

HILLYAR, Robert Purkis, RN (*d* 1855)
Inspector-general of hospitals and fleets, 1841   B i 1478

HOARE, *Adm* Edward Wallis (1778–1870)   M x 195

HOARE, *Capt* Richard, RN (1793–1850)   M vi 13

HOBART, *Vice-Adm* Augustus Charles (1822–1886)   B i 1486

HOBART [*or* HUBBARD], *Capt* Henry, RN (*d* 1711)   *ch* iii 249

HOBART-HAMPDEN, *Adm* Augustus Charles ('Hobart Pasha')
(1828–1882)   CE vii 159; DNB ix
                                                                   930

HOBBS, *Lieut-Cdr* I. Goodwin, USN (*fl* 1864–1880)   H 995

HOBBS, *Capt* James, RN (*d* 1770)   *ch* vi 169

HOBBS, *Lieut* John, RN (*d* 1826)   Tr 287

HOBBS, *Capt* William, RN (*fl* 1672–1678)   *ch* i 337

HOBSON, *Lieut* Joseph B., USN (*fl* 1865–1880)   H 961

HOBSON, *Capt* William, RN (1793–1842)   AE i 617; DAuB i 545;
                                                                   M vi 42

HOBSON, *Capt* William Robert, RN (1831–1880)   B i 1490

HOCKADAY, *Capt* William, RN (*d* 1724)   *ch* iii 33

HOCKINGS, *Capt* Robert, RN (*b* 1776)   M xii 290

HOCKLY, *Lieut* William, RN (*fl* 1805–1823)   Tr 244

HOCQUART, Gilles (1694–1783)
Commissary of marine; intendant of New France   MDC 322

HODDER, *Capt* Edward, RN (*d* 1829)   M xi 395

HODDER, Edward Mulberry (1810–1878)
Surgeon; commodore of Royal Canadian Yacht Club; writer on the Lake Ontario ports   MDC 323

HODDER, *Capt* Richard, RN (*fl* 1664–1684)   *ch* ii 14

HODDESON, *Sir* Christopher (1534–1611)
Master of the Merchant Adventurers Company   DNB xxii 853

HODGE, *Capt* Andrew, RN (*fl* 1800–1807)   M vi 365

HODGE, Arthur (*fl* 1822)
Instrument-maker, inventor of perpetual log   T ii 424

HODGES, *Maj-Gen* Harry Foote, USA (1860–1929)
Engineer in charge of the design of the locks, dams and regulating works on the
Panama Canal   DAB 441

HODGES, *Capt* Richard, RN (*fl* 1660–1664)   *ch* i 15

HODGES, *Sir* William (1808–1868)
Judge of vice-admiralty court, 1858–1868   B i 1492; DNB ix 956

HODGESON, Marmaduke (*fl* 1690)
Teacher of navigation and use of globes   T i 286

HOLDSTOCK, Alfred Worsley (1820–1901)
Marine artist   MDC 324

HOLE, *Cdr* Charles, RN (*b* 1781)   M vii 76

HOLE, *Adm* Lewis (1779–1870)   B i 1505; M xi 182;
                                                                            Tr 106

HOLGATE, *Lieut* Robert, RN (*b* 1784)   Tr 54

HOLLAND, *Capt* Edward, RN (*d* 1724 *or* 1736)   *ch* iii 399

HOLLAND, John Philip (1840–1914)   DAB 446

HOLLAND, *Capt* John Wentworth, RN (*fl* 1789–1806)   M ix 31

HOLLAND, *Capt* Philip, RN (*fl* 1666–1682)   *ch* i 236

HOLLAND, *Capt* Robert, RN (*fl* 1673)   *ch* i 396

HOLLAND, Samuel (1728?–1801)
Cartographer   CE vii 175; T ii 263

HOLLAR, Wenceslaus (1607–1677)
Czech; engraver of maps, plans and views; surveyor   CE vii 179; *chb* 433;
                                                                            Md xix 554; T ii 211

HOLLES, *Capt Sir* Frescheville, RN (1641–1672)   *ch* i 236; DNB ix 1060

HOLLES, John, *first Earl of Clare* (1564?–1637)
Soldier and politician; served as a volunteer against the Armada (1588) and on the
Azores expedition (1597)   DNB ix 1062

HOLLINS, George Nichols, CSN (1799–1878)   DAB 446

HOLLINGWORTH, *Adm* John Ibbetson (*d* 1861)   B i 1511; M x 349

HOLLIS, *Vice-Adm* Aiskew Paffard (1764–1844)   DNB ix 1070; M iii
                                                                            115

HOLLIS, Ira Nelson (1856–1930)
Engineer in the USN, 1878–1893   DAB 446

HOLLOND [*or* HOLLAND], John (*fl* 1638–1659)
Naval writer   DNB xxii 861

HOLLOWAY, *Adm* John (*d* 1826)   M i 101; *Md* xix 557;
                                                                            NA ii 90; NC xix 353;
                                                                            R ii 209

HOLLOWAY, *Gen-Sir* Thomas, KCB, RM (1810–1875)   B i 1512

HOLLWALL [*or* HOLLWELL], *Capt* John, RN (*d* 1775)   *ch* vi 106

HOLMAN, Francis (*fl* 1760–1790)
Marine painter   DNB ix 1076

HOLMAN, James (1786–1857)
Blind traveller; became totally blind at the age of 25 and was compelled to resign
his naval commission 1810. Wrote an account of his voyage round the world,
1827–32   B i 1513; DNB ix 1076

HONYMAN, *Adm* Robert (*fl* 1782–1847)   M iii 179

HOOD, *Adm* Alexander, *first Viscount Bridport* (1727–1814)   CE vii 205; DNB ix
                                                                         1147; M*d* xix 596;
                                                                         NA i 98; NC i 165;
                                                                         R i 202

HOOD, *Capt* Alexander, RN (1758–1798)   DNB ix 1146; NC vi
                                                                         173; R iv 48

HOOD, *Adm* Arthur William Acland, GCB, *first Baron Hood* (1824–1901)   DNB xxiiib 293

HOOD, *Rear-Adm Sir* Horace Lambert Alexander, KCB, DSO (1870–1916)   DNB xxiv 266

HOOD, John (1720–1783?)
Surveyor and inventor; published: 'Tables of difference of latitude & departure for
navigators, land surveyors, &c.' (1772); is said to have anticipated the invention of
Hadley's Quadrant   DNB ix 1152; T ii 290

HOOD, *Adm* Samuel, *first Viscount Hood* (1724–1816)   CE vii 206; DNB ix
                                                                         1157; NC ii 1; R i 242

HOOD, *Vice-Adm Sir* Samuel (1752–1814)   DNB ix 1155; NC xvii 1

HOOD, *Cdr* Silas Thomson, RN (*b* 1789)   M vii 357

HOOD, Thomas (*fl* 1582–1598)
Mathematician; author of: 'The Mariners Guide' (1596); corrected Bourne's: 'A
Regiment for the Sea' in 1592   DNB ix 1164; T i 179

HOOD, *Capt* William John Thomson, RN (1794–1857)   M viii 257; T ii 424;
                                                                         Tr 164

HOOKE, *Capt* Edmund, RN (*d* 1733)   *ch* iv 36

HOOKE, John (*fl* 1677)
Compass-maker; possibly worked for Narborough   T i 274

HOOKE, Robert (1635–1703)   CE vii 207; DNB ix
                                                                         1177; T i 243

HOOKER, *Lieut-Cdr* Edward, USN (*fl* 1861–1880)   H 925

HOOKER, *Sir* Joseph Dalton, OM, GCSI (1817–1911)
Botanist; naturalist on Sir J. C. Ross's 1839–1843 Antarctic expedition DNB xxiiib 294

HOOPPELL, Robert Eli (1833–1895)
Author of: 'A practical introduction to navigation & nautical astronomy' (1871) B v 695

HOOPER, Edward (1795–1865)   B i 1527

HOOPER, Frederic Edward Eden (1842–1886)
Clerk at the Admiralty   B i 1527

HOOPER, *Capt* George Wastell, RN (*fl* 1800–1817)   M xii 138

HOOPER, *Capt* George William, RN (*d* 1839)   Tr 61

HOOPER, *Capt* John, RN (*d* 1692)   *ch* iii 106

HOOPER, *Capt* Robert, RN (*fl* 1665–1671)   *ch* i 168

HOOPER, *Lieut* William Hulme, RN (1827–1854)   B i 1528; DNB ix 1201

HOORE [*or* HORE], Richard (*fl* 1507–1540)
Merchant, navigator; promoter of Newfoundland colonisation DCB i 371

HOPE, *Capt* Charles, RN (*fl* 1799)   NA ii 64

HOPE, *Capt* Charles, RN (*fl* 1816–1826)   M v 281

HOPE, *Capt* Charles Webley, RN (1829–1880)   B i 1529

HOPE, *Capt* David, RN (*b* 1787)   M vi 111

HOPE, *Cdr* George, RN (*fl* 1813–1833)   M viii 266

HOPE, *Rear-Adm* George Johnstone, KCB (1767–1818)   Tr 180

HOPE, *Adm Sir* Henry, KCB (1787–1863)   B i 1530; DNB ix
                                                              1208; M ix 314

HOPE, *Adm of the Fleet Sir* James, GCB (1808–1881)   B i 1531; DNB ix 1212

HOPE, *Vice-Adm* Sackett (*d* 1868)   B i 1532

HOPE, William (1863–1931)
Canadian landscape and marine painter; official war artist MDC 314

HOPE, *Vice-Adm Sir* William Johnstone, GCB (1766–1831)   DNB ix 1223; M ii
                                                              507; NC xviii 269;
                                                              R iii 122

HOPKINS, *Cdr* Alfred, USN (*fl* 1851–1880)   H 903

HOPKINS, Edward Augustus (1822–1891)   DAB 452

HOPKINS, *Cdre* Esek, USN (1718–1802)   CE vii 211; DAB 452;
                                                              H 346

HOPKINS, *Capt* Harry, RN (*fl* 1787–1814)   M xii 272

HOPKINS, Manley (1817/8–1887)
Author of: 'A manual of marine insurance' (1867)   B v 698

HOPKINS, John Burroughs (1742–1796)
American naval officer and privateer   DAB 452

HOPKINS, *Cdre* William E., USN (*fl* 1839–1880)   H 347

HOPKINSON, . . . (*fl* 1783)
Writer on mechanical log   T ii 314

HOPKINSON, Francis (1737–1791)
Chairman of the United States Navy Board, 1776–1778   DAB 453

HOPKINSON, John (1849–1888)
*Electrical engineer; invented the group flash system to enable mariners to distinguish
one lighthouse from another*   B v 698; DNB xxii 864

HOPKINSON, *Cdr* Simon, RN (*fl* 1791–1821)   M viii 68

HOPLEY, William, *Surgeon*, RN (*d* 1815)   DAuB i 553

HOPPER, John, *Purser*, RN (*d* 1837)   Tr 73

HOPPNER, *Capt* Henry Parkyns (*fl* 1815–1825)   M v 279; M*d* xix 623

HOPSON, *Vice-Adm* Edward (*d* 1728)   *ch* iii 128

HOPSON(N), *Vice-Adm Sir* Thomas (1642–1717)   *ch* ii 50; DNB ix 1238

HOPWOOD, Francis John Stephens, GCMG, GCVO, KCB, KCSI, *first Baron Southborough* (1860–1947)
Civil lord of the Admiralty, 1912–1917   DNB xxvii 408

HORD, William T., *Surgeon*, USN (*fl* 1854–1879)   H 969

HORE, *Rear-Adm* Daniel (*d* 1762)   *ch* v 105

HORE, *Cdr* Herbert William, RN (*fl* 1782–1814)   M vii 216

HORE, *Cdr* Samuel Bradstreet, RN (*b* 1791)   M vii 114

HORN, Henry (*d* 1899)
Served in the merchant service and later with the naval brigade during the Crimean War   B v 701

HORN, *Cdr* Philip Thicknesse, RN (*fl* 1801–1816)   M vii 406

HORNBY, *Adm of the Fleet Sir* Geoffrey Thomas Phipps, GCB (1828–1895)   B v 702; DNB xxii 866

HORNBY, *Adm Sir* Phipps, GCB (1785–1867)   B i 1538; DNB ix 1249; M x 70

HORNBY, Thomas Dyson (1822–1889)
Chairman of Liverpool Dock Board, 1876–1889   B v 703

HORNBY, *Adm Sir* William Wyndham, KCB (1812–1899)   B v 703

HORNE, *Capt* Count, RN (*fl* 1671–1672)   *ch* i 337

HORNE, *Capt* Edmund, RN (*d* 1764)   *ch* v 392

HORNE [*or* HERNE], *Capt* John, RN (*d* 1705)   *ch* iii 33

HORNE, Robert Stevenson, KBE, *Viscount Horne of Slamannan* (1871–1940)
Civil lord of the Admiralty, 1918–1919: a director of the Suez Canal Company   DNB xxvi 444

HORNER, Frederick, *Surgeon,* USN (*fl* 1851–1865)   H 985

HORNER, G. R. B., *Medical-Director,* USN (*fl* 1826–1866)   H 981

HORNSBY, Thomas (1733–1810)
Astronomer   DNB ix 1266

HORRIE, *Lieut* James, RN (*d* 1826)   Tr 124

HORROCKS, Jeremiah (1617?–1641)
Astronomer   DNB ix 1267

HORSBURGH, James (1762–1836)
Hydrographer   DNB ix 1270; M*d* xx 1; T ii 314

HORSBURGH, John (1791–1869)
Engraved several plates for E. W. Cooke's: 'Southern Coast of England'   DNB ix 1271

HOTHAM, *Adm* William, KH (1794–1873)   B i 1546; M ii 580;
                                                                v 212; R iii 336

HOUGH, George Washington (1836–1909)
Astronomer   DAB 456

HOUGH, *Cdr* John James, RN (*fl* 1799–1846)   M viii 242

HOULDING, *Capt* William, RN (*d* 1731)   ch iv 11

HOULTON, *Rear-Adm* John (*d* 1791)   ch vi 451

HOUSE, *Lieut* Jerome B., USN (*d* 1881)   H 956

HOUSTON, *Lieut-Cdr* Edwin S., USN (*fl* 1861–1880)   H 937

HOUSTON, *Capt* George P., USN (*fl* 1860–1879)   H 1014

HOUSTON, *Lieut* Nelson, USN (*fl* 1865–1880)   H 961

HOUSTON, *Adm* Wallace (1811–1891)   B i 1550

HOUTMAN, Frederik de (1571?–1627)
Dutch East India Company officer; discovered the western coast of Australia in 1619   DAuB i 555

HOUTMAN, Cornelius de (*ca* 1540–1599)   Md xx 64

HOVELL, William Hilton, *Master*, RN (1786–1875)   AE i 628

HOW [*or* HOWES], *Capt* William, RN (*fl* 1666–1667)   ch i 238

HOWARD, Charles, *Baron Howard of Effingham & Earl of Nottingham*
(1536–1624)   CE vii 270; DNB X 1;
                                                               H 350; Md xx 65; NC
                                                               xvii 89

HOWARD, *Capt* Charles, RN (*fl* 1681–1705)   ch iii 293

HOWARD, *Sir* Edward, KG (1477?–1513)
Lord high admiral   DNB X 10

HOWARD, Edward (*d* 1841)
Novelist; author of: 'Rattlin the Reefer' (1836); served in the Royal Navy up to 1832   DNB X 13

HOWARD, *Adm* Edward Granville George, *Lord Lanerton* (1809–1880)   M viii 390

HOWARD, *Vice-Adm* Edward Henry (1832–1890)   B i 1551

HOWARD, Henry, KG, *first Earl of Northampton* (1540–1614)
Warden of the Cinque Ports   DNB X 28

HOWARD, John, *first Duke of Norfolk* (1430?–1485)
English military and naval commander; deputy-governor of Calais; Lord Admiral of
England, Ireland, and Aquitaine   Md xxxi 34

HOWARD, John (1726?–1790)
Philanthropist; was a passenger on the packet 'Hanover' which was captured by a
French privateer in 1756, obtained a parole and returned to England. There, he brought
the crew's suffering to the notice of the commissioners for sick and wounded sailors
and was instrumental in securing their release   DNB X 44

HUALT DE MONTMAGNY, Charles (*ca* 1583–1653)
*Naval officer in the service of the Order of Malta; first governor and lieutenant-general
of New France*   DCB i 372; MDC 523

HUBBARD, *Lieut* Armiger Watts, RN (*d* 1844)   Tr 34

HUBBARD, Benjamin (*fl* 1647–1656)
Writer on navigation   T i 221

HUBBARD [*or* HOBART], *Capt* Henry, RN (*d* 1711)   ch iii 249

HUBBART, *Capt* John, RN (*fl* 1662–1693)   ch i 81

HUBBARD, *Capt* John, RN (*d* 1668)   ch i 168

HUBBARD, *Capt* John, RN (*fl* 1688–1710)   ch ii 317

HUBBARD, *Capt* John, RN (*d* 1728)   ch iv 68

HUBBARD, *Lieut* John, USN (*fl* 1866–1878)   H 964

HUBBARD, *Capt* Nathaniel, RN (*d* 1731)   ch iv 11

HUBBARD, *Lieut-Cdr* Socrates, USN (*fl* 1861–1879)   H 933

HUBNER, Jean (1608–1671)
German geographer   Md xx 92

HUDDART, James (1847–1901)
Australian shipowner   DNB xxiiib 313

HUDDART, Joseph (1741–1816)
Hydrographer; captain in the East India Company   DNB x 141; T ii 264

HUDSON, . . . (*fl* 1700–1715)
Instrument-maker; backstaff at National Maritime Museum   T i 297

HUDSON, Adrian, *Surgeon*, USN (*fl* 1861–1880)   H 973

HUDSON, *Rear-Adm* Charles (*fl* 1757–1793)   ch vi 565

HUDSON, Henry (*fl* 1607–1611)
Explorer and navigator   CE vii 276; DAB 464;
                                                                                       DCB i 374; DNB x 147;
                                                                                       H 351; MDC 331

HUDSON, John (*ca* 1592–*ca* 1611)
Companion and probably son of Henry Hudson   DCB i 379

HUDSON, *Capt* John, RN (*d* 1823)   M x 220

HUDSON, *Lieut* John, RN (*d* 1848)   Tr 215

HUDSON, *Capt* John, RN (1796–1869)   B v 718; M viii 379

HUDSON, *Capt* Richard, RN (*fl* 1673)   ch i 397

HUDSON, *Capt* Thomas, RN (*d* 1702)   ch iii 219

HUDSON, William, *Master*, RN (*d* 1835)   Tr 96

HUGHES, *Capt* William James, RN (*b* 1804)   M vi 351

HUISH, *Lieut* George, RN (*fl* 1800–1809)   Tr 168

HUISH, *Capt* Henry, RN (*d* 1763)   *ch* v 473

HUISH, Robert (1777–1850)
Miscellaneous author; wrote: 'The last voyage of Captain Sir John Ross . . .' (1835)   DNB xxii 882

HULL, *Cdre* Isaac, USN (1773–1843)   CE vii 283; DAB 466;
                                                                               H 352

HULL, *Capt* John, RN (*fl* 1673)   *ch* i 397

HULL, *Cdre* Joseph, USN (*fl* 1813–1861)   H 352

HULLS [*or* HULL], Jonathan (*fl* 1737)
Inventor; first person to attempt to propel a vessel using steam   DNB x 200

HUMBLE, *Capt* William, RN (*fl* 1666–1672)   *ch* i 238

HUMBOLDT, Friederich Heinrich Alexander, *Baron von* (1769–1859)   CE vii 285

HUME, *Capt* Francis, RN (*d* 1733)   *ch* iv 46

HUME, *Capt* John, RN (*d* 1759)   *ch* v 394

HUMPHREYS, Joshua (1751–1838)
Shipbuilder and naval architect   DAB 467

HUMPHREYS, *Capt Sir* Salusbury Price, CB (*b* 1778)   M iv 591; viii 449;
                                                                               NC xxviii 353

HUNKER, *Lieut* John J., USN (*fl* 1862–1880)   H 944

HUNN, *Capt* Frederick, RN (*fl* 1803–1846)   M xii 435

HUNNEWELL, James (1794–1869)
Sea captain and merchant   DAB 468

HUNT, George, *Chief Engineer*, USN (*fl* 1861–1880)   H 1011

HUNT, Harry (*fl* 1673–1713)
Maker of marine barometers and other instruments; assistant to Robert Hooke T i 266

HUNT, *Cdr* Joseph, RN (*d* 1761)   *ch* vi 400

HUNT, *Maj* Paul, RM (*d* 1818)   Tr 146

HUNT, *Capt* Peter, RN (*d* 1824)   M iv 844

HUNT, Thomas William (*fl* 1805–1848)
Midshipman aboard the 'Prince' at Trafalgar   Tr 81

HUNT, *Cdre* Timothy A., USN (*fl* 1825–1867)   H 353

HUNT, William (*fl* 1673–1698)
Inventor of navigational slide-rule   T i 267

HUNTER, *Capt* Colin, RN (*fl* 1698–1700)   *ch* iii 193

HUNTER, Colin (1841–1904)
Marine artist   DNB xxiiib 328

HUNTER, *Lieut* David, RN (*fl* 1805–1809)   Tr 249

HUSSEY, William Joseph (1662–1926)
Astronomer   DAB 472

HUTCHENSON, *Capt* Thomas Howard, RN (*d* 1758)   *ch* vi 47

HUTCHESON, *Capt* Francis Deans, RN (*fl* 1813–1841)   M viii 301

HUTCHESON, *Adm* Francis Drake (1800–1875)   B i 1604

HUTCHINS, *Lieut* Charles Thomas, USN (*fl* 1862–1880)   H 946

HUTCHINS, *Capt* Stephen, RN (*d* 1709)   *ch* iii 294

HUTCHINS, Thomas (1730–1789)
American surveyor   CE vii 319

HUTCHINSON, *Cdr* Charles, RN (*fl* 1800–1834)   M vii 304

HUTCHINSON, *Cdr the Hon* Coote Hely, RN (*fl* 1817–1834)   M viii 97

HUTCHINSON, *Capt* Edward, RN (*b* 1771)   M vi 267

HUTCHINSON, *Cdr* George, RN (*fl* 1806–1821)   M viii 94

HUTCHINSON, William (1715–1801)
Mariner and writer on seamanship   DNB X 346; T ii 181

HUTCHINSON, *Cdr* William, RN (*fl* 1790–1843)   M viii 255

HUTCHINSON, *Cdr* William, RN (*fl* 1806–1814)   M vii 198

HUTT, *Capt* John, RN (1746–1794)   DNB X 349

HUTTON, *Rear-Adm* Frederick (1804–1866)   B i 1608

HUTTON, *Capt* John, RN (*fl* 1666)   *ch* i 238

HUXLEY, Thomas Henry (1825–1895)
Biologist; accompanied the 'Challenger' expedition, 1846–1850   B V 740; CE vii 320;
                                                                                            DAuB i 577; DNB xxii
                                                                                            894

HUYGENS, Christian (1629–1695)
Dutch astronomer and mathematician   A 261; CE vii 321;
                                                                                            Md xx 222

HYATT, *Capt* Abraham, RN (*fl* 1673)   *ch* i 397

HYDE, *Capt* Frederick, RN (*fl* 1746–1764)   *ch* v 473

HYDE, *Lieut* Frederick G., USN (*b* 1847)   H 949

HYVEE, Ryner (*fl* 1703–1704)
Teacher of navigation   T i 299

IBERVILLE, Pierre Le Moyne, *Sieur d'* (1661–1706)
French-Canadian naval commander; governor of Louisiana   MDC 337

IBN BATUTA, Abu Abdullah Mohammed (1304–1377)
Arabian traveller   CE vii

INGRAM, *Cdr* Robert, RN (*d ca* 1859)   M viii 338

INGRAM, Walter (1855–1888)
Officer in the Middlesex yeomanry; attached to Beresford's naval corps, 1884   DNB X 451

INMAN, *Capt* Henry, RN (1762–1809)   NC XXV 1

INMAN, James (1776–1859)
Professor of navigation and nautical science   B ii 15; DNB X 455;
                                                                                    T ii 342

INMAN, William (1825–1881)
Founder of the Inman Line   B ii 16; DNB X 457

INMAN, *Cdre* William, USN (*d* 1872)   H 361

INNES, *Capt* Alexander, RN (*d* 1785)   *ch* vi 182

INNES, *Capt* Alexander, RN (*fl* 1794–1810)   M X 267

INNES, Archibald Clunes (1800–1857)
Captain of the guard in Australian convict ship, army officer, farmer, police magistrate   DAuB ii 3

INNES, *Capt* James, RN (*d* 1779)   *ch* vi 444

INNES, *Capt* Thomas, RN (*d* 1750)   *ch* v 474

INNES, *Capt* Thomas, RN (*fl* 1790–1810)   M X 213

INNES, W. (*fl* 1818)
Teacher of navigation   T ii 397

INSAM [*or* ENSOM], *Capt* Robert, RN (*d* 1667)   *ch* i 86

INSKIP, *Reverend* Robert Mills, *Chaplain*, RN (1816–1890)   B ii 18

IRBY, *Capt* Charles Leonard, RN (1789–1845)   DNB X 465; M vi 1

IRBY, *Rear-Adm the Hon* Frederick Paul (1779–1844)   DNB X 465; M iii 488;
                                                                                    R iv 422

IRONS, *Cdr* John, RN (*fl* 1790–1811)   M vii 12

IRVINE, *Capt* Charles Chamberlayne, RN (*fl* 1789–1832)   M vi 368

IRVINE, *Lieut* John C., USN (*fl* 1864–1880)   H 956

IRVING, Charles, *Surgeon*, RN (1770–1794)
Inventor of a method of desalination   T ii 290

IRVING, John (*d* 1795)
Surgeon on convict transports to Australia   DAuB ii 4

IRVING, Washington (1783–1859)
Author of: 'History of the life and voyages of Christopher Columbus' (1828)   CE vii 758; DAB 479

IRWIN, Christopher (*fl* 1758–1763)
Inventor of a marine chair for longitude observations   T ii 235

IRWIN, *Cdr* James, RN (*d* 1825)   M vi 294

ISACHSEN, Gunnar Invald (1868–1939)
Norwegian polar explorer   CE vii 759

JACKSON, *Capt* William, RM (*fl* 1795–1819)   Tr 45

JACKSON, *Capt* William Rush, RN (*d* 1835)   M vii 127

JACOB, *Lieut* Edwin, USN (*fl* 1862–1880)   H 949

JACOB, *Vice-Adm* Louis Léon *Comte* (1768–1854)   s i 589

JACOB, *Capt* Thomas, RN (*fl* 1665–1678)   ch ii 56

JACOB, William Stephen (1813–1862)
Astronomer   B ii 44; DNB X 560

JACOBS, *Capt* Maximilian, RN (*d ca* 1802)   ch vi 318

JACOBS, *Capt* Thomas, RN (*d* 1748)   ch iv 11

JACOBY, *Lieut* Henry M., USN (*fl* 1866–1880)   H 984

JACOMB, William (1832–1887)
Assistant to Gainsford in the supervision of the building of the 'Great Eastern'   B ii 46

JAGO, *Lieut* Samuel, RN (*fl* 1805–1819)   Tr 99

JAILLOT, Alexis Hubert(1632–1712)
French cartographer   CE viii 7; Md xx 525

JALOBERT, Macé (*fl* 1528–1555)
Sea-captain and pilot; brother-in-law and companion of Jaques Cartier   DCB i 384

JAMES, *Rear-Adm* Bartholomew (1752–1827)   DNB X 640; M iii 181

JAMES, *Cdr* Edwin, RN (*d* 1827)   M vii 156

JAMES, *Lieut-Gen Sir* Henry (1803–1877)
Superintendent of constructional works at Portsmouth dockyard, 1846–1850;
director-general of the Ordnance Survey, 1854–1875   B ii 49; DNB X 647

JAMES, *Cdr* Jacob, RN (*fl* 1784–1832)   M vi 261

JAMES, *Cdr* James, RM (1760–1845)   M viii 296

JAMES, John (*d* 1746)
Architect; clerk of works at Greenwich Hospital, 1705–1746   DNB X 650

JAMES, *Capt* Joseph, RN (*d* 1837)   M X 39

JAMES, *Capt* Richard, RN (*fl* 1664–1677)   ch i 239

JAMES, Thomas (*ca* 1593–*ca* 1635)
Sea-captain; explorer of North West Passage   DCB i 384; MDC 344

JAMES, *Sir* William (1721–1783)
Commodore of the Bombay Marine   DNB X 664

JAMES, William (*d* 1827)
Writer on naval history; author of: 'The Naval History of Great Britain, from the
declaration of war by France in 1793 to the accession of George IV', 5 vols
(1822–1824)   DNB X 665

JAMESON, *Capt* William, RN (*d* 1706)   ch iii 336

JAMIESON, John Lennox Kincaid (1826–1883)
Marine engineer   B ii 58

JAMIESON, Robert (*fl* 1820)
Instrument-maker; designer of marine thermometer case   T ii 425

JAMIESON, Robert (*d* 1861)
*Merchant; equipped the 'Ethiope' steamer which explored several West African
rivers (1839)*   B ii 59

JAMISON, *Sir* John, *Surgeon*, RN (*d* 1844)   AE i 680; Tr 270;
                                                                                                   DAuB ii 10

JAMISON, Thomas, *Surgeon*, RN (1745–1811)   DAuB ii 12

JANE, *Capt* Henry, RN (*fl* 1810–1835)   M v 223

JANE, *Lieut* John, RN (*d* 1835)   Tr 243

JANSSEN, Pierre Jules César (1824–1907)
French astronomer   CE viii 18

JANSSEN [*or* JANZ], Willem (*fl* 1603–1628)
*Dutch seaman; navigation expert; voyager to Australia; vice-admiral of Anglo-Dutch
fleet of defence in East Indies*   DAuB ii 13

JANSSON, Jan (*fl* 1607–1664)
Dutch map publisher and cartographer   CE viii 18; chb 435

JANVERIN, *Lieut* Thomas, RN (*d* 1826)   Tr 181

JANVRIN, *Capt* Richard Gaire, RN (*d* 1835)   M x 271

JAQUES, *Capt* William, RN (*fl* 1667–1678)   ch i 294

JAQUES, *Lieut* William H., USN (*fl* 1863–1880)   H 948

JARDINE, James (1776–1858)
*Constructed the Union Canal, 1822; first person to determine the mean level
of the sea, 1809*   B ii 61; DNB x 687

JARDINE, *Sir* Robert (1825–1905)   DNB xxii 363

JASPER, *Capt* Richard, RN (*d* 1761)   ch v 394

JASPER, *Lieut* Robert T., USN (*fl* 1864–1880)   H 954

JAUNCEY, *Capt* Henry Fyge, RN (*d* 1834)   M xii 314

JAY, John (*d* 1528)
Shipowner, merchant, promoter of Atlantic voyages, probably an associate of Cabot   DCB i 386

JEAFFRESON, John Cordy (1831–1901)
*Author of: 'Lady Hamilton & Lord Nelson' (1888) and: 'The Queen of Naples &
Lord Nelson' (1889)*   DNB xxiiib 364

JEAN, Philip (1755–1802)
Miniature painter; served at one time in the navy   DNB x 694

JEANS, Henry William (1804–1881)
Mathematical master at Royal Naval College Portsmouth, 1839–1866; writer on
nautical astronomy   B ii 65

JEANS, *Sir* James Hopwood (1877–1946)
Astronomer   CE viii 67; DNB XXVii
                                                                                            430

JEAURAT, Edme-Sébastien (1724–1803)
Astronomer   M*d* xxi 27

JEEJEEBHOY, *Sir* Jamsetjee (1783–1859)
Philanthropist; made several trading voyages to China, 1799–1804   DNB X 700

JEFFERIES, *Capt* John, RN (*fl* 1664–1665)   *ch* i 106

JEFFERIS, *Cdr* Charles, RN (1798–1875)   B ii 68

JEFFERS, *Cdre* William Nicholson, USN (1824–1883)   DAB 492; H 404

JEFFERY, *Cdr* Samuel, RN (*fl* 1805–1807)   M vi 364

JEFFERYS, John (*fl* 1726–1753)
Maker of watches carried on John Campbell's voyages   T ii 162

JEFFERYS, Thomas (*fl* 1732–1771)
Map-engraver and publisher   CE viii 69; *chb* 435;
                                                                                            DNB X 706; M*d* xxi
                                                                                            40; T ii 181

JEFFREYS, *Lieut* Charles, RN (1782–1826)   DA*u*B ii 15

JEFFREYS, *Capt* Robert, RN (*d* 1780)   *ch* v 396

JEKYLL, *Capt* Edward, RN (*d* 1776)   *ch* vi 73

JEKYLL, *Cdr* John, RN (*d* 1839)   M vii 65

JELFE, *Capt* Andrews, RN (*d* 1765)   *ch* v 473

JELLICOE, *Adm of the Fleet* John Rushworth, GCB, OM, GCVO (1859–1935)   CE viii 70; DNB XXVi
                                                                                            474

JEMMETT, *Capt* William, RN (*fl* 1673)   *ch* i 397

JENIFER, *Capt* John, RN (*fl* 1672–1699)   T i 265

JENKIN, Henry Charles Fleming (1833–1885)
Fitted out submarine telegraph cables, 1858–1873   B ii 76; DNB X 733

JENKINS, Charles Frewen, CBE (1865–1940)
First professor of engineering science, Oxford University; served in RNVR,
1914–1918   DNB XXVi 482

JENKINS, David James (1824–1891)
Merchant and shipowner   B ii 76

JENKINS, Philip (1854–1891)
Professor of naval architecture and marine engineering at Glasgow University,
1886–1891   B ii 79

JERVIS, *Adm of the Fleet* John, KB, *Earl of St Vincent* (1735–1823)   CE xi 155; *ch* vi 406; DNB x 792; H 406; M*d* xxi 70; NA i 164; NC iv 1; R i 277

JERVIS, John Bloomfield (1795–1885)
Canal engineer   DAB 497

JERVIS [*formerly* RICKETTS], *Capt* William Henry, RN (1764–1805)   NC XX 1

JERVIS-WHITE-JERVIS, *Cdr Sir* Henry Meredyth, RN (1793–1869)   B V 774

JERVOIS, *Cdr* Sampson, RN (*fl* 1801–1828)   M viii 339

JERVOIS, *Lieut-Gen Sir* William Francis Drummond (1821–1897)   DNB xxii 912

JERVOISE, *Capt* William Clarke (*d* 1837)   M vi 43, 446; Tr 54

JESSON, *Cdr* James, RN (*d* 1707/8)   *ch* iii 73

JESSOP, *Lieut* Samuel, RN (*fl* 1804–1813)   Tr 296

JEWEL, *Lieut-Cdr* Theo F., USN (*fl* 1861–1880)   H 926

JEWELL, Thomas, *Purser*, RN (*d* 1821)   Tr 208

JEWELL, *Lieut* William Nunn, RN (*d* 1847)   Tr 205

JEWERS, *Cdr* Richard Francis, RN (*d* 1872)   B ii 97

JEWETT, David (1772–1842)
Served in the USN 1799–1801 and later in the navies of Argentine and Brazil DAB 499

JEWITT, John R. (1783–1821)
Armourer on American merchant ship   MDC 348

JOCELYN, *Capt* Robert, RN (*fl* 1746–1787)   *ch* vi 369

JOHN, William (1845–1890)
Naval architect   B ii 101

JOHN OF AUSTRIA, *Don* (1547–1578)
The victor of Lepanto (1571)   CE viii 122; M*d* xxi 277

JOHNS, *Capt* Richard, RM (1805–1851)   B ii 102

JOHNSON, *Capt* Andrew W., USN (*fl* 1841–1879)   H 882

JOHNSON, *Capt* Charles (*fl* 1724–1736)
Author of: 'A general history of the robberies and murders of the most notorious pyrates . . .' (1724)   DNB x 893

JOHNSON, *Capt* Charles Alexander, RN (*d* 1861)   Tr 269

JOHNSON, *Cdr* Edward, RN (*b* 1777)   M vii 327

JOHNSON, *Capt* Edward John, RN (1795–1853)   B ii 104; M viii 321; T ii 342

JOHNSON, *Capt* Francis, RN (*fl* 1665)   *ch* i 169

JOHNSTONE, *Cdre* George, RN (1730–1787) *ch* vi 494; DNB x 963; R i 364

JOHNSTONE, *Capt* George James Hope, RN (*d* 1842) M vi 14

JOHNSTONE, *Capt* James, RN (*fl* 1806–1811) M ix 78

JOHNSTONE, *Adm Sir* William James Hope, KCB (1798–1878) B ii 120; M v 96

JOLLIET, Louis Thomas de (1645–1700)
French explorer and discoverer of the Mississippi; cartographer and King's hydrographer DAB 507; DCB i 392; MDC 352

JOLLEY, *Lieut* Charles, RN (*d* 1838) Tr 153

JOLLY, *Cdr* Thomas, RN (*d* 1741) *ch* v 44

JOLY, Charles Jasper (1864–1906)
Astronomer DNB xxiiib 376

JOLY, John (1857–1933)
Pioneer yachtsman; wrote on signalling, a collision predictor and floating breakwaters DNB xxvi 238

JONCAS, Louis Zépherin (1846–1903)
Manager of the Gaspé Fishing Company; writer on Canadian fisheries MDC 353

JONCLAIRE, Louis Thomas de (1670–1739)
Marine officer, French Canada MDC 353

JONES, *Adm* Alexander (1778–1862) B ii 122; M x 390

JONES, *Sir* Alfred Lewis, KCMG (1845–1906)
Shipowner DNB xxiiib 379

JONES, *Capt* Arthur, RN (*d* 1731) *ch* iv 46

JONES, *Cdr* Catesby Ap Roger, CSN (1821–1877) DAB 507

JONES, *Capt* Charles, RN (*fl* 1793–1824) M ix 4

JONES, *Rear-Adm Sir* Charles Thomas, RN (1778–1853) M xii 205

JONES, *Capt* Daniel, RN (*d* 1693) *ch* ii 56

JONES, *Maj* Edward, RM (*fl* 1795–1826) Tr 298

JONES, Ernest Lester (1876–1929)
Director of the U.S. Coast & Geodetic Survey, 1915–1929 DAB 508

JONES, *Gen* George, RM (1780–1857) B ii 125

JONES, *Capt* George, RN (*fl* 1798–1808) M vi 269

JONES, George, *Chaplain*, USN (1832–1902) DAB 508

JONES, *Capt* George Matthew, RN (1785?–1831) DNB x 991; M xii 197; M*d* xxi 142

JONES, *Sir* Harold Spencer, KBE (1890–1960)
Astronomer Royal, 1933–1955 A 523

JONES, William (1762–1831)
Astronomer   M*d* xxi 142; T ii 315

JONES, *Capt* William, RN (*fl* 1807–1815)   M vi 51

JONES, *Vice-Adm* William Gore, CB (1826–1888)   B ii 146

JONES, William H., *Surgeon*, USN (*b* 1840)   H 976

JONGE, Jean-Corneille (1793–1853)
Historian; author of: 'Vies de Jean et de Corneille Evertsen' (1820)   M*d* xxi 143

JORDAN, John W., *Assist-Paymaster*, USN (*fl* 1870–1880)   H 997

JORDAN, *Vice-Adm Sir* Joseph (1603–1685)   c*h* i 108; DNB X 1084

JORDAN, Thomas Brown (1807–1890)
Compass-maker; supplied Ross   DNB X 1088; T ii 453

JORGENSEN, Jorgen (1780–1841)
Danish privateer captain; served also in British Royal and Merchant Navy   AE i 687; DA*u*B ii 26

JOSEPH, Henry (1775–1832)
Canadian shipowner   MDC 356

JOUETT, *Capt* James Edward, USN (*fl* 1841–1880)   H 880

JOUFFROY D'ABBANS, Claude François Dorothée, *Marquis de*
Made experiments with steam navigation, 1776–1832   M*d* xxi 229

JOURDAIN [*or* JOURDAN], Silvester (*d* 1650)
Voyager   DNB X 1102

JOWLES, *Capt* Valentine, RN (*fl* 1660)   c*h* i 20

JOY, *Capt* John, RN (*fl* 1673)   c*h* i 397

JOY, John Cantiloe (1806–1866)
Marine painter   DNB X 1105

JOY, William (1803–1867)
Marine painter   DNB X 1105

JOYCE, *Capt* John, RN (*b* 1768)   M ix 458

JOYEUSE, *Adm* Anne de (1561–1587)   M*d* xxi 275

JUAN Y SANTACILLA, *Don* Jorge (1712–1773)
Explorer and astronomer   M*d* xxi 279

JUCHEREAU DES CHATELETS, Noël (*d* 1648)
French lawyer, Canadian colonial administrator, clerk in charge of naval purchases
at Quebec   DCB 402

JUDD, *Lieut* Charles H., USN (*fl* 1862–1870)   H 945

JUDD, *Cdr* Robert Hayley, RN (*fl* 1777–1840)   M vi 296

JUEL, Niels (1629–1697)
Danish admiral   M*d* xxi 296

KEAN, T. (*fl* 1774)
Perhaps a mariner; writer on longitude at sea   T ii 290

KEANE, *Adm* George Disney, CB (1817–1891)   B ii 166

KEANE, *Cdr* Richard, RN (*d ca* 1837)   M viii 304

KEARLEY, Hudson Ewbanke, *first Viscount Devonport* (1856–1934)
*Business man; steered the Port of London Bill through the House of Commons in
1908; the following year became first chairman of the Port of London Authority*   DNB XXV 501

KEARNY, *Capt* Lawrence, USN (1789–1868)   DAB 516

KEATS, *Adm Sir* Richard Goodwin, KB (1757–1834)   DNB X 1176; M i 342,
ii 865; M*d* xxi 475;
MDC 359; R ii 487

KEATS, *Rear-Adm* William (*d ca* 1869)   M v 283

KECK, *Cdr* Laurence, RN (*d* 1724)   *ch* ii 394

KEEBLE, *Cdr* Henry, RN (*fl* 1667)   *ch* i 294

KEELE, *Capt* Charles, RN (*b* 1795)   M viii 190

KEELER, James Edward (1857–1900)
American astronomer   CE viii 191; DAB 516

KEELER, *Lieut* John, USN (*fl* 1866–1880)   H 965

KEELER, *Rear-Adm* Robert (*fl* 1756–1787)   *ch* vi 433

KEELING, William (*d* 1620)
Naval commander in the East India Company's service   DNB X 1188

KEEN, *Capt* Robert, RN (*fl* 1783–1810)   M x 207

KEENAN, *Cdr* John, RN (*d ca* 1842)   M vii 72

KEENE, *Lieut* Henry C., USN (*fl* 1865–1871)   H 966

KEENE, *Capt* John, RN (*fl* 1673)   *ch* i·317

KEERE, Pieter van den (*fl* 1590–1620)
Dutch engraver and cartographer   *chb* 436

KEIGWIN, Richard (*d* 1690)
Naval and military commander   DNB X 1196

KEILL, John (1671–1721)
Mathematician and astronomer   DNB X 1198

KEITH, *Capt Sir* Basil, RN (*d* 1777)   *ch* vi 401

KEITH, *Cdr Sir* George Mouat, RN (*fl* 1801–1814)   M vii 152

KEITH, James, *Master*, RN (*d* 1838)   T*r* 65

KEITH, Thomas (1759–1834)
Professor of geography; writer on use of globes   DNB X 1219; T ii 315

KEITH, *Capt the Hon* William, RN (1799–1846)   M vi 51

KELLER, *Capt* Edward, RN (*d* 1750)   *ch* vi 77

KEMPENFELT, *Rear-Adm* Richard (1718–1782)   CE viii 196; *ch* vi
                                                              246; DNB X 1283; NA
                                                              i 180; NC vii 365;
                                                              R i 215

KEMPFF, *Cdr* Louis, USN (1841–1920)   DAB 520; H 912

KEMPTHORN, *Capt* John, RN (*fl* 1672–1678)   *ch* i 397

KEMPTHORN, *Cdr* Morgan, RN (*d* 1681)   *ch* i 397

KEMPTHORNE, *Vice-Adm Sir* John (1620–1679)   *ch* i 111; DNB X 1285

KEMPTHORNE, *Capt* John, RN (*fl* 1672–1688)   T i 265

KEMPTHORNE, *Capt* Rupert, RN (*d* 1691)   *ch* ii 320

KEMPTHORNE, *Cdr* Samuel, RN (*fl* 1789)   M vi 249

KEMPTHORNE, *Capt* Thomas, RN (*d* 1736)   *ch* iii 297

KEMPTHORNE, *Capt* William, RN (*d ca* 1667)   *ch* i 169

KEMPTHORNE, *Capt* William, RN (*fl* 1795–1816)   M xii 114

KEMYS, Lawrence (*d* 1618)
*Sea-captain; accompanied Ralegh up the Orinoco, 1595; Ralegh's pilot and captain
on the last expedition to Guiana, 1616*   DNB X 1287

KENDAL, *Capt* Charles, RN (*d* 1743)   *ch* iv 57

KENDALL, Abraham (*d* 1596)
Pilot, shipmaster, explorer with Frobisher, Drake and John Chidley   T i 180

KENDALL, *Lieut* E. N., RN (*fl* 1824–1830)   T ii 426

KENDALL, *Capt* George, RM (*d* 1840)   Tr 66

KENDALL, *Rear-Adm* John (*fl* 1778–1808)   M iii 1

KENDALL, Larcum (1721–1785)
Chronometer-maker; chronometers at National Maritime Museum   T ii 209

KENDRICK, John (*ca* 1740–1794)   Md xxi 518

KENNEDY, *Cdr* Alexander, RN (*fl* 1798–1814)   M vi 385

KENNEDY, *Cdr* Alexander, RN (*d ca* 1862)   M viii 112

KENNEDY, *Capt* Archibald, RN (*d* 1794)   *ch* vi 252

KENNEDY, *Lieut-Cdr* Charles W., USN (*fl* 1861–1880)   H 926

KENNEDY, Duncan, *Master*, USN (*fl* 1864–1880)   H 953

KENNEDY, James (1801–1867)
Manager of the Tay and Tyne Shipping Co   B ii 197

KENNEDY, *Sir* John (1838–1921)
Chief engineer of the Montreal Harbour Commission   MDC 362

KENNEDY, *Lieut-Gen* John Pitt, RE (1796–1879)
Constructed lighthouses at Guardianno and Point Theodore, 1822–1828   DNB X 1318

KENNEDY, Stephen D., *Surgeon*, USN (*fl* 1861–1880)   H 973

KERR, *Capt* Charles Julius, RN (*fl* 1799–1815)   M xii 401

KERR, *Capt* Henry Schomberg, RN (1838–1895)   B v 817

KERR, *Rear-Adm Lord* Mark Robert (1776–1840)   M ii 782

KERR, *Adm of the Fleet Lord* Walter Talbot, GCB (1839–1927)   DNB xxv 469

KERR, *Capt* William, RN (*fl* 1688–1708)   *ch* ii 321

KERSAINT, *Vice-Adm* Armand Gui Simon, *Comte de* (1742–1793)   M*d* xxi 545; S ii 5

KERSHNER, Edward, *Surgeon*, USN (*b* 1839)   H 976

KERWORTH [*or* CARVERTH], *Capt* Richard, RN (*d* 1728)   *ch* ii 394

KESTLE [*or* KISTAL], *Capt* Francis, RN (*d* 1706)   *ch* iii 311

KEULEN, Jan van (*fl* 1681–1696)
Dutch cartographer   CE viii 206

KEY, *Adm Sir* Astley Cooper, GCB (1821–1888)   B ii 214; DNB xi 82

KEYES, *Adm of the Fleet* Roger John Brownlow, GCB, KCVO, DSO, *first
Baron Keyes* (1872–1945)   CE viii 206; DNB
                                                                       xxvii 449

KEYMER [*or* KEYMOR], John (*fl* 1610–1620)
Writer on economics; author of: 'Observations upon the Dutch Fishing' (1664)   DNB xxii 935

KEYSER, *Lieut-Cdr* Edward S., USN (*fl* 1867–1880)   H 929

KIDD, *Capt* Dandy, RN (*d* 1741)   *ch* iv 426

KIDD, William (1645–1701)
Pirate   CE viii 211; DAB 524;
                                                                       DNB xi 93

KIDDER, Jerome H., *Surgeon*, USN (*fl* 1866–1870)   H 977

KIDDER, *Capt* Randolph Breese, USN (*b* 1831)   H 884

KIDWELL, *Cdr* John, RN (*fl* 1693)   *ch* iii 35

KIER, Samuel M. (1813–1874)
Owned and operated canal boats on the Pennsylvania State Canal   DAB 525

KIERSTED, Andrew, *Chief Engineer*, USN (*fl* 1856–1880)   H 1004

KIGGINS, *Cdr* William, RN (*d* 1698)   *ch* ii 276

KIGIVEN [*or* KAGGIVEN], *Capt* Richard, RN (*d* 1689)   *ch* i 337

KILBINGTON, . . . (*fl* 1789)
Compass-maker for Revenue cutters   T ii 316

KILIAN, Jacques (1714–1774)
Astronomer   M*d* xii 615

KILIG-ALI: *see* OCCHALI

KILINICK, *Cdr* Edward, RN (*d* 1830)   M vi 258

KING, *Vice-Adm* Richard Duckworth (1840–1900)   B v 822

KING, *Capt* Richard Henry, RN (*fl* 1805–1838)   M viii 304

KING, *Capt* William, RN (*fl* 1783–1832)   M ix 253

KING, William (1769–1852)
Shipowner   DAB 527

KING, *Lieut* William Elletson, RN (*b* 1776)   NC xxx 449

KING, William H., *Chief Engineer*, USN (*fl* 1857–1880)   H 1005

KINGCOMBE [*or* KINGCOME], *Adm Sir* John, KCB (1794–1871)   B ii 231; M viii 257

KINGDON, *Cdr* John, RN (*d* 1862)   Tr 309

KINGSLEY, George (*fl* 1714–1716)
Almanack-maker; writer on longitude   T i 305

KINGSLEY, *Lieut* Louis, USN (*fl* 1861–1880)   H 938

KINGSMILL, *Adm Sir* Charles Edmund (1855–1935)   MDC 370

KINGSMILL, *Adm Sir* Robert Bruce (1730–1805)   *ch* vi 485; DNB xi
                                                                                                          183; NC v 189; R i
                                                                                                          354

KINGSTON, George Templeman (1817–1886)
Meteorologist; head of the Naval School at Quebec   MDC 370

KINGSTON, *Lieut* John, RN (*d* 1805)   Tr 56

KINSBERGEN, *Compte* Jean Henri van (1735–1819)
Dutch admiral   M*d* xxi 634; S ii 25

KINSMAN, *Cdr* John K., RN (*d* 1831)   M vii 118

KIP, William (*fl* 1598–1635)
Engraver   *chb* 436

KIPPEN, *Capt* George, RN (1781–1826)   M xi 401; Tr 181

KIPPIS, Andrew (1725–1795)
Nonconformist divine and biographer   DNB xi 195

KIRCH, Christfried (1694–1740)
Astronomer   M*d* xxi 639

KIRCH, Gottfried (1639–1710)
Astronomer   M*d* xxi 639

KIRBY, *Capt* Richard, RN (*d* 1703)   *ch* ii 239

KIRBY, *Capt* Robert, RN (*fl* 1660–1664)   *ch* i 20

KIRBY, Thomas (*fl* 1802–1805)
Mathematical and nautical teacher; writer on navigation   T ii 368

KIRBY, *Capt* Walter, RN (1791–1859)   B ii 243; M viii 361

KIRK, Alexander Carnegie (1830–1892)
Senior partner of Robert Napier & Sons, Glasgow   B ii 243

LABELYE, George (*fl* 1736–1737)
Mathematical schoolmaster RN and marine surveyor   T ii 182

LABILLARDIÈRE, Jacques Julien Houton de (1755–1834)
Naturalist; member of d'Entrecasteaux's expedition in search of La Pérouse, 1791   DAuB ii 69; Md xxii
                                                                        273

LABOUCHERE, Henry, *Baron Taunton* (1798–1869)
Served on the Admiralty Board, 1832–1834; carried through a bill repealing the
Navigation Laws, 1849–1850 and was instrumental in passing the Mercantile
Marine Acts, 1850–1852   DNB xi 367

LA BOURDONNAIS, Bertrand François Mahé de (1699–1753)
French naval officer   CE viii 281

LACAILLE, Nicholas Louis de (1713–1763)
French astronomer   CE viii 292

LACKEY, Oscar H., *Chief Engineer*, USN (*fl* 1858–1880)   H 1007

LA CONDAMINE, Charles Marie de (1701–1774)
French geographer   CE viii 296

LA COURT DE PRÉRAVILLON ET DE GRANPRÉ (*fl* 1591)
French financier and possibly sea-captain; discoverer of walrus fishery in the
Magdalen Islands   DCB i 408

LACROIX, Louis Antoine Nicolle de (1704–1760)
Geographer   Md xxii 392

LACROSSE, *Vice-Adm* Jean Raymond, *Baron de* (1760–1829)   Md xxii 406; S ii 25

LACRUZ CANO Y OLMEIDA, *Don* Antonio de (1735–1794)
Geographer   Md xxii 415

LADD, William (1778–1841)
Sea-captain   DAB 537

LADRILLEROS, Juan (*fl* 1557–1558)
Spanish navigator   Md xxii 430

LADRILLEROS, Juan Fernandez de (*fl* 1574)
Spanish navigator   Md xxii 431

LAET, Jean de (*d* 1649)   Md xxii 439

LAFFITE, Jean (*ca* 1780–1821)   DAB 538

LAFONS, John de (*fl* 1805)
Marine chronometer-maker   T ii 361

LAFOREY, *Adm Sir* Francis, KCB (1767–1835)   M ii 446; Tr 113

LAFOREY, *Adm Sir* John (1729?–1796)   Ch vi 319; DNB xi
                                                                        396; R i 231

LAFRERI, Antonio [*otherwise* Antoine Lafrère] (1512–1577)
Italian map publisher   CE viii 303

LAMB, *Capt* James, RN (*fl* 1661–1664)   *ch* i 59

LAMB, *Cdr* John, RN (1790–1862)   DAuB ii 72

LAMB, *Cdr* Philip, RN (*fl* 1782–1802)   M vi 295

LAMBERT, *Cdr* Charles, RN (1790–1856)   Tr 33

LAMBERT, *Cdr* David, RN (*d* 1703)   *ch* i 58

LAMBERT, *Adm Sir* George Robert, GCB (1795–1869)   B ii 283; M v 272

LAMBERT, *Capt* Henry, RN (*d* 1813)   DNB xi 450; M v 256

LAMBERT, *Cdr* John, RN (*fl* 1796–1822)   M vii 221

LAMBERT, *Capt* Robert, RN (*fl* 1754–1760)   *ch* vi 402

LAMBERT, *Vice-Adm* Robert (*d* 1836)   M ii 720

LAMBERT, *Vice-Adm* Rowley, CB (1828–1880)   B ii 284

LAMBERT, *Capt* Thomas, RN (*d* 1700)   *ch* iii 139

LAMBERT, William Blake (1816–1874)
Marine engineer   B ii 285

LAMBERTON, *Rear-Adm* Benjamin Peffer, USN (1844–1912)   DAB 540; H 927

LAMBORN, *Capt* John, RN (*fl* 1794–1810)   M x 267

LAMBORN, Reginald (*fl* 1363)
Astronomer   DNB xi 462

LAMDIN, William J., *Chief Engineer*, USN (*fl* 1851–1880)   H 1003

LAMEY, John Payton, *Purser*, RN (*d* 1834)   Tr 185

LAMMING, *Capt* Thomas, RN (*fl* 1664–1666)   *ch* i 239

LAMONT, Johann von (1805–1879)
Astronomer   B ii 285; DNB xi 467

LA MOTTE DE LUCIÈRE, Dominique (1636–1700)
French army officer; companion of La Salle   DCB i 415

LA MOTTE PICQUET, *Comte* Toussaint Guillaume (1720–1791)   Md xxix 430

LAMPSON, *Sir* Curtis Miranda (1806–1885)
Advocate of the Atlantic cable   DNB xi 473

LANAUDIÈRE, Charles François Xavier Tarieu de (1710–1776)
French-Canadian officer in troupes de la marine; legislative councillor of Quebec MDC 383

LANAUDIÈRE, Charles Louis Tarieu de (1743–1811)
*Son of Charles François; officer in troupes de la marine; legislative councillor of
Lower Canada*   MDC 384

LANÇAROT (*fl* 1444–1447)
Portuguese navigator   Md xxiii 114

LANCASTER, *Cdr* Henry, RN (1791–1862)   Tr 20

LAUZUN, *Cdr* Francis Daniel, RN (*d* 1861)   Tr 43

LA VÉRENDRYE, Pierre Gaultier de Varennes, *Sieur de* (1685–1749)
French-Canadian explorer, fur-trader, captain in troupes de la Marine   MDC 398

LAVILLÉON de la VILLEVALIO du FRESCHESCLOS, *Contre-Adm*
Jean-Baptiste François *Comte de* (1740–1820)   S ii 77

LAW, Edward, *first Baron Ellenborough* (1750–1818)
Lord chief justice of England, presided at Cochrane's trial, 1814   DNB xi 657

LAW, Edward, GCB, *first Earl of Ellenborough* (1790–1871)
First lord of the Admiralty, 1846   B i 975; DNB xi 662

LAW, Homer L., *Assist-Surgeon*, USN (*fl* 1870–1880)   H 980

LAWES [*or* LAWS], *Capt* Joseph, RN (*d* 1733)   ch iv 96

LAWFORD, *Vice-Adm* John (*fl* 1790–1819)   M ii 496

LAWLEY, George Frederick (1848–1928)
Yacht builder   DAB 550

LAWRENCE, *Capt* Daniel, RN (*fl* 1798–1846)   M xii 110

LAWRENCE, *Gen* Elias, RM (*d* 1857)   Tr 172

LAWRENCE [LAUNCE *or* LANCE], *Capt* James, RN (*d* 1695)   ch iii 36

LAWRENCE, *Capt* James, USN (1781–1813)   DAB 550; H 428

LAWRENCE, *Capt* John, RN (*fl* 1798–1846)   M xii 123

LAWRENCE, *Rear-Adm* Peter (*d* 1758)   ch iv 427

LAWRENCE, William Effingham (1781–1841)
*Shipowner in London, Liverpool and New York; founder of the Tamar Steam
Navigation Co*   DAuB ii 93

LAWRY, Walter (1793–1859)
Methodist missionary and shipowner; sailed to New Zealand and Tonga   DAuB ii 95

LAWS, Elijah, *Chief Engineer*, USN (*fl* 1858–1880)   H 1007

LAWS, *Capt* John Milligan, RN (*b* 1799)   M viii 486

LAWS [*or* LAWES], *Capt* Joseph, RN (*d* 1733)   ch iv 96

LAWS, Robert, CMG (1851–1934)
*Pioneer missionary; as medical officer and second in command of Scottish Free Church
expedition he supervised the assembly of a 48-foot sectional steamship which became the
first steamship to float on any African lake, 1875*   DNB xxvi 532

LAWS, *Rear-Adm* William (*fl* 1732–1747)   ch iv 230

LAWSON, *Capt* Henry, RN (*d* 1734)   ch iii 400

LAWSON, Henry (1774–1855)
Astronomer   B ii 333; DNB xi 781;
                                                                        Md xxiii 434

LAWSON, *Adm Sir* John (*d* 1665)   ch i 20; DNB xi 733

LEARY, *Capt* John, RN (*d* 1789)   ch vi 577

LEARY, *Lieut-Cdr* Richard P., USN (*fl* 1860–1880)   H 923

LEATHER, John Towlerton (1804–1885)
Civil engineer; constructed the Portland breakwater, 1848–1856, the sea forts at
Spithead, 1861–1872 and the extension to Portsmouth dockyard   B ii 344

LEATHER, John Wignall (1810–1887)
Engineer of the Aire & Calder navigation   B ii 345

LEAVENWORTH, Francis Preserved (1856–1928)
Astronomer   DAB 552

LEAVITT, Henrietta Swan (1868–1921)
Astronomer   DAB 553

LEBLANC, *Vice-Adm* Louis François Jean (1786–1857)   Md xxiii 467

LECHMERE, *Cdr* Charles, RN (*d* 1823)   M vii 399

LECHMERE, *Cdr* John, RN (1793–1867/8)   Tr 216

LECKY, Squire Thornton Stratford (1838–1902)
Writer on navigation   DNB xxiiib 434

LE CLERC, Jean (*fl* 1585–1621)
French cartographer   CE viii 433

LECOAT, *Contre-Adm* Yves Marie Gabriel Pierre, *Baron de St Haoven*
(1757–1826?)   Md xxiii 536

LECONT, P. (*fl* 1821)
Midshipman RN; writer on ship's compasses and chronometers   T ii 426

LE CREUX DE BREUIL, Nicolas (*fl* 1632)
Lieutenant at Canso and Port-Royal, Nova Scotia; made several voyages to the
colony with colonists and supplies; shipowner   DCB i 442

LE DALL DE KÉREON, *Contre-Adm* Yves Jean (1737–1811)   s ii 87

LE DALL DE TROMELIN, *Contre-Adm* Mathieu Marie (1739–1817)   s ii 88

LEDIARD, Thomas (1685–1743)
Miscellaneous writer; author of: 'The Naval History of England' (1735)   DNB xi 780

LEDYARD, John (1751–1789)   DAB 553; DNB xi 780

LEE, Arthur Hamilton, GBE, GCB, GCSI, *Viscount Lee of Fareham* (1868–1947)
Civil lord of the Admiralty, 1903–1905; Opposition spokesman on naval affairs,
1906–1914; first lord of the Admiralty, 1921–1922   DNB xxvii 494

LEE, *Vice-Adm the Hon* Fitzroy Henry (*d* 1751)   ch iv 195; DNB xi 791

LEE, Richard (*fl* 1532–1540)
Marine surveyor   T i 167

LEE, *Vice-Adm Sir* Richard (1765–1824)   M ii 568; R iii 252

LEE, *Rear-Adm* Samuel Philipps, USN (1812–1807)   DAB 557; H 430

LEE, *Capt* Thomas, RN (*d* 1770)   ch vi 522

BOLTON PUBLIC REFERENCE LIBRARY

LEGUAT, Francois (1638–1735)
Voyager; author of: 'A New Voyage to the East Indies' (1708)   DNB xi 865

LEGUIN, Stephen (*fl* 1790)
Inventor of instrument for finding longitude at sea   T i 344

LE HUNTE, *Capt* Francis, RN (*d* 1859)   M vii 275

LEIF ERICSSON [*or* EIRIKSSON] (*fl* 1000)
First European to visit the American continent   CE viii 460; DCB i 448

LEIGH, Charles (1572–1605)
Merchant and voyager; first English coloniser of the St Lawrence   DCB i 449; DNB xi 871

LEIGH, *Capt* Jodrell, RN (*fl* 1801–1829)   M vi 86

LEIGH, *Cdr* Thomas, RN (*d* 1846)   Tr 154

LEIGHTON, *Capt* Edward, RN (*d* 1750)   ch vi 99

LEIGHTON, *Capt* Henry, RN (*fl* 1673)   ch i 398

LEININGEN, *Adm the Prince* Ernest Leopold Victor Charles Auguste Joseph
Emich, GCB, GCVO (1830–1904)   DNB xxiiib 449

LEISSÈGUES, *Vice-Adm* Corentin Urbain Jacques Bertrand de (1758–1832)   Md xxiv 35; S ii 100

LEITH, *Rear-Adm* John (*d* 1854)   B ii 382; M v 279

LEITH, *Cdr* William Forbes, RN (*fl* 1796–1814)   M vii 239

LE KEUX, Richard (1784–1838)
Instrument-maker and nautical bookseller   T ii 316

LELARGE, *Vice-Adm* Jean Amable (1738–1805)   S ii 102

LELY, *Capt* Peter, RM (*d* 1832)   Tr 109

LE MAIRE, Jacob (*d* 1616)   Md xxiv 58

LÉMERY, Louis Robert Joseph Cornelier (1728–1802)
Astronomer   Md xxiv 84

LEMIEUX, Rodolphe (1866–1937)
Minister of marine and fisheries, Canada   MDC 407

LEMON, *Col* Thomas, CB, RM (1807–1875)   B ii 387; Tr 74

LEMONNIER, Pierre Charles (1715–1799)
Astronomer   Md xxiv 95

LE MOYNE DE CHÂTEAUGUAY, Louis (1676–1694)
Midshipman, French navy; soldier   DCB i 463

LEMPRIÈRE, *Capt* George Ourry, RN (*fl* 1807–1833)   M v 227

LEMPRIÈRE, *Capt* Thomas (*d* 1763)   ch vi 373

LENDRICK, *Capt* John, RN (*d* 1779/80)   ch vi 327

LE NEVE, *Capt* Richard, RN (*d* 1673)   ch i 325

LENNOCK, *Capt* George Gustavus, RN (*fl* 1789–1846)   M xii 254

LEVER, Darcy (1760?–1837)   DNB xi 1019

LEVER, John Orrell (1824–1861)
Shipowner   B vi 45

LEVERRIER, Urbain Jean Joseph (1811–1877)
French astronomer   CE viii 496

LEVERTON, . . . (*fl* 1777)
Optical instrument-maker; octant at National Maritime Museum   T ii 292

LE VESCONTE, *Cdr* Henry, RN (*d* 1850)   M viii 256; Tr 296

LE VESCONTE, *Cdr* Philip, RN (*d* 1850)   M vii 415

LEVESON, *Sir* Richard (1570–1605)
Vice-admiral of England   DNB xi 1024

LEVESON-GOWER, *Rear-Adm* John (1740–1792)   DNB xi 1032

LEVEY, Solomon (1794–1833)
Shipbroker and shipowner in Sydney; shipbuilder; whaler and sealer   DAuB ii 110

LEVY, *Capt* Uriah Phillips, USN (1792–1862)   DAB 564; H 891

LEWE VAN ADUARD, Jean Jonkheer (1774–1832)
Dutch naval officer   Md xxiv 414

LEWIN, John William (1770–1819)
Naturalist and Australian explorer   AE i 734; DAuB ii 111

LEWIN, *Cdr* Richard John, RN (*d* 1827)   M vii 339

LEWIN, Thomas (1805–1877)
*Miscellaneous author; claimed, after a study of Admiralty tidal observations, that Caesar
landed at Hythe, in 55 B.C.*   DNB xi 1047

LEWIS, *Capt* Francis James, RN (*d* 1849)   M vi 151

LEWIS, *Lieut-Gen* George, CB, RM (1770–1854)   B ii 412

LEWIS, *Lieut-Gen* Griffith George, CB, RE (1784–1859)
Served on the Rideau Canal Commission, 1828   DNB xi 1063

LEWIS, *Capt* John Mason, RN (*d ca* 1824)   M iii 324

LEWIS, Richard (*d* 1883)
Secretary of the National Lifeboat Institution, 1850–1883   B ii 417

LEWIS, *Capt* Robert F. R., USN (*fl* 1841–1880)   H 891

LEY, *Capt* Andrew, RN (*fl* 1710–1712)   ch iv 24

LEY, *Adm* James, RN, *third Earl of Marlborough* (1618–1665)   ch i 59

LEYBOURNE, William (1626–1716)
Printer, mathematician, teacher of navigation, surveyor and almanac compiler   DNB xi 1087; Md xxiv
                                                                                 421; T i 230

LEYBOURNE [LEYBURN, LEMBURN *or* LEEBURN], Roger de
(*d* 1271)
Warden of the Cinque Ports, 1263   DNB xi 1088

LILLEY, John (*fl* 1827–1838)
Nautical instrument-maker   T ii 427

LILLICRAP, *Rear-Adm* James (*d* 1851)   M x 221

LILLIE, *Lieut* Abraham B. H., USN (*fl* 1862–1880)   H 946

LILLY, Christian (*d* 1738)
Military engineer; examined Spanish ports on the Peruvian coast and subsequently
reported to the king, 1698; surveyed and improved Jamaican harbours; appointed keeper
of naval ordnance stores at Barbados, 1709; reported on Newfoundland harbours, 1711   DNB xi 1134; T ii 133

LILY, George (*ca* 1693–1739)
Cartographer   CE viii 571

LIMEBURNER, *Capt* Thomas, RN (*d* 1750)   ch v 44

LINCOLN, Charles (*ca* 1744–1807)
Telescope, nautical instrument and globe-maker   T ii 266

LIND, James (1716–1794)
Surgeon Royal Navy, physician, writer on scurvy, student of navigation   A 137; DNB xi 1150;
                                                                                        M*d* xxiv 547; T ii 237

LIND, James (1736–1812)
Physician; surgeon on an East Indiaman, 1766; published an account of his
observations of the transit of Venus, 1769; accompanied Banks' expedition to
Iceland, 1772   DNB xi 1192

LIND, *Capt Sir* James, RN (*d* 1823)   M iv 873

LINDENAU, *Baron* Bernard August de (1779–1854)
Astronomer   M*d* xxiv 552

LINDENKOHL, Adolph (1833–1904)
Oceanographer and cartographer   DAB 571

LINDSAY, *Lieut* James, RN (1783–1845)   Tr 124

LINDSAY, James Ludovic, KT, *twenty-sixth Earl of Crawford and ninth*
Earl of Balcarres (1847–1913)
Astronomer   DNB xxiv 337

LINDSAY, *Rear-Adm Sir* John (1737–1788)   ch vi 256; DNB xi
                                                                                        1186; NA i 128

LINDSAY, William Schaw (1816–1877)
Shipbroker; author of: 'History of merchant shipping & ancient commerce', 4 vols.
(1874–1876)   B ii 439; DNB xi 1195

LINDSEY, *Capt* Michael, RN (*fl* 1661–1665)   ch i 171

LINDSEY, *Cdr* William, RN (*d* 1694)   ch iii 73

LINGEN, *Capt* Joshua [*or* Joseph], RN (*d* 1752)   ch iv 196

LINIERS BREMONT, *Don* Santiago de (*ca* 1760–1809)
Spanish naval officer   M*d* xxiv 568

LIVINGSTON, *Vice-Adm Sir* Thomas (*d* 1853)   M iii 244

LIVINGSTONE, Andrew (*fl* 1820)
Teacher of navigation   T ii 454

LIVINGSTONE, William (1844–1925)
Shipowner   DAB 577

LLEWELLYN, David Herbert (1838–1864)
Surgeon of the C.S.S. 'Alabama'   B ii 456

LLOYD, *Capt* Charles, RN (*fl* 1673)   *ch* i 399

LLOYD, *Capt* David, RN (*d* 1699)   *ch* iii 73

LLOYD, *Capt* David, RN (*d* 1716)   *ch* ii 14; DNB xi 1296

LLOYD, Edward (*fl* 1688–1726)
Founder of Lloyd's   DNB xi 1297

LLOYD, *Rear-Adm* Edward (*d* 1855)   B ii 457; M xii 292, 457

LLOYD, *Rear-Adm* George, RN (1793–1860)   M vi 56

LLOYD, *Capt* James, RN (*d* 1761)   *ch* iv 428

LLOYD, *Lieut* James Lewin (*d* 1806)   Tr 71

LLOYD, *Capt* John, RN (*d* 1745)   *ch* i 115; v 396

LLOYD, *Capt* John, RN (*d* 1778)   *ch* v 478

LLOYD, John Augustus (1800–1854)
Engineer; surveyed the Panama isthmus and reported on the best means of
inter-oceanic communication, 1827; under the joint direction of the Admiralty and the
Royal Society determined the difference in level of the Thames between
London Bridge and the sea, 1830   DNB xi 1306

LLOYD, Meyrick, *Midshipman*, RN (*fl* 1805–1806)   Tr 305

LLOYD, Richard, *Surgeon*, RN (*fl* 1781–1816)   Tr 34

LLOYD, *Vice-Adm* Robert (1765–1846)   M iii 242

LLOYD, *Lieut* Robert, RN (*d* 1805)   Tr 152

LLOYD, Thomas, CB, RN (1803–1875)
Chief engineer, 1847–1869   B ii 463

LLOYD, *Capt* William, RN (*d* 1723)   *ch* iv 46

LLOYD, *Capt* William, RN (*d* 1796)   *ch* vi 79

LOADES, *Capt* Edmund, RN (*d* 1707)   *ch* iii 45

LOANE, Rowland (Roland) Walpole (*d* 1844)
Claimed to have been naval officer; shipowner; merchant   DAuB ii 120

LODGE, Thomas (1558?–1625)
*Author; sailed to the islands of Terceras and the Canaries, ca 1588; and with
Cavendish to South America, 1591*   DNB xii 60

LOFTIN, George (d 1848)
*Served as a midshipman in the 'Neptune' at Trafalgar; second lieutenant, RM in
1807; placed on half-pay, 1809*   Tr 63

LOFTING, *Capt* Samuel, RN (*fl* 1742–1745)   ch v 347

LOGAN, James Richardson (d 1869)
*Scientist who settled in Penang; prevailed upon the Peninsular & Oriental Steam
Navigation Co to maintain direct communication between Penang and the United
Kingdom*   DNB xii 83

LOGAN, *Lieut* Leavitt C., USN (*fl* 1863–1880)   H 952

LOGGIE, *Capt* James, RN (d 1779)   ch vi 328

LOK, Michael (*fl* 1615)
*Traveller; governor of the Cathay Company, 1577; financed Frobisher's voyages,
1577–1579; translated part of Martyr's: 'Historie of the West Indies' (1612)*   DNB xii 92

LONDON, *Capt* Richard, RN (*fl* 1665–1675)   ch i 317

LONEY, *Lieut* Henry, RN (d 1827)   Tr 236

LONEY, *Adm* Robert (1787–1882)   B ii 483

LONG, *Capt* Charles, RN (d 1761)   ch v 107

LONG, Edward (1734–1813)
Judge of Admiralty Court of Jamaica; historian of Jamaica, writer on the slave trade DNB xii 100; Md xxv
                                                                                       68

LONG, *Lieut-Cdr* George Washington, USN (1844–1881)   CE iv 424; DAB 228;
                                                                                       H 933

LONG, *Capt* Henry, RN (d 1723)   ch iii 345

LONG, John, *Chief Engineer*, USN (*fl* 1861–1880)   H 1005

LONG, *Cdr* Richard, RN (*fl* 1664)   ch i 115

LONG, *Capt* Richard, RN (d 1717)   ch iii 167

LONG, *Cdr* Robert, RN (*fl* 1666–1668)   ch i 312

LONG, *Capt* Robert, RN (d 1771)   ch iv 182

LONG, Roger (1680–1770)
Astronomer   DNB xii 108; Md xxv
                                                                                       67

LONG, *Rear-Adm* Samuel (1840–1893)   B ii 485

LONG, *Capt* Thomas, RN (d 1710)   ch iii 140

LONG, *Capt* William, RN (*fl* 1668–1678)   ch i 398

LONG, *Capt* William, RN (d 1780)   ch vi 403

LOTI, Pierre [i.e. Louis Marie Julien Viaud] (1850–1923)
French naval officer   CE viii 694

LOTTIN, Victor Charles (1795–1858)
Captain French Navy; on 'L'Astrolabe' expedition, 1785-8   M*d* xxv 143

LOUIS, *Major-Gen Sir* Charles, RM (1818–1900)   B vi 80

LOUIS, *Cdr* Charles Belfield, RN (*d* 1824)   M viii 40

LOUIS, *Adm Sir* John (1785–1863)   B ii 501; M ix 118

LOUIS, *Rear-Adm Sir* Thomas (1759–1807)   DNB xii 151; NC xvi
                                                                                 177

LOUIS, *Adm* William (1810–1877)   B ii 501

LOUTHEAN, Robert, *Master*, RN (*d* 1836)   Tr 249

LOUVILLE, Jacques Eugéne d'Allonville, *Chevalier de* (1671–1731)
Astronomer   M*d* xxv 356

LOVE, *Adm* Henry Ommanney (1793–1872)   B ii 502; M viii 185

LOVE, James (*fl* 1690–1700)
Writer on navigation   T i 286

LOVE, *Cdr* William, RN (1764–1839)   M vi 353, 455

LOVEKYN, John (*d* 1368)
Four times lord mayor of London; claimed the right as a citizen of London to bring
a freight of sea-coal from Newcastle to London free of custom, 1358   DNB xii 164

LOVELL, *Cdr* Thomas, RN (*fl* 1672–1677)   ch i 347

LOVELL, *Vice-Adm* William Stanhope (1787–1859)   B ii 506; Tr 63

LOVENEWTON, Samuel, *Carpenter*, RN (*fl* 1805–1816)   Tr 290

LOVET, *Capt* John, RN (*d* 1758)   ch v 109

LOVETT, Richard (*fl* 1756–1774)
Writer on mariner's compass   T ii 266

LOW, Edward (*d* 1724)
English pirate in the West Indies   M*d* xxv 374

LOW, *Cdr* John M'Arthur, RN (*d* 1840)   M viii 7

LOW, Peter Albert (1861–1943)
Geologist, Arctic voyager   MDC 423

LOW, *Lieut* William F., USN (*fl* 1865–1877)   H 963

LOWBER, William, *Surgeon*, USN (*fl* 1847–1872)   H 984

LOWCAY, *Cdr* Henry, RN (*d* 1859)   M vii 127

LOWCAY, *Capt* William, RN (1787–1852)   Tr 234

LOWDER, *Gen* Samuel Netterville, CB, RM (1812–1891)   B ii 511

LOWE, *Rear-Adm* Abraham (1771–1854)   B ii 511; M xi 296

LOWE, *Adm* Arthur (1814–1882)   B ii 511

LUCAS, Jean Jacques Étienne (1764–1829)
Captain French Navy; commanded 'Redoubtable' at Trafalgar   Md xxv 409

LUCAS, *Cdr* John, RN (*fl* 1673)   ch i 399

LUCAS, *Cdr* Mark Robinson, RN (*d* 1834)   M viii 67

LUCAS, Paul (1664–1737)
Frenchman; Venetian naval commander; explorer of the Nile and Levant   Md xxv 407

LUCAS, Richard (*ca* 1656–*after* 1686)
Sea-captain Hudson's Bay Co   DCB i 476

LUCE, *Cdr* John, RN (*d* 1827)   M vi 261

LUCE, *Rear-Adm* Stephen Bleeker, USN (1827–1917)   DAB 592; H 877

LUCH [*or* LUCK], *Capt* James, RN (*d* 1736)   ch iv 83

LUCKRAFT, *Adm* Alfred (1792–1871)   M viii 341; Tr 126

LUDIUS (1st century B.C.)
Roman fresco painter of sea scenes, ports, etc.   Md xxv 445

LUDLAM, William (1717–1788)
Mathematician; one of the 'three gentlemen skilled in mechanics' appointed to report
on the merits of John Harrison's watch, 1765   DNB xii 254; T ii 183

LUDLOW, *Lieut-Cdr* Nicoll, USN (*fl* 1859–1880)   H 922

LUDMAN, *Capt* Bernard, RN (*d ca* 1673)   ch i 241

LUFFMAN, John (*fl* 1776–1820)
Geographer, engraver, publisher and goldsmith   chb 439

LUKE, *Cdr* George, RN (*d* 1824)   M vi 250

LUKE, *Cdr* George, RN (*fl* 1804)   M vii 283

LUKIN, Lionel (1742–1834)
Inventor of lifeboats; constructed an 'unsubmergible' boat in 1785   DNB xii 266

LUKIN, *Rear-Adm* William (*fl* 1793–1814)   M ii 701

LUMLEY, *Capt* George, RN (*d* 1710)   ch iii 346

LULL, *Cdr* Edward Phelps, USN (1836–1887)   H 901

LUNY, Thomas (1759–1837)
Marine painter   DNB xii 283

LUSHINGTON, *Capt* Franklin, RN (*d* 1743)   ch iv 428

LUSHINGTON, Stephen (1782–1873)
Judge of the high court of Admiralty, 1838–1867   B ii 535

LUSHINGTON, *Adm Sir* Stephen, GCB (1803–1877)   B ii 535; DNB xii 291;
                                                                                        M vi 88

LUSSAN, Raveneau de (1663–*after* 1688)
Frenchman; cadet in marine regiment; filibuster in West Indies; author of history
of the filibusters   Md xxv 493

LYON, *Capt* George Francis, RN (1795–1832)   DNB xii 345; M v 100;
                                                               M*d* xxv 561

LYON, *Lieut* Henry Ware, USN (*fl* 1862–1880)   H 943

LYON, John (1734–1817)
Historian of Dover; author of: 'History of the town and port of Dover and
Dover Castle, with a short account of the Cinque Ports', 2 vols. (1813–1814)   DNB xii 350

LYON, Primrose, *Surgeon*, RN (*fl* 1805–1827)   Tr 34

LYON, *Adm of the Fleet Sir* Algernon McLennan, GCB (1833–1908)   DNB xxiiib 496

LYONS, *Adm* Edmund, GCB, *first Baron Lyons* (1790–1858)   DNB xxii 355; M xi
                                                               38; M*d* xxv 566

LYONS, *Adm* John (*d* 1872)   B ii 548; M vi 139;
                                                               T ii 267

LYONS, *Lieut-Cdr* Timothy A., USN (*fl* 1862–1880)   H 933

LYSAGHT, *Adm* Arthur (1782–1859)   B ii 549; M ix 184

LYSTER, George Fosbery (1822–1899)
Civil engineer; engineer-in-chief of Mersey Docks and Harbour Board, 1861–1897   B vi 98

LYCOTT [*or* LYDCOTT], *Cdr* John, RN (*d* 1697)   *ch* iii 48

LYTTLETON, William Thomas (*ca* 1786–1839)
Lieutenant 73rd Regiment; naval officer at Port Dalrymple   DAUB ii 143

MABBOT, *Capt* Thomas, RN (*d* 1712)   *ch* iv 30

MACALESTER, Charles (1765–1832)
Merchant and shipowner   DAB 598

McALLISTER, Charles Albert (1867–1939)
Marine engineer   DAB 598

McALPINE, William Jarvis (1812–1890)
Civil engineer; chief engineer of the eastern division of the Erie Canal, and later
to the Government dry-dock at Brooklyn, N.Y.   DAB 598

MACANSH, John, *Surgeon*, RN (*d* 1830)   Tr 297

McARTHUR, Charles (1844–1910)
Politician and writer on marine insurance   DNB xxiiib 499

McARTHUR, John (1755–1840)
Author; enntered the navy as an assistant-clerk, 1755; appointed secretary to Lord
Hood, 1791; commenced publication, in conjunction with James Stanier Clarke, of the:
'Naval Chronicle', 1799; co-author with Clarke of the: 'Life of Lord Nelson',
2 vols. (1809)   DNB xii 402

MACARTHUR, John (1767–1834)
Army officer, shipowner, whale fisher, sheep farmer, merchant   DAUB ii 153; DNB xii
                                                               401

M'CREA, *Adm* Robert Contart (1793–1874)   M viii 135; Tr 225

McCULLOCH, Andrew, *Midshipman*, RN (*b* 1785)   Tr 72

McCULLOCH, Kenneth (*fl* 1787–1791)
Ship's compass-maker   T ii 319

M'CULLOCH, *Cdr* Thomas, RN (*d* 1830)   M vii 80

M'CULLOCH, *Capt* William, RN (*b* 1780)   M xi 398

McCULLUM, *Col* John, RM (*d* 1851)   Tr 73

McCURLEY, *Lieut-Cdr* Felix, USN (*fl* 1861–1880)   H 929

McDANIEL, Charles A., *Paymaster*, USN (*fl* 1865–1880)   H 993

MACDONALD, Andrew Archibald (1829–1912)
Canadian merchant and shipowner; lieutenant-governor of Prince Edward Island   MDC 435

MACDONALD, *Rear-Adm* Colin, CB (*d* 1857)   M xi 275

MACDONALD, *Lieut-Col* John (1759–1831)
*Scottish engineer; as a field officer in the corps of Cinque Ports Volunteers he made
a reconnaissance in an open boat of the preparations for invasion at Bolougne. Devoted
much time to the improvement of naval and military telegraphs*   DNB xii 484; Md xxv
                                                                 611

MACDONALD, *Sir* John Davis, KCB, RN (1826–1908)
Inspector-general of hospitals and fleets; author of: 'Outlines of naval hygiene' (1881)   DNB xxiiib 517

MACDONALD [*or* MACDONEL], *Capt* Randall, RN (*fl* 1678–1687)   ch ii 89

MACDONALD, *Adm Sir* Reginald John, KCB, KCSI (1820–1899)   B vi 110

MACDONALD, William, *Surgeon*, RN (*d* 1823)   Tr 171

MACDONOUGH, *Capt* Thomas, USN (1783–1825)   DAB 609; H 490

M'DOUALL, *Cdr* James, RN (*d* 1845)   M viii 2

McDOUGAL, *Cdr* Charles, USN (*fl* 1852–1880)   H 902

McDOUGAL, *Rear-Adm* David Stockton, USN (1809–1882)   DAB 609; H 490

McDOUGALL, Alexander(1845–1923)
Shipbuilder   DAB 609

M'DOUGALL, *Vice-Adm Sir* John, KCB (1790–1865)   B ii 593; M viii 44;
                                                                 DNB xii 508

M'DOUGALL, *Cdr* William Howard, RN (*fl* 1807–1826)   M viii 182

McELMELL, Jackson, *Chief Engineer*, USN (*fl* 1855–1880)   H 1004

M'FARLAND, *Capt* James, RN (*fl* 1781–1840)   M vi 311

MACFARLANE, James, *Purser*, RN (*d* 1849)   Tr 100

McGIFFIN, Philo Norton (1860–1897)
Served in the USN, 1882–1884, and in the Chinese navy from 1885   DAB 612

MACGILLIVRAY, John (1821–1867)
Naturalist on surveys of H.M.S. 'Fly', 1842–1846; H.M.S. 'Rattlesnake', 1846–1850;
H.M.S. 'Herald', 1852–1855   AE ii 8; B ii 604;
                                                  DAUB ii 167; DNB xii
                                                  535

McGLENSEY, *Cdr* John F., USN (*fl* 1857–1880)   H 911

McGOWAN, *Lieut-Cdr* John, USN (*fl* 1867–1880)   H 929

McGOWAN, William, *Assist-Paymaster*, USN (*fl* 1870–1880)   H 997

McGREGOR, *Cdr* Charles, USN (*fl* 1860–1880)   H 915

MACGREGOR, Donald Robert (1824–1889)
Shipowner   B vi 117

MACGREGOR, *Sir* Evan, GCB (1842–1926)
Civil servant; entered Admiralty, 1860; private secretary to successive senior lords,
1869–1879; permanent secretary, 1884–1907   DNB xxv 538

MACGREGOR, John (1825–1892)   B ii 611; DNB xii 541

McGREGOR, John James (1775–1834)
Historian and topographer; author of: 'Narrative of the loss of the Sea Horse
transport. . . . also some account of the wreck of the Lord Melville. . . . ' (1816)   DNB xii 543

M'GWIRE, *Capt* William, RN (1766–1847)   M vi 264

MACHA-ALLAH (MESSA HALA) (*fl* 700)
Arabian astronomer and writer on navigation   Md xxv 622

MACHAM, Robert (*fl* 1344)
English gentleman, discoverer of Madeira   DNB xii 554; Md xxv
                                                   622

MACHAN, R. (*fl* 1824–1827)
Author of a mariner's guide to the stars   T ii 428

M'HARDY, *Adm* John Bunch Bonnemaison (1801–1882) B ii 611; M viii 367

MACHETTE, Henry C., *Assist-Paymaster*, USN (*b* 1842)   H 995

MACHIN, John (*d* 1751)
Astronomer   DNB xii 554; Md xxv
                                                   635

McILVAINE, *Lieut* Bloomfield, USN (*fl* 1862–1880)   H 947

McINTOSH, William Carmichael (1838–1931)
Marine zoologist   DNB xxvi 573

McINTYRE, John (*d* 1900)
General manager of Palmer & Co, shipbuilders at Jarrow   B vi 119

M'KERLIE, *Rear-Adm* John (1774–1848)   M xi 186; Tr 114

MACKESON, Charles (1842–1899)
Clerk to the director-general of the medical department of the navy, 1861–1879   B vi 123

MACKIE, Benjamin S., *Surgeon,* USN (*fl* 1869–1879)   H 978

McKILLOP, *Lieut* Archibald, RN (*fl* 1805–1820)   Tr 80

M'KILLOP, *Rear-Adm* Henry Frederick, CB (*d* 1879)   B ii 636

M'KILLOP, *Cdr* John Gardner M'Bride, RN (*d* 1829)   M vii 198

MACKINDER, *Sir* Halford John (1861–1947)   DNB xxvii 556

M'KINLEY, *Adm* George (*d* 1852)   B ii 637; M iii 441

MACKINNON, *Capt* Lauchlan Bellingham, RN (1815–1877)   B ii 638

MACKINNON, *Sir* William, CIE (1823–1893)
*Founded Mackinnon, Mackenzie & Co, for coastal trading in the Bay of Bengal;
took a major part in the founding of the British India Steam Navigation Co*   B ii 638; DNB xxii 999

MACKINTOSH, *Lieut* John, RM (1786–1850)   Tr 250

MACKINTOSH, Thomas (*fl* 1780–1782)
Instrument-maker, writer on and teacher of navigation   T ii 317

MACKLY, *Capt* John, RN (*fl* 1673)   ch i 399

M'KONOCHIE, *Cdr* Alexander, RN (*fl* 1805–1818)   M vii 399

MACKY, John (*d* 1726)
*Government agent or spy; directed the packet boat service between Dover, France
and Flanders, 1697–1702, and 1706–1708*   DNB xii 633

McLACHLAN, Charles (*ca* 1795–1855)
*Official of the Australian Company at Leith – a shipowning firm – and the company's
agent at Hobart Town*   DAuB ii 175

McLAREN, David (1785–1850)
*Clyde shipping agent, promoter of missions to seamen, emigration agent, expert on
Australian shipping*   DAuB ii 176

MACLAURIN, *Sir* Henry Normand (1835–1914)
Surgeon in the navy until 1871; migrated to New South Wales, settling in Sydney   AE ii 11

MACLAY, Edgar Stanton (1863–1919)
Author of works on naval history   DAB 621

MACLEAN, *Sir* Andrew (1828–1900)
Partner in the shipbuilding firm of Barclay, Curle & Co   B vi 129

M'LEAN, *Capt* Archibald, RN (*fl* 1816–1822)   M xii 402

M'LEAN, Frank (1837–1904)
Engineer and astronomer   DNB xxiiib 505

MACLEAN, *Capt* Rawdon, RN (*d* 1863)   M viii 127; Tr 171

McLEAN, *Lieut* Thomas C., USN (*fl* 1864–1880)   H 955

McLEAN, Walter, USN (1855–1930)   DAB 621

MACLEAR, *Adm* John Fiot Lee Pearse (1838–1907)   DNB xxiii b 539

MACNEILL, *Sir* John Benjamin (1793?–1880)
Civil engineer; conducted a series of experiments in canal-boat traction; suggested
boats carrying sixty passengers drawn by two horses at the rate of eight miles per hour   B ii 672; DNB xii 695

MACOMB, David B., *Chief Engineer*, USN (*fl* 1849–1880)   H 1001

MACONOCHIE, *Capt* Alexander, RN (1787–1860)   AE ii 14; B ii 673;
                                                                                            DAuB ii 184

MACPHERSON, David (*fl* 1805)
Writer on navigation   T ii 369

M'PHERSON, *Cdr* George, RN (*d* 1824)   M vii 409

M'QUHAE, *Capt* Peter, RN (*fl* 1803–1844)   M vii 272

McRITCHIE, *Lieut* David G., USN (*fl* 1861–1880)   H 941

M'VICAR, *Capt* Alexander, RN (*d* 1840)   M xii 122; Tr 144

McWILLIAM, James Ormiston, CB, *Surgeon*, RN (1808–1862)   DNB xii 731

MACY, Benjamin (*fl* 1700–1731)
Mathematical and nautical instrument-maker and bookseller; instruments
at National Maritime Museum   T i 297; ii 134

MACY, Josiah (1785–1872)
Shipowner   DAB 627

MADDEN, *Cdr* Charles, RN (*fl* 1811–1846)   M viii 331

MADDEN, *Adm of the Fleet* Sir Charles Edward, GCVO, GCB, KCMG
(1862–1935)   DNB xxvi 594

MADDY, Watkin (*d* 1857)
Astronomer   DNB xii 743

MADOG AB OWAIN GWYNEDD (1150–1180?)
Welsh prince or member of royal bodyguard; reputed voyager to North America   DCB i 677; DNB xii
                                                                                            746; Md xxvi 11

MADRIGNANI, *Abbé* Archangèle (*fl* 1400–1420)
Editor of collection of Spanish and Portuguese voyages to East Indies   Md xxvi 12

MAFFIT, David (*d* 1838)
American privateer   DAB 630

MAFFIT, John Newland (1819–1886)
Served in the U.S.N., 1832–1861, and the C.S.N.   DAB 630

MAGALHAENS DE GANDAVO, Pedro de (*ca* 1550–*after* 1576)
Portuguese historian of Brazil and the discovery of America   Md xxvi 22

MAGAW, *Cdr* Samuel, USN (*fl* 1841–1868)   H 919

MAGEE, George W., *Chief Engineer*, USN (1861–1880)   H 1010

MAGELLAN, Ferdinand (*ca* 1480–1521)   A 56; H 462; CE viii
                                                                                            790; Md xxvi 27

MAINGAY [*or* MAINGY], *Cdr* Peter, RN (*b* 1784)   M vii 364

MAINGON, Jacques-Remi (1765–1809)
Captain French Navy, hydrographer   Md xxvi 145

MAINWARING, *Lieut* Benjamin, RN (1794–1852)   Tr 55

MAINWARING, *Capt* Edward Reeves Philip (*b* 1788)   M viii 182

MAINWARING [*or* MANWARING *or* MAYNWARINGE], *Sir* Henry
(1587–1653)
Vice-admiral RN, privateer, pirate and naval lexicographer   DCB i 481

MAINWARING, *Rear-Adm* Rowland (1783–1862)   B ii 699; DNB xii 792;
                                                                                    M vi 126

MAINWARING, *Rear-Adm* Thomas Francis Charles (1780–1858)   M x 310; Tr 295

MAINWARING, *Capt* William, RN (*d* 1763)   ch vi 444

MAIONE DE BARI (*fl* 1155–1160)
Grand admiral of Sicily   Md xxvi 160

MAIR [*or* MARR], John (*fl* 1614–1647)
Dial and compass-maker; supplied needles to Captain Thomas James' Arctic expedition
of 1631   T i 203

MAIR [*or* MARR], John (*fl* 1683–1689)
Mariner, marine surveyor and teacher of navigation   T i 279

MAISEAU, Raymond-Balthasard (1782–1843)
French police official; writer on nautical and commercial statistics and trade   Md xxvi 166

MAISTERSON, *Capt* Samuel, RN (*d* 1762)   ch v 396

MAISTRAL, Désiré-Marie (1764–1842)
Captain French Navy; brother of Esprit-Tranquille Maistral   Md xxvi 173

MAISTRAL, Esprit-Tranquille (1763–1815)
French rear-admiral   Md xxvi 171

MAITLAND, *Capt the Hon* Frederick, RN (1730–1786)   ch vi 374

MAITLAND, *Rear-Adm Sir* Frederick Lewis, KCB (1776–1839)   M iii 381

MAITLAND, *Rear-Adm* John (*fl* 1793–1821)   M ii 840

MAITLAND, *Adm of the Fleet* Thomas, GCB, GCMG, *tenth Earl of Lauderdale*
(1785–1863)   DNB xxi 801; M ix
                                                                                    188

MAITLAND, *Adm of the Fleet* Thomas, GCB, *eleventh Earl of Lauderdale*
(1803–1878)   DNB xii 820; M viii
                                                                                    230

MAITLAND, William (*fl* 1740–1757)
Schoolmaster RN, writer on navigation   T ii 211

MAITLAND-DOUGALL, *Adm* William Heriot (1819–1890)   B vi 144

MANBY, Charles (1804–1884)
*Civil engineer; took part in Sir John Ross's enterprise for running steamers to India,
which was absorbed by the Peninsular & Oriental Co in 1838*   B ii 714; DNB xii 901

MANBY, George William (1765–1854)
Inventor of apparatus for saving life from shipwreck   B ii 715; CE ix 49;
DNB xii 901; M*d* xxvi 309

MANBY, *Rear-Adm* Thomas (1769–1834)   DNB xii 903; M iii 199

MANDELSLO, Jean Albert de (1616–1644)
German voyager to East Indies, China, Japan, Africa; travel writer   M*d* xxvi 323

MANDERSON, *Capt* James, RN (*fl* 1795–1806)   M vi 345; NC xxx 89

MANDEVILLE, *Sir* John (*d ca* 1372)
Author of a famous book of travels, now known to be fabulous   CE ix 86; DNB xii 908

MAGIN, *Rear-Adm* Reuben Caillard (1780–1846)   M ix 240

MANGLES, *Capt* James, RN (1786–1867)   B ii 718; DNB xii 918; M vii 361

MANLEY, *Capt* Francis, RN (*d* 1693)   ch ii 400

MANLEY, *Vice-Adm Sir* Isaac George (*fl* 1790–1821)   M i 386

MANLEY, *Capt* John, USN (*ca* 1734–1793)   DAB 634; H 464

MANLEY, *Cdr* John, RN (*fl* 1782–1802)   M vi 295

MANLY, *Cdr* Henry de Haven, USN (*fl* 1856–1880)   H 909

MANN, Gerard (1821–1855)
Oarsman   B ii 721

MANN, *Gen* Gother, RE (1747–1830)
*Employed on the defences of Sheerness and the Medway, 1763–1775; reported on
the East Coast defences, 1779*   DNB xii 925

MANN, Henry (1806–1879)
Astronomer   B ii 720

MANN, James (*ca* 1685–1750)
Optical instrument-maker; writer on latitude at sea   T ii 134

MANN, *Capt* Robert, RN (*d* 1762)   ch vi 262

MANN, *Capt* Thomas, RN (*d* 1719)   ch iii 312

MANN, Thomas (1856–1941)
*First president of Dockers' Union; founder of the International Federation of Ship,
Dock and River Workers; later revived the fortunes of the National Amalgamated
Sailors' and Fireman's Union*   DNB xxvii 568

MANN, William (1817–1873)
Astronomer   B ii 720; DNB xii 931

MANNERS, *Capt Lord* Robert, RN (1758–1782)   DNB xii 939; NA ii 33

MARCIANUS (early 5th century B.C.)
Greek geographer   Md xxvi 498

MARCONI, Marchese Guglielmo (1874–1937)
Italian electrical engineer, pioneer of radio communications at sea   A 463 ; CE ix 90

MARE, Charles John (1814–1898)
Shipbuilder   B vi 156

MAREC, Pierre (1759–1828)
Commissioner on the 'Bureau de contrôle de l'administration de la marine', at Brest;
inspector of ports   Md xxvi 514

MARESTIER, Jean Baptiste (d 1832)
French marine engineer and naval architect; pioneer of steam navigation   Md xxvi 525

MARGETTS, George (fl 1789–1803)
Instrument-maker, compiler of nautical tables; instruments at National Maritime Museum T ii 318

MARGGRAF, Georg (1610–1644)
German doctor; voyager to Brazil, Guinea; astronomer   Md xxvi 541

MARGUERIE, Jean-Jacques de (1742–1779)
Lieutenant French Navy; mathematician, writer on naval matters   Md xxvi 543

MARGUERIT [or MARGARIT], Berenger (fl 1188)
Sicilian naval commander   Md xxvi 547

MARGUERIT, Pierre (fl 1492)
Courtier of King Ferdinand of Spain; sailed with Columbus, 1492; supposed discoverer
of Ile Marguerite   Md xxvi 548

MARICOURT, Paul le Moyne, *Sieur de* (1663–1704)
French-Canadian soldier and naval captain   MDC 495

MARIGNY, Augustin Étienne Gaspard de Bernard de (1754–1794)
French marine artillery officer   Md xxvi 657

MARIGNY, Charles René Louis de Bernard, *Viscomte de* (1740–1816)
French vice-admiral   Md xxvi 658

MARIN, *Capt* Mathias C., USN (fl 1832–1868)   H 898

MARINAS, Enrico Las (1620–1680)
Spanish marine painter   Md xxvi 672

MARINUS (fl A.D. 100)
Geographer of Tyre, from whom Ptolemy borrowed material   Md xxvi 662

MARION DU FRESNE (fl 1746–1773)
Captain French Navy; explorer of the Pacific   Md xxvi 680

MARITZ, Jean (1711–1790)
Naval cannon founder; inspector of foundries in France; inspector-general of
naval foundries in Spain   Md xxvi 682

MARIX, *Lieut* Adolph, USN (fl 1864–1880)   H 953

MARJORIBANKS, Edward, KT, *second Baron Tweedmouth* (1849–1909)   DNB xxiiib 569

MARSH, *Capt* Henry, RN (*d* 1772)   ch vi 80

MARSH, Humphrey (*fl* 1690)
Instrument-maker; wheel-cutting machine at National Maritime Museum   T i 286

MARSH, John (junior) (*fl* 1810–1838)
Optician; instruments at National Maritime Museum   T ii 399

MARSH, *Rear-Adm* William (*d* 1765)   ch v 247

MARSHALL, *Lieut* Charles Henry, RN (*d* 1835)   Tr 226

MARSHALL, Charles Henry (1792–1865)
Sea-captain, commanded Black Ball packets, 1822–1834, and later became owner of
the line   DAB 642

MARSHALL, *Cdr* Henry Masterman, RN (*b* 1784)   M viii 278

MARSHALL, *Capt* James, RN (*fl* 1815–1832)   M viii 485

MARSHALL, *Cdr* James Nasmyth, RN (*d* 1830)   M vi 290

MARSHALL, John (1663–1725)
Optical instrument-maker; instruments at National Maritime Museum   T i 280

MARSHALL, *Capt* John, RN (*fl* 1672)   ch i 348

MARSHALL, John (1783–1841)
English economist; writer on shipping   DNB xii 1125; M*d*
                                                                             xxvii 78

MARSHALL, *Lieut* John, RN (1784?–1837)   DNB xii 1125

MARSHALL, *Capt Sir* John, CB, RN (*b* 1785)   M xi 390

MARSHALL, *Cdr* John Houlton, RN (*d* 1837)   M vi 402; Tr 40

MARSHALL, *Capt* John Willoughby, RN (*d* 1824)   M x 270

MARSHALL, *Capt* Samuel, RN (*d* 1768)   ch vi 51

MARSHALL, *Capt* Samuel, RN (*fl* 1789)   NA ii 27

MARSHALL, *Capt* Thomas, RN (*d* 1690)   ch i 242

MARSHALL, *Capt* Thomas, RN (*d* 1690?)   ch ii 277

MARSHALL, *Brig-Gen* William Louis, USA (1846–1920)
In charge of river and harbour improvements in Wisconsin and Illinois; completed
the Ambrose Channel, New York   DAB 645

MARSHAM, *Capt* Henry Shovell Jones, RN (1794–1875)   B ii 761; M viii 527

MARSOLET DE SAINT-AIGNAN, Nicolas (*ca* 1587–1677)
French ship's master; fur-trader   DCB i 493

MARSTON, *Cdre* John, USN (*b* 1796)   H 485

MARTEL, *Contre-Adm* Léandre François (1737–1817)   S ii 159

MARTEN, *Sir* Henry (1562?–1641)
Judge of Admiralty court, 1617–1641   DNB xii 1146

MARTIN, *Capt* Robert, RN (*fl* 1660)   *ch* i 25

MARTIN, *Rear-Adm* Roger (*d* 1779)   *ch* v 47

MARTIN, *Capt* Samuel, RN (*d* 1705)   *ch* iii 167

MARTIN [*later* LEAKE], *Capt* Stephen, RN (*d* 1735/6)   *ch* iii 233

MARTIN, *Adm* Thomas (1787–1868)   B ii 773; M v 284

MARTIN, *Adm of the Fleet Sir* Thomas Byam, GCB (1773–1854)   B ii 773; DNB xii
                                                                                  1183; M ii 491; R iii
                                                                                  47

MARTIN, *Rear-Adm* Thomas Hutchinson Mangles (1829–1896)   B vi 169

MARTIN, *Capt* William, RN (*d* 1666)   *ch* i 171

MARTIN, *Adm* William (*d* 1756)   *ch* iv 69

MARTIN, *Capt* William, RN (*d* 1766)   *ch* vi 81

MARTIN, *Cdr* William, RN (1783–1866)   M viii 84; Tr 145

MARTIN, *Adm Sir* William Fanshaw, GCB (1801–1895)   B vi 170; DNB xxii
                                                                                  1017; M v 182

MARTINDALE, Adam (1623–1686)
Mathematician and writer on navigation   DNB xii 1189; T i 227

MARTINES, Joan [*or* Juan] (*fl* 1550–1586)
Hydrographer   CE ix 129

MARWOOD, *Capt* Thomas, RN (*d* 1731)   *ch* iv 46

MARYCHURCH, *Capt* Isaac (*fl* 1661)   *ch* i 61

MASIG, Johann Martin [*or* Willebrand?] (*fl ca* 1700)
Instrument-maker; dials at National Maritime Museum   T i 297

MASKELYNE, Nevil (1732–1811)
Astronomer-Royal   CE ix 141; DNB xii
                                                                                  1299

MASON, Charles (1730–1787)
Astronomer; James Bradley's assistant at Greenwich, 1756–1760   DNB xii 1302; Md
                                                                                  xxvii 194; T ii 239

MASON, *Capt* Christopher, RN (*fl* 1666–1699)   *ch* i 348

MASON, *Vice-Adm Sir* Francis, KCB (1779–1853)   B ii 780; M ix 55

MASON, *Capt* Henry Browne, RN (1791–1870)   M vii 369; Tr 83

MASON, John (1586–1635)
Founder of New Hampshire; nominated 'vice-admiral of New England', 1635   DNB xii 1313; MDC
                                                                                  501

MASON, *Capt* John, RN (*fl* 1679)   *ch* ii 61

MASON, *Capt* John, RN (*d* 1691)   *ch* ii 335

MASON, John Charles (1798–1881)
Marine secretary to the Indian government, 1837–1867   DNB xii 1317

MASON, Joseph, *Purser*, RN (1789–1863)   Tr 250

MASON, Martin (*d* 1821)
Surgeon on H.M.S. 'Buffalo'   DAuB ii 213

MASON, *Lieut* Newton E., USN (*fl* 1865–1880)   H 958

MASON, Samuel (*ca* 1750–1803)
Ohio river pirate   DAB 650

MASON, *Lieut* Theodorus Bailey Myers, USN (*b* 1848)   H 954

MASON, *Adm* Thomas Mason (1811–1900)   B vi 175

MASON, *Capt* Thomas Monck, RN (*fl* 1807–1828)   M vi 31

MASON, William Garn, *Purser*, RN (*d* 1857)   Tr 236

MASPOLI, Augustus (*fl* 1837)
Nautical instrument-maker   T ii 375

MASQUELIER, Louis Joseph (1741–1811)
French engraver of naval battles, etc   Md xxvii 207

MASQUELIER, Nicolas François Joseph (1760–1809)
French engraver; illustrator of Lescallier's: 'Dictionnaire de Marine   Md xxvii 208

MASSAM, *Capt* William, RN (*d* 1708)   ch iii 401

MASSEY, Edward (*fl* 1800–1838)
Chronometer and log-maker; instruments at National Maritime Museum   T ii 369

MASSEY, Frederick Henry (1812–1897)
Civil engineer; supervised the establishment of shipbuilding and engineering works
at Odessa and Sevastopol for the Russian Government   B vi 177

MASSIE, *Adm* Thomas Leeke (1802–1898)   B vi 177; DNB xii
          1023

MASSINGBERD, *Adm* Vincent Amcotts (1808–1889)   B ii 787

MASTER [*or* MASTERS], *Capt* Harcourt, RN (*d* 1762)   ch iv 382

MASTER, *Capt* James, RN (*fl* 1802–1804)   M iv 890

MASTER, *Capt* Streynsham, RN (*d* 1724)   ch iv 24; DNB xii 22

MATCHAM, George (1789–1877)
Nephew of Lord Nelson; author of: 'Notes on the character of Admiral Lord
Nelson' (1861)   DNB xiii 27

MATELIEF, Cornelius (*fl* 1605–1608)
Dutch admiral   Md xxvii 245

MATHER, *Capt* William, RN (*fl* 1672–1673)   ch i 348

MATHER, *Cdr* William, RN (*fl* 1799–1813)   M vi 362

MATHESON, John Augustus (*b* 1780)
Clerk aboard the 'Téméraire' at Trafalgar   Tr 56

MATHEWS, *Sir* Lloyd William, KCMG (1850–1901)   DNB xxiiib 591

MATHEWS, *Adm* Thomas (1676–1751)   *ch* iii 252; DNB xiii
43; M*d* xxvii 282

MATHON DE LA COUR, Jacques (1712–1770)
French mathematician; writer on the handling of large sailing ships   M*d* xxvii 268

MATRA [*or* MAGRA], James Mario (*d* 1806)
A member of the 'Endeavour' 's crew on Cook's first voyage and published an
anonymous account of it in 1771. He spelt his surname Magra up to 1775   AE ii 45

MATSON, *Cdr* George William, RN (*b* 1794)   M viii 366

MATSON, *Capt* Henry, RN (*fl* 1790–1810)   M iv 743

MATSON, *Adm* Richard (*d* 1848)   M iii 213

MATTHEWS, *Cdr* Alfred, RN (*fl* 1803–1833)   M viii 99

MATTHEWS, *Cdr* Edmund O., USN (*fl* 1851–1880)   H 901

MATTHEWS, *Cdr* Michael, RN (*fl* 1799–1816)   M vii 401

MATTHEWS, *Sir* William, KCMG (1844–1922)
Civil engineer; partner in the firm Coode, Son & Matthews, a firm frequently
employed by the Admiralty on naval base contracts   DNB xxv 569

MATTICE, Asa Martines (1853–1925)
USN engineer, 1874–1890   DAB 655

MAUDE, *Capt the Hon* Francis, RN (1798–1886)   B ii 800; M viii 230

MAUDE, *Capt the Hon Sir* James Ashley, CB (1786–1841)   M vii 424; xi 249

MAUDE, *Capt* William, RN (*fl* 1805–1821)   M ix 213

MAUDSLAY, Henry (1771–1831)
Engineer; employed by Marc Brunel to construct machinery for making ships' blocks
which was later erected at Portsmouth dockyard; designed improvements for
marine engines   CE ix 165; DNB xiii
81

MAUDSLAY, Joseph (1801–1861)
Marine engine builder   B ii 800; DNB xiii 82

MAUDSLAY, Thomas Henry (1792–1864)
Marine engine builder   B ii 901; DNB xiii 82

MAUDUITH [*or* MANDUIT], John (*fl* 1310)
Astronomer   DNB xiii 84

MAUGHAM, *Capt* George, RN (*d* 1702)   *ch* iii 168

MAULE-RAMSAY, *Adm* George, CB, *twelfth Earl of Dalhousie* (1806–1880)   B i 804

MAULSBY, George, *Surgeon*, USN (*fl* 1838–1879)   H 982

MAUND, *Capt* Christopher, RN (*d* 1692)   *ch* ii 428

MAUNSELL, *Capt* Robert, CB, RN (1786–1845)   M xi 36

MAUPERTUIS, Pierre-Louis Moreau de (1698–1759)
French astronomer who made a scientific voyage to the Arctic; writer on navigation;
translator of Newton   A 124

MAURICE, *Capt* James Wilkes, RN (1775–1857)   B ii 804; DNB xiii 106;
    M ix 434

MAURICE [*or* MORRICE *or* MORRIS], *Vice-Adm* Salmon (*d* 1741)   Ch iii 169

MAURO, Fra (*fl* 1444–1459)
Geographer, produced map of the world, 1457   Md xxvii 348

MAURVILLE, *Comte* Bidé de (1752–1840)
French rear-admiral   Md xxvii 355

MAURY, Matthew Fountaine (1806–1873)
U.S. naval officer; oceanographer; founder of U.S. Naval Observatory; Confederate
head of coast, harbour and river defences; inventor of a torpedo; pioneer of wind and
current charts   A 253; CE ix 170;
    DAB 656; H 489

MAWBEY, *Lieut* John, RN (*d* 1852)   Tr 116

MAWE, John (1764–1829)
English voyager to South America and travel writer   DNB xiii 110; Md
    xxvii 365

MAWSON, *Sir* Douglas (1882–1958)
Australian Antarctic explorer; accompanied Shackleton expedition, 1907–1909   AE ii 46; CE ix 171

MAXIM, *Sir* Hiram Stevens (1840–1916)
Inventor of the Maxim gun, adopted by the Royal Navy in 1892   DNB xxiv 376

MAXSE, *Adm* Frederick Augustus (1833–1900)   B vi 185; DNB xxii
    1029

MAXWELL, Charles D., *Medical Director*, USN (*fl* 1837–1868)   H 982

MAXWELL, *Cdr* George, RN (*fl* 1780–1790)   M vi 249

MAXWELL, *Capt* George Berkley (*fl* 1796–1830)   M vi 160

MAXWELL, *Capt* John, RN (*d* 1826)   M x 94

MAXWELL, *Capt* John Balfour (1799–1874)   B ii 809; M viii 218

MAXWELL, *Capt* Keith, RN (*d* 1823)   M iv 884

MAXWELL, *Capt Sir* Murray, CB, RN (*fl* 1796–1822)   DNB xiii 130; M iv
    797; Md xxvii 387

MAXWELL, *Gen* William Robert, RM (*d* 1892)   B ii 810

MAY, Edward, *Pay Inspector*, USN (*fl* 1861–1880)   H 987

MAY, George Ernest, KBE, *first Baron May* (1871–1946)
Financial expert; a member of the Navy and Army Canteen Board during
the First World War   DNB xxvii 582

MAY, Henry (*fl* 1591–1594)
Mariner; purser on Sir James Lancaster's East Indies voyage, 1591   DCB i 499

MAY, *Capt* Richard, RN (*d* 1665)   *ch* i 171

MAY, *Lieut* Sidney H., USN (*fl* 1864–1878)   H 964

MAY, *Lieut* Stephen Yonge, RN (*d* 1828)   Tr 306

MAY, *Capt* Walter William, RN (1830–1896)   B vi 189

MAY, *Cdr* William, RN (*fl* 1798–1814)   M vi 393

MAY, *Adm of the Fleet Sir* William Henry, GCB, GCVO (1849–1930)   DNB xxv 571

MAYER, Tobias (1723–1762)
German astronomer   CE ix 174; T ii 268

MAYNARD, Félix (1813–1858)
French merchant marine surgeon; voyager to Australia   Md xxvii 404

MAYNARD, *Capt* Francis, RN (*d* 1693)   *ch* ii 401

MAYNARD, *Capt* Henry Lord, RN (*d* 1742)   *ch* iii 240

MAYNARD, *Cdr* Joseph, RN (*fl* 1808–1844)   M viii 175

MAYNARD, *Capt* Thomas, RN (*fl* 1780–1840)   M vi 322

MAYNARD, *Lieut* Washburne, USN (*fl* 1862–1880)   H 942

MAYNE, *Capt* Covill, RN (*d* 1746)   *ch* iv 30

MAYNE, *Capt* Dawson, RN (*b* 1799)   M viii 334

MAYNE [*or* MAINE], *Capt* John, RN (*d* 1712)   *ch* ii 334

MAYNE, *Vice-Adm* Perry (1700?–1761)   *ch* iv 137; DNB xiii 164

MAYNE, *Adm* Richard Charles, CB (1835–1892)   B ii 818; DNB xiii 166

MAYNE, *Cdr* Robert, RN (1783–1846)   Tr 249

MAYO, Henry O., *Surgeon*, USN (*fl* 1846–1872)   H 984

MAYO, *Adm* Henry Thomas, USN (1856–1937)   DAB 659

MAYO, John Joseph (*d* 1874)
Registrar-general of seamen and shipping, 1862–1874   B vi 191

MAYO, *Capt* Thomas, RN (*fl* 1672)   *ch* i 348

MAYO, *Cdre* William Kennon, USN (1829–1900)   DAB 660; H 879

MAZARREDO Y SALAZAR, Jose Maria (1744–1812)
Spanish admiral   Md xxvii 426

MEAD, *Capt* Joseph, RN (1707–1799)
Merchant navy captain; writer on ocean currents; inventor of a method for cleaning ships'
bottoms   *ch* vi 440; T ii 239

MEAD, Richard (1673–1754)
Physician; writer on maps and globes   DNB xii 181; T ii 239

MELLERSH, *Adm* Arthur (1812–1894)   B vi 193

MELVILL, Pierre, *Baron de Garnbeé* (1743–1826)
Dutch vice-admiral   M*d* xxvii 591

MELVILL, Pierre, *Baron de Garnbeé* (1816–1856)
Lieutenant-captain, Dutch Navy; hydrographer   M*d* xxvii 591

MELVILLE, *Rear-Adm* George Wallace, usn (1841–1912)   DAB 667

MELVILLE, Herman (1819–1891)   CE ix 245; DAB 667

MENDAÑA DE NEYRA, Alvaro (1541–1595)
Spanish voyager to South America and Pacific and discoverer of the Solomon Islands   M*d* xxvii 616

MENENDEZ DE AVILES, Pedro (1519–1574)
Spanish officer   H 493

MENDOZA Y RIOS, Joseph de (1762–1816)
Spanish naval officer, astronomer and writer on navigation   DNB xiii 251; M*d* xxvii 626; T ii 319

MENDS, *Cdre Sir* Robert, RN (1767?–1823)   DNB xiii 251; M iii 270

MENDS, *Adm* William Bowen (1781–1864)   B ii 843; M xi 253

MENDS, *Adm Sir* William Robert, GCB (1812–1897)   B vi 197; DNB xxii 1031

MENNIS [*or* MINNS *or* MYNGS], *Adm Sir* John (1599–1671)   *ch* i 61; DNB xiii 253

MENOCAL, Aniceto Garcia (1836–1908)
Naval officer, engineer in U.S. Navy, 1874–1898   DAB 669

MENZIES, *Gen Sir* Charles, KCB, RM (1783–1866)   B ii 845

MENZIES, Thomas, *Purser*, RN (*d* 1835)   T*r* 297

MERCADELL, *Cdr* Alexander, RN (*fl* 1808–1814)   M vii 331

MERCATOR, Gerhardus (1512–1594)   CE ix 297

MERCER, James (1883–1932)
Mathematician; served as naval instructor, 1914–1918 and was present at Jutland   DNB xxvi 611

MERCER, *Cdr* John Davis, RN (*fl* 1798–1824)   M viii 144

MERCER, *Capt* Paul, RN (*fl* 1672–1680)   *ch* ii 63

MEREDITH, *Capt* Richard, RN (1789–1850)   M viii 132; T*r* 289

MERRELL, *Lieut* John P., usn (*fl* 1863–1880)   H 947

MERRIFIELD, Charles Watkins (1827–1884)
Mathematician; became the first vice-principal of the Royal School of Naval Architecture & Marine Engineering at South Kensington in 1867 and soon afterwards succeeded as principal   DNB xiii 291

MERRIMAN, *Cdr* Edgar C., usn (*fl* 1856–1880)   H 911

MIDDLETON, *Sir* Henry (*d* 1613)
Merchant and sea-captain   DNB xiii 350; M*d*
                                                                    xxviii 261

MIDDLETON, *Capt* Henry, RN (*d* 1703)   c*h* iii 74
MIDDLETON, *Capt* Hugh, RN (*fl* 1660)   c*h* i 25
MIDDLETON, *Capt Sir* Hugh, RN (*fl* 1717–1740)   c*h* iv 47

MIDDLETON, John (*d* 1603)
Relative of Henry Middleton; British East India Co naval commander   M*d* xxviii 261

MIDDLETON, Joseph (*fl* 1717–1736)
Marine surveyor; teacher of mathematics on RN ships   T ii 135

MIDDLETON, *Capt* Robert Gambier, RN (*fl* 1793–1816)   M iii 85

MICHEL(L)S, *Vice-Adm* James (1665–1734)   c*h* iii 74

MIGHELLS, *Capt* Josiah [or Joseph], RN (*d* 1707)   c*h* iii 273

MIGHELS, *Capt* John, RN (*fl* 1708–1733)   c*h* iii 401

MIHILL, Richard (*fl* 1754–1755)
Midshipman RN; geography teacher   T ii 240

MILBANKE, *Lieut* Henry, RN (*fl* 1804–1808)   T*r* 169

MILBANKE, *Adm* Mark (1725?–1805)   c*h* vi 81; DNB xiii
                                                                    369; NA i 70

MILLBANKE, *Capt* Ralph, RN (*d* 1823)   M iii 72

MILDMAY, *Capt* George William St John, RN (*fl* 1805–1838)   M vi 50

MILIUS, Pierre Bernard (1773–1829)
French rear-admiral   M*d* xxviii 290

MILL, Hugh Robert (1861–1950)
Geographer and meteorologist   CE ix 411; DNB xxvii
                                                                    591

MILLAR, *Capt* Archibald, RN (*d* 1766)   c*h* vi 439

MILLER, Andrew (*d* 1790)
Member of Vice-Admiralty Court, New South Wales   DA *u*B ii 229

MILLER, *Lieut* F. Augustus, USN (*fl* 1861–1880)   H 939

MILLER, *Lieut* Henry, RM (*d* 1849)   T*r* 228

MILLER, J. Dickinson, *Surgeon*, USN (*fl* 1836–1872)   H 982

MILLER, *Lieut* Jacob W., USN (*fl* 1863–1880)   H 950

MILLER, *Lieut* James M., USN (*fl* 1863–1871)   H 950

MILLER, John (*fl* 1793–1825)
Instrument-maker; instruments at National Maritime Museum   T ii 345

MILLER, *Capt* John, RN (*fl* 1797–1821)   M iii 114

MILLER, *Cdr* Joseph N., USN (*b* 1836)   H 900

MINCHIN, *Cdr* William, RN (*d* 1845)   M viii 60

MINGAYE, *Adm* William James (1785–1865)   B ii 898; M xii 379

MINGEN, *Capt* John, RN (*fl* 1666)   *ch* i 243

MINNS [*or* MENNIS *or* MYNGS], *Vice-Adm Sir* John (*d* 1671)   *ch* i 61

MINORS, *Capt* Richard, RN (*fl* 1665–1672)   *ch* i 61

MINTERNE, *Capt* William, RN (*fl* 1666–1667)   *ch* i 243

MIRIEL, Jean Joseph Yves Louis (1780–1829)
Surgeon, French Navy   M*d* xxviii 389

MIR-MAHNNA (1735–1769)
Arab pirate in the Red Sea   M*d* xxviii 393

MISSELDEN, Edward (*fl* 1608–1654)
Deputy-governor of the Merchant Adventurers Company at Delft, 1623–1633   DNB xiii 498

MISSIESSY, *Comte* Edward-Thomas Burgues de (1756–1837)
French vice-admiral   M*d* xxviii 398; S ii 206

MITCHELL, Alexander (1780–1868)
Civil engineer; inventor of the Mitchell screw-pile which was first used as
foundation of the Maplin Sand Lighthouse in the mouth of the Thames, 1838; designed
and constructed the Fleetwood-on-Wyre lighthouse, 1839; his improved method
of mooring ships was generally adopted   B ii 901; DNB xiii 509

MITCHELL, *Capt* Andrew, RN (*fl* 1677–1682)   *ch* ii 15

MITCHELL, *Adm Sir* Andrew, KB (1757–1806)   DNB xiii 511; M*d* xxviii 401; NC xvii 89; R ii 91

MITCHELL, *Capt* Andrew, RN (*fl* 1805–1822)   M xii 380

MITCHELL, *Capt Sir* Battimore, RN (*fl* 1667)   *ch* ii 15

MITCHELL, *Capt* Charles, RN (*fl* 1805–1825)   M v 215

MITCHELL, Charles (1820–1895)
Shipbuilder   B vi 219

MITCHELL, *Lieut-Col Sir* Charles Bullen Hugh, GCMG, RM (1836–1899)   B vi 219

MITCHELL, *Capt* Cornelius, RN (*d* 1749)   *ch* iv 230; DNB xiii 512

MITCHELL, *Vice-Adm Sir* David (1650?–1710)   *ch* ii 105; DNB xiii 513

MITCHELL, *Capt* Henry, RN (*d* 1705)   *ch* iii 168

MITCHELL, Henry (1830–1902)
Hydrographer   DAB 684

MOCENIGO, Pedro (*d* 1476)
Doge of Venice: naval commander   Md xxviii 432

MOCKLER, *Lieut* Thomas, RN (*d* 1840)   Tr 296

MOCQUET, Jean (1575–*after* 1617)
French voyager to Africa, South America, the East Indies and India   Md xviii 435

MODÈNE, Charles de Raimond (*fl* 1761, *d* 1772)
Captain French navy   Md xxviii 439

MODÈNE, Henri de Raimond (*fl* 1720, *d* 1727)
Commodore French navy   MD xxviii 439

MODÈNE, Jean François de Raimond de Mormoiron de (1652–1705)
Naval commander for Knights of Malta   Md xxviii 439

MODSLEY, Samuel (*fl* 1774)
Writer on Captain Phipps' voyage to the North Pole, 1773   T ii 292

MOFFITT, *Rear-Adm* William Adger, USN (1869–1933)   DAB 687

MOGG, *Capt* Thomas, RN (*d* 1756)   ch v 348

MOHUN, *Capt* Robert, RN (*fl* 1660–1662)   ch i 82

MOISSON, Henri Félix Antoine (1784–1832)
Captain French navy   Md xxviii 502

MOLÉ, Mathieu (*d* 1688)
Naval commander for Knights of Malta   Md xxviii 536

MOLESWORTH, *Cdr* Bourchier, RN (*fl* 1798–1814)   M vii 154

MOLESWORTH, *Lieut* Francis, RN (*d* 1812)   Tr 62

MOLESWORTH, *Capt* John, RN (1789–1858)   M viii 177

MOLINEUX, *Cdr* James, RN (*fl* 1794–1827)   M vi 399

MOLL, Herman (*d* 1732)
Cartographer   CE ix 476; *chb* 440;
                                                                                 DNB xiii 575

MOLLOY, *Capt* Anthony James Price, RN (*fl* 1768–1778)   NA ii 71

MOLLOY, *Capt Sir* Charles, RN (*d* 1760)   ch v 203

MOLSON, John (1764–1836)
Canadian capitalist and pioneer of St Lawrence steam navigation   MDC 518

MOLYN (TEMPESTA), Pierre (1637–1701)
Dutch marine painter   Md xxviii 588

MOLYNEUX, Emery (*fl* 1587–1605)
Compass, globe, and nautical running-glass maker; explorer   T i 188

MOLYNEUX, Robert (*fl* 1815–1838)
Chronometer maker for Admiralty   T ii 399

MOLYNEUX, Samuel (1687–1728)
Astronomer   DNB xiii 583; T ii 135

MONTAGU, *Capt* Montagu, RN (1787–1863)   B ii 929

MONTAGU, *Adm* Robert (*fl* 1788–1810)   M i 135

MONTAGU, *Capt the Hon* William, RN (*d* 1759)   *ch* v 400; DNB xiii
                                                                                   720

MONTAGU, *Vice-Adm Sir* William Augustus, CB (1785–1852)   B ii 929; M ix 219

MONTAGU-DOUGLAS-SCOTT, *Adm Lord* Charles Thomas, GCB
(1839–1911)   DNB xxiiic 277

MONTAUBAND (*d* 1700)
French filibuster in America and Africa   Md xxix 42

MONTGOMERIE, *Capt* Alexander, RN (*fl* 1802–1846)   M xii 227

MONTGOMERIE, *Rear-Adm* Robert Archibald James, CB, CMG, CVO
(1855–1908)   DNB xxiiib 642

MONTGOMERY, *Lieut* Hugh, RN (1776–1837)   Tr 296

MONTGOMERY, *Capt* James, RN (*fl* 1673–1689)   *ch* ii 133

MONTGOMERY, *Rear-Adm* John Berrien, USN (1794–1873)   DAB 690; H 501

MONTGOMERY, John James (1832–1884)
Private secretary to Sir George B. Airy   B ii 936

MONTGOMERY, *Cdr* Thomas, RN (*b* 1786)   M vii 363

MONTLIVAULT, Eléonore Jacques François de Sales Guyon de Diziers,
Comte de (1765–1846)
Captain French navy; astronomer   Md xxix 156

MONTMAGNY, Charles Hualt de: *see* HUALT DE MONTMAGNY

MONTORGUEUIL, Dauphin de (*fl* 1689)
French naval lieutenant   DCB i 250

MONTRESOR, *Adm* Frederick Byng (*d* 1887)   B ii 939

MONTRESOR, *Capt* Henry, CB, RN (*fl* 1809–1816)   M xii 20

MONTS, Pierre du Guast, *Sieur de* (*fl* 1604–1610)
Companion of Champlain on 1604 Expedition to Canada; explorer, coloniser   Md xxix 201

MOODIE, *Cdr* Donald, RN (*d* 1861)   DNB xiii 776

MOODIE [*or* MUDIE *or* MOODY], *Capt* James, RN (*d* 1724)   *ch* ii 336

MOORE, Alexander (1809–1878)
Master shipwright   B ii 943

MOORE, Andrew M., *Assist-Surgeon*, USN (*fl* 1869–1880)   H 979

MOORE, *Cdr* Charles, RN (*fl* 1813–1819)   M vii 418

MOORE, *Capt* Christopher, RN (*d* 1696)   *ch* iii 107

MOORE, Edward (*fl* 1751)
Teacher of navigation and writer on globes   T ii 240

MOORE, *Lieut* Edward, RN (*d* 1857)   Tr 64

MORARD DE GALLE, Justin Bonaventure (1741–1809)
Vice-admiral French navy   Md xxix 237; s ii 225

MORAS, Gaspard Balthasar Melchior (1772–1824)
French naval pilot; naval artillery officer; colonel of the 2nd Regiment of the flotilla   Md xxix 238

MORCE, *Cdr* William, RN (*d* 1823)   M vi 293

MORDAUNT, *Adm* Charles, KG, *third Earl of Peterborough* (1658–1736)   CE x 609; ch iii 314;
DNB xiii 840; Md
xxxii 574

MORDAUNT, *Capt* Henry, RN (1681?–1710)   ch iii 274; DNB xiii
852

MORDECAL, Moses Cohen (1804–1888)
Merchant and shipowner   DAB 696

MORDEN, Robert (*d* 1703)
Geographer; prepared: 'Sea Atlas, drawn according to Mr Wright's alias Mercator's
projection' (1699) and: 'A new draft of the harbours of Vigo and Bayonna, shewing
the late action of the English fleet . . .' (ca 1702)   chb 440; DNB xiii
857; T i 237

MORE-MOLYNEUX, *Adm Sir* Robert Henry, GCB (1838–1904)   DNB xxiiib 646

MORESBY, *Adm of the Fleet Sir* Fairfax, GCB (1787–1877)   B ii 963; DNB xiii
904; M xi 363

MORESBY, *Adm* John (1830–1922)   DNB xxv 613

MORETON, *Capt* Francis Reynolds, RN, *third Baron Ducie* (1739–1808)   ch vi 474

MOREY, *Lieut* George, RN (*d* 1842)   Tr 43

MOREY, *Lieut* John Doling, RN (*fl* 1805–1825)   Tr 31

MORGAN, Charles (1795–1878)
Shipowner   DAB 696

MORGAN, David Lloyd, CB, RN (1823–1892)
Inspector-general of hospitals and fleets   B ii 964

MORGAN, *Sir* Henry (1635?–1688)   CE ix 533; DNB xiii
914; Md xxix 305

MORGAN, Henry, *Midshipman*, RN (*fl* 1805–1860)   Tr 128

MORGAN, *Capt* James, RN (*fl* 1798–1836)   M viii 79

MORGAN, James Morris, CSN (1845–1928)   DAB 697

MORGAN, *Lieut* Jeremiah, RN (*d* 1817)   Tr 144

MORGAN, John (*ca* 1792–1866)
Royal Marines officer   DAuB ii 258

MORGAN, *Cdr* John Fortescue, RN (*fl* 1803–1815)   M vii 335

MORGAN, *Cdr* Richard, RN (*fl* 1805–1840)   M viii 394

MORGAN, Thomas, *Midshipman*, RN (*fl* 1805–1806)   Tr 305

MORRIS, Edward Patrick, KCMG, *first Baron Morris of St John's and of the City of Waterford* (1859–1935)
Premier of Newfoundland; counsel for the British government in the North Atlantic fisheries dispute conducted at The Hague, 1910; leading figure in the organisation of the Royal Newfoundland Regiment and the enlistment of Newfoundlanders in the Royal Navy in the First World War   DNB xxvi 631; MDC 529

MORRIS, *Lieut-Cdr* Francis, USN (*fl* 1860–1880)   H 923

MORRIS, Frederick, *Chaplain*, RN (*d* 1799)   M viii 156

MORRIS, Gael (*fl* 1752–1765)
Astronomer, assistant observer at Greenwich   T ii 241

MORRIS, *Rear-Adm* George (*b* 1778)   M xi 14

MORRIS, *Adm* Henry Gate (1811–1891)   B ii 982; M xi 105

MORRIS, *Vice-Adm Sir* James Nicoll, KCB (1763–1830)   DNB xiii 993; M ii 488; Tr 167

MORRIS, John B. (*fl* 1825)
Instrument-maker   T ii 430

MORRIS, *Cdr* John Chafin, RN (*fl* 1797–1825)   M viii 154

MORRIS, *Cdr* John Row, RN (*fl* 1787–1832)   M vii 221

MORRIS, Lewis (1700–1765)
Welsh poet, philologist and antiquary; surveyed an area of the Welsh coast for the Admiralty, 1737–1744; this was published in 1748 as: 'Plans of harbours, bars, bays and roads in St George's Channel'   DNB xiii 999; T ii 163

MORRIS, *Capt* Richard Valentine, USN (1768–1815)   DAB 702

MORRIS, *Lieut* Robert, RN (*d* 1823)   Tr 70

MORRIS [*or* MAURICE *or* MORRICE], *Vice-Adm* Salmon (*d* 1741)   ch iii 169

MORRIS, Samuel Sheppard Oakley, *Chaplain*, RN (1847–1893)   B ii 986

MORRIS, *Brig-Gen* Thomas Armstrong, USA (1811–1904)
Canal engineer   DAB 703

MORRISON, *Lieut-Cdr* George F., USN (*fl* 1849–1860)   H 936

MORRISON, *Capt* Isaac Hawkins, RN (*fl* 1795–1846)   M xi 304

MORRISON, Richard James (1795–1874)
Inventor and astrologer; served in the Royal Navy, 1806–1829; presented a plan to the Admiralty 'for registering merchant seamen', 1824; a plan 'for propelling ships of war in a calm', 1827; and a further one 'for providing an ample supply of seamen for the Fleet without impressment', 1835   B ii 988; DNB xiii 1006

MORSE, *Lieut* Jerome E., USN (*fl* 1862–1874)   H 966

MORSE, Samuel Finley Breese (1791–1872)   CE ix 542; DAB 705

MOTTLEY, *Capt* Samuel, RN (*fl* 1782–1803)　　　　　　　　M iv 684

MOUAT, *Capt* Patrick, RN (*d* 1790)　　　　　　　　　　　ch vi 248

MOUAT, *Cdr* Stephen Peter, RN (*fl* 1787–1814)　　　　　　M vi 248

MOUBRAY, *Capt* George, RN (1773–1856)　　　　　　　　M xi 111; Tr 248

MOUBRAY, *Vice-Adm* Richard Hussey, GCMG, KCB (1776–1842)　　M ii 804, 881; R iv 116

MOULAC, Vincent Marie (1780–1836)
Captain French navy　　　　　　　　　　　　　　　　　　Md xxix 444

MOULD, *Capt* James, RN (*d* 1819)　　　　　　　　　　　Tr 51

MOULTON, *Capt* Robert, RN (*fl* 1664–1665)　　　　　　　ch i 116

MOUNSEY, *Capt* William, RN (*fl* 1780–1815)　　　　　　M x 20; R iv 313

MOUNSHER, *Capt* Eyles, RN (*d* 1836)　　　　　　　　　M xi 179; Tr 192

MOUNT, Richard (*d* 1722)
Chart-maker　　　　　　　　　　　　　　　　　　　　　T i 280

MOUNT & PAGE (*fl* 1675–1800)
Nautical stationers and chart publishers　　　　　　　　　T ii 136

MOUNTAGU, Edward, *first Earl of Sandwich: see* MONTAGU

MOUNTAINE, William (*fl* 1736–1778)
Writer on naval gunnery and navigation; pamphlets at National Maritime Museum　　T ii 186

MOUNTBATTEN, Louis Alexander, *first Marquis of Milford Haven, formerly styled Prince Louis Alexander of Battenberg, Admiral of the Fleet* (1854–1921)　　DNB xxiv 394

MOUNTBATTEN, *Adm of the Fleet* Louis Francis Albert Victor Nicholas, *first Earl Mountbatten of Burma* (*b* 1900)　　　　　　　CE ix 583

MOUNTGARRETT, Jacob, *Surgeon*, RN (*ca* 1773–1828)　　DAuB ii 264

MOURGES, Jacques-Augustin (1734–1818)
Director of port works at Brest; writer on the navigation laws　　Md xxix 476

MOUTRAY, *Capt* John, RN (*d* 1785)　　　　　　　　　ch vi 331; DNB xiii 1113

MOWATT, *Lieut* William, RN (*d* 1832/5)　　　　　　　Tr 61

MOWBRAY, Robert (*fl* 1805–1848)
Volunteer first-class in the 'Leviathan' at Trafalgar　　　　Tr 194

MOXON, James (*senior and junior*) (*fl* 1647–1696)
Booksellers and map-engravers　　　　　　　　　　　　T i 231

MOXON, Joseph (1627–1700)
Hydrographer and mathematician　　　　　　　　　　　DNB xiii 1139; T i 233

MOYLE, John, *Surgeon*, RN (*d* 1714)　　　　　　　　　DNB xiii 1141

MUDDLE, *Capt* Richard Henry, RN (*fl* 1803–1807)　　　M xii 119

MUNSON, Walter David (1843–1908)
Shipowner   DAB 715

MUNSTER, Sebastian (1489–1552)
Cosmographer   CE ix 599; Md xxix
                                                                        574

MURDOCH, George, RN (1815–1888)
Chief inspector of machinery, 1866–1870   B ii 1034

MURDOCK, *Rear-Adm* Joseph Ballard, USN (1851–1931)   DAB 715; H 965

MURLEY, *Capt* William, RN (*d* 1870)   M vii 132; Tr 99

MURPHY, Dominic Ignatius (1847–1930)
Secretary of the Isthmian Canal Commission, 1904–1905   DAB 716

MURRAY, *Capt* Alexander, USN (1754/5–1821)   DAB 717

MURRAY, Andrew (1813–1872)
Chief engineer, Portsmouth Dockyard, 1846–1869; consulting engineer to the
Admiralty, 1869–1870   B ii 1040

MURRAY, *Adm* George, sixth Baron Elibank (1706–1785)   Ch v 51; NC xviii 177

MURRAY, *Vice-Adm Sir* George, KCB (1759–1819)   DNB xiii 1258

MURRAY, George Robert Milne (1858–1911)
Botanist; director of civilian scientific staff on Scott's 1901 Antarctic expedition   DNB xxiiib 667

MURRAY, Hugh (1779–1846)
Geographer; author of: 'Southern Seas' (1826) and: 'Polar Seas' (1830)   DNB xiii 1265

MURRAY, *Capt* James, RN (*fl* 1809–1821)   M xii 188

MURRAY, James (*fl* 1824–1830)
Chronometer-maker for Admiralty   T ii 430

MURRAY, *Vice-Adm* James Arthur (1790–1860)   M xii 117

MURRAY, James D., *Pay-Director*, USN (*fl* 1858–1880)   H 986

MURRAY, *Cdr* James Hamilton, RN (*fl* 1812–1828)   M viii 308

MURRAY, John (*ca* 1775–*after* 1807)
Acting lieutenant Royal Navy, hydrographer   DAUB ii 272

MURRAY, John (1804–1882)
Engineer to the commissioners of River Wear   B ii 1048

MURRAY, John (*fl* 1837)
Nautical instrument-maker   T ii 476

MURRAY, *Sir* John (1841–1914)
Oceanographer   CE ix 603; DNB xxiv
                                                                        401

MURRAY, Mungo (*d* 1770)
Author of: 'Treatise on shipbuilding and navigation' (1754)   DNB xiii 1296; T ii
                                                                        456

NANSEN, Fridtjof (1861–1930)

CE ix 656

NAPIER, *Adm Sir* Charles John (1786–1860)

B ii 1073; CE ix 658; DNB xiv 38; M x 1; M*d* xxx 43

NAPIER, David (1790–1869)

B ii 1075; DNB xiv 54

NAPIER, *Capt* Henry Edward, RN (1789–1853)

B ii 1076; DNB xiv; M vi 164

NAPIER, James Robert (1821–1879)

B ii 1077

NAPIER, Robert (1791–1876)
Marine engineer

B ii 1079; CE ix 659; DNB xiv 74

NAPIER, Robert D. (1821–1885)

B ii 1079

NAPIER, *Capt* William John, RN, *eighth Baron Napier* (1786–1834)

DNB xiv 87; M xi 255; T*r* 183

NAPPER, William, *Midshipman*, RN (1783–1809)

T*r* 54

NARBETH, John Harper, CB, CBE, MVO (1863–1944)
Naval architect

DNB xxvii 615

NARBONNE, Charles Henri (*ca* 1627–1681)
French-Canadian soldier; buccaneer with Sir Henry Morgan in West Indies

MDC 545

NARBOROUGH [*or* NARBROUGH], *Adm Sir* John (1640–1688)

ch i 245; DNB xiv 89

NARES, *Adm Sir* George Strong, KCB (1831–1915)

CE ix 673; DNB xxiii 404

NARES, *Capt* William Henry, RN (*d ca* 1867)

M vii 281

NARVAEZ, Panfilo de (*d* 1526)
Spanish soldier, explorer of America, lieutenant to Cortes

M*d* xxx 217

NASH, *Capt* James, RN (*fl* 1802)

M iv 577

NASH, John (*fl* 1666–1689)
Instrument-maker, map and globe-seller

T i 253

NASH, *Capt* John, RN (*fl* 1802)

M iv 560

NASH, *Lieut* William Graves, RN (*fl* 1803–1806)

T*r* 168

NAVARETTE, Martin Fernández de (1765–1846)
Captain Spanish navy; naval historian

M*d* xxx 253

NAVARRO, Pedro (1460–1528)
Spanish naval commander

M*d* xxx 251

NAYLOR, James (1817–1894)
Inventor of the floating graving dock

B ii 1087

NAYLOR, Richard Christopher (1814–1899)
Yachtsman

B vi 276

NELSON, Thomas (1807–1890)
Constructed the Cardiff dock   B ii 1104

NELSON, *Lieut-Cdr* Thomas, USN (*fl* 1862–1880)   H 929

NELSON, William, *first Earl Nelson* (1757–1835)
Brother of Horatio Nelson; a chaplain in the Navy, September 1784–October 1786   DNB xiv 215; M*d* xxx
                                                                306

NEPEAN, *Sir* Evan (1751–1822)
First secretary of the Admiralty, 1795–1804   DA*u*B ii 281; DNB xiv
                                                                222

NEPEAN, *Rear-Adm* Evan (*d* 1864)   M viii 131

NEPEAN, Nicholas (1757–1823)
Lieutenant Royal Marines; lieutenant-colonel 93rd Regiment   DA*u*B ii 281

NESBITT, *Cdr* Alexander, RN (*d* 1824)   M vi 371

NESHAM, *Adm* Christopher John Williams (1771–1853)   B ii 1110; DNB xiv
                                                                227; M iv 587

NETTLE, Richard (1815–1905)
*Author; served in the Royal Navy until 1842; superintendent of fisheries for Lower
Canada, 1857–1864*   MDC 548

NEVELL, *Vice-Adm* John (*d* 1697)   *ch* ii 63; DNB xiv 242

NEVILE, *Cdr* Christopher, RN (*fl* 1790–1797)   M vi 260

NEVILL, *Capt the Viscount* Ralph, RN (1786–1826)   M x 316; Tr 21

NEVILL, *Capt* William, RN (*fl* 1807–1846)   M viii 148

NEVILLE, *Cdr Hon* Edward, RN (1664–1701)   *ch* ii 341

NEVILLE, George, KG, *third Baron of Bergavenny* (1461?–1535)
Became warden of the Cinque Ports in 1513   DNB xiv 257

NEVILLE, *Cdr* James, RN (*fl* 1794–1828)   M viii 307

NEVILLE, John de, KG, *fifth Baron Neville of Raby* (*d* 1388)
Naval and military commander   DNB xiv 262

NEVILLE, *Cdr* Martin, RN (1780–1803)   NC xxix 265

NEVILLE, Richard Griffin, *third Baron Braybrooke* (1783–1858)
First editor of Pepys' Diary   B i 386; DNB xiv 298;
                                                                M*d* xxx 355

NEVILLE, *Maj-Gen* Wendell Cushing, USMC (1870–1930)   DAB 725

NEVILLE, William, KG, *Baron Fauconberg & afterwards Earl of Kent* (*d* 1463)
Appointed admiral of England, 1462   DNB xiv 304

NEVILLE, William de (*d* 1389?)
Appointed admiral of the fleet north of Thames, 1372   DNB xiv 303

NEW, *Capt* Thomas, RN (*d* 1824)   M xii 55

NEWALL, Hugh Frank (1857–1944)
Astronomer
CE ix 815; DNB xxvii 621

NEWALL, Robert Stirling (1812–1889)
Submarine cable manufacturer
B ii 1114; DNB xiv 309

NEWBERY, John (1713–1767)
Bookseller and publisher
Chb 442; DNB xiv 312

NEWBERY, Ralph [or Rafe] (*fl* 1590)
Publisher of Hakluyt's Voyages, 1584
DNB xiv 314

NEWBOLT, *Sir* Henry John, CH (1862–1938)
DNB xxvi 650

NEWCOMB, Simon (1835–1909)
Astronomer
A 333; CE ix 821; DAB 726

NEWCOMBE, *Capt* Francis, RN (*fl* 1794–1825)
M ix 454

NEWELL, John, *Midshipman*, RN (*fl* 1804–1805)
Tr 250

NEWELL, *Lieut-Cdr* John Stark, USN (*fl* 1861–1880)
H 933

NEWELL, *Rear-Adm* Julius James Farmer (*d* 1863)
M viii 318

NEWLAND, *Cdr* Robert, RN (*fl* 1666–1667)
ch i 295

NEWMAN, Edward (1832–1882)
Superintendent of the Admiralty steam department, 1872–1882
B ii 1122

NEWMAN, *Capt* James Newman, RN (*d* 1811)
NC xxx 361

NEWMAN, John (*fl* 1816–1838)
Barometer and electrical instrument-maker; instruments at National Maritime Museum
T ii 400

NEWMAN, *Lieut* William B., USN (*fl* 1861–1880)
H 940

NEWPORT, Christopher (1565?–1617)
Sea-captain; made five voyages to Virginia, 1606–1610; made two successful voyages for the East India Company, 1612 and 1615
DAB 728; DNB xiv 356

NEWSAM, Bartholomew (*d* 1593)
Maker of clocks and nautical dials
DNB xiv 360; T i 176

NEWTON, *Sir* Isaac (1642–1727)
Mathematician, astronomer; designer of a sea quadrant
A 105; CE ix 847; DNB xiv 370; Md xxx 366; T i 251; ii 136

NEWTON, John (1622–1678)
Mathematician and astronomer
DNB xiv 394

NEWTON, John (1725–1807)
CE ix 850; DNB xiv 395; Md xxx 406

NEWTON, John (1810–1868)
Globe-maker and land-surveyor; instruments at National Maritime Museum   T ii 401

NEWTON, John (1832–1899)
Teacher of navigation at the Board of Trade navigation schools at Leith and later at
Glasgow   B vi 291

NEWTON, *Lieut* Robert, RN (*d* 1856)   Tr 65

NEWTON, *Capt* Roger, RN (*d* 1690)   *ch* ii 341

NEWTON, Samuel (*fl* 1694–1709)
Ran a mathematical school for Marines   T i 290

NEWTON, *Cdr* Vincent, RN (*fl* 1803–1804)   M vii 198

NEYRA, Alvaro Mendaña de: *see* MENDAÑA DE NEYRA

NIAS, *Adm Sir* Joseph, KCB (1793–1879)   B ii 1130; M viii 254;
                                                                                                          DNB xiv 410

NIBBS, Richard Henry (1815/16–1893)
Marine artist   B vi 291

NIBLACK, *Rear-Adm* Albert Parker, USN (1859–1929)   DAB 729

NICHOL, John Pringle (1804–1859)
Astronomer   B ii 1131; DNB xiv
                                                                                                          412

NICHOLAS, *Cdr* John, RN (*d* 1831)   M vii 198

NICHOLAS, John Liddiard (1784–1868)
Ironfounder; served on and wrote about missionary voyages to New Zealand   DAUB ii 282

NICHOLAS OF LYNNE (*fl* 1360)
English Franciscan friar, writer on Greenland and Arctic Canada, reputed voyager to
the North Pole   DCB i 678; DNB xiv
                                                                                                          418

NICHOLL, *Sir* John (1759–1838)
Judge; appointed judge of the High Court of Admiralty, 1809   DNB xiv 435

NICHOLLS, Edward (*fl* 1617)
Sea-captain; commanded the 'Dolphin' which was attacked by five Turkish men-o-war;
the Turks were compelled to retire   DNB xiv 437

NICHOLLS, *Sir* George, KCB (1781–1865)
Poor-law reformer and administrator; joined the East India company as a midshipman,
1797 and was a commander, 1809–1815; became practically the controller of the
Berkley & Gloucester Ship Canal, 1823; a director of the Birmingham
Canal Navigations   DNB xiv 438

NICHOLLS, *Adm Sir* Henry (*d ca* 1825)   M i 336; R ii 479

NICHOLLS, Sutton (*fl* 1695–1740)
Draughtsman and engraver   *chb* 442; DNB xiv 445

NICHOLS, *Lieut* Frank W., USN (*fl* 1863–1880)   H 953

NIELLY, Joseph-Marie (1751–1833)   M*d* xxx 582; s ii 256

NIELLY, Patrice-Joseph-Marie-Théodore (1781–1799)   M*d* xxx 585

NIEUHOF [*or* NIEUWHOF], Johann (*fl* 1640–1672)
Westphalian traveller; official of Dutch East India Co.; voyager to Brazil and
East Indies; travel writer   M*d* xxx 593

NIGHTINGALE, *Capt* Gamaliel, RN (*d* 1791)   *ch* vi 334

NIKITIN, Afanasy (*ca* 1420–1472)
Russian merchant; traveller to India via the Volga; travel writer   M*d* xxx 600

NILES, *Lieut* Kossuth, USN (*fl* 1865–1880)   H 962

NILES, *Lieut* Nathan, USN (*fl* 1864–1880)   H 958

NIMMO, Alexander (1783–1832)
Civil engineer; engaged on the construction of Dunmore Harbour; employed by the
fishery board to survey the harbours of Ireland; consulting engineer to the Mersey &
Irwell Navigation   DNB xiv 513

NIND, George, *Midshipman*, RN (1776–1805)   Tr 99

NINIS, *Cdr* George, RN (1799–1814)   M vii 221

NISBET, *Sir* Alexander, RN (*d* 1874)
Inspector-general of hospitals and fleets, 1855–1861   B ii 1152

NISBET, *Capt* Josiah, RN (*fl* 1797–1800)   M iii 184

NIXON, *Capt* Christopher, RN (*d ca* 1842)   M v 217

NIXON, *Capt* Edward, RN (*fl* 1660–1664)   *ch* i 26

NIXON, *Cdr* Horatio Stopford, RN (*fl* 1819–1830)   M viii 333

NOAILLES, Antoine de (1504–1561)
French admiral and soldier; diplomat   M*d* xxx 614

NOAILLES, Louis-Marie, *Vicomte de* (1756–1804)
French army officer; commanded troops on schooner 'Le Courrier' in boarding and
capture of H.M. corvette 'Hasard' off Cuba, 1803   M*d* xxx 628

NOBBS, George Hunn (1799–1884)
Served in the Royal Navy, 1811–1816 and later in the Chilean navy   B ii 1155; DA*u*B ii 288

NOBLE, Aldred (1844–1914)
Canal engineer   DAB 734

NOBLE, *Sir* Andrew, KCB (1831–1915)
Chairman of Armstrong, Whitworth & Co, 1900–1915   DNB xxiv 412

NOBLE, Constantin (*fl* 1661–1669)
Dutch navigator; Rear-Admiral of Batavia fleet commanded by Balthazar Bord;
voyager to China   M*d* xxx 634

NOBLE, *Vice-Adm* James (1774–1851)   B ii 1156; DNB xiv
                                                                    525; M iv 565

NOBLE, *Cdr* Mark, RN (*d* 1701)   *ch* iii 171

NORMAN, Robert (*fl* 1560–1596)
Mathematician; author of the: 'Safegarde of Saylers' (1590)   DNB xiv 559; T i 173

NORMAN, *Capt* Thomas, RM (*d* 1805)   Tr 128

NORMAN, *Cdr* William, RN (*d* 1810)   Tr 241

NORMANDY, Alphonse René Le Mire de (1809–1864)
Patented a desalination machine, 1851   B ii 1168

NORONHA, Antoine de (*fl* 1553–1568)
Portuguese naval commander   Md xxxi 49

NORONHA, Ferdinand de (*fl* 1502–1504)
Portuguese navigator   Md xxxi 50

NORONHA, Garcia de (*ca* 1470–1540)
Portuguese admiral   Md xxxi 47

NORRINGTON, *Lieut* Charles Harvey, RN (*d* 1839)   Tr 153

NORRIS, *Sir* Edward (*d* 1603)
Governor of Ostend, 1590–1599; accompanied Drake's expedition to Portugal, 1589 DNB xiv 562

NORRIS, *Lieut* George A., USN (*fl* 1862–1880)   H 945

NORRIS, *Rear-Adm* Harry (*d* 1764)   ch v 53

NORRIS, *Sir* John (1547?–1597)
Military commander; joint commander with Drake of the expedition to Portugal, 1589 DNB xiv 572

NORRIS, *Adm of the Fleet Sir* John (1660?–1749)   ch ii 341; DNB xiv
                                                                                 579; NC xxxv 353

NORRIS, *Lieut* John A., USN (*fl* 1865–1880)   H 961

NORRIS, *Capt* Matthew, RN (*d* 1738)   ch iv 136

NORRIS, Richard (*fl* 1622–1686)
Ship's master; teacher of navigation   T i 208

NORRIS, *Capt* Richard, RN (*fl* 1735–1744)   ch iv 299

NORTH, *Capt* Abraham, RN (*d* 1781)   ch vi 148

NORTH, Dudley, *third Baron North* (1581–1666)
Admiralty commissioner, 1645   DNB xiv 594

NORTH, *Cdr* John, RN (*fl* 1665)   ch i 252

NORTH, Roger (1585?–1652?)
*Colonial projector; accompanied Ralegh's last voyage to Guiana, 1617; made further
voyages to Guiana*   DNB xiv 618

NORTHALL, William (*fl* 1671–1680)
Mate RN; teacher of mathematics; writer on longitude   T i 264

NORTHCOTE, *Sir* Stafford Henry, GCB, *first Earl of Iddesleigh* (1818–1887)
*Governor of the Hudson's Bay Company, 1869–1874; commissioner for the settlement
of the 'Alabama' claims, 1871; author of: 'A Short review of the navigation laws
from the earliest times, by a Barrister' (1849)*   B ii 5; DNB xiv 639

NUGENT, Patrick Roonier (*fl* 1798–1799)
Land-surveyor; inventor of certain navigation instruments   T ii 346

NULTON, *Capt* Michael, RN (*fl* 1660)   ch i 26

NÚÑEZ, Cabeza de Vaca Alvar (*ca* 1490–*ca* 1557)   DAB 740

NUNNEZ DE SEPULVEDA (*fl* 1640)
Spanish painter; in charge of painters decorating royal ships and galleys   Md xxxi 115

NURSE, *Capt* Edward, RN (*fl* 1713)   ch iv 48

NURSE, *Cdr* Hugh, RN (*fl* 1809–1828)   M viii 263

NUTT, John (*fl* 1620–1632)
Gunner RN, ship's master; pirate; privateer   DCB i 522

NUTT, *Capt* Justinian, RN (*d* 1758)   ch v 404

NYEL (*fl* 1703–1705)
French missionary and explorer of South and Central America   Md xxxi 119

NYENDAEL, David (*fl* 1702)
Dutch voyager; explored West Africa, including Benin   Md xxxi 120

OAKDEN, Philip (*ca* 1784–1851)
Founder of Launceston Shipping Company; merchant   DAuB ii 290

OAKE, *Capt* John, RN (*d* 1699)   ch iii 193

OAKE, *Capt* Josiah, RN (*fl* 1806–1846)   M viii 217

OAKES, *Cdr* Orbell, RN (*b* 1800)   M viii 295

OAKLEY, *Cdr* Edward, RN (*d* 1693)   ch ii 362

OATES, *Capt* Chr, RN (*d* 1740/1)   ch iv 432

OATES, Lawrence Edward Grace (1880–1912)   CE X 142; DNB xxiv
                                                                               414

OBÉRÉA (*ca* 1729–*ca* 1772)
Queen of Otahiti; described by Cook and Banks   Md xxxi 126

OBERLY, Aavon S., *Surgeon*, USN (*b* 1837)   H 973

O'BERNE, John Pritchard, *Surgeon*, RN (*d* 1821)   Tr 117

OBET, Yves-Louis (1738–1810)
Captain French Navy; merchant seaman   Md xxxi 134

O'BRIEN, *Capt* Christopher, RN (*d* 1743)   ch iv 48

O'BRIEN, *Rear-Adm* Donat Henchy (1785–1857)   DNB xiv 756; M xii
                                                                               231

O'BRIEN, Edward George (1798–1875)
Midshipman RN; later an army officer   MDC 556

OGDEN, Herbert Gouverneur (1846–1906)
Cartographer .... DAB 745

OGERON DE LA BOUÈRE, Bertrand d' (*ca* 1615–1676)
French captain in 'troupes de la marine': coloniser; founder of San Domingo ... Md xxxi 204

OGILBY, John (1600–1676)
Cartographer and geographer .... *chb* 444; DNB xiv 908

OGILVIE, *Lieut* David, RN (*fl* 1805–1822) .... Tr 18

OGILVIE, *Capt the Hon* John, RN (*fl* 1715) .... *ch* iv 36

OGILVY, *Lieut* Alexander William, RN (*d* 1887) .... B ii 1219

OGILVY, *Rear-Adm Sir* William (*d* 1823) .... M iii 42

OGLE, *Adm of the Fleet Sir* Chaloner (1681?–1750) .... *ch* iii 402; DNB xiv 785

OGLE, *Adm Sir* Chaloner (*d* 1816) .... *ch* vi 194; NC xxii 265

OGLE, *Adm of the Fleet Sir* Charles (1775–1858) .... B ii 1220; DNB xiv 930

OGLE, *Capt* Thomas, RN (1794–1886) .... B ii 1222; M viii 295

O'GRADY, *Adm* Hayes (1787–1864) .... B ii 1223; M xii 353

O'HARA, *Capt* Francis, RN (*d* 1769) .... *ch* vi 572

O'HARA, *Capt* James, RN (*fl* 1748–1793) .... *ch* vi 545

O'HARA, *Capt* Patrick, RN (*d* 1774) .... *ch* v 349

O'HEA, *Lieut* Daniel, RN (*d* 1834) .... Tr 287

O'KANE, *Cdr* James, RN (*fl* 1856–1880) .... H 908

OLDFIELD, *Maj* Thomas, RM (1756–1799) .... DNB xiv 997

OLDHAM, John (1779–1840)
Engineer; patented paddle-wheels for steamers, 1817, 1820 and 1827 ... DNB xiv 1004

OLDMIXON, John (1673–1742)
Historian and pamphleteer; probable author of the: 'History and life of Robert Blake . . . written by a gentleman bred in his family' (ca 1740) ... DNB xiv 1009

OLDYS, William (1696–1761)
Norroy king-of-arms and antiquary; commissioned by the London booksellers to edit a new edition of Ralegh's: 'History of the World', to which he prefixed: 'The Life of the author, newly compil'd from materials more ample and authentick than have yet been publish'd . . .' (1736) ... DNB xiv 1015

OLEARIUS (ADAM OELSCHLAGER) (*ca* 1600–1671)
German traveller to Russia and geographer .... Md xxxi 234

OLIPHANT, *Capt* John, RN (*d* 1743) .... *ch* iv 383

OLIVER, Brinley Sylvester, *Purser*, RN (*d* 1827) .... Tr 34

ONLEY, *Capt* John, RN (*fl* 1728)　　　　　　　　　　　　*ch* iv 207

ONSLOW, *Capt* John James, RN (*fl* 1810–1854)　　　　M viii 531

ONSLOW, *Adm Sir* Richard, GCB (1741–1817)　　　　*ch* vi 478; DNB xiv
　　　　　　　　　　　　　　　　　　　　　　　1119; M*d* xxxi 285;
　　　　　　　　　　　　　　　　　　　　　　　NC xiii 249; R i 350

ORAM, *Engineer Vice-Adm Sir* Henry John, KCB (1858–1939)　DNB xxvi 660

ORCHARD, *Cdr* William, RN (*fl* 1673)　　　　　　　　*ch* i 399

ORCHERTON, William (*fl* 1755–1764)
Schoolmaster RN, writer about a log-board　　　　　　T ii 269

ORDE, *Adm Sir* John (1752–1862)　　　　　　　　　　M i 69, ii 863; NC II
　　　　　　　　　　　　　　　　　　　　　　　177; R ii 57

O'REILLY, *Cdr* John Roberts, RN (1794–1873)　　　　B vi 329

O'REILLY, *Rear-Adm* Montagu Frederick (1822–1888)　B ii 1254

ORFILA, Matthieu Joseph Bonaventure (1787–1853)
Minorcan, later naturalised French; pilot, merchant service; chemist, toxicologist　M*d* xxxi 333

ORFIREUS [*or* ORFFYRÉ; *formerly* BESSLER], Jean Ernest Elie
(1680–1745)
German scientist and inventor; inventor of life-saving machine for shipwrecks, etc　M*d* xxxi 335

ORIANI (*Abbé* BARNABÉ) (1752–*post* 1831)
Italian astronomer; friend of Herschel, measurer of arc of meridian; compiler of
astronomical tables　　　　　　　　　　　　　　M*d* xxxi 340

ORLEANS, Louis-Philippe Joseph, *Duc d'* (1747–1793)
French naval commander　　　　　　　　　　　　M*d* xxxi 377

ORLEBAR, *Adm* John (1810–1887)　　　　　　　　　B ii 1255

ORME, *Capt* Humphrey, RN (*fl* 1720)　　　　　　　*ch* iv 84

ORMEROD, *Capt* Charles, RN (*fl* 1697)　　　　　　*ch* iii 171

ORMOND, *Capt* Francis, RN (*d* 1851)　　　　　　　M viii 157

ORR, William Morgan (*d* 1843)
Shipowner, shipping agent, whaler and sealer at Hobart　DA*u*B ii 302

ORSBON, George (*fl* 1812)
Possibly mariner, writer on navigation　　　　　　T ii 401

ORTEGA, Jean de (*fl* 1624)
Ensign, Spanish Navy　　　　　　　　　　　　　M*d* xxxi 426

ORTELIUS [ORTELL, *or* OERTEL], Abraham (1527–1598)
Flemish geographer and cartographer　　　　　　　CE x 250; DNB xiv
　　　　　　　　　　　　　　　　　　　　　　　1163; M*d* xxxi 427

ORVILLIERS, Louis Guillouet, *Comte d'* (1708–*post* 1793)
French naval commander　　　　　　　　　　　　M*d* xxxi 432

OSBECK, Pierre (1722–1805)
Swedish traveller, almoner on Dutch East India Co ship, travel writer and naturalist   Md xxxi 434

OSBORN, *Lieut* Arthur P., USN (*fl* 1865–1880)   H 958

OSBORN, *Rear-Adm* Sherard, CB (1822–1875)   B ii 1265; CE X 257;
                                                                                           DNB xiv 1176

OSBORNE, George (*fl* 1625–1628)
Teacher of mathematics and navigation almanac compiler   T i 209

OSBORNE [*or* OSBORN], *Adm* Henry (1698?–1771)   *ch* iv 197; DNB xiv
                                                                                           1239

OSBORNE, *Capt* James, RN (*d* 1754)   *ch* v 350

OSBORNE, *Adm* Peregrine, *Duke of Leeds* (*d* 1729)   *ch* ii 396

OSBORNE, *Capt* Peter, RN (*d* 1754)   *ch* v 54

OSGOOD, *Cdr* Henry, RN (*fl* 1665–1666)   *ch* i 172

OSLER, Abraham Follett (1808–1903)
*Meteorologist; inventor of the first self-recording pressure plate anemometer and rain
gauge 1835, which was adopted by the Royal Greenwich Observatory in 1847*   DNB xxiiic 57

OSLER, Edward (1798–1863)
Miscellaneous writer; author of: 'Life of Admiral Viscount Exmouth' (1835)   DNB xiv 1206

OSMAN, John, *Master*, RN (*d* 1832)   Tr 135

OSMAND, James, *Surgeon's Mate*, RN (*d* 1848)   Tr 228

OSTERHAUS, *Lieut* Hugo, USN (*fl* 1865–1880)   H 965

OSTERMANN, André, *Comte d'* (*ca* 1682–1747)
Born in Germany; Russian naval officer and chancellor of Russia   Md xxxi 460

OTHER [OHTHER *or* OTTAR] (9th century A.D.)
Norwegian voyager, Arctic explorer, whale and seal fisherman   Md xxxi 469

OTOO [*or* OTOU (POMORÉ I)] (1762–1803)
Tahitian King, nephew of Queen Oberea; met Bligh   Md xxxiv 1

OTTER, *Capt* Charles, RN (*d ca* 1831)   M iv 553

OTTER, *Rear-Adm* Henry Charles (1807–1876)   B ii 1274

OTTLEY, *Rear-Adm Sir* Charles Langdale, KCMG, CB, MVO (1858–1932)   DNB xxvi 663

OTTLEY, William, *Master*, RN (*d* 1806)   Tr 257

OTTY, *Capt* Allen, RN (*d* 1859)   M vii 373

OTWAY, *Adm Sir* George Graham (1816–1881)   B ii 1275

OTWAY, *Adm Sir* Robert Waller (1772–1846)   DNB xiv 1239; M ii
                                                                                           691, 880; viii 427

OTWAY, *Vice-Adm* William Albany (*b* 1756)   NC xxx 441

OUDNEY, Walter, *Surgeon*, RN (1790–1824)   CE X 276; DNB xiv
                                                                                           1248

OUGHTON, *Capt* James, RN (*fl* 1783–1808)   M iii 221

OULD, Henry (*fl* 1794)
Writer on longitude   T ii 347

OURAY, *Rear-Adm* George (*d ca* 1799)   *ch* vi 516

OURRY, *Capt* Isaac Florimond, RN (*d* 1773)   *ch* vi 439

OURRY, *Capt* Paul Henry, RN (*d* 1783)   *ch* vi 265

OUTLAW [OUTLAN *or* LOUTLAS], John (*fl* 1682, *d ca* 1697)
English sea-captain for Hudson's Bay Co; shipwright   DCB i 528

OUTRAM, *Sir* Benjamin Fonseca, KCB, RN (1774–1856)
*Joined the naval medical service in 1796 and became medical inspector of fleets and
hospitals in 1841*   B ii 1277; DNB xiv
                                                                   1259

OVEREND, William Heysham (1851–1898)
Marine artist; member of the council of the Navy Record Society B vi 335

OVERTON, Edward, *Master*, RN (*d* 1805)   Tr 203

OVERTON, Henry (*fl* 1706–1764)
Bookseller   *chb* 444

OVIEDO (Gonçalo Hernandez de Oviedo y Valdez) (*ca* 1478–*after* 1535)
Spanish explorer and coloniser of Haiti   Md xxxi 546

OVINGTON, John (*fl* 1689–1693)
English voyager to Africa and India   Md xxxi 547

OWEN, Alfred M., *Surgeon*, USN (*fl* 1869–1880)   H 978

OWEN, *Cdr* Charles Cuncliffe, RN (*fl* 1801–1854)   M vii 342

OWEN, *Capt* Edward, RN (*d* 1707)   *ch* iii 82

OWEN, *Adm Sir* Edward William Campbell Rich, GCB (1771–1849)   DNB xiv 1299; M iii
                                                                   126; Md xxxi 549

OWEN, *Lieut-Gen Sir* John, KCB, RM (1780–1857)   B ii 1287; Tr 100

OWEN, *Capt* Richard, RN (*fl* 1811–1854)   M viii 211

OWEN, *Capt* Thomas, RN (*d* 1796)   *ch* vi 335

OWEN, *Capt* William, RN (*d* 1722)   *ch* iv 49

OWEN, *Vice-Adm* William Fitzwilliam (1774–1857)   B ii 1293; DNB xiv
                                                                   1352; M x 738; T ii
                                                                   347

OWENS, Owen (*fl ca* 1800–1810)
Optical instrument-maker; sextant at National Maritime Museum   T ii 401

OXENDEN, *Sir* George (1694–1775)
Lord of the Admiralty   DNB xv 11

PAGE, *Sir* Thomas Hyde (1746–1821)
Military engineer; constructed the ferry at Chatham; chief consulting engineer for the
improvement of the port of Dublin, of Wicklow harbour, the inland navigation of
Ireland, and of the Royal Shannon and Newberry canals   DNB XV 43

PAGE, William Lucian, CSN (1807–1901)   DAB 759

PAGÈS, Pierre-Marie-François, *Vicomte de* (1748–1793)
French naval officer; explorer of Pacific and Arctic   Md xxxi 612

PAGET, *Vice-Adm Sir* Charles (1778–1839)   DNB XV 49; M ii 854

PAGET, *Capt* Charles Henry, RN (1806–1845)   M vi 88

PAGET, *Adm Lord* Clarence Edward, GCB (1811–1895)   DNB XV 57

PAGET, *Capt Rt Hon Lord* William, RN (1803–1873)   B ii 1307; M v 287

PAILLETERIE, *Le Bailli de la* (d 1720)
Maltese and French naval officer   Md xxxi 622

PAINE, *Brig-Gen* Charles Jackson, USA (1833–1916)
Yachtsman   DAB 759

PAINE, *Lieut* Frederick H., USN (*fl* 1863–1880)   H 952

PAINE, *Cdr* Joseph, RN (*fl* 1665–1667)   *ch* i 173

PAINE, *Cdr* Reuben, RN (*fl* 1801–1831)   M viii 296

PAINE, *Lieut* Sumner C., USN (*fl* 1865–1880)   H 958

PAINTER, *Cdr* Richard, RN (*fl* 1673)   *ch* i 399

PAIXHANS, Henri-Joseph (1783–*post* 1834)
French general of artillery, writer on naval artillery   Md xxxi 634

PAKENHAM, *Adm* John (1790–1876)   B ii 1309; M v 287

PAKENHAM, *Adm the Hon Sir* Thomas, GCB (1757–1836)   DNB XV 85; M i 117;
                                                                                 NA ii 93; R ii 260

PAKENHAM, *Adm Sir* William Christopher, KCB, KCVO, KCMG (1861–1933)   DNB xxvi 668

PALLISER, *Adm Sir* Hugh (1723–1796)   *ch* v 483; DNB XV
                                                                                 114; NC xxxix 89;
                                                                                 MDC 572

PALMER, Alexander, *Midshipman*, RN (1783–1805)   Tr 20

PALMER, *Lieut* Charles, RN (1792–1861)   B vi 347

PALMER, Charles John (1805–1882)
Proctor to the Admiralty Court, Yarmouth. 1827   B ii 1315

PALMER, *Sir* Charles Mark (1822–1907)
Shipowner, established a shipbuilding yard at Jarrow, 1851   DNB xxiiic 66

PALMER, *Capt* Edmund, CB, RN (*fl* 1804–1817)   M ix 215

PALMER, *Cdr* Edward, RN (*d* 1807)   NC xxii 89

PARISH, James (*d* 1861)
Oarsman — B ii 1337

PARISH, *Capt* John, RN (*fl* 1806–1817) — M xii 120

PARISH, *Vice-Adm* John Edward (1823–1894) — B ii 1337

PARK, Mungo (1771–1806)
Scottish explorer — CE X 441; DNB XV 218; M*d* xxxii 149

PARKER, Benjamin (*fl* 1725–1753)
Instrument-maker, writer on longitude at sea — T ii 164

PARKER, *Cdr* Charles, RN (*fl* 1812–1831) — M viii 388

PARKER, *Adm Sir* Charles Christopher (*d* 1765) — B ii 1341; M xii 388; DNB XV 266

PARKER, *Rear-Adm* Christopher (*d* 1765) — *ch* iv 49

PARKER, *Cdre* Foxhall Alexander, USN (1821–1879) — DAB 765; H 635

PARKER, *Cdr* Frederick Augustus Hargood, RN (*fl* 1799–1813) — M vii 240

PARKER, George, *second Earl of Macclesfield* (1697–1764)
Astronomer — DNB XV 234

PARKER, *Adm Sir* George, KCB (1767–1847) — DNB XV 236; M ii 639; R iv 93

PARKER, *Capt* George Charles, RIM (1836–1890) — B ii 1342

PARKER, *Capt* Henry, RN (1788–1873) — M vii 280; Tr 98

PARKER, *Sir* Henry Watson (1825–1894)
A member of the Royal Commission on the loss of life at sea, 1884–1887 — B ii 1343

PARKER, *Vice-Adm Sir* Hyde (1714–1782) — *ch* vi 83; DNB XV 242; NA i 175; NC xx 337; R i 161

PARKER, *Adm Sir* Hyde (1739–1807) — CE X 442; *ch* vi 523; DNB XV 244; M*d* xxxii 154; NC V 281; R i 377

PARKER, *Vice-Adm* Hyde, CB (1784?–1854) — B ii 1343; DNB XV 245; M ix 262; M*d* xxxii 155

PARKER, *Capt* John, RN (*d* 1666) — *ch* i 62

PARKER, John (1799–1881)
Politician; first secretary of the Admiralty, June–Sept, 1841 and 1849–1852 — DNB XV 265

PARKER, *Capt* John, RN (*fl* 1805–1842) — M viii 321

PARKER, Joseph B., *Surgeon*, USN (*fl* 1863–1880) — H 978

PARKER, *Capt* Nicholas, RN (*fl* 1661–1668) — *ch* i 62

PARLOUR, S. (*fl* 1824–1825)
Instructor at East India Company's Academy; writer on naval telescope   T ii 430

PARMENIUS, Stephanus (ISTVÁN PAIZSOS: BUDAI PARMENIUS STVÁN) (*d* 1583)
First Hungarian to visit North America; contributor to Hakluyt   DCB i 531

PARMENTIER, Jean (1494–1529)
French navigator, cartographer and poet; voyager to East Indies and possibly to Newfoundland   DCB i 532

PARNELL, *Sir* Henry Brooke, *first Baron Congleton* (1776–1842)
Politician; appointed treasurer of the Navy in April, 1835   DNB xv 343

PARR, *Lieut* Alexander Forsyth, RN (*d* 1856)   Tr 269

PARREY, *Capt* Edward Iggulden, RN (*fl* 1809–1843)   M viii 350

PARREY, *Cdr* Robert, RN (*d* 1832)   M vi 368

PARROCEL, Joseph (1646–1704)
French military and marine painter   Md xxxii 175

PARROTT, *Rear-Adm* Enoch Greenleafe, USN (1815–1879)   DAB 768

PARRY, *Capt* Francis, RN (*d* 1742)   ch v 204

PARRY, *Cdr* Howard Lewis, RN (*fl* 1803–1833)   M viii 379

PARRY, *Capt* Thomas Parry Jones, RN (1784–1845)   M vi 371

PARRY, *Capt* William, RN (*d* 1753)   ch iv 233

PARRY, *Adm* William, RN (*d* 1779)   ch v 350

PARRY, *Rear-Adm Sir* William Edward (1790–1855)   AE ii 271; B ii 1367; CE x 456; DNB xv 392; H 635; M xii 315; Md xxxii 179; MDC 582; T ii 402

PARRY, *Capt* William Henry Webley, CB, RN (*fl* 1790–1822)   M iv 645

PARSEVAL-DESCHÈNES, Alexandre-Ferdinand (1790–1860)
French admiral   Md xxxii 181

PARSON, *Capt* John, RN (*d* 1847)   M vii 408

PARSONS, Abraham (*d* 1785)
English traveller to Africa and Asia; consul and naval agent in Syria   DNB xv 395; Md xxxii 184

PARSONS, *Sir* Charles Algernon, OM, KCB (1854–1931)
British inventor of marine steam turbine   A 394; CE x 458; DNB xxvi 672

PARSONS, *Capt* Daniel, RN (*fl* 1679)   ch ii 61

PARSONS, *Cdr* George Samuel, RN (1783–1854)   B ii 1369

PARSONS, *Cdr* John, RN (1791–1864)   Tr 138

PATERSON, James (*fl* 1681–1693)
Mathematician, navigational instrument-maker and seller   T i 277

PATEY, *Lieut* Benjamin, RN (*fl* 1801–1809)   Tr 123

PATEY, *Adm* Charles George Edward (1811–1881)   B ii 1381; DNB XV 475

PATEY, *Cdr* George Edward, RN (*b* 1789–1865)   Tr 125

PATEY, *Vice-Adm Sir* George Edwin (1859–1935)   AE ii 279

PATON, Richard (1716–1791)
English marine painter   DNB XV 482; Md xxxii 256

PATOUN, Archibald (*fl* 1725–1738)
Writer on navigation   T ii 164

PATTERSON, *Capt* Daniel Todd, USN (1786–1839)   DAB 771; H 637

PATTERSON, *Rear-Adm* Thomas Harman, USN (1820–1889)   DAB 772; H 637

PATTERSON, John Coleridge (1827–1871)   B ii 1387; DNB XV 510

PATTERSON, *Cdre* Thomas, USN (1822–1891)   DAB 772; H 637

PATTON, *Capt* Charles, RN (1741–1837)   DNB XV 511

PATTON, *Adm* Hugh (1804–1864)   B ii 1391; Tr 205

PATTON, *Adm* Philip (1739–1815)   DNB XV 510; Md xxxi 268; R iii 387

PATTON, *Adm* Robert (1791–1884)   B ii 1392; M v 299; Tr 206

PATTRICK, Thomas (*fl* 1800–1803)
Instrument-maker, writer on armillary sphere and nautical angle; pamphlets at National Maritime Museum   T ii 371

PAUL, *Lieut* Allen G., USN (*fl* 1862–1880)   H 952

PAUL, Friedrich Wilhelm, *Duke of Wurtemberg* (1797–1860)
German naturalist; voyager to North and Central America, Asia, Melanesia and Australia   Md xxxii 288

PAUL, Henry Martyn (1851–1931)
Astronomer   DAB 772

PAUL, *Capt* John, RN (*d* 1720)   ch iii 347

PAULDING, *Rear-Adm* Hiram, USN (1797–1878)   DAB 773

PAULDING, James Kirke (1778–1860)
Secretary of the United States Navy, 1838–1841   DAB 773

PAULET [*or* POWLETT], *Adm* Harry, *sixth Duke of Bolton* (1719–1794)   ch v 55; DNB XV 532

PAULET, Harry (*d* 1804)
Master mariner; claimed to have brought information to Britain which led to Wolfe's expedition to Quebec 1759, and gave Hawke news of the escape of Conflans   DNB XV 533

PEARCE, *Lieut* John Street, RN (*fl* 1800–1809)   Tr 256

PEARCE, *Capt* Joseph, RN (*fl* 1799–1819)   M xi 274

PEARCE, *Capt* Mark, RN (*fl* 1665–1666)   ch i 173

PEARCE, Nathaniel (1779–1820)
English seaman, explorer of Abyssinia   DNB xv 594; Md xxxii
                                                                        333

PEARCE [*or* PEARSE], *Capt* Vincent, RN (*d* 1665)   ch i 174

PEARCE [*or* PEARSE], *Capt* Vincent, RN (*d* 1745)   ch iv 58

PEARCE [*or* PEARSE], *Capt* Vincent, RN (*d* 1759)   ch vi 90

PEARCE, *Sir* William (1833–1888)
Naval architect; founded the Fairfield Shipbuilding & Engineering Company 1878   B ii 1416; DNB xv 595

PEARCE, *Sir* William George (1861–1907)
Chairman of the Fairfield Shipbuilding & Engineering Company, 1888–1907   DNB xxiiic 89

PEARD, *Cdr* George, RN (*b* 1793)   M viii 232

PEARD, *Vice-Adm* Shuldham (1761–1832)   DNB xv 599; M iii 23

PEARETH, William (1808–1854)
Yachtsman   B vi 370

PEARL, *Cdr Sir* James, RN (*d* 1839)   M viii 243; Tr 65

PEARSE, *Capt* Henry Whitmarsh, CB (*fl* 1796–1809)   M x 60

PEARSE [*or* PEARCE], *Capt* Jeffrey, RN (*d* 1672)   ch i 116

PEARSE, *Cdr* John, RN (1780–1864)   B ii 1420

PEARSE, *Adm* Richard Bulkeley (1830–1895)   B ii 1420

PEARSE, *Capt* Thomas, RN (*fl* 1667)   ch i 295

PEARSE, *Rear-Adm* Thomas (*fl* 1796–1819)   M iii 34

PEARSE [*or* PEARCE], *Capt* Vincent, RN (*d* 1665)   ch i 174

PEARSE [*or* PEARCE], *Capt* Vincent, RN (*d* 1745)   ch iv 58

PEARSE [*or* PEARCE], *Capt* Vincent, RN (*d* 1759)   ch vi 90

PEARSON, *Cdr* Alexander Stevenson, RN (*fl* 1799–1839)   M viii 50

PEARSON, Bartholomew (*fl* 1612–1634)
*English yeoman and settler in Newfoundland; member of John Guy's expedition to
Trinity Bay, 1612*   DCB i 534

PEARSON, *Capt* Charles, RN (*fl* 1800–1837)   M vii 307

PEARSON, *Cdr* Frederick, USN (*fl* 1859–1880)   H 914

PEARSON, *Lieut* George, RN (*d* 1816)   Tr 207

PEARSON, *Cdr* Hugh, RN (*fl* 1797–1814)   M vii 202

PEARSON, James (1825–1886)
Author of : 'A Treatise on tides' (1881)   B vi 373

PELL, *Adm Sir* Watkin Owen (1788–1869)   B ii 1440; DNB XV
                                                                                                      708; M xi 162

PELLEGRIN, Simon Joseph (1663–1745)
Ship's almoner; poet and abbé   M*d* xxxii 393

PELLERIN, Joseph (1684–1745)
French official in the bureau de la marine; commissaire de la marine; inspector-general
of classes of sailors at all ports; numismatist   M*d* xxxii 400

PELLEW, *Adm* Edward, G C B, *first Viscount Exmouth* (1757–1833)   CE V 518; DNB XV
                                                                                                      711; NC xviii 441;
                                                                                                      R ii 404

PELLEW, *Adm Sir* Fleetwood Broughton Reynolds, C B (1789–1861)   B ii 1442; DNB XV
                                                                                                      715; M ix 402

PELLEW, *Adm Sir* Israel (1758–1832)   DNB XV 716; M ii 454;
                                                                                                      M*d* xxxii 412; Tr 150

PELLEW, *Capt* Pownall Bastard, R N, *second Viscount Exmouth* (1786–1833)   M ix 108

PELLEW [*or* PELLOW], Thomas (*fl* 1738)
Sailor; a captive of Barbary corsairs, 1715–1738   DNB XV 718

PELLHAM, Edward (*fl* 1630)
Sailor; stranded with seven others in Greenland (1630–1631); later wrote an account
of his experiences   DNB XV 719

PELLIEUX, Jacques-Nicolas (1749–1832)
French naval surgeon   M*d* xxxii 412

PELLOWE, *Capt* Richard, R N (*fl* 1790–1805)   M iv 557

PELLY, *Sir* John Henry (1777–1852)
Governor of the Hudson's Bay Company; instrumental in sending out exploring parties
under Dease & Simpson; elected elder brother of Trinity House, 1823   B ii 1443; DNB XV
                                                                                                      720; MDC 588

PELLY, Robert Parker (*fl* 1790–1825)
Captain East India Co, governor of Assinibois   MDC 588

PELSAERT, Francisco (*ca* 1591–1630)
Captain Dutch East India Co, explorer of Australia and Sumatra   DA*u*B ii 322

PEMBERTON, Charles Reece (1790–1840)   DNB XV 723

PEMBERTON, *Cdr* Henry Charles, R N (*fl* 1809–1818)   M viii 12

PENCHESTER [PENCESTER *or* PENSHURST], Stephen de (*d* 1299)
Appointed Warden of the Cinque Ports, 1271   DNB XV 731

PENDER, *Capt* Daniel, R N (1833–1891)   B ii 1446

PENDER, *Sir* John, K C M G (1815–1896)
A pioneer of submarine telegraphy   DNB xxii 1130

PENDLETON, *Lieut-Cdr* Charles H., U S N (*fl* 1860–1880)   H 923

PERCEVAL, *Capt* Westby, RN (*fl* 1800–1814)   M ix 155

PERCIVAL, *Capt* John, USN (1779–1862)   DAB 787

PERCY, *Adm of the Fleet* Algernon, *tenth Earl of Northumberland* (1602–1668)   DNB xv 830

PERCY, *Adm* Algernon, KG, *fourth Earl of Northumberland* (1792–1865)   B ii 1177; DNB xv
                                                                      835; M xii 39

PERCY [*or* PIERCEY], *Capt* Francis, RN (*d* 1741)   ch iii 407

PERCY, *Vice-Adm* Josceline, CB (1784–1856)   B ii 1464; DNB xv
                                                                      872; M ix 184

PERCY, *Rear-Adm* William Henry (1788–1855)   B ii 1465; DNB xv
                                                                      872; M viii 454
                                                                      xi 64

PERDU, *Capt* John, RN (*fl* 1665–1667)   ch i 295

PEREGRINUS, Petrus (Petrus de MARICOURT) (*fl* 1270)
French military engineer, writer on the mag netic compass   A 48

PERIGAL, Henry (1801–1898)
Astronomer   B vi 387

PERKINS, *Lieut* Charles P., U S N (*fl* 1865–1880)   H 958

PERKINS, George Clement (1839–1923)
Shipowner   DAB 787

PERKINS, *Cdre* George Hamilton, USN (1836–1899)   DAB 788; H 902

PERKINS, *Lieut* Hamilton, USN (*fl* 1863–1880)   H 952

PERKINS, Peter (*fl* 1677–1680)
Writer on navigation   T i 274

PERKINS, *Cdr* Thomas Paul, RN (*d* 1815)   Tr 286

PERKINS, *Lieut* Thomas Steele, RN (*fl* 1798–1816)   Tr 298

PÉRON, François (17 75–1810)
French explorer and natu r alist   DAuB ii 323; Md
                                                                      xxxii 509

PÉROUSE, Jean-François Galaup, *Comte de la* (1741–1788)
French naval officer and exp lo rer   DAuB ii 85

PERRÉE, Jean-Baptiste-Em manuel (1761–1800)
French admiral and captain in m erchant marine   Md xxxii 533; s ii 302

PERRIGNY, Taillevis de (1720–1757)
French navy captain and hydrogr apher   Md xxxii 536

PERRING, John Shae (18 13–1869)
*Civil engineer; articled to the surv eyor of Boston harbour, 1826–1833; engineering
superintendent of the Llanelly railw ay docks and harbour, 1841–1844*   DNB xv 901

PERRONET, Jean-Rodolphe (1708–1794)
French inventor; bridge and canal engineer   Md xxxii 542

PETT, *Capt* Phineas, RN (*fl* 1661–1666)   ch i 62

PETT, *Capt* Phineas, RN (*fl* 1693–1694)   ch iii 49

PETT, *Capt* Robert, RN (*d* 1776)   ch v 54

PETTET, *Cdr* Robert, RN (*fl* 1794–1809)   M vi 321

PETTIGREW, Thomas Joseph (1791–1865)
Surgeon and antiquary; author of: 'Life of Vice-Admiral Lord Nelson' (1849)   DNB xv 994

PETTIGREW, *Capt* William, RN (*d* 1756)   ch vi 148

PETTMAN, *Capt* Thomas, RN (*d* 1828)   M v 94

PETTY, *Sir* William (1623–1687)
Served in Royal Navy; M.P.; inventor of 'an unsinkable ship'   chb 445; DNB xv 999;
                                                                 M*d* xxxii 628

PEYTON, *Cdre* Edward, RN (*d* 1749)   ch v 55; DNB xv 1021

PEYTON, *Capt Sir* John Strutt, RN (1786–1838)   DNB xv 1024; M x
                                                                        438

PEYTON, *Adm* Joseph (*fl* 1743–1799)   ch vi 269; NA i 134

PEYTON, *Capt Sir* Yelverton, RN (*d* 1748/9)   ch iv 138

PHELPS, John (1805–1890)
Oarsman   B ii 1489

PHELPS, Thomas (*fl* 1685)
*Mariner; author of: 'A true account of the captivity of Thomas Phelps at Machaness
in Barbary, and of his strange escape' (1685)*   DNB xv 1036

PHELPS, Thomas (*fl* 1750)
Astronomer   DNB xv 1036

PHELPS, *Lieut* Thomas, USN (*fl* 1865–1880)   H 961

PHELPS, *Rear-Adm* Thomas Stowell, USN (1822–1901)   DAB 793; H 644

PHENN(E)Y, *Capt* John, RN (*fl* 1665)   ch i 175

PHEPOE, *Cdr* John, RN (1786–1862)   Tr 234

PHILIP, George (*b* 1799)
Cartographic publisher   chb 446

PHILIP, *Rear-Adm* John Woodward, USN (1840–1900)   DAB 793; H 910

PHILIPPS, *Lieut* Baker, RN (1718?–1745)   DNB xv 1054

PHILIPPS, Owen Crosby, GCMG, *Baron Kyslant* (1863–1937)
Shipowner   DNB xxvi 696

PHILIPS, *Lieut-Gen* John Alexander, RM (1790–1865)   Tr 99

PHILIPS, Miles (*fl* 1587)
*Mariner; sailed with Hawkins in 1568 to the Indies; was captured in Mexico,
eventually escaped and returned to England in 1582*   DNB xv 1069

PHILLIMORE, *Adm of the Fleet Sir* Augustus, GCB (1822–1897)   B vi 392

PHIPPS, Henry, GCB, *first Earl of Mulgrave & Viscount Normanby* (1755–1831)
First lord of the Admiralty, 1807–1810   DNB XV 1119

PHIPPS, *Capt* Weston, RN (*d* 1847)   M xi 348

PHIPPS [*or* PHIPS], *Sir* William (1651–1695)
Governor of Massachusetts; became a merchant captain at Boston; raised a Spanish
treasure ship sunk off the Bahamas, 1667   DAB 794; DCB i 544;
                                                                                  DNB XV 1133; MDC
                                                                                  594

PHYTHIAN, *Cdr* Robert L., USN (*fl* 1852–1880)   H 902

PIALI (*fl* 1526–1571)
Turkish captain pasha and naval commander   Md xxxiii 165

PIAZZI, *le Père* Joseph (1746–1826)
Italian astronomer, worked at Greenwich, and a friend of Maskelyne and Herschel Md xxxiii 168

PIBUS, *Capt* John, RN (*fl* 1666–1672)   ch i 253

PICARD, Jean (1620–1682)
Astronomer   CE X 717

PICCARD, Auguste (1884–1962)
Swiss physicist; pioneer of stratospheric ballooning and deep-ocean exploration;
invented bathyscaphe   A 497; CE ix 718

PICCHIANI, Francesco (*d* 1690)
Italian architect; designer of naval docks at Naples   Md xxxiii 184

PICHARD [*or* PICKARD], *Capt* Peter, RN (*d* 1701/2)   ch ii 74

PICKERING, Charles (1805–1878)
Chief zoologist of the Wilkes South Seas exploring expedition, 1838–1842   DAB 795

PICKERING, Edward Charles (1846–1919)
Astronomer   CE X 718; DAB 795

PICKERING, William Henry (1858–1938)
Astronomer   CE X 719

PICKERNELL, *Cdr* Peter Giles, RN (1772–1859)   M vi 401; Tr 107

PICKFORD, *Cdr* Charles, RN (*fl* 1794–1809)   M vi 321

PICKFORD, William, *Baron Sterndale* (1848–1923)
Judge; leading counsel for Great Britain at the inquiry in Paris following the
Dogger Bank incident, 1905; active in promoting movement for the unification of
maritime law; president of the Probate, Divorce and Admiralty division of the High
Court, 1918   DNB XXXV 679

PICKING, *Cdr* Henry F., USN (*b* 1840)   H 910

PICKING, *Cdr* William, RN (*fl* 1799–1834)   M viii 317

PICOT, Bernard François Bertrand, *Marquis de la Motta* (1734–1797)
French naval officer; commandant general of Malabar coast; governor of Mahé   Md xxxiii 202

PILCH, *Lieut* William, RN (*d* 1863)   Tr 206

PILCHER, *Maj-Gen* John Montresor, RM (*d* 1873)   B ii 1536

PILES, Ludovic, *Baron de Baumes* (*ca* 1603–1646)
French officer in 'régiment de la marine'   M*d* xxxiii 330

PILES, Paul de Fortia, *Seigneur de* (1559–1621)
French army officer and naval captain   M*d* xxxiii 330

PILES, Paul de (1600–1682)
Son of Paul de Fortia; French army officer and naval captain   M*d* xxxiii 330

PILES, *Capt* Thomas, RN (*fl* 1664–1672)   ch i 372

PILFORD, *Capt* John, CB, RN (1776?–1834)   DNB xv 1178; M iv
                                                                               963; Tr 232

PILGRIM, Thomas (1800–1871)   B ii 1536

PILKINGTON, *Cdr* Edward William, RN (*b* 1803)   M viii 365

PILLSBURY, *Rear-Adm* John Elliott, USN (1846–1919)   DAB 800; H 953

PIM, *Adm* Bedford Clapperton Trevelyan (1826–1886)   B ii 1538; DNB xv
                                                                               1192

PINDAR [*or* PINDER], *Capt* Thomas, RN (*d* 1699)   ch iii 140

PINE, John (1690–1756)
*Engraver; published: 'The tapestry hangings of the Houses of Lords, representing
the several engagements between the English and Spanish fleets in the ever-
memorable year MDLXXXVIII'* (*1739*)   DNB xv 1198; M*d*
                                                                               xxxiii 353

PINGO, Thomas (1692–1776)
Medallist; his medals include: 'Defeat of the French fleet off Cape Finisterre', 1747   DNB xv 1201

PINGRÉ, Alexandre-Gui (1711–1796)
*French astronomer, author of lunar tables used in British Nautical Almanac;
tester of marine chronometers on voyages of Courtanvaux, 1767; Fleurieu 1769 and
Verdun de la Crenne, 1771*   M*d* xxxiii 364

PINKERTON, John (1758–1826)
Scottish historian and geographer, editor of collective voyages   DNB xv 1219; M*d*
                                                                               xxxiii 370

PINN, *Capt* Edward, RN (*fl* 1662–1680)   ch i 372

PINTO, Fernand Mendez (1510–1583)
Portuguese explorer   CE x 737; M*d* xxxiii
                                                                               381

PINTO, *Capt* Thomas, RN (1772–1851)   M vi 366; Tr 268

PINZON, Vincent Yañez (1460?–1524?)
Spanish explorer, lieutenant of Columbus   M*d* xxxiii 387

PLASKETT, John Stanley, CBE (1865–1941)
Astronomer
CE X 774; DNB xxvii 675

PLATEN, *Baron* Pierre-Jean-Bernard (1766–1830)
Governor-general of Norway; served in merchant navy and Swedish Royal Navy; engineer; director-general of Gotha Canal project
Md xxxiii 485

PLATT, John Laurio (*ca* 1782–1836)
Served in Royal Navy; harbourmaster at Heligoland
DAIIB ii 337

PLAYFORD, Francis (1825–1896)
Oarsman
B vi 406

PLÉVILLE LE PELLEY, Georges René (1726–1805)
Vice-admiral French Navy; minister of marine; fisherman; privateer
Md xxxiii 353; S ii 319

PLIMSOLL, Samuel (1824–1898)
B vi 406; CE X 798; DNB xxii 1145

PLUMBRIDGE, *Adm Sir* James Hanway, KCB (1787–1863)
B ii 1562; DNB xv 1326; M xii 402; Tr 181

PLUMMER, Henry Crozier Keating (1875–1946)
Astronomer
DNB xxvii 677

PLUMTRE, John Pemberton (1791–1864)
Deputy lord warden of the Cinque Ports, 1858–1861; a commissioner of Dover Harbour for many years
B vi 407

PLUNKETT, *Rear-Adm* Charles Peshall, USN (1864–1931)
DAB 805

PLUNKETT, *Adm* Edward, *sixteenth Baron Dunsany* (1808–1889)
B i 940

POCKLINGTON, *Rear-Adm* Christopher (*d* 1766)
ch iv 183

POCOCK, *Adm Sir* George, KCB (1706–1792)
CE X 810; ch iv 383; DNB xvi 1; NC viii 441

POCOCK, Nicholas (1741?–1821)
Marine painter
DNB xvi 5

POCOCK, *Lieut* William Innes, RN (1783–1836)
DNB xvi 7

POCZOBUT, Martin Odlanicki de (*ca* 1734–1810)
Polish astronomer, born in Lithuania; visited Greenwich Observatory in 1768 and established observatory on similar lines at Vilna in 1773
Md xxxiii 556

POGSON, *Cdr* Henry Freeman Young, RN (*fl* 1793–1819)
M viii 28

POGSON, Norman Robert (1828–1891)
Astronomer
B ii 1567; CE X 819; DNB xvi 15

PONTEVEZ-GIEN (PONTEVÈS-GIEN), Henri Jean Baptiste, *Vicomte de*
(*d* 1790)
French naval officer; major-general of marine at Brest   M*d* xxxiv 80

POOLE, *Capt* Benjamin, RN (*fl* 1677–1680)   *ch* ii 76

POOLE, *Capt* Charles, RN (*d* 1737/8)   *ch* iv 50

POOLE, Jonas (*d* 1612)
Mariner; made a voyage to Virginia, 1607; visited Spitzbergen, 1610–1612   DNB xvi 98

POOLE, *Capt* Jonas, RN (*fl* 1661–1666)   *ch* i 26

POOLE, *Capt* Richard, RN (*fl* 1665)   *ch* i 175

POOLE, Stanley Edward Lane (1854–1931)
Orientalist and historian; author of: 'The Barbary Corsairs' (1890)   DNB xxvi 715

POOLE, *Capt Sir* William, RN (*fl* 1661–1685)   *ch* i 26

POOLEY, *Capt* William, RN (*fl* 1672–1688)   *ch* i 374

POOR, *Rear-Adm* Charles Henry, USN (1808–1882)   DAB 811; H 655

POPE, James Colledge (1826–1885)
Canadian shipbuilder; minister of marine and fisheries for Canada   MDC 599

POPE, *Capt* Percival, USN (*fl* 1861–1880)   H 1015

POPE, Walter (*d* 1714)
Astronomer   DNB xvi 138

POPE, William (*fl* 1813–1825)
Nautical instrument-maker   T ii 402

POPHAM, *Adm* Brunswick (1805–1878)   B ii 1588; M viii 266

POPHAM, Edward (1610?–1651)
Admiral and general-at-sea   DNB xvi 141

POPHAM, *Rear-Adm Sir* Home Riggs, KCB (1762–1820)   DNB xvi 143; M*d*
                                                                        xxxiv 97; NC xvi
                                                                        265, 353

POPHAM, *Capt* Joseph Lamb, RN (*fl* 1794–1806)   M iv 1006

POPHAM, *Capt* Stephen, RN (*b* 1780)   M xii 85

POPHAM, *Adm* William (1791–1864)   B ii 1588; M xii 204

POPINJAY, Richard (*fl* 1563–1587)
Engineer, surveyor, and cartographer; surveyor of works at Portsmouth   T i 174

POPPLEWELL, *Adm* George Otway (*d* 1889)   B ii 1588

POPPLEWELL, *Cdr* Matthew James, RN (*fl* 1796–1813)   M vii 132

POPOV, Alexander Stepanovich (1859–1905)
Russian physicist; first man to send long-distance ship-to-shore radio signals using
aerial; pioneer of fitting of radio equipment in Russian warships   A 464

POTEMKIN, Grigory Alexandrovich (1724–1791)
Favourite of Catherine the Great; military commander; grand admiral of the
North Sea, Sea of Azov, and Caspian sea fleets   CE xi 142; Md xxxiv
                                                                    177

POTTER, *Capt* Abraham, RN (*d* 1695)   ch ii 189

POTTER, *Capt* Edward E., USN (*fl* 1850–1880)   H 895

POTTER, J. D. (*fl* 1830–1861)
Chart-agent to the Admiralty and instrument-maker; instruments at National
Maritime Museum   T i 458

POTTER, Thomas M., *Surgeon*, USN (*fl* 1839–1876)   H 983

POTTER, *Lieut* William P., USN (*fl* 1865–1880)   H 958

POTTINGER, *Capt* Ewdard, RN (*d* 1690)   ch ii 363

POTTS, *Lieut* John, RN (*d* 1847)   Tr 154

POTTS, Robert, *Chief Engineer*, USN (*fl* 1862–1880)   H 1009

POULDEN, *Rear-Adm* Richard (*d* 1845)   M iv 553

POULETT, *Vice-Adm the Hon* George (1786–1854)   B ii 1606; M ix 160

POULTON [*or* POULSEN], *Capt* Edward, RN (*d* 1695)   ch ii 190

POULTON [*or* POLTON], *Capt* Thomas, RN (*d* 1699)   ch iii 109

POUND, *Adm of the Fleet Sir* Dudley, GCB (1877–1943)   CE xi 146; DNB xxvii
                                                                    689

POUND, James (1669–1724)
Mathematician, astronomer, uncle and colleague of James Bradley   DNB xvi 232; T ii 139

POUND, Thomas (*ca* 1650–1703)
Pirate and hydrographer   DAB 817

POUND, *Capt* Thomas, RN (*fl* 1691–1695)   ch ii 401

POUTRINCOURT (*fl* 1605)
French voyager to Canada   Md xxxiv 251

POUYER, *Baron* Pierre Charles Toussaint (1774–1838)
French naval administrator   Md xxxiv 251

POWELL, *Capt* Edward, RN (*fl* 1666)   ch i 253

POWELL, Edward (1762–1814)
Seaman in Second Fleet to Australia; fisherman, farmer   DAuB ii 347

POWELL, *Cdr* George, RN (1795–1822)   Md xxxiv 253

POWELL, *Cdre* George Eyre, RN (1792–1856)   Md xxxiv 253

POWELL, *Capt* Herbert Brace, RN (*fl* 1797–1822)   M xii 430

POWELL, *Rear-Adm* Levin M., USN (*fl* 1817–1872)   H 661

POWELL, Nathaniel (*d* 1622)
Navigator and colonist; explored Chesapeake Bay with John Smith, 1608 DNB xvi 246

PRESTON, *Capt* William, RN (*fl* 1811–1833)   M viii 392

PRESTON, William, *Assist-Paymaster*, USN (*fl* 1869–1880)   H 996

PREVOST, *Rear-Adm* James (*fl* 1784–1846)   M ix 454

PREVOST, *Adm* James Charles (1810–1891)   B ii 1633

PRICE, Abel F., *Surgeon*, USN (*fl* 1868–1880)   H 978

PRICE, Charles (*fl* 1680–1718)
Cartographer, globe-maker and hydrographer   T i 276

PRICE, Charles (1807–1891)
Congregational minister, chaplain on Australian emigrant ship   AE ii 332; DAuB ii 350

PRICE, *Cdre* Cicero, USN (*fl* 1826–1867)   H 664

PRICE, *Rear-Adm* David (1790–1854)   B ii 1636; DNB xvi
                                                                                        326; M xii 31

PRICE, *Cdr* Francis Swaine, RN (1783–1853/4)   Tr 52

PRICE, *Capt* George, RN (*d* 1840)   M xi 1

PRICE, *Capt* John, RN (*d* 1709)   *ch* ii 282

PRICE, *Capt* Samuel, RN (1793–1852)   M vi 166

PRICE, *Maj Sir* Rose Lambart, RM (1837–1899)   B vi 428

PRICE [*or* PRYS], Thomas (*fl* 1586–1632)
Captain and Welsh poet; served on expeditions under Drake and Ralegh   DNB xvi 339

PRICE, *Cdr* William, RN (*d* 1835)   M viii 60

PRICKETT, *Cdr* John, RN (*d* 1823)   M vii 75

PRIDEAUX, *Capt* John, RN (*fl* 1667)   *ch* i 296

PRIDHAM, *Vice-Adm* Richard (1779–1864)   B ii 1642; M vi 138

PRIESTMAN, *Capt* Henry, RN (*d* 1712)   *ch* i 400

PRIME, *Lieut* Ebenezer S., USN (*fl* 1863–1880)   H 957

PRIMROSE, Archibald (1809–1851)
A lord of the Admiralty, 1835–1841   B ii 1644

PRINCE, Charles Lesson (1821–1899)
Astronomer   B vi 431

PRINCE, Nathan (1698–1748)
Naval schoolmaster   T ii 139

PRING, *Capt* Daniel, RN (*d* 1847)   M xii 93

PRING, Martin (1580–1626?)
*Sea-captain; entered the East India Company's service in 1608 and became general
of the company's ships, 1619; joined the Virginia Company, 1622*   DAB 826; DNB xvi 384

PRINGLE, *Capt* George, RN (*fl* 1807–1814)   M xi 316

PRINGLE, *Vice-Adm* James (*d* 1859)   M xi 75

PROUT, Samuel (1783–1852)
English landscape and marine painter   DNB xvi 426; M*d*
                                                                      xxxiv 420

PROVANA, Andrea (1511–1592)
Piedmontese admiral   M*d* xxxiv 421

PROWER [*or* PROWTHER], *Capt* William, RN (*fl* 1691–1703)   *ch* ii 401

PROWEZ, John (*fl* 1591–1596)
Seaman, gunner and cartographer   T i 190

PROWSE, *Cdr* Thomas, RN (*d* 1806)   Tr 233

PROWSE, *Rear-Adm* William (1753–1826)   DNB xvi 427; M ii
                                                                      779; Tr 303; R iv 112

PROWSE, *Capt* William Jones, RN (*fl* 1801–1841)   M viii 182

PROWTHER [*or* PROWER], *Capt* William, RN (*fl* 1691–1703)   *ch* ii 401

PRUDHOE, *Adm the Lord: see* PERCY, Algernon, *fourth Duke of Northumberland*

PRYCE, *Capt* Henry, RN (*b* 1786)   M viii 77

PRYNN, *Cdr* Parkins, RN (*d* 1838)   Tr 160

PTOLEMAEUS (PTOLEMY) (*fl* 90–168 A.D.)
Greek astronomer and geographer   A 34; CE xi 345; M*d*
                                                                      xxxiv 487

PUCKFORD, *Cdr* James, RN (*fl* 1810–1827)   M viii 255

PUDDICOMBE, William (*fl* 1773)
Seaman, teacher of and writer on navigation   T ii 294

PUDNER, *Capt* Humphrey, RN (*d* 1753)   *ch* iii 277

PUGET, Pierre (1620–1694)
French naval architect, painter, sculptor and architect   CE xi 364; M*d* xxxiv
                                                                      505

PUGH, *Capt* Richard, RN (*d* 1692)   *ch* ii 402

PULHAM, *Capt* John, RN (*fl* 1677)   *ch* ii 15

PULLEN, Henry William (1836–1903)
Miscellaneous writer; served as surgeon aboard the 'Alert' during the Nares Arctic
expedition, 1875–1876   DNB xxviiic 145

PULLEN, Joseph (1807–1877)
Astronomer   B ii 1666

PULLEN, Thomas Francis, RN (1851–1887)   B ii 1666

PULLEN, *Vice-Adm* William John Samuel (1813–1887)   B ii 1666; DNB xvi
                                                                      465

PULLEY, *Capt* Joseph, RN (*d* 1715)   *ch* iv 34

PULLING, *Capt* James, RN (*fl* 1803–1845)   M viii 336

PYRARD, François (*fl* 1601–1615)
French voyager to East Indies   M*d* xxxiv 579

PYTHEAS (*fl* 325 B.C.)
Greek geographer, Arctic explorer   M*d* xxxiv 593

QUACKENBUSH, *Cdr* John N., USN (*fl* 1847–1880)   H 903

QUACKENBUSH, *Rear-Adm* Stephen Platt, USN (1823–1890)   DAB 833

QUARTLEY, Arthur (1839–1886)
Marine artist   DAB 833

QUASH, *Capt* Kempthorne Charles, RN (*d* 1816/17)   Tr 277

QUEEN, *Capt* Walter W., USN (1824–1893)   DAB 834; H 883

QUELCH, John (*ca* 1665–1704)
Pirate   DAB 834

QUETELET, Lambert Adolphe Jacques (1796–1874)
Astronomer   CE xi 419

QUILLIAM, *Capt* John, RN (*d* 1839)   M iv 962; Tr 12

QUIN, *Adm* Michael (*d* 1861)   B ii 1691; M viii 145

QUINTON, *Capt* Cornelius, RN (*fl* 1794–1802)   M iv 613

QUIROS (QUEIROS), Pedro Fernandez de (*ca* 1560–1614)
Spanish explorer   DA*u*B ii 357; M*d* xxxiv 677

QUIQUERAN DE BEAUJEU, Paul Antoine de (*fl* 1637–1671)
Knight of Malta; naval commander   M*d* xxxiv 673

QUIRINO, Pietro (*fl* 1431)
Venetian voyager to East Indies   M*d* xxxiv 675

QUIROGA, Antonio (1784–1841)
Spanish military commander; served in marine guard   M*d* xxxiv 675

QUIROGA, Joseph (1707–1784)
Spanish Jesuit; royal surveyor of sites for ports and harbours in South America;
writer on navigation   M*d* xxxiv 675

RABAN, *Lieut* Herbert, RM (*fl* 1804–1807)   Tr 271

RABY, Augustin (1702–1782)
Quebec pilot and navigator   MDC 615

RABY, *Rear-Adm* James Joseph, USN (1874–1934)   DAB 835

RADCLIFFE, *Lieut* Copleston, RN (1785–1814)   Tr 117

RADCLIFFE, *Cdr* William, RN (*b* 1796)   M viii 362

RALFE, Charles Henry (*d* 1896)
Physician at Seamen's Hospital, Greenwich   B iii 19

RALFE, James (*fl* 1820–1829)
Writer on naval history; author of: 'The Naval chronology of Great Britain . . . '
3 vols (1820) and: 'The Naval biography of Great Britain . . . ', 4 vols (1828)   DNB xvi 651

RALLEAU [*or* RALLUAU], Jean (*fl* 1604–1615)
French explorer; with Champlain; secretary to Dugua de Monts on Nova Scotia
expedition of 1604   DCB i 564

RAM, *Lieut* William Alexander, RN (1784–1805)   Tr 14

RAMAGE, *Capt* William, RN (*d* 1828)   M xii 121

RAMEZAY, Claude de (1657–1724)
French; lieutenant in troupes de la marine; governor of Montreal   MDC 617

RAMSAY, *Adm Sir* Bertram Home, KCB, KBE (1883–1945)   DNB xxvii 705

RAMSAY, David (1794–1860)
Ship's surgeon and merchant   DAuB ii 361

RAMSAY, *Rear-Adm* Francis Munroe, USN (1835–1914)   DAB 838; H 890

RAMSAY, *Adm* George, CB, *twelfth Earl of Dalhousie* (1806–1880)   B i 804; DNB xvi 685

RAMSAY, *Capt* Robert, RN (*d* 1850)   M xii 23

RAMSAY, *Adm Sir* William, KCB (1793–1871)   B iii 29; M viii 376

RAMSDEN, *Cdr* Frank, RN (*b* 1797)   M viii 214

RAMSDEN, Jesse (1735–1800)
Optical instrument-maker, supplier to Captain Phipps, Board of Longitude, and others;
instruments at National Maritime Museum   DNB xvi 713; T ii 244

RAMSDEN, *Rear-Adm* William (*d* 1854)   M xii 421

RAMSEY, *Capt* George, RN (*d* 1717)   *ch* iii 407

RAMSEY, *Cdr* Samuel, RN (*fl* 1803–1804)   M viii 302

RAMUSIO, Giovanni Baptista (1485–1557)
Venetian historian and travel writer   Md xxxv 163

RAND, J. (*fl* 1799)
Optical instrument-maker; writer on a naval telescope   T ii 348

RAND, Stephen, *Assist-Paymaster*, USN (*fl* 1869–1880)   H 996

RAND, *Cdr* Thomas, RN (*fl* 1666)   *ch* i 254

RANDAL, *Capt* Edward, RN (*fl* 1681–1682)   *ch* ii 90

RANDALL, John (1755–1802)
Shipbuilder   DNB xvi 713

RANDALL, Robert Richard (*ca* 1750–1801)
American merchant and privateer   DAB 839

RANDALL, *Lieut* William, RN (*fl* 1805–1814)   Tr 20

RATSEY, *Rear-Adm* Edward (*fl* 1793–1854)   M ix 175

RATTRAY, *Vice-Adm* James (1790–1862)   M xii 103; Tr 42

RAUDOT, Jacques (1647–1728)
Intendant of New France, councillor of marine in France   MDC 620

RAVARDIÈRE (*fl* 1604–1611)
French traveller to Brazil, coloniser   Md xxxv 245

RAVEN, William (1756–1814)
Master RN, merchant captain, fisherman, lieutenant in Trinity House Volunteers –
Thames Flotilla   DAuB ii 364

RAVENHILL, John Richard (1824–1894)
Engineer; assessor to the wreck commissioners   B iii 48

RAVENHILL, Richard (1800–1887)
Marine engineer   B iii 48

RAWLING, *Capt* John, RN (*d* 1757)   ch vi 148

RAWLINS, *Cdr* Thomas, RN (*d* 1860)   Tr 127

RAWLINS, *Cdr* William, RN (*d* 1818)   Tr 144

RAWSON, *Adm Sir* Harry Holdsworth, GCB, GCMG (1843–1910)   AE ii 375; DNB xxiiic
                                                                              167

RAYLEY, *Capt* Charles, RN (*d* 1863)   M vii 135

RAYMOND, *Capt* Baymont [*or* Beaumont], RN (*d* 1718)   ch iii 279

RAYMOND, *Brig-Gen* Charles Walker, USA (1842–1913)
Supervised many important river and harbour improvements   DAB 846

RAYNER [*or* REYNER], John (*fl* 1661–1772)
Sea-captain; deputy governor of Newfoundland   DCB i 567

RAZILLY [*or* RASILLY], Claude Delaunay de (*ca* 1590–1642)
French naval captain, governor of Ile de Ré, Viceroy of Acadia   Md xxxv 274

RAZILLY [*or* RASILLY], Isaac de (1587–1635)
French naval captain, brother of Claude; coloniser, governor of Acadia   DCB i 567; MDC 620

REA, *Maj-Gen* Edward, RM (1805–1862)   B iii 60

READ, Charles William, CSN (1840–1900)   DAB 847

READ, *Capt* Francis, RN (*fl* 1666–1678)   ch i 374

READ, *Adm* George Campbell, USN (1787–1862)   DAB 847; H 680

READ, George Frederick (1788–1860)
Seaman East India Company, merchant captain, shipowner   DAuB ii 365

READ, John (*fl* 1582–1610)
Instrument and compass-maker   T i 185

READ, *Cdr* John, USN (*fl* 1858–1880)   H 914

REES, Abraham (1743–1825)
Encyclopaedist; editor of: 'Chambers's Cyclopaedia' (1778) and of his own:
'Cyclopaedia' (1819)   DNB xvi 840; M*d*
xxxv 319; T ii 270

REES, James (1821–1889)   DAB 851

REES, John, CB, RN (1808–1878)
Naval medical officer   B iii 87

REES, John Krom (1851–1907)
Astronomer   DAB 851

REES, *Lieut* Thomas Gwynne, RN (*d* 1811)   T*r* 169

REEVE, *Rear-Adm* John (*d* 1868)   M viii 350; T*r* 268

REEVES, *Capt Sir* William, RN (*fl* 1664–1673)   c*h* i 122

REEVES, *Cdr* Daniel, RN (*d* 1702)   c*h* iii 109

REEVES, *Lieut* Lewis Buckle, RN (*d* 1861)   T*r* 23

REEVES, *Lieut* Thomas, RN (*d* 1845)   T*r* 146

REEVES, *Cdr* William, RN (*d* 1693)   c*h* iii 84

REFORD, Robert (1831–1913)
Born Ireland; Canadian capitalist; founder of the Robert Reford Company, steamship
agency for the Donaldson Line, Thomson Line, etc.   MDC 622

RÈGEMORTES, Louis de (*fl* 1726)
French canal engineer   M*d* xxxv 322

RÈGEMORTES, Louis de (*fl* 1750–1771)
French canal engineer   M*d* xxxv 322

RÈGEMORTES, Noel de (*fl* 1700–1790)
French canal engineer   M*d* xxxv 322

REGNAULT, Jean-Baptiste (1754–1829)
French merchant seaman and painter   M*d* xxxv 334

REGNAULT DE SAINT-JEAN D'ANGÉLY, Michel Louis Étienne
(*ca* 1760–1819)
French administrator and lawyer   M*d* xxxv 336

REHÉ [*or* RHEE], Samuel (*fl* 1770–1792)
Instrument-maker; member of the Society for Naval Architecture   T ii 295

REHN, Franck Knox Morton (1848–1914)
Astronomer   DAB 852

REIBEY, Thomas (1769–1811)
Employee of East India Company, sea-captain, pilot, sealer, shipowner on the
Hawkesbury River, merchant   AE ii 378; DA*u*B ii 373

REID, *Capt* Charles Hope, RN (*d ca* 1852)   M xii 404

REID, David, *Surgeon*, RN (1777–1840)   DA*u*B ii 375

RENDEL, James Meadows (1799–1856)
Civil engineer; constructed many canals, harbours and docks, including the Birkenhead
docks, 1843; Portland harbour, 1846 and Grimsby docks, 1844–1853   B iii 108; DNB xvi
896; M*d* xxxv 413

RENFORTH, James (1842–1871)
Oarsman   B iii 110

RENNELL, James (1742–1830)
Geographer; served both in the Royal Navy and the East India Company service;
drew many charts   CE xi 600; DNB xvi
900; M*d* xxxv 429;
T ii 271

RENNIE, George (1791–1866)
Civil engineer; his company constructed the engines for 'Archimedes' (in which Sir
Francis Pettit Smith's screw was tried), and the 'Dwarf', the Royal Navy's first
screw-driven ship   B iii 111; DNB xvi 904
RENNIE, *Capt* George, RN (*fl* 1809–1822)   M xii 366
RENNIE, John (1761–1821)   CE xi 601; DNB xvi
905; M*d* xxxv 434;
T ii 322

RENNIE, *Sir* John (1794–1874)
Civil engineer; succeeded his father, John Rennie, as engineer to the Admiralty   B iii 112; DNB xvi 906
RENNOLOSON, J. (*fl* 1817–1822)
Mathematical instrument-maker; instruments at National Maritime Museum   T ii 403
RENNY, *Capt* Alexander, RN (*fl* 1807–1825)   M xii 122
RENOU, *Lieut* Timothy, RN (1789–1849)   Tr 171
RENTONE, *Capt* James, RN (*d* 1748)   *ch* v 62
RENWICK, *Capt* Thomas, RN (*d ca* 1852)   M vii 407
RENWICK, William, *Surgeon*, RN (1740?–1814)   DNB xvi 911
REPINGTON, *Vice-Adm* Edward Henry A'Court (1783–1835)   B iii 116
REQUESENS, Louis de Zuniga y (*fl* 1564–1576)
Spanish naval commander; lieutenant-general to Don John of Austria at the Battle
of Lepanto, 1571   M*d* xxxv 451
RESSEL, Josef (1793–1857)
German marine engineer, inventor of screw propeller   M*d* xxxv 460
RETZ DE ROCHEFORT (*fl* 1778–1891)
Surgeon, French Navy   M*d* xxxv 479
REVANS, *Cdr* Thomas, RN (*b* 1781)   M vi 407
REVELEY, Henry Willey (1788–1875)
Canal and harbour engineer in Australia   DA*u*B ii 376

RICH, *Capt Sir* Charles, RN (*d* 1706)   *ch* iii 280

RICH, *Capt* Charles, RN (*fl* 1801–1838)   M vii 406

RICH, *Capt* Edward, RN (*d* 1753)   *ch* v 411

RICH, *Capt* Edwin Ludlow, RN (*fl* 1804–1841)   M viii 112

RICH, *Vice-Adm* George Frederick (1787–1863)   B iii 135; M v 94

RICH, *Cdr* Henry, RN (1787–1864)   Tr 136

RICH, *Lieut* John C., USN (*fl* 1862–1880)   H 944

RICH, *Sir* Nathaniel (1585?–1636)
Merchant adventurer; contributed to the financing of the first voyage of discovery to
Providence Island, off the north-east of Yucatan, 1629   DNB xvi 1005

RICH, Richard (*fl* 1610)
Sailed with Christopher Newport to Virginia, 1609 and on his return in 1610
published a narrative in verse, entitled: 'Newes from Virginia', which contained an
account of his shipwreck on the Bermudas   DNB xvi 1012

RICH, Robert, KB, *second Earl of Warwick* (1587–1658)
Took part in colonizing voyages to America and in privateering ventures; appointed
lord high admiral in 1643   DNB xvi 1013

RICH, Robert (*d* 1679)
Quaker; wealthy shipowner and merchant   DNB xvi 1019

RICHAN, *Cdr* William, RN (*d* 1829)   M vi 294

RICHARDS, *Lieut* Benjamin S., USN (*fl* 1861–1880)   H 947

RICHARDS, *Capt* Charles, RN (*d* 1703/4)   *ch* iii 84

RICHARDS, *Cdr* Edwin, RN (*fl* 1803–1839)   M viii 217

RICHARDS, *Adm Sir* Frederick William, GCB (1833–1912)   DNB xxiv 459

RICHARDS, *Cdr* Harry Brown, RN (1790–1839)   Tr 154

RICHARDS, *Cdr* Harry Lord, RN (*fl* 1798–1828)   M viii 302

RICHARDS, Jacob, *Midshipman*, RN (*fl* 1804–1808)   Tr 279

RICHARDS, *Capt* James, RN (*d* 1711)   *ch* iv 37

RICHARDS, *Capt* John, RN (*fl* 1775–1809)   M x 9

RICHARDS, *Adm Sir* Peter, KCB (1787–1869)   B iii 141; M vi 76

RICHARDS, *Cdr* William, RN (*fl* 1806–1819)   M vii 261

RICHARDSON, *Vice-Adm Sir* Charles (*d* 1851)   M iv 902

RICHARDSON, Henry Thomas (*d* 1878)
Lifeboat inventor   B iii 148

RICHARDSON, Hugh (1784–1870)
Canadian steamship owner and captain   MDC 626

RICHARDSON, James (1791–1875)
Served in the Upper Canada Provincial Marine in the War of 1812; Methodist bishop   MDC 627

RIDGE, *Cdr* John James, RN (*d* 1809)   Tr 115

RIDGELY, *Capt* Charles Goodwin, USN (1784–1848)   DAB 865

RIDGELY, *Cdre* Daniel Newly, USN (1813–1868)   DAB 865

RIDLEY, *Capt* Hugh, RN (*fl* 1667–1699)   ch i 296

RIDLEY, *Sir* Matthew White, *fifth Viscount Ridley* (1842–1904)
Chairman of the Blyth board of dock commissioners   DNB xxiiic 196

RIETSCHOOF, Hendrick (*b* 1678)
Dutch marine painter; son of Jan Klaas   Md xxxvi 18

RIETSCHOOF, Jan Klaas (1652–1719)
Dutch marine painter   Md xxxvi 18

RIGAUD, Stephen Peter (1774–1839)
Mathematical historian and astronomer   DNB xvi 1196

RIGBY, *Capt* Edward, RN (*fl* 1693–1711)   ch iii 50

RIGGE, William Francis (1857–1927)
Astronomer   DAB 865

RIGNY, Henri Gauthier de (1783–1835)
French admiral   Md xxxvi 30

RILEY, *Cdr* Charles, RN (*fl* 1665)   ch i 175

RILEY, *Vice-Adm* Charles Wilson (1792–1877)   B iii 177

RING, James A., *Assist-Paymaster*, USN (*fl* 1870–1880)   H 996

RINGGOLD, *Rear-Adm* Cadwalader, USN (1802–1867)   DAB 866

RINGROSE, Basil (*d* 1686)
Buccaneer   DNB xvi 1196

RIOU, *Capt* Edward, RN (1758–1901)   AE ii 388; DNB xvi
                                                                                1201; NC v 482

RIPLEY, *Capt* Lionel, RN (*d* 1725)   ch iii 51

RIPLEY, Thomas (*d* 1758)
Architect; engaged in building the Admiralty, 1724–1726; designed the interior and
roof of the chapel at Greenwich Hospital   DNB xvi 1203

RIPLEY, Thomas (*fl* 1773–1802)
Instrument-maker; instruments at National Maritime Museum   T ii 295

RIPLEY, *Capt* William, RN (*d* 1697)   ch iii 110

RIPPE, *Cdr* James de, RN (*d* 1828)   M vii 6

RIQUET, Pierre Paul de (1604–1680)
French canal engineer   Md xxxvi 54

ROBERTS, *Cdr* George, RN (*fl* 1665–1672)   *ch* i 175

ROBERTS, George (*fl* 1726)
Mariner; reputed author of: 'The four years' voyages of Capt George Roberts . . . '
(1762), which is sometimes attributed to Defoe   DNB xvi 1264

ROBERTS [*or* ROBARTS], Henry (*fl* 1606)
Author of: 'A most friendly farewell to . . . Sir Francis Drake . . . ' (1585)   DNB xvi 1265

ROBERTS, Isaac (1829–1904)
Astronomer   DNB xxiiic 209

ROBERTS, *Capt* John, RN (*d* 1744)   *ch* iii 348

ROBERTS, *Capt* John Charles Gawen, RN (*b* 1787)   M xii 23

ROBERTS, *Capt* John Walter, RN (1792–1845)   M v 90

ROBERTS, Lewes [*or* Lewis] (1596–1641)
Merchant, writer on merchant shipping and trade; visitor to Newfoundland   DCB i 574; DNB xvi
                                                                                   1274

ROBERTS, Marshall Owen (1814–1880)
Shipowner   DAB 870

ROBERTS, *Cdr* Mitchell, RN (*d* 1859)   M vii 333

ROBERTS, Nathan S. (1776–1852)
Canal engineer   DAB 871

ROBERTS, Richard Francis, *Midshipman*, RN   Tr 18

ROBERTS, *Capt* Sir Samuel, RN (1787–*ca* 1846)   M vi 440; xii 28

ROBERTS, Solomon White (1811–1882)
Canal engineer   DAB 871

ROBERTS, *Capt* Thomas, RN (*b* 1779)   M vii 1

ROBERTS, *Cdr* William, RN (*fl* 1810–1816)   M vii 406

ROBERTS, *Cdr* William Gilbert, RN (*b* 1791)   M vii 401

ROBERTS, *Capt* William Pender, RN (*fl* 1797–1845)   M vii 69

ROBERTSON, Abraham (1751–1826)
Astronomer and mathematician   DNB xvi 1284

ROBERTSON, Ashley Herman, USN (1867–1930)   DAB 871

ROBERTSON, David (1806–1896)
Marine biologist; worked on the research ship 'Ark'   B iii 205

ROBERTSON, John (1712–1776)
Mathematician; first master of the Royal Naval Academy, Portsmouth, 1755–1756;
author of: 'The Elements of navigation' (1754)   DNB xvi 1299; T ii
                                                                                   189

ROBERTSON, Morgan Andrew (1861–1915)
Merchant seaman and author of sea stories   DAB 872

ROBERTSON [*or* ROBINSON], *Capt* Nicholas, RN (*d* 1753)   *ch* iv 302

ROBINSON, *Adm Sir* Robert Spencer, KCB (1809–1889)   B iii 230; DNB xvii 43

ROBINSON, Somerset, *Surgeon,* USN (*fl* 1861–1880)   H 972

ROBINSON, *Rear-Adm Sir* Tancred (*d* 1754)   ch iii 408

ROBINSON, *Capt* Thomas, RN (*d* 1703)   ch ii 190

ROBINSON, Thomas, *Boatswain,* RN (*d* 1805)   Tr 208

ROBINSON, Thomas Charles (*fl* 1821–1835)
Instrument-maker and quadrant-designer; dip-circle at National Maritime Museum   T ii 433

ROBINSON, *Capt* Thomas Pitt, RN (1792–1861)   M viii 303; Tr 31

ROBINSON, Thomas Romney (1792–1882)
Astronomer   B iii 232; DNB xvii 53

ROBINSON, William (1801–1870)
Author of: 'Reports of cases in the High Court of Admiralty, 1838–1850', 3 vols. (1844–1852)   B iii 233

ROBINSON, William Braham (1819–1888)
Chief constructor at Portsmouth dockyard, 1869–1881   B iii 234

ROBINSON, John (1739–1804)
Scientist, surveyor and teacher of naval cadets   Md xxxvi 192

ROBSON, T. C. (*fl* 1834)
Marine surveyor   T ii 459

ROBSON, Thomas (*d* 1864)
Patented a marine signal light   B v 491

ROBYNS, *Maj-Gen* John, RM (1780–1857)   B iii 240

ROCHE, *Le Marquis de la* (*fl* 1598)
French voyager to America   Md xxxvi 206

ROCHFORT, *Cdr* Robert, RN (*b* 1789)   M viii 267

ROCHFORT, *Capt* William, RN (*d* 1847)   M v 282

ROCHEGUDE, *Contre-Adm* Henri de Pascal, *Marquis de* (1741–1834)   s ii 380

ROCHE-SAINT-ANDRÉ, Gilles, *Chevalier de la* (1621–1668)
French military and naval commander, hydrographer   Md xxxvi 211

ROCHE-SAINT-ANDRÉ, Louis *de la* (*d* 1732)
Captain French Navy   Md xxxvi 212

ROCHE-SAINT-ANDRÉ, . . . (*fl* 1747)
Ensign in French navy   Md xxxvi 212

ROCHETTE, Nicolas Gargot *de la: see* GARGOT DE LA ROCHETTE

ROCHON, Alexis Marie de (1744–1817)
Librarian of Royal Naval Academy at Brest; astronomer of the navy; explorer; hydrographer; writer on navigation and optics   Md xxxvi 258

ROGERS, *Capt* George, RN (*d* 1729) — *ch* iii 283

ROGERS, *Cdr* John, RN (*fl* 1673–1678) — *ch* i 402

ROGERS, *Capt* Josias, RN (1755–1795) — DNB xvii 134

ROGERS, Moses (*ca* 1779–1821)
Steamboat captain — DAB 881

ROGERS, Robert David (1809–1885)
Canadian militia officer; took part in capture of steamer 'Caroline' during 1837
rebellion, of which he wrote an account — MDC 644

ROGERS, *Capt* Robert Henley, RN (*b* 1783) — M xii 112

ROGERS, Thomas Eales (*d* 1859)
H.E.I.C. naval officer; superintendent of the Calcutta Marine Department, 1846–1857 — B iii 263

ROGERS, *Capt* William, RN (*d* 1848) — M vi 344

ROGERS, William Augustus (1832–1898)
Astronomer — DAB 882

ROGERS, Woodes (*d* 1732) — DNB xvii 146; M*d* xxxvi 317

ROGGEWEEN [*or* ROGGEVIN], Jacob (1669–*post* 1723)
Naval commander for Dutch East India Company; explorer — M*d* xxxvi 320

ROHAN-MONTEBAZON, Louis Armand Constantin, *Prince de* (1730–1794)
French vice-admiral — M*d* xxxvi 344

ROHDE, Lévin Joergen (1786–1856)
Danish naval captain; inventor of telegraphic signals system — M*d* xxxvi 346

ROHRER, *Lieut* Karl, USN (*fl* 1865–1880) — H 961

ROKEBY, *Cdr* Henry Ralph, RN (*d ca* 1830) — M vii 368

ROLETTE, Frédéric (1785–1831)
Served in the Royal Navy until 1805; later an officer in the Canadian provincial
marine — MDC 644

ROLLAND, Pierre Elisabeth (*d* 1811)
French naval architect — M*d* xxxvi 367

ROLLAND, Pierre Jacques Nicolas (1779–1837)
French naval architect — M*d* xxxvi 367

ROLLES, *Vice-Adm* Robert (*fl* 1793–1832) — M ii 676

ROLLESTON, *Sir* Humphrey Davy, GCVO, KCB (1862–1944)
Consulting physician to the Royal Navy with the temporary rank of surgeon
rear-admiral, 1914–1918 — DNB xxvii 733

ROLT, Peter (1798–1882)
Connected with the Thames Iron Works and the construction of the 'Warrior', 1860 — B iii 270

ROMEGAS, Mathurian d' Aux-Lescaut (*d* 1581)
Knight of Malta and naval commander — M*d* xxxvi 407

ROQUEFEUIL, Jacques Aymar, *Comte de* (1665–1744)
Lieutenant-general de la marine; naval commander   Md xxxvi 443

ROQUEMONT DE BRISON, Claude (*fl* 1627–1629)
Admiral of the Fleet of the Compagnie des Cent-Associés   DCB i 579

ROS, *Rear-Adm* John Frederick Fitzgerald de (1804–1861)   B i 864; M viii 261

ROSA, Narcisse (1823–1907)
Quebec shipbuilder and writer on Quebec maritime history   MDC 646

ROSAMEL, Claude Charles Marie du *Comte de* (1774–1848)
French vice-admiral   Md xxvi 461

ROSE, *Cdr* Alexander, RN (*d* 1826)   M vi 407

ROSE, George (1744–1818)
Treasurer of the Navy, president of the Board of Trade   DNB xvii 226; Md xxxvi 475

ROSE, *Cdr* James, RN (*d* 1841)   M vii 119

ROSE, John Holland (1855–1842)
Naval historian   DNB xxvii 736

ROSEWELL, *Capt* Henry, RN (*d* 1771)   ch v 412

ROSIER, James (1575–1635)
Sailed with Bartholomew Gosnold to New England, 1602; and with George Weymouth, 1605; published an account of the latter voyage   DNB xvii 251

ROSILY-MESROS, *Amiral* François Étienne, *Comte de* (1748–1832)   Md xxxvi 493; s ii 390

ROSKRUGE, *Lieut* Francis, RN (*d* 1805)   Tr 40

ROSS, Alexander, *Surgeon*, RN (*d* 1819/20)   Tr 279

ROSS, Charles, *Purser*, RN (*d* 1816)   Tr 270

ROSS, *Vice-Adm* Charles Bayne Hodgson (*d* 1849)   M iv 735

ROSS, *Capt* Daniel, RN (*d* 1827)   M xii 109; T ii 373

ROSS, *Cdr* David, RN (*fl* 1795–1827)   M viii 231

ROSS, Henry Page Bailey (*fl* 1805–1848)
Served as a volunteer in the 'Agamemnon' at the battle of Trafalgar   Tr 270

ROSS, *Rear-Adm Sir* James Clark (1800–1862)   B iii 297; CE xii 1; DNB xvii 265; H 701; M viii 535; MDC 649; T ii 434

ROSS [*or* ROTZ], Jean [*or* John] (*fl* 1540–1548)
Hydrographer to the King; Dieppe pilot; chart-maker and writer on navigation   T i 169

ROSS, *Capt* John, RN (*d* 1731)   ch iv 63

ROUSE, *Capt* Augustus, RN (*d* 1714) — ch iv 34

ROUSSEAU, *Rear-Adm* Harr y Harwood, USN (1870–1930) — DAB 892

ROUSSIN, Albin-Reine (1781–1854)
French admiral; minister of marine — Md xxxvi 640

ROUTH, *Capt* Robert, RN (*d* 1760) — ch vi 149

ROWAN, *Vice-Adm* Stephen Clegg (1808–1890) — H 703

ROWE, *Capt* Henry Nathaniel, RN (*d* 1860) — M vi 397; Tr 233

ROWE, Jacob (*fl* 1725–1734)
Sea-captain and writer on navigation — T ii 165

ROWE, *Capt* Robert, RN (*fl* 1703–1725) — T ii 140

ROWE, Robert (*ca* 1775–1843)
Engraver, geographer and map-publisher — chb 448

ROWE, *Cdr* Symon, RN (*fl* 1682–1686) — ch ii 133

ROWE, William, *Midshipman*, RN (*fl* 1804–1849) — Tr 99

ROWED, *Cdr* Henry, RN (*d* 1831) — M vii 218

ROWLAND, David (*fl* 1814–1833)
Instrument-maker; inventor of naval quadrant — T ii 404

ROWLAND, Richard (*fl* 1807–1819)
Instrument-maker; improver of steering wheel, compass and log — T ii 404

ROWLANDSON, *Cdr* Francis, RN (*fl* 1671) — ch i 328

ROWLES, Richard (*fl* 1608)
English navigator; with Admiral Sharpey — Md xxxvi 662

ROWLEY, *Adm Sir* Charles, GCB (1770–1845) — DNB xvii 359; M ii 672; viii 419

ROWLEY, *Cdr* Edward, RN (*d* 1817) — Tr 185

ROWLEY, John (*d* 1728)
Mathematical instrument and globe-maker; instruments at National Maritime Museum — T i 294; T ii 140

ROWLEY, *Vice-Adm Sir* Joshua (1734–1790) — ch vi 107; DNB xvii 361; NA i 78; NC xxiv 89; R i 170

ROWLEY, *Vice-Adm Sir* Joshua Rickets (*ca* 1789–1857) — B vi 506; M xi 116

ROWLEY, *Adm Sir* Josias, GCB, GCMG (1765–1842) — DNB xvii 361; M ii 622, 872

ROWLEY, *Capt* Richard Freeman, RN (*b* 1806) — M vi 125, 453

ROWLEY, *Capt* Robert, RN (*fl* 1810–1822) — M xii 39

ROWLEY, *Rear-Adm* Samuel Campbell (1774–1846) — M iv 683

ROWLEY, *Adm of the Fleet Sir* William, KB (1690?–1768) — ch iv 63; DNB xvii 365; NC xxii 441

RUSH, *Lieut* Richard, USN (*fl* 1863–1879)   H 951

RUSH, William (1756–1833)
Carver of ships' figureheads   DAB 899

RUSHOUT, *Sir* John (1684–1775)
Politician; treasurer of the navy, 1743–1744   DNB xvii 418

RUSHWORTH, *Capt* John, RN (*d* 1779)   *ch* vi 336

RUSSEL, *Cdr* Robert, RN (*fl* 1805–1815)   M vi 416

RUSSEL, *Cdr* William, RN (*d* 1703)   *ch* iii 110

RUSSELL, Alexander W., *Pay Director*, USN (*fl* 1842–1880)   H 986

RUSSELL, Charles Arthur, GCMG, *first Baron Russell of Killowen* (1832–1900)
Counsel for Great Britain in Bering Sea arbitration, 1893   B vi 514

RUSSELL, *Adm of the Fleet* Edward, *Earl of Orford* (1653–1727)   DNB xvii 429; Md xxxvii 131

RUSSELL, *Adm Lord* Edward, CB (1805–1887)   B iii 347; DNB xvii 431; M viii 527

RUSSELL, George Horne (1861–1933)
Scot; settled in Canada; marine painter   MDC 658

RUSSELL, Henry Chamberlaine, CMG (1836–1907)
Astronomer   DNB xxxiiic 238

RUSSELL, Henry Norris (1877–1959)
Astronomer   CE xii 62

RUSSELL, Henry Stuart (1818–1889)
Explored coast from Brisbane to Wide Bay in a whale-boat; farmer and historian of Queensland   DAuB ii 406

RUSSELL, John, KG, *first Earl of Bedford* (1486?–1555)
Lord high admiral of England, 1540–1542   DNB xvii 444

RUSSELL, John, KG, *fourth Duke of Bedford* (1719–1771)
First lord of the Admiralty, 1744   DNB xvii 447

RUSSELL, *Cdr* John, RN (*d ca* 1745)   *ch* iv 309

RUSSELL, *Cdr* John, RN (*fl* 1815–1833)   M viii 97

RUSSELL, *Capt* John Henry, USN (1827–1897)   DAB 900; H 881

RUSSELL, John Scott (1808–1882)
Naval architect; was a shipbuilder on the Thames for many years; his company constructed the 'Great Eastern', 1854; joint-designer of the 'Warrior', the Royal Navy's first iron-clad   B iii 352; DNB xvii 465

RUSSELL, Joseph (1719–1804)
Shipowner   DAB 900

RUSSELL, *Capt* Robert, RN (*fl* 1820–1834)   M viii 346

RYMER, James (*fl* 1775–1822)
Ship's surgeon, Royal Navy; writer on navigation   DNB xvii 554; T ii
                                                                      296

RYMER-JONES, Thomas Manson (1839–1894)
Patented a method for ventilating steamships   B iii 369

RYTHER, Augustine (*fl* 1576–1590)
Engraver; associated with Jodocus Hondius and others in engraving charts for: 'The
Mariner's Mirrour' (1588); translator of Ubaldini's: 'Expeditionis Hispaniorum in
Angliam vera descriptio' (1590)   *ch*b 448; DNB xvii
                                                                      561; T i 179

RYVES, *Rear-Adm* George Frederick (1758–1826)   DNB xvii 561; M iii
                                                                      136

RYVES, *Rear-Adm* George Frederick, CB (1792–1858)   B iii 370; M vi 156

SAAVEDRA, Alvaro de (*fl* 1526)
Spanish explorer   M*d* xxxvii 166

SABBEN, *Lieut* James, RN (1787–1849)   T*r* 72

SABINE, *Gen Sir* Edward, KCB, RA (1788–1883)
Astronomer on John Ross's 1818 Arctic expedition and on Parry's of 1819–1820;
joint commissioner with Sir John Herschel in determining the difference of longitude
between Paris and Greenwich, 1825; appointed scientific adviser to the Admiralty, 1828 B iii 371; DNB xvii
                                                                      563; MDC 662; T ii
                                                                      405

SACHEVERELL, William (1638–1691)
Lord of the Admiralty, 1688–1689   DNB xvii 572

SACKLER, *Capt* Tobias, RN (*fl* 1660–1663)   *ch* i 29

SACKVILLE, Lionel Cranfield, KG, *first Duke of Dorset* (1688–1765)
Lord Warden of the Cinque Ports, 1708–1713 and 1757–1765   DNB xvii 581

SADD, *Capt* Simon, RN (*fl* 1660–1665)   *ch* i 176

SADE, Hippolyte, *Comte de* (*d* 1780)
Commodore French Navy   M*d* xxxvii 218

SADE, *Le Chevalier* Louis de (1753–1832)
Captain in French Marine Artillery; writer on navigation   M*d* xxxvii 224

SADLEIR, *Cdr* Richard, RN (1794–1889)   DA*u*B ii 414

SADLER, *Lieut* John Thomas, RN (*fl* 1805–1807)   T*r* 268

SADLER, Samuel Whitchurch (*d* 1886)
Paymaster-in-chief, Royal Navy   B vi 523

SADLER, Thomas (*fl* 1753–1773)
Teacher of mathematics and navigation   T ii 245

SADLINGTON, *Capt* Richard, RN (*d* 1673)   *ch* i 375

SAGHANY, Ahmed Ben Mohammed al (*d* 989 A.D.)
Arab astronomer; improver of the astrolabe   *Md* xxxvii 22?

SAID PASHA, Mohammed (1822–1863)
Viceroy of Egypt, Grand Admiral of the Fleet   *Md* xxxvii 238

SAINT-ANDRÉ, Jean Bon (1749–1813)
French merchant seaman; naval administrator and Protestant clergyman   *Md* xxxvii 254

ST CLAIR, *Capt* David Latimer, RN (*b* 1786)   M vii 83

SAINT-CRICQ, Jean (*ca* 1775–*ca* 1828)
Captain French Navy   *Md* xxxvii 266

SAINTE-CROIX, *Don* Alvarez de Bassano, *Marquis de* (*d* 1587)
Spanish admiral   *Md* xxxvii 281

SAINT-ÉTIENNE DE LA TOUR (TURGIS), Claude de (*ca* 1570–*post* 1636)
French sea-captain, trader, adventurer and coloniser   DCB i 596

SAINT-FÉLIX, Armand Philippe Germain, *Marquis de* (1737–1819)
French vice-admiral   *Md* xxxvii 306; s ii 411

ST GEORGE, *Lieut* William Molyneux, RN (*d* 1805)   *Tr* 152

SAINT-GEORGES, Jacques François Grout, *Chevalier de* (1704–1763)
Naval officer in French East India Company; captain French Navy   *Md* xxxvii 317

SAINT-GREY, Joseph de (1590–1674)
Frenchman in naval service of Grand Duke of Tuscany; army officer and scientist   *Md* xxxvii 325

SAINT-HAOUEN, Yves-Marie Gabriel Pierre Lecoat, *Baron de* (1756–1826)
French rear-admiral   *Md* xxxvii 326

SAINTHILL, *Capt* George Augustus, RN (*fl* 1810–1838)   M viii 362

SAINT-HIPPOLYTE, Jacques Philippe Pradin de Biarges, *Comte de* (1762–1830)
French rear-admiral   *Md* xxxvii 329

SAINT-JACQUES DE SYLVABELLE, Guillaume de (1722–1801)
French astronomer; writer on naval architecture and navigation   *Md* xxxvii 335

ST JOHN, Charles Edward (1857–1935)
Astronomer   DAB 905

ST JOHN, Frederick Edward Molyneux (1838–1904)
Officer, Royal Marines; journalist in Canada   MDC 664

ST JOHN, *Capt the Hon* Henry, RN (*d* 1780)   *ch* vi 509

SAINT-JULIEN DE CHABON, *Contre-Amiral* Jean René César de (1752–1799)   s ii 415

ST LO, *Rear-Adm* Edward (1682?–1729)   ch iii 284; DNB xvii 660

ST LO, *Capt* George, RN (*d* 1718)   ch ii 95; DNB xvii 661

ST LO [*or* ST LOE *or* ST LOO], *Rear-Adm* John (*d* 1757)   ch iv 50

SAINT-LUSSON, Simon François Daumont de (*d* 1677)
French explorer and army officer   DCB i 248; MDC 664

SAINT-PIERRE, Jacques Bernardin Henri de (1737–1814)
French author, army engineer and voyager to Mauritius   CE xii 151

ST QUINTON, *Cdr* James, RN (1791–1864/5)   Tr 270

ST VINCENT, *Adm of the Fleet the Earl of*: *see* JERVIS, John

SALES, Charles de (1625–1666)
Frenchman; naval commander for Knights of Malta; governor of Antilles   Md xxxvii 489

SALMA, Van (17th century)
Dutch marine painter   Md xxxvii 525

SALMON, *Sir* James, RN (1811–1886)
Naval surgeon   B iii 390

SALMON, *Capt* Robert, RN (*fl* 1664–1678)   ch i 135

SALMON, Robert (*fl* 1803)
Navigational instrument-maker   T ii 374

SALT, Henry (*fl* 1802, *d* 1827)
English traveller to Africa, India, etc.; travel writer; topographical artist; cartographer   DNB xvii 701; Md xxxvii 548

SALTER, *Lieut* Daniel, RN (*d* 1842/3)   Tr 18

SALTER, *Capt* Elliot, RN (*fl* 1788)   NA ii 44

SALTING, Severin Kanute (1805–1865)
Born in Denmark; marine store-keeper and shipchandler at Sydney   DAuB ii 415

SALTONSTALL, Charles (*fl* 1627–1665)
*Sea-captain; author of: 'The Navigator, shewing and explaining all the chiefe
principles and parts both theorick and practick that are contained in the famous art of
navigation . . . ' (1642)*   DNB xvii 711; T i 211

SALTONSTALL, Dudley (1738–1796)
American naval officer   DAB 906

SALVIN, Hugh, *Chaplain*, RN (1773–1852)   B iii 395

SAMPSON [*or* SAMSON], *Capt* Michael, RN (*d* 1711)   ch iii 409

SAMPSON, Ralph Allen (1866–1939)
Astronomer   DNB xxvi 781

SAMPSON, *Rear-Adm* William Thomas, USN (1840–1902)   DAB 907; H 910

SAMSON, *Air-Cdre* Charles Rumney, CMG (1883–1931)   DNB xxvi 781

SANDWELL, John (*fl* 1783)
Instrument-maker; octant at National Maritime Museum   T ii 322

SANDWICH, *The Earl of: see* MONTAGU, Edward

SANDWITH, *Col* John Hartley, CB, RM (1846–1895)   B iii 407

SANDYS, *Capt* Jordan (*d* 1734)   ch iii 287

SANÉ, Jacques Noel, *Baron* (1740–1831)
French naval architect   Md xxxvii 633

SANSON, Guillaume (*d* 1718)
French geographer   Md xxxvii 655

SANSON, Nicolas (1600–1676)
French geographer   CE xii 210; Md xxxvii
                                                                                          654

SANSON, Nicolas (*ca* 1626–1648)
French geographer   Md xxxvii 654

SANSUM [*or* SAMPSON *or* SANSOME], *Rear-Adm* Robert (*d* 1665)   ch i 135; DNB xvii
                                                                                          787

SANTA CRUZ, *Don* Alonzo de (*before* 1500–1572)
Spanish cartographer, historian and writer on navigation; treasurer of Sebastian
Cabot's expedition   Md xxxvii 664

SANUTO, Livio (*ca* 1532–1588)
Venetian geographer and cartographer   Md xxxvii 691

SAPSFORD, *Capt* John, RN (*fl* 1709)   ch iv 16

SARCEL DE (DU) PREVERT, Jean (*d* 1622)
French shipowner and merchant; voyager to Canada   DCB i 601

SARIS, John (*d* 1646)
Merchant and sea-captain; voyager to Japan   DNB xvii 793

SARGEANT, *Capt* William, RN (*fl* 1799–1819)   M xii 215

SARJANT, Thomas (*fl* 1713)
Instrument-maker; slide-rule at National Maritime Museum   T ii 141

SARMIENTO DA GAMBOA, Pedro (*fl* 1579–1586)
Spanish naval officer, explorer of South America   Md xxxviii 19

SARMON, *Cdr* George Woods, RN (*fl* 1808–1815)   M vii 367

SARTAIN, *Capt* Stephen, RN (*fl* 1664–1669)   ch i 136

SARTIGES, Charles Gabriel Eugéne, *Vicomte de* (1771–1827)
Captain French Navy   Md xxxviii 36

SARTINE, Antoine Raimond Jean Gualbert Gabriel de (1729–1801)
French minister of marine   Md xxxviii 36

SARTORIUS, *Adm of the Fleet Sir* George Rose, GCB (1790–1885)   B iii 417; DNB xvii
                                                                                          797; M xi 267; Tr 90

SAUVAGE, Pierre Louis Frédéric (1785–1857)
French marine architect and pioneer of steam navigation   M*d* xxxviii 81

SAVAGE, Arthur (1798–1853)
Surgeon superintendent Royal Navy   DA*u*B ii 418

SAVAGE, *Adm* Henry (*fl* 1758–1814)   M i 124; ii 602

SAVAGE, *Cdr* William, RN (*fl* 1796–1830)   M viii 367

SAVARY, Daniel (1743–1808)
Captain French Navy and merchant captain   M*d* xxxviii 106; s ii
                                                                                                            428

SAVERY, Thomas (1650?–1715)
Engineer; patented invention for propelling ships by means of paddle-wheels, 1696;
appointed treasurer of the hospital for sick and wounded seamen, 1705   DNB xvii 843

SAVIGNON (*fl* 1610–1611)
Red Indian of the Huron tribe who accompanied Champlain   DCB i 603

SAVILE, Henry (1642–1687)
Commissioner of the Admiralty, 1682–1684   DNB xvii 859

SAWYER, *Lieut-Cdr* George A., USN (*fl* 1861–1869)   H 998

SAWYER, *Adm* Herbert (1731?–1798)   c*h* vi 336; DNB xvii
                                                                                                            870; NA i 148; R i 239

SAWYER, *Vice-Adm Sir* Herbert, KCB (*fl* 1788–1820)   M i 337

SAXBY, Stephen Martin (1804–1883)
Served in the Royal Navy; lecturer on H.M.S. 'Worcester' training ship for cadets;
invented spherograph for correcting the compass; a pioneer weather forecaster   B vi 531

SAXTON, *Sir* Charles (1732–1808)
Commissioner of the Navy, 1789–1806   c*h* vi 461; DNB xvii
                                                                                                            873; NC xx 425

SAXTON, Christopher (1542–1610)
Cartographer   CE xii 240; c*h*b 449;
                                                                                                            DNB xvii 874; T i 175

SAYER, *Rear-Adm* George, CB (*fl* 1790–1816)   M iii 350

SAYER, *Capt* George, RN (*d* 1846)   M x 208

SAYER, *Vice-Adm* James (*d* 1777)   c*h* v 504

SAYER, Robert *and* BENNETT (1744–1794)
Map and chart dealers, atlas publishers   c*h*b 450; T ii 217

SAYLE [*or* SEALE], *Capt* William, RN (*fl* 1666–1667)   c*h* i 178

SCAIFE, *Capt* John, RN (*d* 1773)   c*h* vi 377

SCALE, Bernard (*fl* 1765–1776)
Land surveyor and hydrographer   T ii 271

SCALLEY [*or* SCALLY], *Capt* William, RN (*d* 1703)   c*h* iii 198

SCHOMBERG, *Capt Sir* Alexander, RN (1720–1804)   *ch* vi 272; DNB xvii
                                                                          911

SCHOMBERG, *Adm Sir* Alexander Wilmot (1774–1850)   DNB xvii 912; M iii
                                                                          325; vi 174

SCHOMBERG, *Capt Sir* Charles Marsh (1779–1835)   DNB xvii 913; M iv
                                                                          817

SCHOMBERG, *Capt* Isaac, RN (1753–1813)   DNB xvii 922

SCHONER, Johannes (1477–1547)
Mathematician and cosmographer   CE xii 269

SCHOONMAKER, *Cdr* C. M., USN (*b* 1839)   H 908

SCHOULER, *Lieut-Cdr* John, USN (1861–1880)   H 928

SCHOUTEN, Gautier (1567?–1625)
Dutch East India Company naval surgeon   Md xxxviii 431

SCHOUTEN, Willem Cornelissen (*fl* 1615–1625)
Dutch navigator   Md xvxiii 430

SCHRAEMBL, Franz Anton (1751–1803)
Austrian cartographer; publisher of a general atlas, 1786–1800   Md xxviii 432

SCHREIBER, Aloys Wilhelm (1763–1841)
German historian; writer on steam navigation on the Rhine and Lake Constance   Md xxxviii 436

SCHROEDER, *Rear-Adm* Seaton, USN (1849–1922)   DAB 921; H 954

SCHROTER, Johann Hieronymus (1745–1816)
Astronomer   CE xii 273

SCHUMACHER, Heinrich Christian (1780–1850)
*German astronomer; established observatory at Altona and fixed its position in
relation to Greenwich in co-operation with the Board of Longitude on board an
Admiralty steamer*   Md xxxviii 473

SCHWABE, Heinrich Samuel (1789–1875)
Astronomer   CE xii 277

SCHWATKA, Frederick (1849–1892)
Arctic explorer   CE xii 278; DAB 924

SCIPIO, Gnaeus Cornelius Asina (*fl* 260–256 B.C.)
Roman naval commander and consul   Md xxxviii 511

SCLATER [*or* SLATER *or* SLAUGHTER], *Capt* George, RN (*d* 1750)   *ch* iv 294

SCOBELL, *Capt* Edward, RN (1784–1825)   M x 351

SCOBELL, *Capt* George Treweeke, RN (1785–1869)   B iii 444; M vii 34

SCOLVUS, John (*fl ca* 1470–1480)
Probably Danish; navigator and pilot and possible voyager to Labrador   DCB i 679

SCOTT, *Vice-Adm* Matthew Henry (*fl* 1793–1819)   M ii 538

SCOTT, Michael (1789–1835)
Author of: 'Tom Cringle's Log' (1836) and: 'The Cruise of the Midge' (1836)   DNB xvii 1000

SCOTT, *Adm Sir* Percy Moreton, KCB, CVO (1853–1924)   DNB xxv 753

SCOTT, Robert (*b* 1797)
Engraver   *chb* 450

SCOTT, *Capt* Robert Falcon, CVO, RN (1868–1912)   A 460; CE xii 331; DNB xxiv 485

SCOTT, Samuel (1710?–1772)
Marine artist   DNB xvii 1004; M*d* xxxviii 551

SCOTT, *Capt* Samuel, RN (*d* 1774)   *ch* vi 92

SCOTT, *Capt* Theophilus, RN (*fl* 1666–1672)   *ch* i 254

SCOTT, *Capt* Thomas, RN (*fl* 1665)   *ch* i 254

SCOTT, *Capt* Thomas, RN (*d* 1725)   *ch* iii 302

SCOTT, William, *Baron Stowell* (1745–1836)
Maritime and international lawyer; appointed advocate-general for the office of the lord high admiral, 1782   DNB xvii 1046

SCOTT, *Capt* William Isaac, RN (*fl* 1792–1814)   M xi 357

SCOTT-ELLIS, Thomas Evelyn, *eighth Baron Howard de Walden & fourth Baron Seaford* (1880–1946)
Writer and sportsman; yachtsman and early exponent of motor-boat racing   DNB xxvii 764

SCOTTI, Marcel Eusébe (1742–1800)
Neapolitan scholar and priest; author of: 'Nautical catechism for the Navy and maritime history of Naples'   M*d* xxxviii 582

SCRIVEN, Thomas, *Master*, RN (*d* 1805)   T*r* 169

SCRIVEN, *Cdr* Timothy, CB, RN (*d* 1824)   M vii 122

SCROPE, *Capt* Adrian, RN (*fl* 1672–1682)   *ch* ii 96

SCROPE, *Capt* Carr, RN (*d* 1762)   *ch* vi 101

SCUDAMORE-STANHOPE, *Capt Sir* Edwyn Francis, RN (1793–1874)   B vi 538

SCYLAX (sixth century B.C.)
Greek geographer, navigator and travel writer   M*d* xxxviii 602

SCYMNUS of Chios (*fl* 80 B.C.)
Greek geographer and explorer   M*d* xxxviii 603

SEAGER, *Cdr* John, RN (*d* 1846)   M vii 221

SEAL, Charles (1801–1852)
Shipowner and whaler at Hobart   DA*u*B ii 433

SEALE, *Capt* Charles Henry, RN (*b* 1790)   M viii 184

SEEMANN, Berthold Carl (1825–1871)
Naturalist on board H.M.S. 'Herald' in the Pacific and Arctic, January 1847–June 1851   B iii 479; DNB xviii 1132

SEGOVIA, Juan de (*d ca* 1655)
Spanish marine painter   M*d* xxxviii 655

SELFRIDGE, *Lieut* James, USN (*fl* 1864–1880)   H 956

SELFRIDGE, *Rear-Adm* Thomas O., USN (*b* 1818)   H 730

SELFRIDGE, *Rear-Adm* Thomas Oliver, USN (1836–1924)   DAB 933; H 878

SELKIRK, Alexander (1676–1721)
English seaman and castaway; the inspiration of Defoe's: 'Robinson Crusoe'   DNB xvii 1162; M*d* xxxix 24

SELLER, Jeremiah (*fl* 1698–1707)
Instrument-maker, hydrographer, atlas and chart-seller, compass-maker for the navy   T i 295

SELLER, John (*fl* 1658–1698)
Hydrographer to the King; compass-maker for the navy; nautical instrument-maker; publisher of atlases and charts; teacher of and writer on navigation and gunnery   CE xii 407; C*hb* 451; DNB xvii 1165; T i 244

SELLERS, Isaiah (*ca* 1802–1864)
Pioneer American steamboat captain; an authority on the navigation of the Mississippi   DAB 934

SELSEY, *Capt the Lord: see* PEACHEY, Henry John

SEMMES, *Capt* Alexander A., USN (*fl* 1841–1880)   H 878

SEMMES, *Capt* Raphael, CSN (1809–1877)   DAB 935

SÉNÉCAL, Louis Adélard (1829–1887)
Canadian shipbuilder and politician   MDC 681

SENEX, John (*d* 1740)
Engraver; map, globe and instrument-maker   C*hb* 452; DNB xvii 1182; T i 301; ii 143

SENHOUSE, *Capt Sir* Humphrey Fleming (*d* 1841)   M xi 405; T*r* 152

SENHOUSE, *Sir* Joseph (*fl* 1793–1818)
Designer of a marine chair   T ii 349

SENNETT, Richard (1847–1891)
Engineer-in-chief at the Admiralty, 1886–1889   B iii 493

SENSER, George W., *Chief Engineer*, USN (*fl* 1860–1880)   H 1009

SEPMANVILLE, Lieudé François Cyprien Antoine, *Baron de*
French seaman and astronomer   M*d* xxxix 82

SEPPING, *Sir* Robert (1767–1840)
Naval architect   DNB xvii 1187

SEYMOUR, *Cdr* Joseph, RN (*d* 1862)   Tr 155

SEYMOUR, *Rear-Adm Sir* Michael, KCB (1768–1834)   B iii 506; DNB xvii
                                                                                1262; M iii 294; NC
                                                                                xxi 89; R iv 307

SEYMOUR, *Adm Sir* Michael, GCB (1802–1887)   DNB xvii 1264; M V
                                                                                286

SEYMOUR, Thomas, KG, *Baron Seymour of Sudeley* (1508?–1549)
Appointed lord high admiral, 1547   DNB xvii 1268

SEYMOUR-SYMERS, Thomas Lyell (1797–1884)
Mate, East India Company; shipowner   DAuB ii 435

SHACKLETON, *Sir* Ernest Henry, CVO, OBE (1874–1922)   DNB xxv 758; CE xii
                                                                                447

SHADWELL, *Rear-Adm Sir* Charles Frederick Alexander, KCB (1814–1886)   B iii 508; T ii 480;
                                                                                DNB xvii 1276

SHAFTO [*or* SHASTO], *Capt* RN (*fl* 1666)   ch i 254

SHAIRP, *Cdr* Alexander, RN (*fl* 1808–1838)   M viii 219

SHAKERLEY, Jeremy (*fl* 1650)
Mathematician and astronomer   DNB xvii 1283

SHAKESPERE, *Lieut* Arthur, RN (1788–1847)   Tr 194

SHALES, *Capt* John, RN (*d* 1720)   ch iii 393

SHAND, *Sir* Charles Farquhar (1912–1889)
Judge of the Vice-Admiralty court at Mauritius, 1860–1879   B iii 513

SHANNON, *Capt* Rodney, RN (*fl* 1801–1826)   M V 284; viii 533

SHAPLEY, Harlow (*b* 1885)
Astronomer   CE xii 456

SHARP, Abraham (1651–1742)
Mathematician, teacher, assistant to Flamsteed at Greenwich; instruments at National
Maritime Museum   CE xii 459; DNB xvii
                                                                                1338; T i 265

SHARLAND, *Capt* James, RN (*fl* 1664–1665)   ch i 45

SHARPE, *Rear-Adm* Alexander Renton, CB (*fl* 1799–1848)   M xi 122

SHARPE, Bartholomew (*fl* 1679–1682)
Buccaneer   ch ii 96; DNB xvii
                                                                                1357

SHARPE, *Capt* Robert, RN (*fl* 1807–1848)   M viii 212

SHARPEIGH, Alexander (*fl* 1607–1613)
Merchant and sea-captain; captain in the service of the East-India Company and
general of the fourth voyage to the East Indies, 1608   DNB xvii 1365

SHARRER, *Lieut* William O., USN (*fl* 1864–1880)   H 955

SHEPHEARD, *Capt* William, RN (*b* 1769)   M xi 21

SHEPHEARD, *Vice-Adm* William (1793/4–1870)   B iii 541; M viii 369;
                                                                                                   Tr 54

SHEPHERD, Anthony (1721–1796)
Astronomer   DNB xviii 52

SHEPHERD, *Cdr* John, RN (*fl* 1799–1812)   M viii 76

SHEPHERD, *Capt* Robert, RN (*fl* 1664–1668)   ch i 136

SHEPPARD, *Lieut-Cdr* Francis H., USN (*fl* 1861–1869)   H 935

SHERE [*or* SHERES], Henry (*fl* 1669–1698)
Marine engineer and surveyor   T i 261

SHERER, *Capt* James, RN (*fl* 1811–1841)   M viii 348

SHERIDAN, *Capt* John, RN (*fl* 1795–1846)   M xii 21

SHERIVE, *Capt* James, RN (*fl* 1672–1673)   ch i 375

SHERWIN, *Cdr* Thomas Cowper, RN (*fl* 1788–1843)   M viii 150

SHERWIN, *Capt* William, RN (*fl* 1673)   ch i 431

SHERWOOD, . . . (*fl* 1838)
Maker of longitude-compass   T ii 480

SHREVE, Henry Miller (1785–1851)
Steamboat captain   DAB 955

SHIFFNER, *Vice-Adm Sir* Henry (1789–1859)   B vi 553; M xxi 221

SHILLING, Andrew (*d* 1621)
*One of the chief masters of the navy, 1608; commander in the East India Company
service, 1617–1621*   DNB xviii 107

SHILLINGLAW, John Joseph (1830–1905)
*Went to Australia in 1852; superintendent of the Melbourne water police,
1854–1856; in 1856 was made shipping master to the Port of Melbourne*   AE ii 455

SHIPLEY, *Capt* Conway, RN (1782–1808)   M ix 389; NC xxxix
                                                                                                   345

SHIPPARD, *Rear-Adm* Alexander (1771–1841)   DNB xviii 116

SHIPPARD, *Capt* William, RN (1764–1856)   DNB xviii 116; M vii
                                                                                                   75

SHIPPEN, Edward, *Medical Director*, USN (*fl* 1849–1880)   H 967

SHIRLEY, *Vice-Adm* George James (*d* 1845)   M viii 421; iii 135

SHIRLEY, *Capt* James, RN (*d* 1774)   ch vi 483

SHIRLEY, *Rear-Adm* Thomas (1733–1814)   ch vi 378

SHIRLEY, *Vice-Adm* Washington, *fifth Earl Ferrers* (1722–1778)   ch v 452; DNB xviii
                                                                                                   135

SHIRREFF, *Rear-Adm* William Henry (*d* 1847)   M x 52

SICKLEMORE [or RATCLIFFE], John (d 1610)
Governor of Virginia; sailed from London in command of the 'Discovery', in
company with Christopher Newport and Gosnold, December 1606   DNB xviii 192

SIDDINS, Richard (ca 1770–1846)
Master mariner; whaler; pilot; lighthouse-keeper   DAuB ii 444

SIDGREAVES, Sir Arthur Frederick, OBE (1882–1948)
Businessman; served in the R.N.A.S. in the First World War   DNB xxvii 788

SIEBE, Augustus (1788–1872)   B iii 570

SIEGFRIED, Charles A., Surgeon, USN (fl 1872–1880)   H 980

SIEMENS, Sir William (1823–1883)
Metallurgist and electrician; laid the Atlantic cable 1874 and designed the
cable-ship 'Faraday', 1874   B iii 570; CE xii 537;
                                                                              DNB xviii 240

SIGSBEE, Rear-Adm Charles Dwight, USN (1845–1923)   DAB 958; H 923

SILLERY, Alexis Brulart, Marquis de (1737–1793)
French seaman and statesman   Md xxxix 345

SILVER, Capt John, RN (fl 1665–1666)   ch i 178

SILVESTER, Capt Sir Philip Carteret, CB, RN (1777–1828)   DNB xviii 251; M ix
                                                                              66

SIMCOE, Capt John, RN (d 1759)   ch v 259

SIMEON, Rear-Adm Charles (1791–1858)   M v 291

SIMMONDS, Cdr Joseph, RN (d 1838)   M vi 396; Tr 30

SIMMONDS, Cdr Richard Smith, RN (1788–1865)   Tr 184

SIMMONS, Lieut Edward, RN (1790–1849)   Tr 145

SIMMONS, John, Midshipman, RN (1784–1805)   Tr 206

SIMMS, Frederick Walter (1793–1860)
Mathematical instrument-maker; astronomer at Royal Greenwich Observatory   B iii 577; DNB xviii
                                                                              261; T ii 480

SIMON, William J., Surgeon, USN (fl 1864–1880)   H 977

SIMONS, Manley H., Surgeon, USN (1872–1880)   H 980

SIMONS, Lieut Thomas, RN (d 1805)   Tr 134

SIMPKINSON DE WESSELLOW, Lieut Francis Guillemard, RN
(1819–1906)   DAuB ii 446

SIMPSON, Charles Walter (1878–1942)
Canadian marine painter   MDC 693

SIMPSON, Rear-Adm Edward, USN (1824–1888)   DAB 961; H 755

SIMPSON, George (1791–1858)
English traveller   Md xxxix 397

SKINNER, Aaron Nicholas (1845–1918)
Astronomer   DAB 963

SKINNER, *Cdr* Arthur MacGregor, RN (*b* 1799)   M viii 311

SKIPSEY, *Cdr* Robert, RN (*fl* 1790–1815)   M vii 396

SKIPSEY, *Rear-Adm* William (*d* 1846)   M iii 488

SKYNNER, *Capt* Lancelot, RN (*d* 1760)   *ch* vi 338

SKYNNER, *Capt* Lancelot, RN (1766?–1799)   DNB xviii 361

SLADE, *Vice-Adm Sir* Adolphus, KCB (1802–1877)   B iii 599; DNB xviii
                                                                                362

SLADE, *Cdr* Henry, RN (*fl* 1800–1825)   M viii 156

SLADE, *Capt* James, RN (1786–1846)   M x 213

SLAMM, Charles W., *Paymaster*, USN (*fl* 1862–1880)   H 994

SLAUGHTER [*or* SCLATER *or* SLATER], *Capt* George, RN (*d* 1750)   *ch* iv 294

SLAUGHTER, *Adm* William (1787–1872)   B iii 604; M vi 413

SLINGSBY, *Sir* Robert (1611–1661)
Comptroller of the navy, 1550–1551   DNB xviii 378

SLITER, Robert (*fl* 1652–1677)
Master rope-maker at Chatham Docks; mathematician, teacher of navigation   T i 239

SLOAT, *Rear-Adm* John Drake, USN (1781–1867)   DAB 965

SLOCUM, Joshua (1844–*ca* 1910)   DAB 965

SMART, *Capt* Alexander, RN (*fl* 1673)   *ch* i 431

SMART, John (*fl* 1690–1700)
Instrument-maker; scales at National Maritime Museum   T i 287

SMART, *Adm Sir* Robert, KCB (1796–1874)   B iii 610; M viii 267

SMART, *Capt* Thomas, RN (*d* 1722)   *ch* iv 58

SMART, *Sir* William Richard Edwin, KCB, RN (1817–1889)
Surgeon   B iii 610

SMEATON, John (1724–1792)
Engineer, surveyor and instrument-maker; writer on mariner's compass, quadrant,
canals and perpetual logs   CE xii 610; DNB xviii
                                                                                393; M*d* xxxix 445;
                                                                                T ii 218

SMITH, Aaron (*ca* 1793–*ca* 1852)
Seaman tried at the Old Bailey on charges of piracy, but was able to prove that he
had done so under compulsion and was acquitted, 1823   B iii 615; DNB xviii
                                                                                410

SMITH, *Capt* Abel, RN (*d* 1756)   *ch* v 508

SMITH, *Capt* George, RN (1797?–1850)   DNB xviii 446; M viii
                                                         481

SMITH, George Charles (1782–1863)
Known as 'Boatswain Smith'; pressed into the Royal Navy, 1796 and left the
service in 1803; became a Baptist pastor and devoted himself to open air preaching
to sailors and watermen; opened the first sailors' home in London, 1828   B iii 628; DNB xviii
                                                         450

SMITH, *Capt* George Sidney, RN (*fl* 1804–1828)   M vi 52

SMITH, *Capt* Henry, RN (*fl* 1756)   ch vi 202

SMITH, *Adm Sir* Henry, KCB (1803–1887)   B iii 631; M vi 87

SMITH, Henry Gilbert (1802–1886)
Shipbuilder and shipowner at Sydney   DAuB ii 451

SMITH, *Sir* Herbert Llewellyn, GCB (1864–1945)
Civil servant and social investigator; helped Ben Tillett at the time of the
London dock strike; co-author, with Vaughan Nash of: 'The story of the Dockers'
strike' (1890)   DNB xxvii 794

SMITH, Howard, *Surgeon*, USN (*fl* 1871–1880)   H 979

SMITH, *Rear-Adm* Isaac (1753–1831)   AE ii 468; M iii 5;
                                                         T ii 247

SMITH, *Capt* James, RN (*fl* 1747–1770)   ch vi 339

SMITH, James (1782–1867)
Yachtsman   B iii 633; DNB xviii
                                                         467

SMITH, James (1805–1872)
Member of the Liverpool local marine board and Mersey docks and harbour board   B iii 633

SMITH, *Adm Sir* Jeremiah [Jeremy] (*d* 1675)   ch i 136

SMITH, *Capt* John (1580–1631)
Explorer and colonizer   CE xii 614; DAB 973;
                                                         DNB xviii 478; H
                                                         760; Md xxxix 454;
                                                         T ii 195

SMITH, John (*fl* 1633–1673)
Author of: 'The trade and fishing of Great Britain displayed . . .' (1661)   DNB xviii 483

SMITH, *Capt* John, RN (*d* 1729)   ch iv 203

SMITH, *Capt* John, RN (*d* 1772)   ch iii 386

SMITH, *Cdr* John Bernard, RN (*fl* 1805–1812)   M vii 90

SMITH, *Cdr* John Langdale, RN (1767–1827)   M vi 344

SMITH, *Lieut* John Samuel, RN (*d* 1840)   Tr 145

SMITH, *Capt* Thomas, RN (*d* 1847)   M v 272, vii 428

SMITH, Thomas L., *Surgeon*, USN (*fl* 1828–1862)   H 981

SMITH, Thomas Whistler (1824–1859)
Businessman; director of the Australian Steam Navigation Company   DAUB ii 453

SMITH, Walker D., *Chief Engineer*, USN (*fl* 1861–1880)   H 1011

SMITH, *Capt* William, RN (*fl* 1667–1673)   ch i 431

SMITH, *Capt* William, RN (*d* 1695)   ch iii 87

SMITH, William (*fl* 1726)
Surveyor to Royal African Company; published a survey of Guinea in 1726 DNB xviii 554; M*d* xxxix 457

SMITH, *Capt* William, RN (*fl* 1728)   ch iv 203

SMITH, *Capt* William, RN (*d* 1756)   ch iv 66

SMITH, *Cdr* William, RN (*fl* 1798–1826)   M viii 181

SMITH, *Cdr* William, RN (*d* 1825)   M vi 396

SMITH, William, *Midshipman*, RN (*fl* 1805–1848)   Tr 236

SMITH, *Capt* William, RN (*fl* 1806–1846)   M viii 187

SMITH, William Henry (1825–1891)
First Lord of the Admiralty, 1877–1880   B iii 651; DNB xviii 565

SMITH, William Henry (*fl* 1846–1851)
English ship's surgeon; author of a gazetteer and history of Canada   MDC 703

SMITH, *Capt* William Richard, RN (*fl* 1800–1817)   M xii 139

SMITH, *Capt* William Robert, RN (*fl* 1793–1840)   M vi 382

SMITH, William S., *Chief Engineer*, USN (*fl* 1861–1880)   H 1010

SMITH, *Adm Sir* William Sidney, KCB (1764–1840)   CE xii 616; DNB xviii 570; M i 291, ii 800, 808; NC iv 445; R iv 201

SMITH, *Adm* William Sidney (1799–1892)   B iii 652; M viii 363

SMITH, Willoughby (1828–1891)
Submarine cable engineer; in charge of the French Atlantic cable expedition, 1869   B iii 653; DNB xviii 576

SMITHSEND, Nicholas (*fl* 1685–1699)
Hudson's Bay Co captain   DCB i 611

SMITHSEND, Richard (*ca* 1653–*after* 1691)
Hudson's Bay Co captain   DCB i 611

SMOLLETT, *Capt* John Rouett, RN (*fl* 1794–1802)   M iv 689

SOLANDER, Daniel Charles (1736–1782)
Swede; naturalist on Cook's 'Endeavour' voyage; secretary and librarian to
Joseph Banks   DAuB ii 456; DNB
                                                                                xviii 620

SOLEY, James Russell (1850–1911)
Assistant-secretary United States Navy, 1890–1893   DAB 982

SOLEY, *Lieut* John Codman, USN (1862–1877)   H 944

SOLGARD, *Capt* Peter, RN (*d* 1740)   ch iv 98

SOLIS, Jean Diaz de (*ca* 1450–1516)
Spanish explorer of South America; companion of Pinzon   CE xii 694; Md xxxix
                                                                                581

SOLVYNES, François Balthazar (1760–1824)
Belgian seascape painter and traveller; sailed with Sir Home Popham to India;
captain of the port of Antwerp   Md xxxix 592

SOMERS [*or* SUMMERS], *Sir* George (1554–1610)
Virtual discoverer of the Bermudas; served on a buccaneering voyage, 1595;
took part in the 'Islands voyage', 1597; commanded the Virginia Company's fleet,
1609; wrecked on the Bermudas, 1609   DNB xviii 628

SOMERS, *Lieut* Richard, USN (1778–1804)   DAB 982

SOMERS, *Capt* Thomas, RN (*fl* 1744–1748)   ch v 353

SOMERSET, *Capt* John Stuckley, RN (*fl* 1758)   ch vi 341

SOMERSET, *Adm* Leveson Eliot Henry (1829–1900)   B vi 594

SOMERVILLE, *Adm of the Fleet Sir* James Fownes, GCB, GBE, DSO
(1882–1949)   DNB xxvii 810

SOMERVILLE, *Adm* Kenelm, *seventeenth Lord Somerville* (1787–1864)   B iii 669; M xi 381

SOMNER, William (1598–1669)
Antiquary; writer on the Roman harbours and forts of Kent   Md xxxix 607

SONNERAT, Pierre (*ca* 1745–1814)
French explorer of Madagascar and the Moluccas; travel writer; official of
ministry of marine   Md xxxix 610

SOPER, Edward, *Master*, RN (*fl* 1799–1806)   Tr 89

SORELL, William (1800–1860)
Registrar of Tasmania vice-admiralty court   DAuB ii 462

SOSISTRATUS OF CNIDUS (*fl* 280 B.C.)
Egyptian architect; builder of the Pharos of Alexandria (lighthouse)   Md xxxix 651

SOTHEBY, *Rear-Adm* Charles (*fl* 1795–1848)   M xi 62

SOTHEBY, *Adm Sir* Edward Southwell, KCB (1813–1902)   DNB xxiiic 281

SOTHEBY, *Adm* Thomas (*fl* 1783–1809)   M i 323

SOTHERON, *Vice-Adm* Frank (*b* 1765)   M ii 499

SPENCE, Graeme (*fl* 1784–1812)
Chief maritime surveyor at the Admiralty   T ii 323

SPENCE, *Cdr* Henry Francis, RN (*d* 1856)   Tr 194

SPENCE, *Capt* Henry Hume, RN (*fl* 1797–1809)   M x 48

SPENCER, *Lord* Charles (1740–1820)
Lord of the Admiralty, 1779   DNB xviii 760

SPENCER, *Rear-Adm* Frederick, KG, CB, *fourth Earl Spencer* (1798–1857)   B iii 685; M xii 401;
                                                                           M*d* xl 32

SPENCER, George John, KG, *second Earl Spencer* (1758–1834)
First lord of the Admiralty, 1794–1801   DNB xviii 763; M*d* xl 30

SPENCER, John Poyntz, KG, *fifth Earl Spencer* (1835–1910)
Statesman, first lord of the Admiralty, 1892–1895   DNB xxiiic 371

SPENCER, John Richard (*fl* 1796)
Mariner, author of a manuscript on navigation   T ii 323

SPENCER, *Adm* John Welbore Sunderland (1813–1888)   B iii 686

SPENCER, *Capt Sir* Richard, CB, RN (1779–1839)   DA*u*B ii 465; M xi 40

SPENCER, *Capt Sir* Robert Cavendish, RN (1791–1830)   DNB xviii 785; M xi 256

SPENCER, *Capt* Samuel, RN (*d* 1795)   *ch* vi 273

SPENCER, *Lieut* Samuel, RN (*d* 1850)   Tr 15

SPENCER, BROWNING & RUST (*fl* 1781–1838)
Instrument-makers; instruments at National Maritime Museum   T ii 323

SPERRY, *Lieut* Charles S., USN (*fl* 1862–1880)   H 943

SPERRY, Elmer Ambrose (1860–1930)
Inventor of gyroscopic compass used by the Navy   A 386; DAB 988

SPEYERS, *Lieut* Arthur B., USN (*fl* 1863–1880)   H 957

SPICER, Edward *and* LYNCH, James (*fl* 1760–1772)
Makers of navigational instruments   T ii 273

SPICER, *Capt* Peter, RN (*fl* 1795–1816)   M iv 577

SPILBERGEN, Georg de (*fl* 1601–1625)
Dutch navigator   M*d* xl 55

SPILLER, Joel (1790–1873)
*Marine engineer; established steam navigation on the Thames between Putney and
London, 1833*   B iii 689

SPILSBURY, Francis Brockell, *Surgeon*, RN (1756–1823)   M xii 89; MDC 708

SPILSBURY, *Capt* George (*fl* 1672)   *ch* i 376

SPODE, Josiah (1790–1858)
Australian landowner and public servant; served in the Royal Navy   DA*u*B ii 466

STANDRIDGE [or STAYNRED], Philip (*fl* 1621–1669)
Mathematician, instrument-maker and almanac compiler, contributor to Sturmy's:
'*Mariners Magazine*'   T i 208

STANFELL, *Capt* Francis, RN (*fl* 1795–1814)   M x 7

STANFIELD, Clarkson (1793–1867)
Marine and landscape painter   DNB xviii 884

STANFIELD, Daniel (*d* 1826)
Australian settler; served in the Royal Marines until 1794   DAuB ii 469

STANHOPE, *Capt* Chandos Scudamore, RN (1823–1871)   B vi 606

STANHOPE, Charles, *third Earl of Stanhope* (1753–1816)
Politician and man of science; took out patents for steam-vessels, 1790 and 1807   DNB xviii 888

STANHOPE, Edward (1840–1893)
Politician; largely responsible for the passing of the Merchant Shipping Act of 1876;
introduced and passed the Imperial Defence Act, 1888, which was devoted to
strengthening the defences of coaling stations and the improvement of military garrisons
at home and overseas   DNB xviii 895

STANHOPE, *Cdr Sir* Edwyn Francis, RN (1793–1874)   M viii 1

STANHOPE, *Adm* Henry (1788–1865)   B iii 707; M xii 433

STANHOPE, *Adm the Hon Sir* Henry Edyn (*fl* 1754–1814)   NC xv 91

STANHOPE, *Capt* Philip, RN (*d* 1708)   *ch* iii 302

STANHOPE, *Cdr* Robert Henry, RN (*fl* 1824–1888)   M viii 264

STANHOPE, *Capt Sir* Thomas, RN (*d* 1770)   *ch* v 417

STANIFORTH, Thomas (1807–1887)
Oarsman   B vi 606

STANLEY, *Capt* Edward, RN (*d* 1693)   *ch* ii 112

STANLEY, *Adm* Edward (1798–1878)   B iii 710; M viii 381

STANLEY, Frederick Arthur, KG, GCB, GCVO, *sixteenth Earl of Derby*
(1841–1908)
Lord of the Admiralty, 1868   DNB xxiii 381

STANLEY, Hans (1720?–1780)
Lord of the Admiralty, 1757–1765   DNB xviii 955

STANLEY, *Capt* John, RN (*d* 1740)   *ch* iv 204

STANLEY, Owen (1811–1850)
Hydrographer and explorer of New Guinea   DAuB ii 470

STANLEY, *Capt* William Pearce, RN (*fl* 1798–1839)   M viii 90

STANLY, *Rear-Adm* Fabius, USN (*b* 1815)   H 771

STANSEL, Valentin (1621–1690)
Astronomer   *vd* xl 161

STEFANSSON, Vilhjalmur (1879–1962)
Arctic explorer   CE xiii 169

STEMBEL, *Rear-Adm* Roger N., USN (*fl* 1832–1875)   H 776

STEPHENS, . . . (*fl* 1699)
Teacher of navigation   T i 295

STEPHENS, *Capt* Daniel, RN (*fl* 1666)   *ch* i 255

STEPHENS, *Cdr* Edward, RN (*fl* 1796–1819)   M viii 216

STEPHENS, George Washington (1866–1942)
Canadian official and broker; chairman of the Montreal Harbour Commission;
writer on the St Lawrence Seaway project   MDC 713

STEPHENS, James Francis (1792–1852)
Clerk in the Admiralty Office, 1807–1845   B iii 731

STEPHENS, *Capt* John, RN (*fl* 1661)   *ch* i 77

STEPHENS, *Capt* Nathaniel, RN (*d* 1747)   *ch* v 909

STEPHENS, *Sir* Philip (1725–1809)
Secretary of the Admiralty, 1763–1795   DNB xviii 1066

STEPHENS [*formerly* WILKINSON], *Adm* Philip (*d* 1846)   M ii 576

STEPHENS, *Adm* William Knighton (1815–1897)   B iii 733

STEPNEY, *Capt* George, RN (*d* 1753)   *ch* v 260

STEPNEY, *Capt* Rowland, RN (*fl* 1665–1676)   *ch* i 376

STEPNEY, *Capt* Thomas, RN (*d* 1740)   *ch* iii 52

STERETT, *Lieut* Andrew, USN (1778–1807)   DAB 1001

STERNE, Thomas (*fl* 1619–1631)
Globe-maker   T i 206

STERROP, George (*ca* 1715–1756)
Optical instrument-maker; instruments at National Maritime Museum   T ii 144

STEUART, *Capt* Hew, RN (*d* 1820)   M xi 116

STEVENS, Edwin Augustus (1795–1868)
Experimented with the construction of armour-plated ships   DAB 1005

STEVENS, *Cdr* George A., USN (*fl* 1840–1880)   H 903

STEVENS, *Capt* John, RN (*d* 1731)   *ch* iv 67

STEVENS, Marshall (1852–1936)
A founder and first general manager of the Manchester Ship Canal Company   DNB xxvi 831

STEVENS, *Capt* Robert, RN (*d* 1703/4)   *ch* iii 88

STEVENS, Robert Livingston (1787–1856)
Naval architect   DAB 1007

STEVENS, *Lieut* Thomas H., USN (*fl* 1863–1878)   H 957

STEVENS, *Capt* Thomas Holdup, USN (1795–1841)   DAB 1008; H 777

STEWART, *Capt* John, RN (1774–1811)   NC xxviii 1

STEWART, *Maj-Gen* John Henry, RM (1822–1880)   B iii 753

STEWART, *Vice-Adm the Hon* Keith (d 1795)   ch vi 471

STEWART, *Adm* Keith, CB (1814–1879)   B iii 753

STEWART, *Adm Sir* William Houston, GCB (1822–1900)   DNB xxiiic 419

STIERNSKÖLD, Nils (d 1627)
Swedish general and admiral   Md xl 249

STILES, *Capt* John, RN (fl 1781–1806)   M iii 228

STIRLING, *Vice-Adm* Charles (1760–1833)   DNB xviii 1271; M i
                                                                       402; ii 865; R iii 73

STIRLING, *Vice-Adm* Frederick Henry (1829–1885)   B iii 759

STIRLING, *Vice-Adm Sir* James (1791–1865)   AE ii 499; B iii 759;
                                                                       M vii 273; DNB xviii
                                                                       1267; DAuB ii 484

STIRLING, *Capt Sir* Walter, RN (1718–1786)   ch vi 379; DNB xviii
                                                                       1271

STIRLING, *Lieut-Cdr* Yates, USN (fl 1860–1880)   H 921

STOAKES, *Capt* John, RN (fl 1660–1664)   ch i 46

STOCKDALE, John (b 1658)
Engraver   chb 454

STOCKHAM, *Capt* John, RN (d 1814)   Tr 241

STOCKLER DE BORJA GARÇAO, François de (1759–1829)
Professor of mathematics at the Portuguese Marine Academy   Md xl 266

STOCKTON, *Lieut* Charles H., USN (fl 1861–1880)   H 938

STOCKTON, George (fl 1830–1837)
Nautical instrument-maker   T ii 461

STOCKTON, *Lieut* Henry T., USN (fl 1865–1879)   H 963

STOCKTON, *Capt* Robert Field, USN (1796–1866)   DAB 1015; H 781

STOCKWELL, John Nelson (1832–1920)
Calculator at the United States Naval Observatory   DAB 1015

STODDART, *Adm* James (1813–1892)   B iii 766

STODDART, *Capt* John, RN (fl 1797–1846)   M v 227

STODDART, *Rear-Adm* Pringle (1768–1848)   M ix 255

STODDERT, Benjamin (1751–1813)
First secretary of the United States Navy, 1798–1801   DAB 1016

STOKES, *Sir* Frederick Wilfried Scott, KBE (1860–1927)
Civil engineer; inventor of a canal sluice   DNB xxv 813

STUART, William (1773–1854)
Civil engineer; superintendent of Plymouth breakwater, 1830–1854   B iii 812

STUCLEY [*or* STUKELY], *Adm Sir* Lewis (*d* 1620)   DNB xix 122

STUDDERT, *Adm* John Fitzgerald (1790–1867)   B vi 645; M vi 23

STUDLEY, *Capt* James, RN (*d* 1697)   *ch* iii 143

STUDLEY, *Capt* Robert, RN (*d* 1717)   *ch* iii 410

STUPART, *Rear-Adm* Augustus (*fl* 1790–1846)   M x 268

STURDEE, *Adm of the Fleet Sir* Frederick Charles Doveton (1859–1925)   CE xiii 234; DNB xxv 820

STURDY, *Lieut* Edward W., USN (*fl* 1863–1880)   H 952

STURMY, Samuel (1633–1669)
Sea-captain, customs official and writer on mathematics and navigation   T i 265

STURT, *Capt* Henry Richard (*fl* 1813–1844)   M viii 357

STURTON, *Capt* Thomas, RN (*d* 1754)   *ch* v 261

STYLE, *Capt* William, RN (*b* 1785)   M vii 37

SUCKLING, *Capt* Maurice, RN (1725–1778)
Comptroller of the Navy, 1775–1778   *ch* vi 149; DNB xix 146; NC xiv 265

SUCKLING, *Capt* William Benjamin, RN (*fl* 1803–1841)   M vii 282

SUDBURY, John (*fl* 1610–1615)
Bookseller   *chb* 455

SUDDARDS, James, *Surgeon*, USN (*fl* 1849–1880)   H 967

SUFFREN SAINT-TROPEZ, Pierre André de (1729–1788)
French seaman   CE xii 262; M*d* xl 404

SUGAR, John (*fl* 1645–1653)
Globe-maker   T i 240

SULIVAN, *Adm Sir* Bartholomew James, KCB (1810–1890)   B iii 821; DNB xix 156

SULIVAN, *Lieut* Daniel Hunt, RN (*d* 1836)   Tr 64

SULIVAN, *Lieut* Samuel Hood, RN (*d* 1836)   Tr 162

SULIVAN, *Rear-Adm* Thomas Bell, CB (1780–1857)   B iii 822; DNB xix 157; M xi 408

SULLIVAN, *Adm Sir* Charles (1789–1862)   M xi 388

SULLIVAN, John C., *Assist-Paymaster*, USN (*fl* 1870–1880)   H 997

SULLIVAN, *Lieut* John T., USN (*fl* 1862–1879)   H 948

SULLY, Henry (1680–1728)
Inventor of a marine chronometer   T ii 145

SUMERS, *Capt* John, RN (*fl* 1673–1678)   *ch* i 431

SUMNER, *Cdr* George W., USN (*fl* 1858–1880)   H 912

SWANN [*formerly* SCWANN], *Air Vice Marshall* Sir Oliver, KCB, CBE, RAF
(1878–1948)
Assistant to Sueter in construction and development of the naval airship, 1909;
later Sueter's deputy at the newly-formed air department; transferred to the Royal Air
Force, 1918   DNB xxvii 855

SWANN, *Cdr* Thomas L., USN (*fl* 1856–1877)   H 918

SWANSON, Claude Augustus (1862–1939)
Secretary of the United States Navy, 1933–1939   DAB 1036

SWANTON, *Rear-Adm* Robert (*d* 1765)   *ch* v 354

SWANTON, *Capt* Thomas, RN (*d* 1723)   *ch* iii 111

SWANTON, *Capt* Thomas, RN (*d* 1744)   *ch* v 127

SWAYNE, *Capt* John, RN (*fl* 1667)   *ch* i 299

SWAYNE, *Cdr* Thomas, RN (*fl* 1672–1688)   *ch* ii 193

SWAYSLAND, *Rear-Adm* Henry (*d* 1757)   *ch* v 127

SWENY, *Capt* Mark Halpen, RN (1785–1865)   M viii 78; Tr 169

SWOFT, *Lieut* Willie, USN (*fl* 1863–1880)   H 949

SWINBURNE, *Adm* Charles Henry (1797–1867)   B iii 849; M viii 219

SWINBURNE, *Lieut* William T., USN (*fl* 1862–1880)   H 946

SWINEY, *Adm* William (*fl* 1779–1808)   M i 94

SWINFEN, *Cdr* William Clement, RN (*fl* 1816–1829)   M viii 336

SYEDS, John (*fl* 1790–1810)
Mariner, compass-maker and writer on navigation   T ii 350

SYER, *Rear-Adm* Joseph (1785–1856)   Tr 89

SYKES, *Adm* John (1773–1858)   B iii 853; M ix 1

SYKES, *Cdr* John, RN (*fl* 1789–1816)   M vii 336

SYKES, *Capt* Thomas, RN (*d* 1855)   M vii 133

SYMES, *Rear-Adm* Joseph (1785–1856)   M xi 63; Tr 89

SYMINGTON, William (1763–1831)   CE xiii 395; DNB xix
                                                                                  269

SYMONDS, *Capt* Benjamin, RN (*fl* 1666–1668)   *ch* i 255

SYMONDS, *Lieut* Frederick M., USN (*fl* 1867–1879)   H 949

SYMONDS, *Capt* George, RN (*fl* 1693–1698)   *ch* iii 54

SYMONDS, *Cdr* John, RN (*fl* 1807–1814)   M vii 312

SYMONDS, *Capt* Joseph, RN (*fl* 1663)   *ch* i 88

SYMONDS, *Capt* Richard, RN (*d* 1740)   *ch* iv 208

SYMONDS, *Capt* Thomas, RN (*d* 1694)   *ch* ii 364

SYMONDS, *Adm* Thomas Edward (1781–1858)   B iii 859; M xi 154

TANGYE, *Sir* Richard (1833–1906)
Engineer; supplied hydraulic jacks used for launching the 'Great Eastern'   DNB xxiiic 475

TANNER, *Cdr* John, RN (*fl* 1666)   ch i 255

TANNER, Joseph Robson (1860–1931)
Historian; published several works on Samuel Pepys   DNB xxvi 846

TANNER, *Lieut* Zera L., USN (*fl* 1862–1880)   H 941

TAPLEY [*or* TORPLEY], *Capt* John, RN (*d* 1699)   ch i 255

TAPP, John (*fl* 1596–1631)
Writer on navigation; author of: 'The Arte of Navigation . . .' (1596)   DNB xix 304; T i 193

TAPSON, *Capt* Richard, RN (*fl* 1670–1678)   ch i 431

TARBELL, John F., *Paymaster*, USN (*fl* 1862–1880)   H 995

TARBELL, *Capt* Joseph, USN (*ca* 1780–1815)   DAB 1044

TARDREW, *Cdr* George, RN (1784–1871)   Tr 81

TARLETON, *Adm Sir* John Walter, KCB (1811–1880)   B iii 877

TASMAN, Abel Janszoon (*ca* 1603–1659)
Dutch naval commander, merchant seaman and explorer   CE xiii 471; DAuB ii
                                                                            503; Md xii 48

TATERSAL, *Cdr* Nicholas, RN (*fl* 1660)   ch i 47

TATHAM, *Rear-Adm* Edward, CB (1811–1880)   B iii 880

TATHAM, *Rear-Adm* Sandford (*fl* 1791–1813)   M iii 9

TATHAM, William (1752–1819)
Soldier and engineer; superintendent of the London Docks, Wapping, 1801–1805   DAB 1044; DNB xix
                                                                            386

TATNALL, *Cdr* James Barnwell, RN (1790–1850)   M viii 30

TATNELL, *Cdr* Valentine, RN (*fl* 1660)   ch i 47

TATTNALL, Josiah (1795–1871)   DAB 1045

TAUNT, *Lieut* Emory H., USN (*fl* 1865–1880)   H 962

TAUSSIG, *Lieut* Edward D., USN (*fl* 1863–1880)   H 953

TAYLER, *Adm* Joseph Needham, CB (1785–1864)   B iii 885; DNB xix
                                                                            400; M xi 131; viii
                                                                            454

TAYLOR, *Capt* Bushrod B., USN (*fl* 1850–1880)   H 893

TAYLOR, *Rear-Adm* David Watson, USN (1864–1940)   DAB 1046

TAYLOR, George (*fl* 1775–1781)
Surveyor   chb 455

TAYLOR, George (*fl* 1833–1845)
Teacher of navigation, publisher   T ii 461

TAYLOR, *Cdr* Henry, RN (*fl* 1806–1814)   M vii 242

TAYLOR, *Rear-Adm* William Rogers, USN (1811–1889)   DAB 1049; H 802

TAYLOR, *Capt* William Vigneron, USN (1780–1858)   DAB 1049

TAYLOR, *Capt* Witteronge, RN (1719–1760)   *ch* vi 151; DNB xix
                                                                    479

TCHING-TCHING-KONG (*fl* 1646–1670)
Chinese admiral and pirate   M*d* xli 105

TCHITCHAGOFF, Paul Wassilewitsch (1767–1849)
Russian admiral   M*d* xli 106

TEACH [*or* THATCH], Edward (*d* 1718)
Pirate; commonly known as 'Blackbeard'   DNB xix 481; M*d* xli
                                                                    107

TEATE, *Capt* Mathew, RN (*d* 1718)   *ch* iii 306

TEATE, *Cdr* Richard, RN (*fl* 1661–1665)   *ch* i 77

TEDDEMAN, *Vice-Adm Sir* Thomas (*d* 1668)   DNB xix 482

TEDMAN, *Capt* Henry, RN (*fl* 1664)   *ch* i 139

TEGETTHOFF, Wilhelm, *Baron von* (1827–1871)
Austrian naval commander   CE xiii 496

TEGG, Thomas (1776–1845)
Published: 'The whole life of Nelson' (November 1805) and: 'The Mariner's
mavellous magazine . . . ', 4 vols. (1809)   DNB xix 486

TEIXEIRA, Pedro (1575?–1640)
Portuguese traveller, soldier and explorer   M*d* xli 206

TELFORD, Thomas (1757–1834)
Engineer; engineer of the Ellesmere Canal, 1793; reported on Scottish harbours,
1801–1803; constructed the Caledonian Canal; drew up a plan for the improvement
of Dover harbour, 1834   CE xiii 522; DNB xix
                                                                    489

TEMPEST, *Cdr* John, RN (*d* 1673)   *ch* i 377

TEMPLE, *Vice-Adm* Francis (*d* 1863)   M iv 911

TEMPLE, Henry, *second Viscount Palmerston* (1739–1802)
Lord of the Admiralty, 1777–1782   DNB xix 495

TEMPLE, Henry John, KG, GCB, *third Viscount Palmerston* (1784–1865)
Statesman; lord of the Admiralty, 1807–1809; became lord warden of the Cinque
Ports, 1861; master of Trinity House, 1862–1825   B ii 1325; DNB xix
                                                                    496

TEMPLE, *Cdr* John, RN (*fl* 1660–1685)   *ch* i 328

TEMPLE, *Capt* John, RN (*d* 1734)   *ch* iv 37

THIRAT DE CHAILLY, *Contre-Adm* Charles Louis (1749–1812)   s ii 495

THIRKILL, Lancelot (*fl* 1498–1501)
Merchant, shipowner, and explorer; sailed with John Cabot   DCB i 641

THOMAS, *Cdr* Abel Wantner, RN (*fl* 1793–1814)   M vii 238

THOMAS, *Capt* Alan Brodrick, CB, RN (1844–1894)   B iii 923

THOMAS, Andrew (*ca* 1773–1810)
Shipbuilder and shipowner on the Hawkesbury River, Australia   DAuB ii 519

THOMAS, *Capt* Charles, USN (*fl* 1829–1867)   H 899

THOMAS, *Lieut-Cdr* Charles M., USN (*fl* 1861–1880)   H 934

THOMAS, David John (1813–1871)
Ship's surgeon   DAuB ii 514

THOMAS, *Lieut* Davis, RN (*fl* 1805–1811)   Tr 193

THOMAS, *Capt* Edmund Fanning, RN (*d* 1842)   Tr 203

THOMAS, *Lieut* Eugene B., USN (*fl* 1861–1879)   H 937

THOMAS, *Rear-Adm* Frederick Jennings (1786–1855)   B iii 926; DNB xix
                                                                     660; M xi 205; Tr 115

THOMAS, George (1758–1802)
Master compass-maker at Deptford Dockyard   T ii 298

THOMAS, George (*fl* 1803–1846)
Naval schoolmaster and head maritime surveyor, RN   T ii 377

THOMAS, Jean (*fl* 1635)
French sea-captain and fur-trader   DCB i 642

THOMAS, Pascoe (*fl* 1740–1745)
Schoolmaster, Royal Navy; on Anson's voyage   T ii 219

THOMAS, *Adm* Richard (1777–1857)   DNB xix 669; M iv
                                                                     953

THOMAS, *Adm* Richard Darton (1777–1857)   B iii 931

THOMAS, *Capt Sir* William Sidney, RN (1807–1867)   B vi 679

THOMPSON, *Capt* Bradshaw, RN (*d* 1756)   ch v 63

THOMPSON, *Adm Sir* Charles (1740?–1799)   DNB xix 689; R ii 1

THOMPSON, Charles P., *Paymaster*, USN (*fl* 1865–1880)   H 991

THOMPSON, Curtis, *Assist-Paymaster*, USN (*fl* 1869–1880)   H 996

THOMPSON, *Capt* David, RN (1789–1834)   T ii 407

THOMPSON, *Cdre* Edward, RN (1738?–1786)   DNB xix 696; Md xli
                                                                     414; NC vi 437; vii 93

THOMPSON, *Capt* Egbert, USN (1822–1881)   DAB 1060; H 898

THOMSON, *Sir* Edward Deas, KCMG, CB
Navy Office official; writer on United States navy; Australian administrator   DAuB ii 523; DNB xix 719

THOMSON, *Cdr* Henry, RN (*d* 1827)   M vi 401

THOMSON, *Capt* John, RN (*fl* 1815)   M xii 85

THOMSON, *Capt* Lenox, RN (*fl* 1780–1802)   M iii 482

THOMSON, *Capt* Ormond, RN (*d* 1753)   ch v 358

THOMSON, William, OM, *first Baron Kelvin of Largs* (1824–1907)   CE xiii 194; DNB xxiiic 434

THOMSON, *Cdr* William Augustus, RN (*fl* 1806–1854)   M viii 380

THOMSON, William J., *Paymaster*, USN (*fl* 1865–1880)   H 994

THOREZ, Philip, *Midshipman*, RN (*d* 1839–1840)   Tr 18

THORFINNR THORDARSON (*fl* 1000–1020)
Icelandic explorer; first coloniser of North America   DCB i 642

THORNBROUGH, *Adm Sir* Edward, GCB (1754–1834)   DNB xix 767; M i 165; NA ii 118; R ii 357

THORNBROUGH, *Capt* Edward le Gras, RN (*b* 1795)   M v 292

THORNDYKE, Israel (1755–1832)
American Revolutionary privateer   DAB 1064

THORNE, *Adm* James (*d* 1870)   B iii 957; M vi 81

THORNE, Robert (*d* 1519)
Bristol merchant and shipowner, associate of the Cabots   DCB i 643

THORNE, Robert (1492–1532)
Bristol merchant and shipowner, associate of the Cabots   DCB i 643; DNB xix 774

THORNHILL, *Sir* James (1675–1734)   CE xiii 609; DNB xix 775

THORNLEY, John, *Surgeon*, USN (*fl* 1840–1871)   H 984

THORNTON, John (*fl* 1679–1740?)
Hydrographer   CE xiii 610; T i 257

THORNTON, *Capt* Samuel, RN (*b* 1797)   M v 300

THORNYCROFT, *Sir* John Isaac (1843–1928)
Shipbuilder and naval architect   CE xiii 610; DNB xxv 839

THROSBY, Charles, *Surgeon*, RN (1777–1828)   DAuB ii 530

THRUSH, *Capt* Thomas, RN (*fl* 1802–1825)   M x 20

THRUSHTON, *Capt* Charles Thomas, RN (*d* 1858)   M vii 37

TOTTEN, *Brig-Gen* Joseph Gilbert, USA (1788–1864)
Military engineer; engaged on coastal defences and harbour works; gained a high
reputation in lighthouse construction   DAB 1075

TOTTY, *Cdr* John, RN (*fl* 1665–1668)   ch i 182

TOUCHE-TRÉVILLE, Louis René Madelene Levason de la (1745–1804)
French vice-admiral   Md xlii 10

TOUR DU PIN-MONTAUBAN, *Le Marquis* David Sigsmond (1751–1810)
French naval officer   Md xlii 36

TOURNEUR, Laurent (1762–1820)
French seaman   Md xlii 52

TOURVILLE, Anne Hilarion de Contentin, *Comte de* (1642–1701)
French naval officer   CE xiii 700; Md xlii
                                                                     63

TOVEY, *Cdr* Nicholas, RN (*fl* 1666)   ch i 272

TOWER, *Rear-Adm* John (*d* 1837)   M iv 897

TOWERSON, Gabriel (*d* 1623)
Captain and agent for the East India Company; made several voyages to India DNB xix 1019

TOWERSON, William (1555–1577)
Merchant and navigator; made three voyages to the Guinea coast, 1555–1557   DNB xix 1020

TOWNLEY, *Cdr* Edmund, RN (*d* 1759)   ch vi 206

TOWNS, Robert (1791–1873)
Visited Australia in his own ship 'The Brothers', 1828; this was the first passenger
ship to take home a cargo consisting entirely of wool. Towns became a pioneer in the
South Sea trade   AE ii 571

TOWNSEND, *Capt* Bryant, RN (*d* 1690/1)   ch ii 289

TOWNSEND, *Adm the Hon* George (1715–1769)   ch iv 434; DNB xix
                                                                     1048

TOWNSEND, *Capt Sir* Isaac, RN (*d* 1731)   ch ii 364

TOWNSEND, *Adm* Isaac (*d* 1765)   ch iv 85; DNB xix
                                                                     1032

TOWNSEND, *Capt* James, RN (*d* 1864)   M vii 277

TOWNSEND, *Capt* Robert, USN (1819–1866)   DAB 1077

TOWNSHEND, *Maj-Gen Sir* Charles Vere Ferrers, KCB, DSO (1861–1924)
Served in the Royal Marine Light Infantry, 1884–1885   DNB xxv 848

TOWNSHEND, *Capt* Horatio, RN (*d* 1698)   ch iii 56

TOWNSHEND, *Capt Lord* James, RN (*b* 1785)   M x 18

TOWNSHEND, *Rear-Adm* John, *fourth Marquess Townshend* (1798–1863) M iii 999; M viii 534

TOWRY, *Capt* Henry John Philip, RN (*d* 1762)   ch vi 275

TRELAWNY-JAGO, *Vice-Adm* Charles (1829–1891)   B ii 46

TREMAIN, *Lieut* Hobart L., USN (1864–1880)   H 954

TREMENHEERE, *Gen* Walter, RM (1761–1855)   B iii 1011

TREMETT, *Vice-Adm* William Henry Brown (*b* 1777)   M iv 712

TREMLETT, *Rear-Adm* Francisco Sangro Robert Dawson (1815–1897)   B iii 1011

TREMLETT, *Adm* William Henry Brown (1777–1866)   B iii 1012

TRENCH, Melesina (1768–1827)   DNB xix 1116

TRENCH, *Rear-Adm the Hon* William le Poer (1771–1846)   M iv 697

TRENCHARD, *Cdr* George, RN (*d* 1696)   *ch* iii 90

TRENCHARD, *Rear-Adm* Stephen Decatur, USN (1818–1883)   DAB 1078; H 819

TRENGROUSE, Henry (1772–1854)
Inventor of 'rocket' life-saving apparatus, 1808   B iii 1015; DNB xix
                                                                                1137

TREVALYAN, *Sir* George Otto, OM (1838–1928)
Historian and statesman; Parliamentary secretary to the Admiralty, 1881   DNB xxv 853

TREVANION, *Capt Sir* Nicholas, RN (*d* 1737)   *ch* iii 144

TREVANION, *Capt* Richard, RN (*fl* 1666–1688)   *ch* i 273

TREVENEN, James (1760–1790)   DNB xix 1137

TREVITHICK, Richard (1771–1833)   CE xiii 766; DNB xix
                                                                                1140

TREVOR, *Capt* John, RN (*d* 1735)   *ch* iv 184

TREVOR, *Capt* Robert, RN (*d* 1740)   *ch* iv 19

TREVOR, *Sir* Sackvill (*fl* 1632)
Naval commander   DNB xix 1154

TREVOR, *Cdr* Thomas, RN (*d* 1743)   *ch* iv 234

TREVOR, *Capt* Tudor, RN (*d* 1739/40)   *ch* iii 173

TREWORGIE [TREWORGY *or* TREWERGHEY], John (*ca* 1618–1663)
Merchant, fisherman and coloniser; governor of Newfoundland   DCB i 652

TRILLEY, Joseph, *Chief Engineer*, USN (*fl* 1861–1880)   H 1009

TRIPPE, *Lieut* John, USN (1785–1810)   DAB 1080

TRISCOTT, *Capt* Richard Shepheard, RN (*d* 1858)   M viii 351

TRISTAN, Nuno (*d* 1447)
Portuguese navigator   M*d* xlii 173

TRITTON, *Sir* William Ashbee (1875–1946)
Engineer; employed by J. I. Thornycroft & Co, Chiswick in the 1890's; played
a prominent part in the design and construction of tanks for Churchill's Admiralty
Landship Committee   DNB xxvii 888

TRUGUET, *Adm* Laurent Jean François, *Comte* (1752–1839)   M*d* xlii 220; s ii 515

TRUPPO, *Lieut* Peter, RN (*d* 1822)   Tr 97

TRUSCOTT, *Cdr* Francis, RN (*d* 1827)   M vii 336

TRUSCOTT, *Capt* George, RN (*d ca* 1852)   M vii 68

TRUSCOTT, *Rear-Adm* William (1734–1798)   NC xxx 177

TRUSSON, *Lieut* Charles Almond, RM (*fl* 1804–1809)   Tr 251

TRUXTUN, *Capt* Thomas, USN (1755–1822)   DAB 1083; H 822

TRUXTUN, *Cdre* William Talbot, USN (1824–1887)   DAB 1084; H 878

TRYON, *Vice-Adm Sir* George, KCB (1832–1893)   AE ii 598; B iii 1029;
                                                                  CE xiii 788; DNB ix
                                                                  1199

TRYON, J. Rufus, *Surgeon*, USN (*fl* 1863–1880)   H 976

TUCKER, Benjamin (1762–1829)
Secretary of the Admiralty under Lord St Vincent   DNB xix 1206

TUCKER, *Rear-Adm Sir* Edward (*d* 1864)   M ix 197

TUCKER, John (*b* 1793)
A volunteer first class on the 'Bellerophon' at Trafalgar   Tr 206

TUCKER, *Adm* John Jervis (1802–1886)   B iii 1031; M vi 385

TUCKER, *Capt* John Randolph, USN (1812–1883)   DAB 1085

TUCKER, *Capt* Robert, RN (*b* 1769)   M vi 385

TUCKER, Samuel (1747–1833)
Served in both the United States Navy and merchant marine   DAB 1086; H 823

TUCKER, *Rear-Adm* Thomas (*d* 1766)   c*h* v 127

TUCKER, *Rear-Adm* Thomas Tudor (1775–1852)   B iii 1032; DNB xix
                                                                  1211; M x 419

TUCKER, *Capt* William, RN (*d* 1772)   c*h* vi 276

TUCKER, *Cdr* William, RN (*d* 1852)   M viii 213

TUCKEY, *Cdr* James Kingston, RN (1776–1816)   DNB xix 1212; M*d*
                                                                  xiii 241; NC xl 165,
                                                                  245

TUCKEY, *Cdr* John, RN (*d* 1696)   c*h* iii 90

TUDOR, *Capt* Abraham, RN (*d* 1708)   c*h* iii 393

TUKE, Francis Edward (1825–1898)
Oarsman   B vi 715

TULLIDGE, *Capt* Joseph Crew, RN (*d* 1845)   M vii 15

TUPINIER, *Le Baron* (1779–1850)   M*d* xlii 287

TUPMAN, *Cdr* George, RN (1785–1847)   M vii 405

TYLER, *Capt* Charles, RN (*d* 1846)   M vii 37

TYLER, *Vice-Adm Sir* George (1792–1862)   B iii 1060; DNB xix
                                                              1346; M xii 404

TYLER, *Lieut* George Whittelsey, USN (*b* 1847)   H 955

TYNG, Edward (1683–1755)
Merchant; officer in the Colonial Massuchusetts Navy   DAB 1093

TYRREL, *Capt* Richard, RN (*d* 1766)   *ch* v 264; NC X 353

TYRRELL, *Capt* John, RN (*d* 1689)   *ch* ii 32

TYSON, George Emory (1829–1906)
*American whaling captain; second-in-command of the 'Polaris' Arctic expedition,
1871–1873*   DAB 1093

TYSON, John (*fl* 1816)
Writer on navigation   T ii 409

TYRWHIT, *Capt* John, RN (*d* 1687)   *ch* i 50

UFFORD, Robert de, KG, *first Earl of Suffolk* (1298–1369)
Naval and military commander; admiral of the Northern Fleet, 1344–1347   DNB XX 9

ULLOA, Antonio de (1716–1795)
Spanish naval officer   M*d* xlii 346

UNDERDOWN, *Capt* John, RN (*d* 1728)   *ch* iii 140

UNDERWOOD, James (*ca* 1776–1844)
Shipbuilder on Hunter River; sealing shipowner   DA*u*B ii 546

UNDERWOOD, Joseph (1779–1833)
Sealing shipowner and captain   DA*u*B ii 547

UNDERWOOD, *Cdr* William, RN (*d* 1814)   M viii 359

UNDRELL, *Cdr* John, RN (*fl* 1805–1815)   M vii 361

UNWIN, William Cawthorne (1838–1933)
*Engineer; instructor in marine engineering at the Royal School of Naval
Architecture, South Kensington, 1869–1872*   DNB xxvi 878

UPSHUR, *Rear-Adm* John Henry, USN (1823–1917)   DAB 1097; H 827

URING, John (*fl* 1735–1771)
Ship-chandler and optical instrument-maker; instruments at National Maritime Museum T ii 193

URRY, *Cdr* Thomas, RN (*d* 1699)   *ch* ii 365

URRY, *Capt* William, RN (*fl* 1695)   *ch* iii 116

USHER, *Capt* Arthur, RN (*d* 1763)   *ch* vi 421

USHER, *Rear-Adm* Nathaniel Reilly, USN (1855–1931)   DAB 1097

USSHER, Henry (*d* 1790)
Astronomer   DNB XX 63

VAN DE VELDE, Willem (1633–1707)
Dutch marine painter   CE xiv 245; DNB xx
                                                                             103; M*d* xliii 81

VAN DE ZANDE (*fl* 1798)
French privateer   M*d* xliii 570

VAND HORN (*fl* 1635)
Buccaneer   M*d* xlii 571

VANE, *Sir* Henry (1613–1662)
Joint treasurer of the Navy, 1639–1641   CE xiv 247; DNB xx
                                                                             140

VANE, *Capt the Hon* Raby, RN (1736–1769)   *ch* vi 380

VAN NEK, Jan Cornelius (*fl* 1598)
Dutch seaman   M*d* xlii 501

VAN NOORT, Olivier: *see* NOORT

VANSITTART, *Vice-Adm* Edward Westby, CB (1818–1904)   DNB xxiiic 548

VANSITTART, *Vice-Adm* Henry (1777–1843)   DNB xx 140; M iii
                                                                             329; MDC 768

VANSTABEL, *Contre-Adm* Pierre Jean (1744–1797)   M*d* xlii 610; s ii 532

VARELA Y ULLOA, *Don* Joseph (1748–1797)
Marine surveyor   M*d* xlii 625

VARGAS Y PONCE, *Don* Joseph (1755–1821)
Geographer and seaman   M*d* xlii; 635

VARLEY, Cromwell Fleetwood (1828–1883)
Electrical engineer; consulted about the laying of the second Atlantic cable DNB xx 149

VARLO, *Capt* Weston, RN (*d* 1789)   *ch* vi 381

VASHON, *Adm* James (1742–1850)   DNB xx 154

VASSALL, John (*d* 1625)
Colonial pioneer and mariner; commanded a ship against the Armada, 1588   DAB 1110; DNB xx
                                                                             155

VASSALL, *Capt Sir* Spencer Lambert Hunter, RN (1799–1846)   M viii 226

VASSELL, *Cdr* Nathaniel, RN (*d* 1832)   M vii 217

VAUDREUIL, Louis Philippe Rigaud *Marquis de* (1723–1802)
French naval officer   M*d* xliii 25

VAUDREUIL-CAVAGNAL, Pierre de Rigaud, *Marquis de* (1704–1778)
French-Canadian; captain in troupes de la marine; last governor of New France MDC 768

VAUGHAN, *Capt* Francis, RN (*d* 1706/7)   *ch* iii 328

VAUGHAN, *Capt* Henry, RN (*b* 1757)   M iv 1003

VAUGHAN, *Adm* John (*d* 1789)   *ch* v 509

VAUGHAN, *Cdr* Roger, RN (*d* 1695)   *ch* ii 365

VERNON, Pierre Antoine (1736–1770)
French astronomer and navigator   Md xliii 226

VERNON, William (1719–1806)
Merchant; connected with the founding of the United States navy   DAB 1113

VERNON-HARCOURT, Leveson Francis (1838–1907)
Civil engineer; resident engineer at the East India & West India docks, 1866–1870;
at Alderney Harbour, 1870–1871, and on the Rosslare harbour works, 1872–1874   DNB xxiiic 555

VERY, *Lieut* Edward W., USN (*fl* 1863–1880)   H 952

VERY, *Lieut* Samuel Williams, RN (*b* 1846)   H 944

VESCONTE, *Lieut* James le, RM (*fl* 1805–1814)   Tr 34

VESEY, *Capt* Francis, RN (*d ca* 1828)   M iii 237

VESPUCCI, Amerigo (1451–1512)
Explorer   CE xiv; H 830; Md i
                                                                     582

VESTURME, *Vice-Adm* Louis Hutton (1825–1888)   B vi 743

VIAL DU CLAIRBOIS, Honoré Sebastien (1733–1816)
French shipbuilder   Md xliii 275

VIAN, *Adm of the Fleet Sir* Philip Louis, GCB, KBE, DSO (1894–1968) CE xiv 303

VIAT, *Capt* John, RN (*d* 1701/2)   ch iii 57

VICKARS, *Capt* William, RN (*d* 1693)   ch ii 366

VICARY, *Cdr* William, RN (1792–1882)   Tr 163

VICKERS, Albert (1838–1919)   CE xix 305

VICKERS, Gomersal (1810–1837)
Astronomer   DNB xx 301

VICKERS, Thomas Edward (1833–1919)   CE xiv 305

VICTOR FERDINAND FRANZ EUGEN GUSTAF ADOLF
CONSTANTIN FRIEDRICH of Hohenlohe-Langenburg, *Adm The Prince*,
GCB (1833–1891)
Known as Count Gleichen for many years   DNB xxii 1260

VICTRICIUS, Saint (330?–410)
Patron saint of seamen   Md xliii 339

VIDAL, *Cdr* Richard Emeric, RN (*fl* 1799–1830)   M viii 359

VIENNAY-PACHOIT, François (*d* 1698)
French merchant, fisherman, militia captain; director of the Compagnie du Nord   DCB i 661

VIENNE, Jean de (1342?–1396)
French admiral   Md xliii 360

VIGNAU, Nicolas de (*fl* 1611–1613)
Companion of Champlain on his explorations   DCB i 662

VILLARET DE JOYEUSE, *Vice-Adm* Louis Thomas, *Comte* (1748–1812)   Md xliii 412; S ii 553

WADDELL, *Cdr* James Iredell, CSN (1824–1886)   DAB 1120

WADDINGTON, Robert (*fl* 1747–1778)
Assistant to Maskelyne; writer on navigation and longitude   T ii 219

WADE, *Capt* Caleb, RN (*d* 1732 or 1738)   *ch* iv 21

WADE, *Capt* Cooper, RN (*d* 1703)   *ch* iii 57

WADE, *Lieut* George, RN (*d* 1825)   Tr 82

WADE, *Lieut-Cdr* Thomas F., USN (*fl* 1861–1877)   H 935

WADLEIGH, *Cdr* George H., USN (*fl* 1860–1880)   H 917

WAFER, Lionel (1660?–1705?)
Surgeon, buccaneer and voyager   DNB xx 427; Md xliv
                                                                 188

WAGER, *Capt* Charles, RN (*d* 1665)   *ch* i 50

WAGER, *Adm Sir* Charles (*d* 1743)   *ch* ii 437; DNB xx
                                                                 428; Md xliv 191

WAGER, Richard (*fl* 1728–1756)
Master compass-maker to the Navy   T ii 166

WAGGENER, James P., *Surgeon*, USN (*fl* 1872–1880)   H 980

WAGHENAER, Lucas Jansz (1550–1592?)
Cartographer and navigator; author of: 'The Mariner's Mirrour'   Md xliv 189

WAGHORN, *Capt* Martin, RN (*d* 1787)   DNB xx 431

WAGHORN, *Lieut* Thomas, RN (1800–1850)   DNB xx 431; H 832;
                                                                 Md xliv 192

WAINWRIGHT, Jonathan Mayhew, USN (1821–1863)   DAB 1122

WAINWRIGHT, *Lieut* Richard, USN (1817–1862)   DAB 1123; H 956

WAINWRIGHT, *Rear-Adm* Richard, USN (1849–1926)   DAB 1123

WAKE, *Adm* Charles (1824–1890)   B iii 1129

WAKEFIELD, Charles Cheers, GCVO, *Viscount Wakefield* (1859–1941)
Businessman and philanthropist; owner of the 'Miss England' speedboats   DNB xxvii 914

WAKELIN, *Capt* William, RN (*d* 1705)   *ch* ii 454

WAKELY [*or* WAKERLY], Andrew (*fl* 1631–1665)
Teacher of navigation; nautical instrument-maker, supplied Captain Thomas James
in 1633   T i 213

WAKE-WALKER, *Adm Sir* William Frederic, KCB (1888–1945)   DNB xxvii 913

WALBRAN, John T. (*d* 1913)
English master mariner; served in marine and fisheries service of Canada; commanded
Canadian Government steamer 'Quadra'; author of: 'British Columbia coast names'
(1909)   MDC 777

WALCOTT, *Vice-Adm* Charles (*fl* 1810–1846)   M viii 394

BOLTON PUBLIC REFERENCE LIBRARY

WALKER, *Lieut* Henry, RN (1790–1854)   Tr 55

WALKER, *Lieut* Henry, RN (d 1849)   Tr 206

WALKER, *Rear-Adm Sir* Hovenden (d 1728)   ch ii 455; DNB XX
                                                                       521; MDC 778

WALKER, *Rear-Adm* James, CB (d 1831)   DNB XX 524; M ii
                                                                       848; R iv 155

WALKER, James (1781–1862)
Civil engineer and designer of the Bishop Rock lighthouse   B iii 1147

WALKER, James, *Midshipman*, RN (*fl* 1805–1816)   Tr 100

WALKER, *Capt* James Robertson, RN (1783–1858)   B iii 1148; DNB XX
                                                                       526; M vii 376; Tr 19

WALKER, John (1779–1874)
Merchant, shipowner at Hobart   DAuB ii 563

WALKER, *Cdre* John Grimes, USN (1835–1907)   DAB 1127; H 890

WALKER, Nehemiah (*fl* 1670–1690)
Captain Hudson's Bay Company   DCB i 666

WALKER, *Lieut* Noris, RN (*fl* 1805–1813)   Tr 126

WALKER, Ralph (1749–1824)
Inventor of compass for finding longitude at sea; instruments at National Maritime
Museum   T ii 300

WALKER, *Cdr* Robert, RN (*fl* 1803–1813)   M vii 147

WALKER, Sears Cook (1805–1853)
Astronomer   DAB 1129

WALKER, Thomas Andrew (1828–1889)
Contractor; constructed the Barry docks, Glamorgan; harbour works at Buenos Aires
and a part of the Manchester Ship Canal   B iii 1153

WALKER, William (1787–1854)
Merchant; shipowner; whaler at Sydney   DAuB ii 566

WALKER, William (1793–1863)
Scot; legislative councillor of Canada; part-owner of steamship 'Royal William'   MDC 779

WALKER, *Cdr* William, RN (*fl* 1801–1828)   M viii 303

WALKER, *Sir* William Harrison (1800–1872)
Served in the Hon. East India Company naval service; later a professional member
of the marine department of the Board of Trade, 1850–1872; a conservator of the
River Thames   B iii 1155

WALLACE, Frederick William (1886–1958)
Born in Scotland; Canadian author and journalist; served with several shipping lines;
writer of history of maritime sail and of maritime fiction; founder of the: 'Canadian
Fisherman'   MDC 780

WARD, *Capt* James, RN (*d* 1693)   *ch* ii 289

WARD, James Edward (1836–1894)
Founder of the Ward Line, later the New York & Cuba Mail S.S. Co   DAB 1138

WARD, John (*fl* 1693–1615)
Pirate   DNB XX 777

WARD, *Capt* John, RN (*fl* 1667)   *ch* i 300

WARD, *Capt* John, RN (*d* 1703)   *ch* iii 58

WARD, *Capt* John, RN (*d* 1717)   *ch* iii 116

WARD, John (1679?–1758)
*Author of: 'The lives of the Professors of Gresham College . . .' (1740); was clerk
at the Navy Office until 1710*   DNB XX 779

WARD, *Capt* John, RN (1825–1896)   B iii 1193; DNB XX
                                                                     781

WARD, John Gray (1844–1922)
Submarine cable engineer   DAB 1137

WARD, *Adm* John Ross (1813–1890)   B iii 1193

WARD, *Capt* Thomas, RN (*fl* 1667)   *ch* i 300

WARD, *Vice-Adm* William (1782–1856)   B iii 1195; M iv 736;
                                                                     ix 301

WARD, *Adm* William John Petty (1829–1900)   B vi 783

WARDE, *Adm* Charles (1786–1869)   B iii 1196; M xii 85

WARDE, Luke (*fl* 1588)
*Sea-captain; sailed with Frobisher, 1576–1578, and Fenton, 1582–1583;
commanded a Queen's ship against the Armada, 1588*   DNB XX 807

WARDELL, William Wilkinson (1823–1889)
Civil engineer; constructed several lighthouses on the Australian coast B iii 1197

WARDEN, *Vice-Adm* Frederick, CB (1807–1869)   B iii 1198

WARDEN, William, *Surgeon*, RN (1777–1849)   DNB XX 807

WARELL [*or* WORRELL], *Capt* John, RN (*d* 1716)   *ch* iii 117

WARING, *Cdr* Henry, RN (*fl* 1793–1805)   M vi 296

WARING, *Lieut* James, RN (*d* 1832)   Tr 234

WARING, *Capt* Rupert, RN (*d* 1753)   *ch* v 129

WARNEFORD, *Sub-Lieut* Reginald Alexander John, VC, RN (1891–1915)   DNB xxiv 553

WARNER, *Cdr* Arthur Lee, RN (*d* 1848)   M viii 94

WARNER, Samuel Alfred (*d* 1853)
*Inventor; continually urged the Admiralty and War Office to adopt his 'invisible
shell' (apparently a small torpedo or sea-mine)*   DNB XX 859

WARRAND, *Capt* Thomas, RN (1775–1848)   M v 270

WATERS, Daniel, USN (1731–1816)   DAB 1155

WATERS, *Capt* David, USN (1731–1816)   H 838

WATERS, *Capt* Joseph, RN (*d* 1694)   *ch* ii 290

WATERWORTH, *Capt* John, RN (*d* 1672)   *ch* i 185

WATFORD, *Cdr* William, RN (1788–1859)   Tr 204

WATHAM, *Capt* Jonathan, RN (*fl* 1661–1678)   *ch* i 78

WATHING, *Capt* James, RN (*fl* 1665–1672)   *ch* i 183

WATKINS, Francis (*ca* 1723–1783)
Optical and mathematical instrument-maker; instruments at National Maritime Museum   T ii 220

WATKINS, *Rear-Adm* Frederick (*d* 1856)   B iii 1221; M iii 9

WATKINS, George R., *Assist-Paymaster*, USN (*fl* 1863–1880)   H 993

WATKINS, Henry George ('Gino') (1907–1932)
Arctic explorer   CE xiv 474; DNB xxvii
                                                                                               892

WATKINS, *Capt* John, RN (*d* 1757)   *ch* v 271

WATKINS, *Rear-Adm* Richard (*d* 1770)   *ch* v 270

WATKINS, *Capt* Robert, RN (*fl* 1694)   *ch* iii 90

WATKINS, *Capt* Robert, RN (*d* 1732)   *ch* iii 219

WATKINS, William (*fl* 1791–1825)
Optical instrument-maker; instruments at National Maritime Museum   T ii 351

WATLING, *Adm* John Wyatt (1789–1867)   B iii 1221; M vi 131

WATLY, *Capt* John, RN (*fl* 1665)   *ch* i 183

WATMOUGH, James H., *Pay-Director*, USN (*b* 1822)   H 985

WATMOUGH, William N., *Paymaster*, USN (*fl* 1861–1880)   H 991

WATSON, *Capt* Alexander, RM (*d* 1826)   Tr 45

WATSON, *Sir* Brook (1735–1807)
Seaman; commissary-general of the army in Canada; M.P.   MDC 785

WATSON, *Vice-Adm* Charles (1714–1757)   *ch* iv 407; DNB xx
                                                                                               913; M*d* xliv 383

WATSON, *Capt* Charles Hope, RN (*d* 1836)   M xi 268; Tr 183

WATSON, *Capt* Christopher, RN (*d* 1823)   M x 208

WATSON, *Lieut* Eugene W., USN (*fl* 1862–1880)   H 942

WATSON, *Capt* George, RN (*fl* 1665–1673)   *ch* i 183

WATSON, *Capt* George, RN (*d* 1774)   *ch* vi 382

WATSON, George Lennox (1851–1904)
Naval architect   DNB xxiiic 604

WATSON, *Adm Sir* George Willes, KCB (1827–1897)   B iii 1224

WATTS, *Capt* James, RN (*fl* 1666–1673)   *ch* i 432

WATTS, *Sir* John (*d* 1616)
Merchant and shipowner   DNB xx 981

WATTS, *Capt* Jonathan, RN (*d* 1698)   *ch* iii 151

WATTS, *Sir* Philip, KCB (1846–1926)
Naval architect   DNB xxv 895

WATTS, *Lieut* William, USN (*fl* 1862–1880)   H 944

WATTS, *Cdr* William Barber, RN (*fl* 1808–1830)   M viii 359

WAUCHOPE, *Rear-Adm* Robert (*d* 1862)   B iii 1236; M xi 268

WAVELL, *Capt* David, RN (*d* 1704)   *ch* iii 91

WAYMAN, *Capt* William, RN (*fl* 1667)   *ch* i 300

WAYMOUTH, Bernard (1824–1890)
Secretary of Lloyd's Register of Shipping, 1873–1890   B iii 1239

WAYMOUTH [*or* WEYMOUTH], George (*d ca* 1612)
*Explorer and navigator, sailed to Hudson's Strait and Virginia; writer on navigation
and shipbuilding*   DAB 1158; DCB i 667

WEALE, *Cdr* Edward Taylor, RN (*b* 1785)   M viii 253

WEARING, *Lieut-Gen* Thomas, RM (*d* 1863)   B iii 1240; Tr 156

WEAVER, *Capt* John, RM (*d* 1834)   Tr 101

WEAVER, *Cdr* William, RN (1795–1864)   Tr 270

WEBB, *Sir* Aston, GCVO, CB (1859–1930)
*Architect; designed the Admiralty Arch in Whitehall and the 'Britannia' Royal
Naval College*   DNB xxv 900

WEBB, *Cdr* Edward, RN (*fl* 1813–1827)   M viii 245

WEBB, Edward Brainerd (1820–1879)
*Civil engineer, author of: 'On iron breakwaters & piers' (1862); and, with James
Brunlees: 'The proposed ship railway across the Isthmus of Suez' (1859)*   B iii 1243

WEBB, *Capt* James, RN (*d* 1761)   *ch* v 510

WEBB, James (*d* 1889?)
Marine artist   B vi 814

WEBB, *Sir* John Sydney, KCMG (1816–1898)
Deputy master of Trinity House, 1883–1898   B iii 1245

WEBB, Joseph Benjamin (*fl* 1825–1828)
Nautical instrument-maker   T ii 438

WEBB, *Cdr* Joseph Richard Raggett (*fl* 1806–1828)   M viii 267

WEBB, Matthew (1848–1883)
*Merchant marine captain; a noted swimmer, he swam from Dover to Calais in
twenty-two hours, 1875*   DNB xx 105

WELLARD, *Capt* Robert, RN (*d* 1776)   *ch* v 511

WELLER, *Capt* John, RN (*d* 1752 or 1756)   *ch* iv 95

WELLER, *Rear-Adm* John (*d* 1772)   *ch* v 421

WELLER, John Laing (1862–1932)
Canadian civil engineer; engineer of the Trent and Murray canals, Ontario to
St Lawrence canals, and Welland ship canal   MDC 789

WELLES, Gideon (1802–1878)
Secretary of the United States Navy, 1861–1869   DAB 1168

WELLES, *Rear-Adm* Roger, USN (1862–1932)   DAB 1169

WELLESLEY, *Adm Sir* George Greville, GCB (1814–1901)   DNB xxiiic 631

WELLESLEY, *Capt the Hon* William Henry George, RN (1806–1875)   M vi 77

WELLESLEY-POLE, William, *third Earl of Mornington and first Baron*
Maryborough (1763–1845)
Served in the Royal Navy; entered Parliament, 1790; secretary to the Admiralty, 1807   DNB xx 1134

WELLS, Charles J. S., *Surgeon*, USN (*fl* 1861–1880)   H 976

WELLS, *Cdre* Clarke H., USN (*b* 1822)   H 840

WELLS, Edwin, *Chief Engineer*, USN (*fl* 1861–1880)   H 1011

WELLS, Henry, *Purser*, RN (*d* 1849)   Tr 244

WELLS, John (*fl* 1606–1635)
Seaman, naval storekeeper and mathematician   T i 114

WELLS, *Adm Sir* John, KCB (*fl* 1783–1821)   M i 279

WELLS, *Lieut* John, RN (1784–1841)   Tr 44

WELLS, *Adm Sir* Richard, KCB (1833–1896)   B iii 1266

WELLS, *Capt* Thomas, RN (*d* 1825)   M vi 370

WELLS, *Capt* William, RN (*d* 1826)   M ix 476

WELLSTED, James Raymond (1805–1842)
Surveyor and traveller; served in East India Company vessels, 1830–1839   DNB xx 1147

WELSH [*formerly* WILLIAMS], John (*d* 1832)
Able seaman Royal Navy; merchant captain; superintendent of Government vessels
at Tasmania; port officer at Launceston; hydrographer   DAuB ii 577

WEMYSS, *Lieut-Col* James, RM (*d* 1823)   Tr 208

WEMYSS, *Rear-Adm* James Erskine (1789–1854)   B iii 1269; M xi 397

WEMYSS, *Adm of the Fleet Sir* Rosslyn Erskine, GCB, CMG, MVO, *Baron*
Wester Wemyss (1864–1933)   DNB xxvi 896

WENTWORTH, *Capt* Samuel, RN (*fl* 1665–1672)   *ch* i 184

WENZEL, Charles Frederick (1740–1793)
Naval surgeon and metallurgist   Md xliv 472

WERDEN, *Rear-Adm* Reed, USN (1818–1886)   DAB 1173; H 841

WETWANG, *Capt Sir* John, RN (*d* 1684)   *ch* i 184; DNB XX
                                                                                  1299

WETWANG, *Capt* Joseph, RN (*fl* 1678–1680)   *ch* ii 58

WEYMOUTH, George: *see* WAYMOUTH

WEYMOUTH, *Cdr* Richard, RN (*d* 1832)   M vii 340

WEYMYS, *Capt* John, RN (*fl* 1673)   *ch* i 432

WHALLEY, *Lieut* Francis, RM (*fl* 1804–1806)   Tr 164

WHARTON, Benjamin B. H., *Chief Engineer*, USN (*fl* 1857–1880)   H 928

WHARTON, *Rear-Adm Sir* William James Lloyd (1843–1905)   DNB xxiii c 644

WHATELY, *Capt* John [*or* Thomas], RN (*fl* 1665)   *ch* i 185

WHEATLEY, *Cdr* John, RN (*b* 1801)   M viii 387

WHEATSTONE, *Sir* Charles (1802–1875)
Scientist and inventor; made important improvements to submarine telegraphy   DNB XX 1346

WHEELER, Daniel (1771–1840)
Quaker missionary; apprentice on a merchantman, 1783, midshipman RN, 1784;
served in the army, 1790–1796; made a missionary voyage to Polynesia and
Australasia, 1833–1838   DNB XX 1355

WHEELER, *Capt* Edward, RN (*d* 1761)   *ch* vi 95

WHEELER, Thomas (*fl before* 1779)
Land surveyor; carried out coast and harbour surveys for: 'The Atlantic Neptune' T ii 301

WHEELOCK, *Capt* John, RN (*d* 1778)   *ch* vi 286

WHELER, *Adm Sir* Francis (1656?–1694)   *ch* ii 76; DNB XX
                                                                                  1355

WHETHAM, *Sir* Charles (1811–1885)
Member of the Thames Conservancy board, 1883–1885   B vi 842

WHETSTONE, *Rear-Adm Sir* William (*d* 1711)   *ch* ii 290; DNB XX
                                                                                  1364

WHICHELO, Richard M., *Purser*, RN (1783–1858)   Tr 44

WHICHER, John Cobb, *Chaplain*, RN (*d* 1841)   Tr 164

WHIDDON, Jacob (*d* 1595)
Sea-captain; served against the Armada and later sailed with Ralegh to Guiana, 1595 DNB xxi 4

WHINYATES, *Rear-Adm* William (*fl* 1793–1846)   M xi 107

WHIPPLE, Abraham, USN (1733–1819)   DAB 1182

WHIPPLE, *Cdr* John, RN (*fl* 1782–1842)   M vi 268

WHIPPLE, Thomas (*d* 1805)
Captain's clerk on the 'Victory' at Trafalgar   Tr 22

WHISH, *Adm* William George Hyndman (1797–1884)   B iii 1304; M viii 176

WHISTON, *Capt* John, RN (*fl* 1673–1677)   *ch* ii 33

WILDE, *Capt* Henry, RN (*fl* 1692–1705)   *ch* iii 151

WILDES, *Cdr* Frank, USN (*fl* 1860–1880)   H 918

WILDEY, *Capt* Henry, RN (*fl* 1790–1840)   M vi 399

WILFORD, *Capt* Robert, RN (*fl* 1672–1685)   *ch* ii 59

WILGNESS, *Capt* John, RN (*fl* 1664–1670)   *ch* i 51

WILKES, *Rear-Adm* Charles, USN (1798–1877)   CE xiv 587; DAB
Antarctic and Pacific explorer   1205; H 845

WILKIE, *Lieut* James, RN (*d* 1821)   Tr 125

WILKINS, *Lieut* George F., USN (*fl* 1863–1879)   H 966

WILKINS, *Sir* George Hubert (1888–1958)
Polar explorer   CE xiv 588

WILKINS, *Capt* Michael, RN (*d* 1694)   *ch* iii 91

WILKINSON, *Capt* Andrew, RN (*d* 1785)   *chb* i 287

WILKINSON, *Cdr* Frederick Augustus, RN (*b* 1798)   M viii 133

WILKINSON, Henry Spenser (1853–1937)
Military historian and journalist; author of: 'The Brain of the Navy' (1895)   DNB xxvi 908

WILKINSON, *Capt* James, RN (*fl* 1803–1840)   M viii 264

WILKINSON, *Lieut* John, CSN (1821–1891)   DAB 1207

WILKINSON, *Capt* Robert, RN (*fl* 1665–1687)   *ch* i 187

WILKINSON, *Cdr* William, RN (*d* 1857)   Tr 305

WILLIAMS, Peter William (1851–1892)
Boat-builder   B vi 881

WILLAUMEZ, *Vice-Adm* Jean Baptiste Philibert, *Comte* (1763–1845)   M*d* xliv 626; s ii 570

WILLCOCKS, Samuel (1788–1848)
Served as a clerk in the 'Bellerophon' at Trafalgar   Tr 208

WILLCOX, Brodie McGhie (1785–1862)
Chairman of the Peninsular & Orient Line, 1840–1862   B iii 1356

WILLCOX, *Vice-Adm* James, CB (1812–1877)   B iii 1356

WILLCOX, *Cdr* Robert, RN (*fl* 1795–1846)   M viii 129

WILLDEY, George (*ca* 1681–1738)
Optical instrument-maker; instruments at National Maritime Museum   T ii 148

WILLDEY, Thomas (1718–1750)
Optical instrument-maker; map, instrument and globe-seller   T ii 195

WILLES, George Irwin, RN (*d* 1894)
Deputy inspector-general of hospitals and fleets   B vi 882

WILLES, *Adm Sir* George Ommanney, GCB (1823–1901)   DNB xxiiic 670

WILLES, *Capt* George Wickens, RN (1785–1846)   DNB xxi 286; M xi 349

WILLIAMS, *Vice-Adm* Thomas (*d* 1754)   ch v 360

WILLIAMS, *Adm Sir* Thomas, GCB (1762?–1841)   DNB xxi 455; M i 387;
                                                                                  R iv 477

WILLIAMS, *Cdr* Thomas, RN (*d* 1849)   M vii 277

WILLIAMS [*afterwards* WILLIAMS-FREEMAN], *Adm of the Fleet*
William Peere (1742–1832)   DNB xxi 470; M i 33;
                                                                                  NA ii 20; R i 420

WILLIAMS, William W., *Pay Inspector*, USN (*fl* 1861–1880)   H 987

WILLIAMS, *Adm* Woodford John (1809–1822)   B iii 1382

WILLIAMS, Zachariah (1673?–1753)
Writer on longitude   DNB xxi 471; T ii 148

WILLIAMSON, James (1816–1895)
Astronomer   B vi 900

WILLIAMSON, *Capt* Robert, RN (*fl* 1660)   ch i 51

WILLIAMSON, Thomas, *Chief Engineer*, USN (*fl* 1853–1880)   H 1003

WILLIAMSON, *Capt* William, RN (*d* 1771)   ch vi 345

WILLIS, *Cdr* Cecil Sherlock Wale, RN (*d* 1898)   B vi 902

WILLIS, *Capt* Francis, RN (*d* 1729)   ch iv 56

WILLIS, James W., *Midshipman*, RN (*fl* 1805–1848)   Tr 288

WILLIS, John (*fl* 1819–1821)
*Master Royal Navy, inventor of steering card and compass; card at National
Maritime Museum*   T ii 410

WILLIS, Michael (1810–1888)
Chairman of Lloyd's, 1881   B vi 906

WILLIS, *Rear-Adm* Richard, RN (*fl* 1790–1808)   M iii 8

WILLIS, *Capt* Thomas, RN (*d* 1766)   ch vi 433

WILLOCK, *Capt* Frank George, RN (*fl* 1806–1815)   M xii 108

WILLOUGHBY, *Capt* Digby, RN, *seventh Baron Middleton* (1769–1856)   M vi 298; 454

WILLOUGHBY, *Sir* Hugh (*d* 1554)
Sea-captain and Arctic voyager   CE xiv 595; DNB xxi
                                                                                  507; Md xliv 654

WILLOUGHBY, *Rear-Adm Sir* Nesbit Josiah, CB (1777–1849)   DNB xxi 508; M vii
                                                                                  424; X III; Md xliv
                                                                                  655

WILLOUGHBY, *Capt* Thomas, RN (*d* 1667)   ch i 187

WILLS, *Lieut* Francis, RN (*fl* 1801–1811)   Tr 107

WILLS, Horatio Spencer Howe (1811–1861)
Merchant seaman, farmer   DAuB ii 605

WILSON, Henry (*d* 1810)
English navigator   M*d* xliv 659

WILSON, *Capt* Henry, USN (*fl* 1847–1880)   H 892

WILSON, *Cdr* Henry Smith, RN (*d* 1844)   M viii 68

WILSON, Herbert Wrigley (1866–1940)
Journalist and writer on naval affairs   DNB xxvi 912

WILSON, James (*fl* 1764–1771)
Doctor of medicine; historian; writer on history of navigation   T ii 275

WILSON, James (*fl* 1796–1798)
Commander of the missionary ship 'Duff'   M*d* xliv 660

WILSON, *Cdr* James, RN (*fl* 1806–1854)   M viii 317

WILSON, John (*fl* 1714–1741)
Writer on navigation   T ii 150

WILSON, *Capt* John, RN (*d* 1749)   *ch* v 360

WILSON, *Capt* John, RN (*d* 1796)   *ch* vi 440

WILSON, John (1774–1855)
Sea-painter   DNB xxi 545

WILSON, *Adm* John (1789–1870)   B iii 1417

WILSON, John (1792–1860)
Tyne waterman   B vi 917

WILSON, John (*fl before* 1802)
Master Royal Navy, marine surveyor   T ii 378

WILSON, John (*d* 1800)
Seaman and explorer   DA*u*B ii 610

WILSON, *Major* John, RM (*fl* 1804–1854)   T*r* 209

WILSON, *Capt* John, RN (*fl* 1808–1827)   M xi 316

WILSON, *Capt* John, RN (*fl* 1809–1830)   M vi 159

WILSON, *Lieut-Col* John, RM (*d* 1850)   T*r* 185

WILSON, *Lieut* John C., USN (*fl* 1865–1880)   H 959

WILSON, *Rear-Adm* John Crawford (1834–1885)   B iii 1419

WILSON, Joseph Havelock, CBE (1858–1929)   DNB xxv 916

WILSON, *Capt Sir* John Morillyon, CB, RN   B iii 1420; DNB xxi 588

WILSON, Robert (1803–1882)
Engineer; invented a screw-propeller for vessels, 1832   B iii 1421; DNB xxi 596

WILSON, Theodore Belavan (1840–1896)
Chief of the United States Navy Bureau of Construction, 1882–1893   DAB 1224

WINSLOW, Edward (1595–1655)
'*Mayflower*' *pilgrim*   DAB 1232; DCB 1232;
                                                                          DNB xxi 672

WINSLOW, George F., *Surgeon*, USN (*fl* 1862–1880)   H 977

WINSLOW, *Lieut* Herbert, USN (*fl* 1865–1880)   H 960

WINSLOW, *Rear-Adm* John Acrum, USN (1811–1873)   DAB 1233

WINSLOW, John Flack (1810–1892)
Industrialist; manufactured machinery and plating for the USS 'Monitor' DAB 1233

WINSTANLEY, Henry (1644–1703)
Engineer; constructor and designer of the first Eddystone lighthouse, 1696–1700   DNB xxi 679

WINTER, George Robert (1826–1895)
Oarsman   B iii 1445

WINTER, *Sir* James Spearman, KCMG (1845–1911)
Premier of Newfoundland; represented Newfoundland at the Washington fisheries
conference, 1887–1888   DNB xxiiic 695; MDC
                                                                          808

WINTER, John William de (1750–1812)
Dutch vice-admiral   Md xliv 707

WINTER [*or correctly* WYNTER], *Adm Sir* William (*d* 1589)   DNB xxi 691

WINTERBOTTOM, Thomas (1819–1869)
Bandmaster of the Plymouth division, Royal Marines band, 1852–1869   B iii 1447

WINTERBOTTOM, William (1821–1889)
Bandmaster Woolwich division, Royal Marines Light Infantry   B iii 1447

WINTHROP, John (1714–1779)
Astronomer   DAB 1236

WINTHROP, *Rear-Adm* John (*fl* 1790–1819)   M ii 759, 881

WISE, *Vice-Adm* Charles (1810–1877)   B iii 1450

WISE, *Capt* Henry Augustus, USN (1819–1869)   DAB 1238; H 848

WISE, *Lieut-Cdr* William C., USN (*b* 1842)   H 921

WISE, *Rear-Adm* William Furlong, CB (1784–1844)   DNB xxi 713; M ix
                                                                          150

WISEMAN, *Capt* Robert, RN (*d* 1693/4)   ch ii 213

WISEMAN, Solomon (1777–1838)
Thames lighterman; shipowner in New South Wales   DAuB ii 617

WISEMAN, *Capt Sir* William, RN (1845–1893)   B iii 1453

WISEMAN, *Cdr Sir* William Saltonstall, RN (*b* 1814)   M xii 228

WISHART, *Adm Sir* James (*d* 1723)   ch ii 299; DNB xxi
                                                                          724; NC xxvii 177

WOOD, Benjamin (*fl* 1596)
English navigator   M*d* xlv 56

WOOD, *Lieut* Charles, RN (*d* 1819/20)   Tr 233

WOOD, *Sir* Charles, GCB, *first Viscount Halifax* (1800–1885)
Secretary of the Admiralty, 1835–1839   DNB xxi 824

WOOD, *Lieut* Edward P., USN (*fl* 1863–1880)   H 949

WOOD, *Cdr* George W., USN (*fl* 1859–1880)   H 915

WOOD, James (1856–1928)
Engineer; manufactured the internal combustion engine fitted in the first Holland
submarine   DAB 1244

WOOD, *Rear-Adm Sir* James Athol, CB (1756–1829)   DNB xxi 831; M ii
                                                                                              784, 881; NC xxiv
                                                                                              177; R iv 173, 527

WOOD, *Capt* John, RN (*fl* 1665–1671)   *ch* i 51, 378

WOOD, John (*d* 1681)
Marine surveyor, explorer   M*d* xlv 55; T i 261

WOOD, *Cdr* John, RN (*d* 1725)   *ch* iv 52

WOOD, John (1811–1871)
Geographer; entered the East India Company's naval service 1826, and rose to the
rank of captain; manager of the Oriental Inland Steam Navigation Company at Sind,
1857; superintendent of the Indus steam flotilla, 1861–1871   B iii 1468; DNB xxi
                                                                                              835

WOOD, Josiah (1843–1927)
Canadian shipbuilder; lieutenant-governor of New Brunswick   MDC 811

WOOD, *Capt* Lambert, RN (*fl* 1664–1669)   *ch* i 139

WOOD, *Capt* Robert, RN (*fl* 1666)   *ch* i 277

WOOD, *Lieut* Theodore T., USN (*fl* 1864–1880)   H 955

WOOD, *Capt* Walter, RN (*d* 1666)   *ch* i 51

WOOD, *Adm* William (1824–1889)   B iii 1477

WOOD, *Lieut* William, USN (*fl* 1865–1880)   H 963

WOOD, William Charles Henry (1864–1947)
Canadian military and naval historian; army officer   MDC 812

WOOD, William Maxwell, *Surgeon*, USN (*d* 1880)   H 848

WOODEN, *Capt* John, RN (*d* 1704)   *ch* iii 91

WOODIN, *Lieut* John, RN (*d* 1805)   Tr 96

WOODHULL, William W., *Paymaster*, USN (*fl* 1863–1880)   H 992

WOODLEY, George (1786–1846)
Divine; claimed to have anticipated Manby's life-saving apparatus   DNB xxi 874

WORTH, *Cdr* John, RN (*fl* 1809)   M vi 393

WORTHINGTON, Nathaniel, (*fl* 1821–1846)

WORTHINGTON, *Cdr* Samuel, RN (*d* 1697)   *ch* iii 119

WRAY, *Capt* Charles, RN (*d* 1773)   *ch* v 511

WRAY, *Cdr* Henry, RN (*d* 1825)   M vi 251

WRAY, *Cdr* Luke Henry, RN (*fl* 1798–1854)   M viii 147

WREN, *Sir* Christopher (1632–1723)
Architect, surveyor and mathematician; architect of Flamsteed House   A 103; CE xiv 755;
                                                                                                   DNB xxi 995; T i 241

WRENCH, *Cdr* Matthew, RN (*d* 1831)   M vi 262

WRENN, *Cdre* Ralph, RN (*d* 1692)   *ch* i 388; DNB xxi
                                                                                                   1013

WRIFORD, *Cdr* Samuel, RN (*fl* 1797–1854)   M vii 405

WRIGHT, *Lieut-Cdr* Arthur H., USN (*fl* 1860–1880)   H 922

WRIGHT, Benjamin (*fl* 1596–1613)
Map-engraver and instrument-maker   T i 193

WRIGHT, Benjamin (1770–1842)
Canal engineer   DAB 1255

WRIGHT, Edward (1558–1615)
Mathematician and hydrographer   DNB xxi 1015; T i 181

WRIGHT, *Cdr* Ezekiel, RN (*d* 1736)   *ch* iv 53

WRIGHT, Fortunatus (*d* 1757)
Merchant and privateer   DNB xxi 1018

WRIGHT, George (*fl* 1780–1783)
Instrument-maker; writer on navigational instruments and globes   T ii 327

WRIGHT, Henry T., *Paymaster*, USN (*fl* 1864–1878)   H 993

WRIGHT, *Sir* James, CB, RN (1823–1899)
Engineer-in-chief of the navy, 1872–1886   B iii 1517

WRIGHT, *Cdr* John, RN (*d* 1691)   *ch* ii 402

WRIGHT, *Capt* John Wesley, RN (1769–1805)   DNB xxi 1029; M*d* xlv
                                                                                                   102; NC xxxiv 1, 89,
                                                                                                   177, 265, 353, 441;
                                                                                                   xxxv 441; xxxvi, 1,
                                                                                                   84, 177, 265

WRIGHT, *Cdre* Lawrence, RN (*d* 1713)   *ch* i 317; DNB xxi
                                                                                                   1033

WRIGHT, *Cdr* Mayson, RN (*fl* 1794–1815)   M vii 118

WRIGHT, *Lieut* Miers Fisher, USN (*fl* 1866–1880)   H 965

YOUNG, *Cdr* George, RN (*b* 1785)   M viii 255

YOUNG, George Frederick (1791–1870)
Member of the Lloyds Committee, 1835–1867   B vi 979

YOUNG, *Cdr* Henry, RN (*fl* 1666)   ch i 279

YOUNG, *Adm* James (*d* 1789)   DNB xxi 1291; NA i
                                                                                      29

YOUNG, *Rear-Adm* James (*d* 1833)   ch v 272; M ii 683

YOUNG, *Capt* Jonathan, USN (*fl* 1841–1862)   H 879

YOUNG, *Cdr* John, RN (*fl* 1672)   ch i 384

YOUNG, John (*d* 1819)
Canadian merchant and executive councillor; chairman of commission for the
regulation of pilots; first master of Trinity House at Quebec   MDC 819

YOUNG, John (1811–1878)
Commissioner of public works for Canada; chairman of the port of Montreal
harbour commissioners   MDC 819

YOUNG, John Radford (1799–1865)
Mathematician; author of: 'The theory and practice of navigation and nautical
astronomy' (1856)   DNB xxi 1298; T ii
                                                                                      440

YOUNG, *Cdr* Michael, RN (*fl* 1665–1667)   ch i 188

YOUNG, *Capt* Robert, RN (*d* 1750)   ch v 130

YOUNG, *Cdr* Robert Benjamin, RN (1773–1846)   M vii 432; vi 403; Tr
                                                                                      312

YOUNG, *Lieut* Thomas, RN (*b* 1794)   M xii 119

YOUNG, Thomas (1773–1829)
Scientist; superintendent of the 'Nautical Almanac'; secretary to the Board of Longitude   DNB xxi 1308; T ii
                                                                                      302

YOUNG, *Cdr* Thomas Bristowe, RN (1767–1846)   M vii 135

YOUNG, *Lieut* Thomas James, VC, RN (1827–1869)   B vi 982

YOUNG, *Adm Sir* William, GCB (1751–1821)   DNB xxi 1315

YOUNG, *Vice-Adm* William (1761–1847)   M iv 628

YOUNG, William (1825–1896)
Member of Lloyd's Registry of British & Foreign shipping   B iii 1580

YOUNGER, *Capt* William, RN (*fl* 1665–1666)   ch i 188

YOUNGHUSBAND, *Cdr* Frank Campbell, RN (1849/50–1894)   B iii 1582

YRALA, Domingo Martinez de (1486–1557)
Spanish explorer   Md xlv 291

YULE, *Capt* Charles Bamfield, RN (1806–1878)   B iii 1583

BOLTON PUBLIC
REFERENCE
LIBRARY
LIBRARIES